PUNJAB PLANTS

PUNJAB PLANTS,

COMPRISING

Botanical and vernacular names, and uses

OF MOST OF THE

TREES, SHRUBS, AND HERBS

OF ECONOMICAL VALUE,

GROWING WITHIN THE PROVINCE.

J. L. STEWART, M. D.

GYAN

Published by

GYAN

Gyan Publishing House
5, Ansari Road
Daryaganj, New Delhi-110002
Phone: 011-47034999, 9811692060
E-mail: books@gyanbooks.com

Distribution Network
gyanbooks.com
India, USA, Canada, UK, Australia, France

ISBN: 978-81-212-8346-5 (PB)
First Published, 1869

2nd Impression 2023

Printed at: Gyan Press, Delhi.

PUNJAB PLANTS
Author: J. L. STEWART

PUNJAB PLANTS,

COMPRISING

Botanical and Vernacular names, and uses

OF MOST OF THE

TREES, SHRUBS, AND HERBS

OF ECONOMICAL VALUE,

GROWING WITHIN THE PROVINCE.

INTENDED AS

A HAND-BOOK

FOR OFFICERS AND RESIDENTS IN THE

PUNJAB.

BY

J. L. STEWART, M.D.,

L.R.C.S.E., F.L.S., F.R.G.S.,

CONSERVATOR OF FORESTS, PUNJAB.

LAHORE:

PRINTED AT THE GOVERNMENT PRESS,

PUBLIC WORKS DEPARTMENT.

MDCCCLXIX.

CHIEF ERRATA AND OMISSIONS.

Page.

2, at Anemone, enter "S. *kukra.*"

3, at Delphinium Brunonianum, enter "S. *supalú, ruskar, liokpa;* Lad., *ládara.*"

7 at Berberis vulgaris, for "Atvensis," read "Ætnensis."

9, at Meconopsis, enter "S. *kanda.*"

10, at Papaver, enter "S. *fim.*"

11, line 11, under Brassica, for "Hyperanthera," read "Moringa."

13, line 19, read "Cheiranthus cheiri," and enter "Wallflower" at ditto.

line 25, enter "Christolea crassifolia. Lad., *shangsho.* Grows from 10,000 to 15,000 feet in Ladák; is browsed by goats, but little by *yáks.*"

14, line 3, enter "Mr. A. O. Hume states to me that the Farsetia is a favourite food of the large bustard."

line 4, enter "Lepidium latifolium. L. Lad., *gonyúch.* Grows in Ladák, 10,000 to 14,000 feet; is browsed by sheep and goats, little by *yáks.*"

at Nasturtium, enter "Water-cress."

20, at Drosera, enter "S. *chitra.*"

line 13, enter "Alsine sp. Lad., *pangdúm.* Grows in Ladák at 15,000 to 18,000 feet. A clumpy prickly species which furnishes a very poor fuel, only used under stress."

21, at Gossypium, enter "Flax."

22, at Linum, enter "Cotton."

26, at Corchorus capsularis, enter "Jute."

29, at line 15, for "Lunetta," read "Limetta,"

31, under Pavia, at S., enter "*kúnor.*"

34, under Cedrela toona serrata, at S., enter "*dallí.*"

35, under Vitis Indica, enter "grapes, *angúr.*"

37, under Fagonia, at T. I., enter "*aghzái,*" and at B. D., &c., "*damá.*"

ERRATA.

Page

44, under ZIZYPHUS VULGARIS, for "*anmia,*" read "*amnia.*"

47, at PISTACIA VERA, enter "Pistachio tree," and under the same, for "*bozaghanj,*" read "*bozghanj.*"

52, line 4, for "*bubbúr,*" read "*babbur.*"

57, under ARACHIS, for "nut," read "seed."

60, under CÆSALPINIA SEPIARIA, for "*relmí,*" read "*relnú.*"

63, at CICER SOONGARICUM, enter "P. *tsarrí.*"

68, under EDWARDSIA MOLLIS, for "*buná,*" read "*búna.*"
under ERVUM, for "*kerge,*" read "*kerze.*"

69, at FABA, enter "Bean."

70, read "LATHYRUS APHACA."

72, after OUGEINIA, enter "OXYTROPIS MACROPHYLLA. DC. Lad., *niargal*; P. *táksha.* Grows in Ladák and Spiti from 12,500 to nearly 18,000 feet; is browsed by sheep and *yáks.*"

73, at PISUM, enter "Pea."

76, at TRIFOLIUM REPENS, enter "Dutch clover."

78, under AMYGDALUS PERSICA var. LÆVIS, for "*shoftálú,*" read "*shaftálú.*"

81, line 6, for "10,000," read "16,000."
read "PRINSEPIA."

85, line 2, for "*sun,*" read "*sún.*"

87, line 9, for "*surgauch,*" read *surganch.*

88, under CONOCARPUS, for "*dhan,*" read "*dhau.*"

96, under CUCUMIS COLOCYNTHIS, for "PTYCHOTIS," read "LIGUSTICUM."

97, under CUCURBITA, enter "Plains, &c.," before *kaddú sufèd.*

99, at Dubiæ, 3, for "PEPO," read "MAXIMA."
at PORTULACA, enter "Purslain."

100, over KALANCHOE, enter "N. O. CRASSULACEÆ."

105, at "CUMINUM," enter "Cumin."
at DAUCUS, enter "Carrot."

106, at FERULA, read "ASAFŒTIDA."

107, under PIMPINELLA CRINITA, for "PTYCHOTIS," read "LIGUSTICUM."

108, line 1, read PLEUROSPERMUM.

116, at RUBIA, read "Wild Madder."

117, under RUBIA TINCTORUM, enter "S. *bacho.*"

Page.

119, at ACHILLEA, enter "Yarrow."

under APLOTAXIS, for "SERRATULA," read "VERNONIA."

121, under ARTEMISIA SACRORUM, for "*zbiir,*" read "*zbür.*"

line 11, before *tatwen*, enter "J."

124, 6th line from below, for "it," read "this plant;" 2nd line from below, after "both," enter "varieties."

129, under SAUSSUREA OBVALLATA, enter "S. *birm-kanwal.*"

139, line 15, after "12,000 feet," enter ("Hf. and T.")

under OLEA, for "*khan,*" read "*khau.*"

140, line 1, for "that," read "the last."

142, line 8 from below, for "said," read "used."

147, under AGATHOTES, for "*chirreta,*" read "*chiretta.*"

150, line 7, after *veri*, enter "Lad., *tiktigma.*" "In Ladák it is eaten by cattle."

154-5, under MACROTOMIA, read "*gao-zabán,*" quater.

157, line 4, for "Marr.," read "Murr."

165, under CALLICARPA, for "*baunú,*" read "*bannú.*"

170, line 14, after "be," enter "used in."

at OCIMUM, enter "Sweet Basil."

line 3 from below, for "*páur,*" read "*pánr.*"

176, line 15, after "uncommon," enter "wild."

178, at CHENOPODIUM ALBUM, enter "Goosefoot."

180, under ÆRUA, at T. I., enter "*spera wanne.*"

182, line 3 from below, for "*pumde,*" read "*punáe.*"

192, at BUXUS, enter "Box."

193, at EUPHORBIA HELIOSCOPIA, enter "Sun Spurge."

198, line 4, after "and," enter "for."

199, line 24, for "others," read "other oaks."

203, line at bottom, for PASTIGIATA, read "NIGRA."

204, line 5, ditto, ditto.

209, at CELTIS, enter "Nettle-tree."

210, under ULMUS, line 1, omit "which grows to a large size," and lines 5 and 6, omit sentence beginning "I may, &c."

215, (and elsewhere), for "NUSSIESSYA," read "MISSIESSYA."

line 2 from bottom, after "common," enter "wild."

220, line 15, after "region," enter "in the Himalaya."

222, under JUNIPERUS, for "*mích, chích,*" read "*núch, chúch.*"

INTRODUCTION.

In the course of 1867, it for the first time struck me that many of the items of information I had accumulated regarding the vegetation and vegetable products of the Punjab, if supplemented by other data available, might well be put into such a shape as to be useful. Accordingly, the compilation of this work was commenced, and His Honor the Lieutenant Governor, and Colonel Maclagan, Secretary Public Works Department, having kindly consented that it should be printed at the expense of Government, and by the Public Works Department Press, the materials were mostly arranged by about the middle of 1868.

Since commencing the work, I have at times thought that its publication might have been deferred with advantage, until, while on furlough, I should have an opportunity of getting correct identifications of all my plants. But this would have entailed great delay and probably considerable alteration in the nature of the work,—while in this form, even with its numerous defects, it will perhaps answer the purpose for which it is intended nearly as well as if it had a more technical arrangement and form, and ranked higher as to scientific accuracy.

It comprizes some notice of almost all the trees of the Province, of most of the shrubs of some size, indigenous or cultivated, and of the herbs wild or cultivated, which are, or are supposed to be, useful or hurtful, or are otherwise interesting. All of these that I have met with in the Punjab, or that are mentioned in such books, reports, and papers as I have access to, get some notice, longer or shorter, according to their apparent importance or interest. As a rule, with the exception of trees of some size, but few plants are inserted which are not considered by natives at least to be of note in themselves or for their products, or are not cultivated as flowers. As a rule also, but with one or two exceptions, plants which are cultivated only by Europeans are not inserted. And on the whole I have tried to err rather on the side of fulness than of scantiness of detail, so far as this could be done without rendering the book too bulky.

The Natural Orders are arranged as in DeCandolle, and under each the genera, and under these the species are given alphabetically, except in the case of doubtful plants, which are entered last under their Natural Order or genus. The scientific nomenclature of the species is perhaps the feeblest part of all; and besides the need for numerous marks of interrogation or other notes of doubt, there are probably many errors as to this. But to those who have worked at a distance from libraries and standard collections, no profuse apologies will be necessary on this score. I can only say I have done my best with the aids at my command.

It would probably be superfluous to dilate on the need for some such work as this is intended to be, for the benefit of Officers and other residents, as well as travellers, in the Province. And however inadequately the present attempt may have been carried out, there may perhaps be room for hope that it will in some degree supply what has hitherto been a desideratum for the Punjab. In it will be found many, though often necessarily meagre, items of some importance or interest in connection with commercial vegetable products, some of them of great antiquity, *e. g.*, Aucklandia root; or peculiar to the Province, *e. g.*, Datisca root, with timbers and their uses, with drugs, with poisons, some hitherto unpublished, *e. g.*, Scopolia, and with adulterations.

And with regard to the identification of even common trees, &c., the work may be of use. For in the Punjab parallels might be found to the well-known story of the English nobleman who went into ecstasies over a fine tree somewhere on the continent, and, after having plants imported, found that it was the ordinary hornbeam, common on his own estate! The similarity of native names of different trees in the several parts of the Province is apt, where there is no guide, to lead to error. For instance, the *báhn*, Populus Euphratica of the southern Punjab, has been reported of as likely to furnish a tanning material, from confusion with the *bhán*, Rhus Cotinus of Hazára. Again, this work will at least help to obviate the recurrence of such errors as the importation from the Nílgiris of seed of Urtica heterophylla, which is common in many parts of our Himalaya.

The following is some account of the sources of information, and of the materials on which the work is founded. From 1856 to 1861, while serving with various regiments, I had an opportunity of studying, with some degree of minuteness, the Flora of parts of the northern Trans-Indus Frontier, including considerable portions of the hills visited on three Military Expeditions, of marching across various parts of the Province, and of botanizing

Hazára and the Kashmír Valley. While holding my present appointment, I have had ample opportunities for investigating the Flora of the Punjab generally, have marched across almost every district in the plains, been a second time through considerable portions of Hazára and Kashmír, and traversed great parts of the intramontane basins of each of our great rivers. An extensive tour in Ladák, south, north, and east of Lê, during 1868, has completed my own wanderings in search of information as to the Flora in and near the Punjab. Some of the data collected in 1861-63 in the upper Gangetic Doáb, Rohilkund, Garhwál, and Kumaon, have also been incorporated with the rest, as well as various items acquired during a short official tour in Sind in 1866.

The very extensive series of vegetable products, collected for the Punjab Exhibition of 1863, now carefully arranged by Mr. Baden Powell in the Lahore Museum, with the reports and notes on these by District Officers, have afforded me great assistance, especially with reference to cultivated plants and their products, as to which perhaps I stood most in need of aid. Regarding these also I have received willing and liberal assistance from Dr. G. Henderson and Dr. T. E. B. Brown, on matters with which they are more familiar than myself.

The published information on which I have drawn most largely comprizes the following. Many items have been excerpted from the printed reports of the Agri-Horticultural Society of the Punjab, and the Selections from its records, and some from the Journal of the Agri-Horticultural Society of India. As to the plains of the Province, I have been largely indebted to Dr. Bellew's Report on Eusufzái; Dr. Aitchison's papers on the Flora of Jhelam in the Journals of the Linnæan Society, and of the Asiatic Society; Mr. Edgeworth's papers on Ambála and Múltán in the Asiatic Society's and Linnæan Society's Journals; Mr. W. Coldstream's paper on the products of Mozaffargarh in the Journal of the Agri-Horticultural Society of India; and the Settlement Reports of certain Punjab districts. Various details have also been supplied by Firminger's work on gardening in India, and many items extracted from Honigberger's book on the Punjab. But I regret to say that items from the latter require very frequent notes of interrogation, both as to names and uses of plants.

Regarding the plants of countries west of the Indus, in particular Afghánistán, I have been chiefly indebted to Irvine's

Report (Journal of the Agri-Horticultural Society of India, 1839), the works of Griffith, Masson, and Vigne, and Bellew's "Kandahár Mission."

Many items of information as to the plants and products of Kashmír and various parts of the Himalaya have been excerpted from Vigne's and Hugel's books on Kashmír; the more scientific works of Royle, Jacquemont and Thomson on the Himalaya; and papers by Lowther on Kashmír (Journal Agri-Horticultural Society of India). and by J. D. Cunningham and Hutton on Kanáwar (Journal of the Asiatic Society); Dr. Cleghorn's Punjab Forest Report, 1864; an official Report by Colonel Lake on the timber trees of Kángra; and Dr. Aitchison's paper (Journal of the Linnæan Society) on the Flora of Lahoul, from specimens and information collected by Reverend H. Jaeschke, a ten years' resident there. Hoffmeister's travels, and various papers by Colonel Madden (Journal of the Asiatic Society) have also been drawn upon as to parts of the Sutlej basin and the Himalaya to the eastward.

Concerning the plants of the plains of the N. W. Provinces, many items have been culled from the Sahâranpúr catalogue of Dr. Jameson, which, however, is perhaps hardly so full upon the uses of plants as that gentleman's great and long experience might have rendered it, and from Mr. Edgeworth's papers on Banda (Journals of the Asiatic Society and Linnæan Society). Notes have also been taken when necessary from Long's papers on the Flora of Bengal (Journal of the Agri-Horticultural Society of India), from Drury's useful plants of India, the Bombay Flora, and Dr. Birdwood's Bombay Products.

For information personally received, I am also indebted especially to Dr. Cayley, British Agent at Lê, Reverend H. Jaeschke, Dr. Bellew, Mr. J. Watson, Madhopúr Workshops, and Mr. G. W. Strettell, Forest Department, Sind, concerning respectively the plants of Ladák, of Lahoul, of the Peshawar Valley and Affghánistán, the uses of certain timbers, and the plants of Sind.

It may be well to make some observations on the native names of plants which are inserted so lavishly. In strictly scientific works, these are frequently entirely ignored; but in what is intended to be in some measure a hand-book for general reference, it appears to me they are a *sine quâ non.* For the most part only names have been inserted which are in use in the Punjab, or in the countries to the north and west (which it has been thought advisable to introduce, as these are not accessible in a collected form) with a few of the N. W. Provinces, &c. The vernacular names given, numerous as they are, do not assume to be exhaustive even of those noted by myself, and many have been left out as merely modifications or corruptions of those that are given. Almost all the vernacular names of growing plants (*i. e.*, exclusive of drugs and commercial products) have been got by my own enquiries on the spot, except where it is otherwise noted or evident from the text.

In the plains, from the greater inter-diffusion of tribes and tongues, some vernacular names extend over wide tracts, though there are marked exceptions to this. In the Himalaya, on the other hand, where, owing to geographical difficulties and peculiarities, as well as comparative sparseness of population, dialects remain more distinct, there are much greater varieties in the names of the same plants, and it is not uncommon for several to be in use for even a tree or a shrub of some size within a space of a few miles on the same river. In other cases again, certain names of trees, &c., extend at times in modified forms over considerable portions of the basins of more than one river. And there may be more marked instances of this than any I have known or noted. It may be remarked that in the Punjab, as in other countries, names of places are not unfrequently derived from those of trees, either from a single large specimen as *Simbal*, Bombax, or from an abundance of a certain tree as *Palosín*, from *palosa*, Pushtú for Acacia modesta.

As in other countries also, so here some marked quality leads to frequent repetitions of the same name more or less modified and applied to different plants. Among the more notable instances are such names as *bánsa, basmatí*, &c., from *bás* smell; *gándla*, &c., also denoting odour; *kandiára*, &c., from *kánta*, a thorn; *khatta* or *amla* implying sourness; *níl kanthí*, &c., "blue-throated," applied to blue-flowered plants; *píú* (strictly *pihú*) *már*, flea-killer; and *chattrí*, &c., umbrella-like, applied to plants such as mushroom, Euphorbia helioscopia, &c. In other cases again, a standard name (such as *rattanjot, bajr-banj*) is at times given to various plants other than that to which it was originally applied, owing to some real or fancied resemblance.

Besides ordinary Punjábí (Pí.) and Hindustání (Hí.) names inserted, the chief linguistic or dialectic varieties of which examples occur are the following. Some Persian names are applied to drugs, or are used in Affghánistán. The Pushtú names include those in use in that country, and those employed in our Trans-Indus territory and the Súlimán Range, &c. Numerous Kashmír and Ladákí (Tibetan) names are given, and a small number of Sind and Belúchistán. A few Arabic and still fewer Greek terms are entered as applied to drugs, the latter having filtered through the Arabian physicians and *hakíms* to the Indian Bazárs, where they are not always very recognizable. Many of the Lahoulí names, included with those of the Chenáb basin, belong to a branch of the Tibetan language, as do those of Spítí.

It would have been difficult in the text to escape entirely the use of some common Indian words, such as *jámpán, sharbat,* &c. These with short definitions have accordingly been included in the vernacular Index. It may be noted that where the spelling of the names given in the Indices differ from that in the text, the former are generally the more correct. Much of the text laboured under the disadvantage of being printed when I was constantly on the march, hundreds of miles in the interior. And the absence of the conjoined letters *kh, gh,* &c., has somewhat affected the correctness of the spelling of vernacular words.

A few words seem necessary as to uses of plants which have been entered. In most cases where these are not the result of my own enquiries, the authority is given. And only in a few instances has it seemed necessary to note uses to which plants or their products are put elsewhere than in the Punjab.

Curious results are at times evolved from comparing the uses of various timbers. Thus we find that several soft or loose grained woods, *e. g.,* Phœnix, Ficus, Bombax, Cedrela toona serrata, &c., are preferred for water conduits, well-curbs, and supports of small bridges, &c., which is perhaps hardly what we should expect. The weights which are here given for some of the kinds of timber are from my own experiments.

Respecting vegetable substances used as drugs, I have constantly been in the habit of making enquiries as to local usage in this matter, and have besides for several years been collecting from dealers, &c., the substances employed under the more or less orthodox systems of native practitioners. And although I have as yet failed to procure no fewer than 350 of the drugs mentioned in various publications on the native Materia Medica of northern India, (partly no doubt through inaccurate names, but chiefly because they are not used in the parts of the country where I have been,) I have got together about 500 vegetable substances applied or given medicinally in the Punjab. In collecting and identifying these, I have been much aided by the collections and lists made for the Punjab Exhibition, and have received much valuable assistance from Dr. T. E. B. Brown, Mr. Baden Powell, Pundit Rádha Kishen, whose knowledge of this subject is very extensive, and Rám Sing, an intelligent native drug-merchant, who does a large business in Lahore and Umritsur. Of the whole number collected, only between 25 and 30 remain completely unidentified, although, as might be expected, there is often in the case of roots, &c., a good deal of doubt as to the plants yielding them. As a rule, only substances used as drugs in the Punjab and Affghánistán have been noted, and those used only in eastern and southern India have been but rarely included. But, when necessary, advantage has been taken of the information contained in Dr. Forbes Watson's list, O'Shaughnessy's Bengal Dispensatory, and Royle's, Irving's, and Butler's lists for the N. W. Provinces, Ajmere, and Oudh. As to identifications, I have been favoured with some hints from Mr. M. C. Cooke, of the India Museum.

Of drugs proper, *i. e.*, those regularly collected and vended in the Bazárs, only the best-known names have been entered, hundreds of others having been left out. And when the ordinary designation of the drug has as adjunct the name of the part, *e. g.*, *bekh*, root, and *tukhm*, seed, the latter has for the most part been omitted. Here frequently crop out errors arising from the confused and uncertain system of native nomenclature: thus, *kálí jarrí* and similar names are locally applied to certain plants often not resembling the real *kálí zírí* (Vernonia anthelmintica) or only like it in some minor particular. In the identification of the medicinal *kankol mirch* (fruit of Celtis Caucasica) one is apt to be led astray by Elæagnus being called *kankolí* in some parts of the Himalaya; and difficulties of this kind frequently occur.

Although considerable care has been bestowed on the collection and identification of these drugs, and their "uses" have been entered. I must confess to a belief that the effects of most of them are *nil* or not of the kind attributed to them. The state of medicine among the natives of India would appear to be very considerably behind what it had reached in England 300 years ago,—when so many substances, now known to be quite ineffective, were included in the Materia Medica. In India now, as in Europe then, almost every substance, especially if possessing any peculiarity of colour, shape, smell, or taste, is believed to have *some* medicinal virtue. And in India now, as during the middle ages in Europe, much reliance is placed on the doctrine of the signatures, *i. e.*, the belief that a substance which has some of the physical characters of an organ or of the symptoms of a disease, will have power over what it resembles; many instances of this are noted in the body of the work. It would even appear that some substances (chiefly animal, however) are considered to have medicinal virtues merely from their oddity, *e. g.*, *píkhái mús*, rats' dung, the gall bladder of the brown bear, the hairs of a tiger's whisker, &c. Difficulty of acquisition would also appear to add virtue; thus it frequently happens that of two kinds of a drug, the one which is more rare is considered much the more powerful, in some cases indeed when neither would appear to have any special virtue. The *hakíms* have curious beliefs as to the plants which produce some of the foreign vegetable drugs, and still more curious theories are held as to the source of some of those of mineral origin. Thus I have been gravely told that *zahrmohra*, which comprizes several mineral substances given medicinally, is formed by the spittle of the *márkhor* (Capra megaceros) falling on stones in the Kohistán, west of the Indus.

The great number of substances to which by natives, and in their books on medicine, aphrodisiac virtues are attributed, is remarkable, some in connection with the doctrine of signatures, and most of them probably quite destitute of the qualities attributed to them.

Of the plants noted in this work, and indeed of all I have ever collected, only a very few are in all probability new to science. Royle, through his collectors, and Falconer and Thomson personally, had so thoroughly botanized the Punjab Himalaya, and the same may be said of Griffith for Affghánistán, that but few new species could have been left to be gleaned by their successors. This the more especially, as, considering the extent of the region, the Flora is not a large one as to number of species, nor is there great variation within it, even at points distant from each other.

A few remarks may not be out of place here as to the geographical and climatic conditions most likely to affect the nature of the Flora in the tract with which we have to do. The two chief modifying circumstances to be noted as to the Punjab are—that cold increases as we rise in the hills or pass more towards the north, and that on the whole the rain-fall is less and the aridity greater as we go further into the Himalaya, or proceed to the west, either in hills or plains. But there are important exceptions as to the latter point in the plains, where distance from the hills also increases the aridity The most arid part of the plains of the Punjab is probably near and to the west of Múltán, where the annual rain-fall is reckoned by fractions of an inch.

In the plains of the Punjab, although certain plants, as Calligonum polygonoides and others, are peculiar or nearly so to the driest tracts, mere aridity does not so much modify the nature as it lessens the amount of vegetation. In the Himalaya, however, the former also is much affected by the diminution of moisture. Thus in passing from the outer and middle ranges into the arid semi-Tibetan tracts on the upper Sutlej and upper Chenáb, not only does vegetation, arboreous, shrubby, and herbaceous, very much diminish in quantity, but there very many of the species are diverse from those in the moister parts. This is still more marked in Spítí and Ladák, where, great elevation being added to intense aridity, trees are almost unknown, and shrubs rare, and where by far the majority of the members of the herbaceous Flora are widely different from those growing in the outer hills. Different families also prevail in either of these tracts.

Some of the results of latitude and aridity on the families most apt to be modified by such conditions, will be apparent from the following. Ferns are nowhere very common in the plains of northern India; but, while Edgeworth found seven species in Banda (N. W. Provinces), only two occur rarely and locally in the Punjab plains, and not more than three have been found in the west, even in the Salt Range, which reaches 5,000, and in the hills Trans-Indus, up to 8,000 feet. In the Himalaya again, seventy kinds of ferns, out of one thousand species of plants collected, were got in the moister climate of Garhwál and Kumaon, while of 870 species collected on the Chenáb and Rávi, only 30, and of nearly 700 species collected in Hazára, only 20, were ferns. And in each of Lahoul and Ladák only three or four ferns have been found. In going west also, epidendric ferns, which require more moisture than others, diminish in numbers, and seem to cease entirely about the Rávi. Actiniopteris radiata, which affects the driest habitats near Dehlí and to the east, has not, so far as I know, been found within the Punjab proper. A small Ophioglossum, which Beddome considers near O. vulgatum, occurs in the Salt Range and (probably the same) in so different a locality as the low land by the great rivers near Ambála.

Orchidaceous plants are rare throughout the plains of northern India, and in the Punjab only the ubiquitous Zeuxine sulcata occurs generally, while Eulophia is found locally,—and only one other was found in the Trans-Indus hills to 8,000 feet. In the Himalaya, this family, like the last, decreases very much in numbers towards the west. Out of one thousand Garhwál and Kumaon plants, more than 20 were orchids, while in Hazára only four out of 516 belonged to this family, and not more than three have been found in each of Lahoul and Ladák, in the latter very sparingly and in a very confined area. Epidendric orchids like epidendric ferns I have not observed west of the Rávi.

Aroid plants diminish very much in number of individuals towards the west, but I found nearly the same number of species in Hazára as in Garhwál and Kumaon. Of Balsams again there are not half the number of species in the former that occur in the latter, while the number of individuals is infinitely smaller. The diminution towards the west of Gesneraceæ and Begoniaceæ, two families which luxuriate in a moist atmosphere, is remarkable; about a dozen species of these were found in Garhwál and Kumaon, while I have only seen a single *specimen* west of the Rávi.

A peculiarity of growth, which doubtless depends on climatic causes, as yet uncertain, is that the deodár, which, like most other conifers, prefers the shady aspects in most parts, undoubtedly-thrives best on the sunnier aspects on the Kishenganga and Kunhár, two tributaries of the Jhelam in the extreme north-west. I am inclined to think this arises from the circumstance that there, from increase of latitude, the tree gets on the shady slopes less heat throughout the year than what is necessary to its well-being.

It may be well to note here various other circumstances as to the distribution of plants not peculiarly affected by drought, &c., and which do not very evidently depend on obvious climatic causes or arise from other conditions. Of each of Urtica and Euphorbia, only a single peculiar species appears to be found in Ladák, while of the former several, and of the latter many, occur in the Himalaya further out. Of Parasites, several Orobanchaceous plants occur in the latter, two extend to Lahoul, and only one to Ladák; several species of Cuscuta are found in the outer and middle Himalaya, and two species occur in Lahoul, while one only has been met with in Ladák; several species of Viscum are common in the outer parts of the hills, one species only is peculiar to the pencil cedar in Lahoul, and none occur in Ladák.

Marrubium vulgare is the most limited as to area of habitats of any plant I have met with. I have only found it over an extent of a few yards at each of six or seven different places, the extremes being hundreds of miles apart from each other in the Himalaya and elsewhere above the plains level, and always near habitations, though there seems no reason to suppose that it was introduced in these places. Mirabilis Jalapa also is for the most part only seen near villages, &c., but its habitats are much more numerous than those of Marrubium.

The frequency of Ficus religiosa and F. Indica depends very much on the proportion of Hindús among the population. In some parts, where the latter is almost entirely Mússalmán, these trees are very rare, even allowing for differences of climate. Of plants now become quasi-indigenous, but which we know to have been introduced within the historical period, the most remarkable is perhaps Argemone Mexicana, which is stated to have been introduced into India from Mexico three centuries ago, and is now abundant wild in many parts of India, including the eastern part of the Punjab. In 1854, Edgeworth states that it had not reached

Múltán, but within the last three years I and others have found it south of that place.

The proportion of grasses relative to the total Flora of this part of India would appear to be larger than that which has been assigned by Hooker and Thomson for the whole country, viz., one-thirtieth. Thus, of 1,000 species collected in Garhwál and Kumaon, 50 were grasses, while of 516 got in Hazára, 36, of 460 near Peshawar, 60, and of 400 Trans-Indus further south, 50 were of this family.

As to extent of range in the plains, a good many plants, some of considerable size, are found from end to end or nearly so. But most plants extend over a much less wide area, generally being found from the outer edge of the Province in any direction only to a certain distance inward. To illustrate this it may be mentioned that of 540 species of plants collected in the Salt Range, a well-defined and somewhat central tract, 56 are Western or Affghán forms which are not found to the east or south, 19 occur to the south, but not to the north of the Range, and 44 species of the Himalaya and Siwáliks to the east have not been found to the north-west or Trans-Indus.

As to plants of considerable elevational range, no great account need be made of such species as have a deep range within the Himalaya themselves (*e. g.*, Saxifraga ligulata) or of such European species occurring at very various heights within our limits as are of extensive distribution in different parts of the world, and tolerant of wide variations of climate. Among the most noted of these which are found in the Punjab plains and to great elevations in the Himalaya, are Silene conica, Stellaria media, Vaccaria, Solanum nigrum, and Poa annua.

More notable perhaps are the following, all of which are found in parts at least of the Punjab plains, and, so far as identifications have yet been made, the same or very nearly allied species occur also at great heights in the mountains. Ranunculus aquatilis, Malcolmia Africana, Tribulus terrestris, Lamium amplexicaule, Salsola Kali, Juncus bufonius, Potamogeton crispus, P. gramineus, and Scirpus maritimus. All occur at 10,500 or 11,000 feet, while Arnebia hispidissima reaches 15,000, and Astragalus multiceps 16,500 feet in Ladák. Of this class, still more notable on account of their size are—Ballota limbata, found by Thomson above Iskardo, and Capparis spinosa, Tamarix Gallica, and Populus Euphratica, which reach 10,500 feet in Ladák.

In conclusion, a few remarks may not be unnecessary as to the geographical divisions which have been adopted for the range and vernacular names of plants. For the Himalayà the main portion of each different river basin has for the most part been kept as a distinct region under the initial letter of its name. But Ladák, a portion of the upper part of the Indus basin with a distinct Flora and a distinct language, of itself constitutes a region, as does the Kashmir Valley, a portion of the Jhelam basin with a distinct language and to some extent a Flora of its own. The Jhelam basin also here includes the whole of Hazára, although a portion of the latter is within the Indus water-shed.

The heights given for the range of Himalayan plants are mostly founded on my own observations supplemented by data from a large set of Hooker and Thomson's East Indian distribution, for which I am indebted to Dr. Hooker's liberality; from Hooker and Thomson's Flora Indica and its continuation the Præcursores in the Journal of the Linnæan Society; from Dr. Thomson's travels in the N. W. Himalaya; from Jacquemont; and from Dr. Aitchison's paper on the Flora of Lahoul already referred to; as well as from information personally received from Revd. H. Jaeschke.

The term Siwálik tract, so frequently used, includes the range so called by Europeans, lying under and external to the Himalaya at from 1,000 to 2,500 and occasionally rising to 3,000 feet. Many of the trees, shrubs, &c., which grow in that tract, extend to some distance within the Himalaya in the valleys of the great rivers to a similar height, and where a similar climate prevails to that of the Siwáliks, nor has it been thought necessary in each instance to note this fact.

As to the range of growth of plants in the plains and the vernacular nam used there, the natural geographical divisions by the great rivers into Doábs (from west to east Sind Ságar, Chuj, Rechnáb, Bári and Jalandar Doábs) has as far as possible been adhered to and the initials of these employed. The most marked exceptions to this are the Salt Range in the upper part of the Sind Ságar Doáb, which, from its somewhat peculiar conditions and Flora, it has been thought well to keep separate, and the tract between the Sutlej and Jumna, which it seems advisable to divide into Ambála to the north, and to the south Ferozepúr and Dehlí, with between them Harriána, a convenient and well known ancient name here applied to the districts of Sirsa, Hissár, and the western part of Rohtuck. Southern Punjab again includes the lowest part of the Sind Ságar and Bárí Doábs. The Trans-Indus plains and lower hills have necessarily been kept distinct, as over the greater part of them the names used (with the language spoken) is either Pushtú or Belúch or largely interlarded with one of these.

Where only "plains" or "Himalaya" is used in the text, it is to be understood that this means within the Punjab. And where no regional letter is prefixed to a vernacular name it is undersood to be used in the Cis-Indus plains generally. Such names as Dehra Gházi Khan, Loodiana, &c., of course, apply to the districts so called.

The diagram, with initials and names, has been introduced in order to render more clear the terms, &c., employed as to distribution of plants and their native names.

J. L. S.

Lahore, February, 1869.

Diagram of the Punjab, &c.

WITH INITIALS OF REGIONS INDICATED IN

PUNJAB PLANTS.

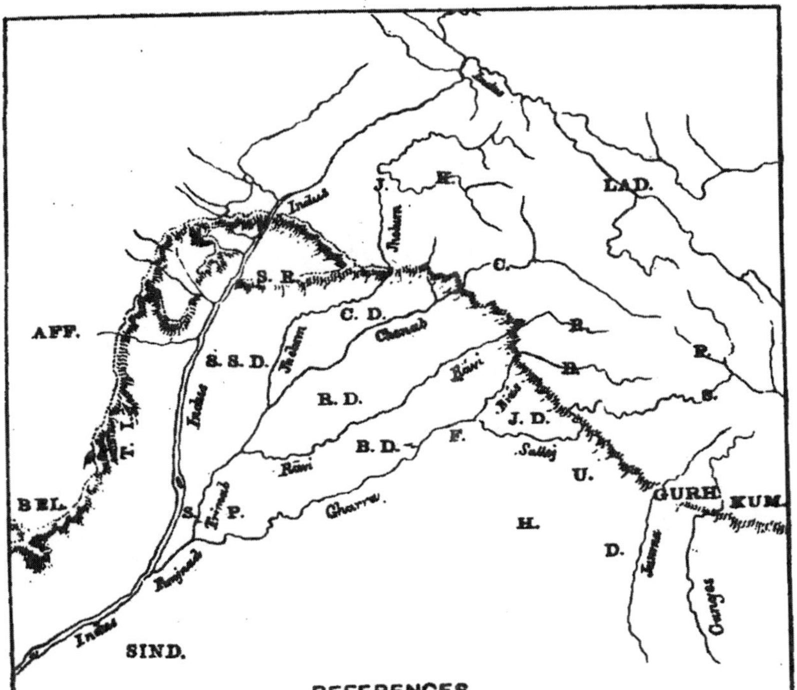

REFERENCES.

LAD. *Ladák.*
K. *Kashmir Valley.*
J. *Jhelam Basin.*
C. *Chenáb Basin.*
R. *Rávi Basin.*
B. *Biás Basin.*
S. *Sutlej Basin.*
P. *Piti or Spiti.*
GURH. *Garhwál.*
KUM. *Kumaon.*

AFF. *Affghánistan.*
BEL. *Belúchistán.*
T. I. *Trans-Indus.*
S. R. *Salt Range.*
S. S. D. *Sind Ságar Doab.*
C. D. *Chuj Doáb.*
R. D. *Rechnáb Doab.*
B. D. *Bári Doáb.*
J. D. *Jalandar Doáb.*
S. P. *Southern Punjab.*

SIND.
U. *Umbála.*
F. *Ferozepur.*
H. *Harriána.*
D. *Dehli.*

Scale 128 Miles = 1 inch.

PUNJAB PLANTS,

COMPRISING NOTES ON MOST OF THOSE OF ANY INTEREST FOUND WILD, OR GROWN BY NATIVES, WITHIN THE PROVINCE.

N. O. RANUNCULACEÆ.

ACONITUM. Aconite, Wolf's-bane.

Several species are common to considerable heights in many parts of the Punjab Himalaya. They are handsome flowering plants. The roots of some are officinal, and those of several are poisonous; the kinds found with native drug-sellers, under the following names, being assigned to Aconites, generally A. FEROX, sometimes A. NAPELLUS—*bíkh, síngía, mítha zahr, mítha tilia, mítha dodia, dúdhia, makrela.* Moorcroft states that the stupefiant effects of honey in certain localities in Kumaon during spring is attributed to the bees feeding on an Aconite.

A. FEROX. Wall.

Vernacular. R. *dúdhia maura*, S. *maura bíkh* Bazár, root, *bíkh, síngía.*

This plant grows in various parts of the Punjab Himalaya at from 10,000 to 14,000 feet. The root is a strong poison. In Bissahir it is used for destroying wild animals. (Cleghorn). In Chumba it is ground and applied externally, after scarification, for headache. It is officinal in the plains, being reckoned anodyne, and used externally and internally in bronchitis, &c.

A. HETEROPHYLLUM. Wall.

Vernacular. J. *súkhí harí* (from the fresh roots springing from the dry ones), *chitijarí, patrís.* C. *bongu*, R. *patís*, B. S. and Bazár, root, *atís.*

In many parts of the Punjab Himalaya this grows at from 8,000 to 12,000 feet. The root is very bitter, and in Hazára is given for the cruptive fevers (?) of children; in Chumba it is taken for indigestion. From some parts of the hills it is largely exported to the plains, where it is officinal. As a tonic and febrifuge, it is undoubtedly of some value.

A. NAPELLUS. L. (A. DISSECTUM. Don). Monkshood.

Vernacular. J. *piún, mohrí.* S. *tilia kachang.* Bazár, root, *dúdhía*

The range of this plant is given at 10,000 to 16,000 feet; it is frequent in parts of the Punjab Himalaya. Cleghorn states that in Bissahir the root is used for destroying wild animals. It is officinal in the plains. Davies' Trade Report gives 20 seers of *mítha tília* as annually exported to Kábul from Peshawar. In Europe, aconitina, the most virulent poison known, is extracted from the root of this plant.

ACTÆA SPICATA. L. Baneberry.

Vernacular. (?)

This plant is found in various parts of the Punjab Himalaya at from 6,000 to 10,500 feet. But I have found no trace of its being used or dreaded, although in Europe the plant is poisonous, and the root is given in catarrh.

ANEMONE OBTUSILOBA. Don. (A. DISCOLOR. Royle).

Vernacular. K. *rattanjog.* R. *padar.*

This appears to be very common at from 7,000 to 13,000 feet in many parts of the Punjab Himalaya. In Hazára the pounded root, which is acrid, is mixed with milk and given internally for contusions. In Bissahir it is said to be used as a blister, but to be apt to produce sores and scars.

CALTHA PALUSTRIS. L. Marsh Marigold.

Vernacular. J. *mamírí.* S. *bairingú.*

Not uncommon in the Punjab Himalaya at from 8,000 to at least 12,000 feet. In Hazára the root is considered poisonous.

CIMICIFUGA FŒTIDA. L. (FRIGIDA. Royle). Bugwort.

Vernacular. C. *jiúntí.*

Occasional in the Punjab Himalaya at from 7,000 to 12,000 feet. Here it appears to be considered inert, though the root is found to be poisonous in some other countries. In Siberia the plant is used to drive away bugs and fleas, whence the generic name.

CLEMATIS.

There are numerous species in the Himalaya; many of them noted for their handsome flowers, and several for their scent. Only one needs special notice here.

C. NEPALENSIS. (C. MONTANUM. Don?)

Vernacular. T. I. *pawanne.* J. *birri.* S. *wandak.*

One of the more rare species occurring at medium heights. In Kanáwar the leaves are said to act deleteriously on the skin, but this seems unlikely.

DELPHINIUM. Larkspur.

There are many species in the Himalaya, and one at least grows in the plains, Trans-Indus. Some of them have fine flowers (all being blue), but otherwise they are not of much importance.

DELPHINIUM AJACIS. L.

Vernacular. *nafurmán.*

Cultivated in flower gardens in the plains. Of no known use.

DELPHINIUM BRUNONIANUM. Royle.

Vernacular. R. *sapfáli.* S. *laskar, spet panní.*

Common in parts of the Punjab Himalaya at from 14,000 to 18,000 feet. On the Chenáb, Rávi, and Sutlej, it is prized for its strong scent of musk, is offered to the deota in temples, and worn in the cap.

D. CÆRULEUM. Jacqt. (?)

Vernacular. S. *dakhangú.*

A slender plant with light blue flowers, apparently near this species, is common on the Sutlej at from 5,500 to 9,000 feet; but the range given for the above is 14,000 to 15,000 feet, so that this may be different. The root of the latter is applied to kill the maggots in the wounds of goats, &c.

D. DENUDATUM. Wall. (D. PAUCIFLORUM. Royle).

Vernacular. (?)

The root of this plant is stated by Madden to be chewed by the Bissahiris for toothache, but on Sundays only!

D. KASHMIRIANUM. Royle. (D. JACQUEMONTIANUM. Camb).

Vernacular. R. *amlín.*

This also has a strong scent of musk. I found what appears to be it at 10,000 to 13,000 feet on the Rávi.

D. SANICULÆFOLIUM. Boiss. (?)

Vernacular. Bazár. flowers K. *asbarg, gháfiz.*

Under the former native name a considerable import takes place from Affghánistán into the Punjab of the flowers of perhaps the species named. They are used in Múltán, &c., with *aklbír* (see Datisca) and alum to dye silk yellow. Mr. Edgeworth first brought this substance to notice many years ago, and supposed these were the flowers of D. altissimum, Wall; but it does not appear to grow so far west. The drug called *gháfiz* consists of the flowers of this or a very similar but larger-flowered species, brought from the west also. They are very bitter, and are given as a febrifuge.

NIGELLA SATIVA. L.

Vernacular. *kálajíra, kalaunjí.* Aff. *shewadárú, siyáhdárú.*

The seeds are found in the bazárs of the Punjab (and the plant has been grown from them by Dr. Brown), being imported from Hindústán and probably the west, for they appear to be the *shewadárú*, which Davies' Trade Report states to be imported from Kábul to Peshawar to the extent of 10 maunds annually. They are reckoned stimulant, and are administered by *hakíms*, often in milk, for rheumatism and cough, especially on the *Yunání* system. They are also said by Honigberger to be put among clothes to keep off insects.

PÆONIA OFFICINALIS. L. Pæony.

Vernacular. T. I. and J. *mamekh.*

This plant occurs frequently in the Western Himalaya generally at about 7,500 to 8,000 feet. Dr. Bellew states that the root is in Bonêr, &c., given to cattle to render them prolific, and in combination is a favorite remedy for bruises, strains, &c. Madden mentions that in Kumaon the young shoots are eaten as a vegetable, and suggests that the long root may furnish one of the kinds of *bíkh* (generally Aconite q. v.)

RANUNCULUS. Crowfoot.

Many species grow in the hills at various elevations, and several in the plains. Only one needs mention here.

Ranunculus arvensis. L.

Vernacular. S. S. D. *chambal.*

Not uncommon in the Himalaya up to 5,000 or 6,000 feet, and common in the plains N. W. Punjab. Madden states that in Kumaon it is frequently fatal to sheep and goats, who eat it greedily.

Thalictrum. Meadow Rue.

There are a good many species in the Punjab Himalaya at various heights. Only one falls to be noticed here.

Thalictrum foliolosum. DC.

Vernacular. B. *gúrbíání.* S. *pashmaran.* Bazár, root, *pílíjarí, mamíra.*

Two centuries ago, Bernier mentions "*mamíron*, a little root, good for the eyes, as being brought (along with rhubarb, musk, and the wood of China) from Cathay to Kashmír by a long journey," in which *jhúlas* are described as being crossed. He afterwards suggests that this is *jinseng*, the "man-root;" but it is now known to be mostly if not entirely derived from the plant named above, which is common in many parts of the Himalaya from 5,000 to 9,500 feet, whence it is exported to the plains. Madden, however, mentions a large kind as brought "from Persia;" and Bellew informs us that the powder of the "leaves and stems" (root?) of *mamíra* is largely used as an *anjan*, or application in ophthalmia, in Affghánistán. This also is the principal use of the root in India; but it is likewise given as a tonic and antiperiodic. A. Delphinium is called *mamíra* in Hazára, so that other roots than the one named may be used under this appellation.

N. O. MAGNOLIACEÆ.

Michelia Champaca. L.

Vernacular. *champa* of Bengál and Hindústán, &c. R. B. and S. *chamba.* Bazár fruit, *chamakhrí, chamotí.*

This tree is prized in many parts of India for furniture, &c., and is said to polish well. It is doubtful whether the planted trees called *chamba*, which occur above Kálka, in Kángra, and Chumba, at 2,000 to 3,000 feet, are the same species, but their wood is prized for similar qualities, and is said not to be subject to worms, or to be apt to warp. In Kángra it was one of the *padsháhí* trees, *i. e.*, reserved for *Rájas*. Most of the larger *chamba* trees in Kángra have long ago been cut, and those left are mostly hollow. Handsome specimens of 7 or 8 feet girth and 60 or 70 feet high may still occasionally be seen near Chumba, &c. Its timber is valued for well-work, verandah-posts, &c. It is a handsome tree, with odorous flowers, which are offered up at Hindu shrines. Its capsules also are odorous, and are rubbed on the body at marriages, &c.

N. O. MENISPERMACEÆ.

Anamirta Cocculus. W. and A.

Vernacular. (?)

One planted tree of this is stated by Edgeworth to exist at Múltán.

Cissampelos Pareira. L.

Vernacular. C. *bat bel*, *parbik*. R. *katorí*. B. *zakhmí haiyát*, *batindú*. S. S. D. *patákí*. R. D. *katorí*. Bazár, leaves, *páth*, root, *pílíjarí* (partly).

Is not uncommon in the outer low hills and in parts of the plains. The leaves are said to be applied to abscesses, and its root is stated to furnish part of the *pílíjarí*—(see Thalictrum).

Cocculus Leæba. DC.

Vernacular. T. I. *parwattí*, *perkhatúna*. S. S. D. *illar billar*, *vehrí*. B. D. *vallúr*.

A climbing plant of the Arabian flora, common Trans-Indus, and extending more sparingly as far as Umritsur, and occasional apparently to some way further east, reaching 3 or 4 feet in girth at times. It is said to be browsed by goats, but by no other animal, and is of no special use.

Tinospora cordifolia. Miers. (Cocculus. DC).

Vernacular. B. *batindú*, *zakhmí haiyát*. Bazár, &c., *gilo*. Dry extract, *sat-gilo*.

Seems to occur (?) as far west as Trans-Indus. The root and extract are esteemed as tonic and febrifuge in native pharmacy, and have been recommended by some Europeans.

N. O. BERBERIDEÆ.

Berberis. Barberry.

Many species occur in the Himalaya from low to very considerable heights. The chief of these must be noted collectively, as they have frequently not been distinguished in practice.

Berberis aristata. DC.
B. Asiatica. Rox.
B. Lycium. Royle.

Vernacular. T.-I. *kúraskái, kwerei*. J. *súmlú*. K. *enkasing*. K. C. & R. *símlú, kemal, kemlú, kamla*, (&c.) B. *kasmal*. S. *kammal, tútrúm, chotra, jataun*. Bazár, root, *dárhald, dárchob*. Extract of root, *rasaut*.

One or other or more of these is common in most parts of the N. W. Himalaya and Trans-Indus hills. The fruit of many is eaten, and of several is very palatable. The fruit of one or other is in Kanáwar used to flavour spirits, and Moorcroft states that the juice of a barberry is in Kumaon boiled with capsicums to be used as sauce. Bellew mentions that in Affghánistán an electuary of the fruit is given as a cooling laxative to children. The latter also states that the stems are used as diaphoretic, and laxative in rheumatism. The root is used in native practice internally as a stomachic, and in diarrhœa, &c., and with oil is rubbed externally in rheumatism. The dried extract of the root *rasaut* is extensively used as a purgative for children, and especially as an application in ophthalmia. I am assured on the best authority that it is an excellent application for sun-blindness. The specific name, Lycium, was given by Royle, under the impression that the *rasaut* was the Lycium of the ancients.

Berberis vulgaris. L. var. Atvensis, &c.

Vernacular. *zirishk*.

This was found by Bellew growing abundantly on the Safêd Koh, and its fruit is stated to be largely dried. It also occurs in the Punjab Himalaya at from 6,000 to 12,000 feet. The dried barberries, which under the name *zirishk tursh* (*i. e.*, sour currants) are imported in small quantity from Kábul (one maund annually according to Davies' Trade Report), are probably, in part at least, supplied by this species. They are also said to be imported from Herát to Kandahár. They are officinal in the Punjab, being given as diuretic, and for the relief of heat, thirst, and nausea.

MAHONIA NEPALENSIS. DC. (BERBERIS N. Spr.)

Vernacular. R. *amúdanda, chiror.*

This handsome shrub, which is sometimes mistaken for holly, seems to come sparingly only to the Rávi (near which it may be seen about 5,000 to 7,000 feet), though it is common in many places east of the Sutlej. Its fruit is eaten.

PODOPHYLLUM EMODI. Wall.

Vernacular. J. *papri, banbakri.* C. *wanwángan chijákri, chimyáka.* R. *bankákra, gúl kákrú.*

Is common in parts of the N. W. Himalaya at from 6,000 to 11,000 feet up to near the Indus. Europeans consider that its handsome red fruit (ripe in September and October) is insipid, and even the natives do not praise it much although they eat it in most parts. In Lahoul it seems to be used medicinally.

N. O. NYMPHÆACEÆ.

EURYALE FEROX. Salisb.

Vernacular. K. *jewar* (Bengál, &c., *makhána*) Bazár, flowers, *phúlmakhána.*

This, which is a common aquatic plant in Bengál, &c., is only known to grow in Kashmír, west of the Satlej. Its seeds are eaten by the Kashmírís.

NYMPHÆA. Water Lily.

There is some uncertainty about the species, but one or other of all of the following is understood to grow in marshes and ponds in various parts of the plains of the Punjab, being more common as the tract is more moist. The first at least grows in Kashmír (5,000 feet).

NYMPHÆA ALBA. L.
N. CÆRULEA. Sav.
N. PUBISCENS. Willd. (N. LOTUS. L.)
N. STELLATA. Willd.

Vernacular. Kí. *brímposh.* Plains, *nílofar.* Bazár, roasted seeds, *kamúd bíj.*

The roasted seeds are officinal in the plains, and the root and seeds are eaten in times of scarcity. An infusion of the flower and fruit is given in diarrhœa, and as a diaphoretic.

N. O. NELUMBIACEÆ.

Nelumbium speciosum. Willd. Pythagorean Bean.

Vernacular. K. *pamposh.* Plains, *kánwal.* Bazár, &c., root, *kánwal kakrí* ; seed, *k. gatte.*

This magnificent flower is common in many tanks and marshes in the plains up to Peshawar; is abundant in Kashmír (5,000 feet), and occurs at Mozaffarabád, &c. The sliced roots, dug about October, when the leaves dry up, are sold as food, and are used cooked or as pickle. Moorcroft states that in Kashmír the stalks are eaten as a vegetable. The broad leaves are sold as plates. The flowers are sold in Kashmír to be used as offerings; and Bellew mentions that in the Peshawar valley they are used in *sharbats.* The seeds are used as food, and are considered somewhat medicinal, being given to check vomiting, and as diuretic and refrigerant to children. According to Moorcroft, this plant in Kashmír supports, perhaps, 5,000 people for eight months of the year.

N. O. PAPAVERACEÆ.

Argemone Mexicana. L.

Vernacular. B. D., &c., *kandiárí.* East, *katelí, bhat kateya.*

This is a cold-weather spinous-leaved plant with yellow flowers, which has been introduced within the historical period. It is only now working up the Punjab, and has not been noted as occurring much to the west of Lahore. In 1854, Edgeworth observes that it had not reached Múltán; but in 1866 it was seen in the extreme south-west of that district, near the junction of the Trimáb (Chenáb), with the Garra (Sutlej), and recently I have heard of it at Bhawulpoor to the south of the latter. It does not appear to be used in the west; but near Dehlí, where it is more abundant, an oil is extracted from the seeds, which is used for burning, and is applied medicinally to indolent ulcers, &c., and to eruptions.

Meconopsis aculeata. Royle.

Vernacular. J. *guddi kúm.* R. *gúdia.*

A blue-flowered spinous-leaved plant common in the Himalaya at 9,000 to 14,000 feet. In Kashmír, according to Honigberger, the root is officinal as a narcotic, and in Chumba it is stated to be poisonous.

Papaver somniferum. L. (var. album generally, nigrum rarely).

Vernacular. T. I. *khash-khash*. Cis-Indus *post*. Bazár, &c., heads, *doda*. Opium, *afím*. Seeds, *khish-khásh*.

Is cultivated (the red-flowered more rarely) throughout the plains of the Province, but less common in the north-west. I have seen it cultivated in the Biás basin to nearly 7,500 feet. The area cultivated with poppy has much increased in certain tracts of late years. The Shahpur Settlement Report gives no less than 3,000 acres for that district in 1865-66, an increase of 800 per cent. in about 10 years. The same report gives a good account of its cultivation, &c. Is generally grown in rich irrigated soil. A good deal is raised in Kashmír, where Rs. 200 per annum is said to be drawn by the Maharaja as duty on it. In Garhwál, Moorcroft states that the young plant is used as a vegetable, raw, or cooked with buttermilk; also that oil is extracted from it, as is likewise the case in some parts of the plains of the Punjab, where it is used medicinally as a narcotic in headache, &c. Davies' Trade Report gives 50 maunds of poppy seed as annually imported from Kábul to Peshawar.

The poppy-heads and seeds are used medicinally as sedatives. But the plant is grown principally for opium, which is largely used by the Sikhs. A considerable quantity of the drug is exported from the British possessions *viâ* Lêh to Yárkand, with some assumption of secrecy, on account of the prohibition of the Chinese Government. Davies' Report puts the quantity exported from Lêh by Yárkand at 210 maunds, worth 50,000 rupees; but for the last two years, since the Chinese were expelled from Western Túrkistán, the trade seems to have ceased. Indeed, Cayley states that in 1867, 24 seers were brought to Lêh from Kúllú, while 12 maunds were sent *back*.

N. O. FUMARIACEÆ.

Corydalis.

A good many species grow in the Himalaya at various elevations. One only needs mention here.

Corydalis Govaniana. Wall.

Vernacular. *budkhes*.

This plant grows in the Punjab Himalaya at 8,000 to 12,000 feet. The native name is given by Jameson; but it is not certain that it is applied to this plant west of the Sutlej—(see Umbelliferæ for uses of *budkhes*).

FUMARIA PARVIFLORA. Lam.

Vernacular. Plains and Bazár, *sháhtara*, *pit-pápra*.

Is abundant in fields, &c., in the Punjab plains in early spring, and occurs to 3,500 feet, Trans-Indus, &c. The seeds and leaves, &c., are considered as cooling, diaphoretic, diuretic, and laxative, and enter into the composition of many *sharbats*.

N. O. CRUCIFERÆ.

BRASSICA.

Includes cabbages, turnips, and mustards (formerly Sinapis). There is considerable complication in the names of these, and their scientific nomenclature has been frequently altered. It would appear that some wild species of mustard are utilized in parts of the Punjab (as in the North Western Provinces), *e. g.*, Bellew mentions that two or three wild mustards are used in the Peshawar valley, some as vegetables and carminatives, the seeds of some for flatulent colic, and the oil of others as an application to skin diseases in man and beast. The medicinal seed, *kamarkas*, would appear also to be in part produced by a wild mustard. The gum of Butea frondosa and Hyperanthera (q. v.), as well as the bark of Cathartocarpus fistula, are also called by this name. And the following species are notable.

BRASSICA CAMPESTRIS. L. (and many synonyms).

Vernacular. Plains, *sarson*, *sarrú*, *sarrí*. Bazár, seeds, *rái Banársi*. (? Edgeworth).

This (which furnishes the colsa oil of Europe, and which is supposed to be the origin of the Swedish turnip) is extensively grown as a cold-weather field crop in the plains. Edgeworth mentions that in parts of Ambála where water is abundant it is grown as a summer crop. It appears to be cultivated in the Himalaya—(see B. sp. p. 13)—up to over 10,000 feet in Tibet; also in Affghánistán. It is said to be subject to be spoiled by frost. When young it is eaten as a pot-herb. But it is chiefly grown for the bland oil extracted from its seeds, which is burned, and which natives use in cooking. The seed has recently begun to be exported largely towards Karráchí from near Lahore. Bellew mentions that in the Peshawar valley the seeds are often roasted and eaten with parched wheat. The *rái Banársi* is reckoned the best for cataplasms, but it is doubtfully furnished by this species.

B. ERUCA. L. (ERUCA SATIVA, Lam). Rocket.

Vernacular. *tara*, *úsí*, *úsán*, *assú*, *kála sarson*.

Is very extensively cultivated, especially in the more arid parts of the Province, for its bitter oil, which is employed for burning, &c. It is generally raised in the cold-weather, but with water is, like the last, said to be grown as a summer crop. The young plant is used as greens, as in France, &c.

B. GRIFFITHII. Hf. and T.

Vernacular. T. I. *sizgái, mole.* S. S. D. *baráni múlí, bíbácha, chináka.*

Has a rather pretty lilac flower, and is not uncommon in parts of the lower hills, Trans-Indus, and of the Salt Range, from 1,000 to 4,500 feet (as well as in Belúchistán and Affghánistán). It is used as a pot-herb.

B. JUNCEA. L. (and many synonyms).

Vernacular. Plains, *rái, túria,* Bazár. Seeds, *khardil.* (?)

Appears to be much less extensively cultivated in the plains than the *sarson,* which it resembles. Appears to be grown also in the Himalaya up to say 10,000 feet in Tibet, as well as in Affghánistán. Its somewhat acrid oil is burned, used for inunction, &c., and occasionally employed in cooking. Its seeds are often added to native pickles, and the *khardil* of the Bazárs, in part doubtfully furnished by this, is held to be diaphoretic in native medicine.

B. OLERACEA, VAR. VULGARIS. DC. Cabbage.

Vernacular. Plains, *gobí, kobí.*

This is at times cultivated by natives in the plains, but is understood to have been introduced by Europeans. I believe, however, that I have seen it grown in the Kashmír valley (5,000 feet), and at 5,500 feet in Chumba.

B. RAPA. L. Turnip.

Vernacular. J. *thipar;* K. *gúnglú, gúgchí;* C. *mokalí, gúnglú, gúglí;* B. *gumbar;* S. *shaghar, shirwa. (?)* Lad. *niúma.* Plains, *shalgham.*

In the plains is extensively grown in Jhang, Mozaffargarh, and Múltán, to feed cattle with, and is held to improve both milk and beef. In the plains also it is eaten raw and as *áchár* (pickles), and sliced and dried in the sun, when it will keep for many months. In some parts of the hills, as on the Chenáb, where it is cultivated up to 8,000 feet, the root is eaten; and Hugel states that in Kanáwar it is dried and pounded with flour for bread; while elsewhere in the hills, as on the Kishenganga, and in Ladák, where it is grown to nearly 13,000 feet, and where the roots are eaten raw, the tops are used as a pot-herb (Moorcroft). Aitchison states that the dry roots are also brought from Ladák to Lahoul;

and Longden mentions that he saw a "few small turnips" grown in the latter. In Kashmír it would seem to be sown in autumn, "when the Elæagnus is ripe," though it is probably for the most part a summer crop in the hills.

BRASSICA SP. (B. napus, L., &c.)

Vernacular. J. *sarri;* CR. *kát kranar, shái, sarria, sarrú;* B. *shái;* S. *shák, cháyang, sharwa;* Lad. *niúnkar, niúskar;* leaves, *chodmal.*

These are cultivated species (probably B. campestris, B. juncea, and B. napus) which in many parts of the hills are often grown at considerable heights (to 11,000 feet, Kanáwar, Hoffmeister and Cleghorn; 10,000, Zanskar; and 12,000, Kanáwar, Thomson; and 13,000, Ladák, Cayley and myself); to furnish oil above where the apricot will flourish (Cunningham). They are also used as pot-herbs.

CARDAMINE HIRSUTA. L.

Vernacular. (?)

This grows at Hassan Abdál, in the plains of the north-west Punjab, where it is freely eaten as water cress—(see Nasturtium).

C. CHEIRI. L.

Vernacular. Bazar, seeds, *todri surkh, and t. nafarmani or t. siyáh.*

The seeds of this plant, which is cultivated for its flower, are officinal with natives, and held to have similar properties to those of Mathiola incana (q. v.)

CRAMBE CORDIFOLIA.

Vernacular. (?)

Thomson mentions a species (probably this) as growing at 12,000 feet on the Sutlej, the young leaves of which are used as a pot-herb.

ERYSIMUM STRICTUM. Gært, (E. ROBUSTUM. Don).

Vernacular. (?)

This is found in the Punjab Himalaya at from 6,000 to 13,500 feet; and under the name "Nepál wall-flower" is mentioned by Madden as grown by natives near Simla, in gardens.

FARSETIA EDGEWORTHII. Hf. and T.
F. JACQUEMONTII. Hf. and T.
F. HAMILTONII. Royle.

Vernacular. T. I. *mulei.* B. D., &c., *fárid búti, láthia.*

One or other of these is common in many parts of the arid tracts throughout the Punjab plains, from Dehlí to Peshawar.

They have a pleasant pungent taste, are pounded and taken as cooling medicine, and are considered specific for rheumatism (Edgeworth).

LEPIDIUM SATIVUM. L.

Vernacular. T. I. *shargundei, sorma.* Cis-Indus and Bazár, *tezak, hálim.*

This is commonly cultivated in the plains, and is probably the "cresses" of Matson, at Kábul. The leaves and seeds are pungent and officinal. The latter are given and applied as lactagogue, and administered after being boiled with milk to cause abortion (Bellew).

MALCOLMIA STRIGOSA. Boiss.

Vernacular. T. I. *khunserdia.* S. S. D. *patthra, páchan, chináka.*

A pretty little lilac flower abundant in many places on the Salt Range and north-west of it, sometimes called "heather" by Europeans. Not known to be of any use. A nearly allied species, M. Africana, grows in the plains of the north-west Punjab, and also apparently at 10,500 feet in Ladák.

MATHIOLA ANNUA. Sw. Stock.

Vernacular. *shab bú.*

Cultivated in European gardens only in the Punjab, but stated by Vigne to be grown at Kábul.

M. INCANA. Br.

Vernacular. *todri safêd, t. lila.*

Grown for its seeds, which constitute some of the several kinds of *todri*, reckoned aphrodisiac.

NASTURTIUM AMPHIBIUM. Br.
N. OFFICINALE. Br.
N. TERRESTRE. Br. (N. PALUSTRE. DC).

Vernacular. (?)

These three species grow at various elevations in the Punjab Himalaya. The first I found wild at 2,000 feet near the Indus, the second grows at a greater elevation, and the third I have found wild in Kashmir up to over 9,000 feet. All more or less resemble the water-cress, but Hf. and T. doubt if the second or true water-cress is really indigenous.

RAPHANUS CAUDATUS.

Vernacular. *múngra.*

First made known from Northern India by Mr. Bell, Saharanpur Gardens. Not uncommon cultivated about Lahore. Its immensely elongated fruit is cooked as a pot-herb.

R. RAPHANISTRUM. DC.

Vernacular. *tára míra.*

Given by Edgeworth as cultivated at Ambála; but Brassica eruca may be meant, especially as Hf. and T. only mention Affghánistán as a habitat of the above.

R. SATIVUS. L. Radish.

Vernacular. *múlí*, fruit, *sengra.*

Commonly grown in the Punjab, and in the Himalaya including (it is said) Ladák, not only for the root, but for the young fruit (and leaves occasionally?) used as a pot-herb. It *has* been stated (A. H. S. Selections) that it is grown for oil, but this seems doubtful. The seeds are officinal, being reckoned emmenagogue.

SISYMBRIUM IRIO. L.

Vernacular. T. I. *janglí sarson.* S. S. D. *naktrúsa.* **Bazár seeds,** *khúb kalán, kháksí.*

Common wild throughout the Punjab plains (Honigberger is probably mistaken in saying it is cultivated at Lahore). Davies' Trade Report gives 5 maunds of its seeds as annually imported from Affghánistán by the Bolan. They are reckoned febrifuge by natives.

S. SOPHIA. L.

Vernacular.

Is also indigenous in the plains of the north-west Punjab, and its seeds are said occasionally to be used under the same name.

N. O. CAPPARIDEÆ.

CAPPARIS APHYLLA. L. (SODADA DECIDUA. Forsk).

Vernacular. T. I. *kirra.* S. S. D. *karia, karín.* B. D., &c., *karíl.* Bud, *tít.* Fruit, *tentí, delha, pínjú.*

A curious, green, twiggy-looking shrub, which has handsome red flowers in spring and red fruit in April. It is characteristic of the Punjab, being common towards Dehlí and along Harriána, and gets abundant in the Sirsa tract, as well as in Múltán, and to the north and west, and Trans-Indus. It is less common outside these tracts, especially where the climate is less arid. It at times attains a considerable size, the largest on record being one of 8 feet girth mentioned by Edgeworth near Chíchawatní; but its ordinary girth is not a fourth of this. It has immense roots, and the natives in some parts assert that it never grows from seed, but that each plant has been growing from all time. I am not aware of any successful attempt in the Punjab to raise it either from seed or by cuttings, even in places where it is very common; but Dr. Anderson has recently informed me that he has grown plants of it in Calcutta from seed sent by me. It is commonly used for fuel by natives, burning with a strong gaseous flame even when green, and does for brick-burning, but is not suited for burning alone in furnaces, &c., on the large scale. Its wood is stated to be very durable, is bitter, and not liable to the attacks of white ants, being often untouched among other timbers destroyed by them. It is much used for the rafters of small buildings, Trans-Indus, in the Southern Punjab, and up as far as the latitude of Lahore to the westward of it. Ploughshares are made of it in Dehra Ghází Khan, and it is said to be used for turning in Jhelam (Aitchison). In Sind the timber is often used for knees in boat-building.

The bud is cooked fresh as a pot-herb. The fruit is about the size of a marble, and is very largely consumed by the natives, great numbers of whom go out for the purpose of collecting it both when green and after it is ripe. In the former state it is generally steeped for 15 days in salt and water, being put in the sun to ferment till it becomes acid, pepper, &c., and oil being then added. It is said that it will thus keep for a year, and is eaten to an ounce or two at a time usually with bread. The ripe fruit is generally made into pickle with mustard or other oil (Hindus are not allowed to use vinegar) to be eaten with bread. In this state it is frequently exported as far east as Cawnpúr.

The top shoots and young leaves are ground to make a blister in native pharmacy.

CAPPARIS HORRIDA. L., OR C. SEPIARIA. L.

Vernacular. B. *hiún garna.* J. D., &c., *hís.* S. P. *karvíla.*

Occasional in the Punjab Siwáliks and in the plains as far west as Lahore, and south to Múltán, &c. The wood is only used for fuel. In the Southern Punjab and Sind the fruit is made into pickle, and in the latter the leaves are applied as a counter-irritant.

C. SPINOSA. L.

Vernacular. Lad. *kábra*. T. I. *kbarra*. S. S. D. *kaur, kiárí, taker, baurí*. C. *ber*. B. *barárí*. S. *bandar, kakrí, bassar*.

This plant, which in Europe furnishes the caper, generally grows in the Punjab exactly as a recent traveller has described it on Sinai: "In bright green tufts hanging down from the clefts of the rocks," and adorned with a very handsome large flower. It is found near Múltán, in the Salt Range, along the Trans-Indus hills to Peshawar, and in the valleys of some of the great rivers, ascending to 5,000 feet at Wangtú, on the Sutlej (8,000 feet, Thomson), and on the Indus above Iskardo to about 10,500 feet (Jacquemont and Thomson), and it occurs to 12,000 near Lêh. The ripe fruit is made into pickles by the natives of the Salt Range, &c.; but in some places at least eaten only by Hindús. Mr. Edgeworth prepared the buds in the European style as capers, and found them first-rate. In Ladák the leaves are used as greens. They are eaten by goats and sheep, and in Kángra the roots are said to be applied to sores.

CLEOME RUTA. DNE.

Vernacular. T. I. *kastere*. B. D. *dandí bútí, búgrí, bújra*.

A small inconspicuous plant, with a yellow flower and a strong Rutaceous smell, which is common in many places in the Punjab plains from the Sutlej westward, and up to the Súlimán range. In the Southern Punjab the plant is pounded and taken for colic.

CRATÆVA RELIGIOSA. Ham. (C. ROXBURGHII. Br.?)

Vernacular. Plains, &c., *barna, barnáhí*.

A handsome tree with a luxuriant flush of pretty white flowers in spring. It is generally of rather small size, but at times reaches a girth of 7 or 8 feet. It occurs in the Síwálik tract in the east of the Punjab, and is frequently seen planted at wells, &c., west as far as Jhelum and south to Múltán. The wood is soft and easily cut, but tolerably tough, and is used for making small wheels, and for carving models, making writing-boards and combs, &c. In Peninsular India, the root, bark, leaves, juice, and seeds of this or allied species, are used for various purposes. Aitchison states that at Jhelum the fruit is mixed with mortar to form a strong cement, and the rind as a mordant in dyeing.

GYNANDROPSIS PENTAPHYLLA. DC. (CLEOME P. L.)

POLANISIA ICOSANDRIA. W. and A. (P. VISCOSA. DC. CLEOME I. L.)

Vernacular. *hulhul, búgra, gandhúlí.*

These herbs, the former with white, the latter with yellow flowers, occur throughout the Province in the plains and to 2,500 feet. They appear to be at times confused by natives. The former is used as a vegetable (Edgeworth), and the seeds of one or other are officinal, being considered stimulant. In Sind, women use the plant (?) for their hair to destroy vermin.

N. O. FLACOURTIANEÆ.

FLACOURTIA SAPIDA. ROX.

Vernacular. T. I. and J. *kúkai.* R. *kangú, kukoa.* S. S. D. *kukoa.* J. D. *kangú.* U. *kandei.*

A large shrub which is found along the lower hills sometimes to 3,500 feet, in the Salt Range, and on the skirts of the Súlimán range, &c. The timber is occasionally employed for ploughs, but is too small for most purposes. It is straight and close-grained, and is used for combs and in turnery. The fruit is eaten.

F. SEPIARIA. ROX. (F. RAMOTCHI. L. Her.)

Vernacular. T. I. *sherawane, zargal, dajkar.* S. R. *dajkar, jidkar.* D. *khatái.* H. *kíngaro.*

A small shrub which occurs about Dehlí, in the arid tract to the west, in the Salt Range, and on the skirts of the Súlimán range. Its wood is too small to be of use (very much the largest trunk I have noted was 3 feet in girth), and the spines are so strong that its twigs cannot be eaten by cattle, but the leaves are thrashed out for them. The fruit is small, hard, and insipid, but is said to be eaten by natives.

N. O. CISTINEÆ.

COCHLOSPERMUM GOSSYPIUM. DC.

Vernacular. *kúmbí.* Bazár, gum, *katíra.*

I have not seen this tree west of the Jumna, but it probably exists in the Siwálik region, in the east of the Punjab. Its gum is officinal, being used as demulcent in coughs, &c. The *katíra,* of which 10 maunds are stated by Davies' Trade Report to be imported annually *viâ* Peshawar, must be entered by mistake, or be the product of a different plant. And odd enough, the same authority gives 50 maunds of this substance as exported from "Loodiana" to Affghánistán by the Bolan.

N. O. VIOLARIEÆ.

VIOLA. Violet.

V. CINEREA. Boiss. grows to the plains level, Trans-Indus, and in the Salt Range, and several species are found in the Himalaya up to 10,000 feet, perhaps the commonest being—

V. SERPENS. Wall.

Vernacular. Him. and Bazár, *banafsha.*

The plant of this (chiefly) and other species is found in the Bazárs, and considered diaphoretic and aperient.

V. PATRINII. DC.

Vernacular. (?)

Found in Hazára, &c. A dark-flowered variety has a particularly fine scent.

N. O. MORINGACEÆ.

MORINGA PTERYGOSPERMA. Gært. (HYPERANTHERA MORINGA. Willd.) Horse-radish tree.

Vernacular. Plains, &c., *soanjna, sánjna, senjna.*

A tree which grows wild in the Siwálik region in the Eastern Punjab, and is seen commonly planted throughout the Province up to 1,200 or 1,500 feet. It is said to be very easily raised from seed, but is almost never grown except by natives. The wood is excessively soft and quite useless, and said to be "not even fit for fuel." In some parts the twigs and leaves are largely lopped for fodder. The roots have the flavour of horse-radish, and are occasionally used for it. The flowers, which are rather handsome, come out about February, preceding the leaves. The long pod-like fruit ripens about April, and is eaten by the natives, cooked as a pot-herb, or in curry, or is made into a pickle described as "most nauseous to Europeans." The fruit is stated by Honigberger to be officinal. Where the tree is plentiful, in the wild state at least, incisions are made in the trunk, from which, in a day or two a gum exudes. This is used in rheumatism, or is given as *kamarkas*—(see Butea frondosa). No oil is known to be extracted from the seeds in the Punjab.

N. O. DROSERACEÆ.

Drosera muscipula.

Vernacular. (?)

The leaves of this plant (or perhaps D. lunata. Ham.) are stated by Madden to be used for blisters in Kanáwar. I do not know of any D. being found to west of the Sutlej.

N. O. CARYOPHYLLEÆ.

This family abounds in the Himalaya, and a few species grow in the plains, but almost all are quite useless.

Goufeia holosteoides. Camb.

R. *kakúa.* S. *gandíal.* Lad. *chíkí.*

This appears to be the herb which, growing at from 5,500 to 10,000 feet, is used as a vegetable in Chumba and Ladák. It is also probably Madden's Stellaria crispata. Wall.—used in a similar way in Bissahir.

Lychnis Indica. Benth.
Silene viscosa. Pers.

Vernacular.

Aitchison states that in Lahoul the root and leaves of these are used for soap.

N. O. LINEÆ.

Linum perenne. L.

Vernacular. (?)

Aitchison states that this is to be found in some quantity in Lahoul, though not used. And it probably furnished the seed of "linseed growing wild in Spiti," which many years ago was sent for trial to the Agri-Horticultural Society at Lahore.

L. trigynum. Rox.

Vernacular. J. *karkún.* S. R. *kaur, gud batal.* C., B., and Plains, *basant, bál-basant.*

A small shrub with a fine yellow flower, common at low elevations in the hills generally, and occasionally seen to 6,000 feet, and cultivated in many gardens in the plains. It is stated to be administered as a medicine for founder in cattle.

L. USITATISSIMUM. L.

Vernacular. K. *alísh.* Plains, *tísí, alsí.*

Not uncommon as a field crop, the seed ripening in April, but more rare towards the north-west. Is grown in the Kashmír Valley (5,000 feet). Being raised only for its oil, is always sown wide, alone, (or sometimes mixed with Cicer); and as the plants are generally only from 18 to 24 inches high, the fibre is useless for textile purposes. By proper treatment, however, good fibre can be got from plants raised from European seed, or even from country seed if properly sown. Operations were carried on by a Company at Sealkôt from 1863; but, owing to various circumstances, these have recently been brought to a close. The seeds are officinal with natives, being given (as infusion ?) for asthma.

N. O. MALVACEÆ.

ABELMOSCHUS ESCULENTUS. L. (HIBISCUS LONGIFOLIUS. W. and A.)

Vernacular. *bhinda torí, rámturái.*

Grown by natives and Europeans in the plains throughout the Punjab. The fruit is cooked and eaten as a vegetable.

A. FICULNEUS. W. and A.

Vernacular. *dúla.*

Occurs in fields in the plains. Seeds put in sweetmeats.

ABUTILON INDICUM. G. Don.

Vernacular. T. I. *súnbal.* S. R. *pílí búti.* B, D. *pataka.*

Not uncommon wild up to the skirts of the Súlimán range. Edgeworth states that it is given in coughs (the seeds. ?)

ALTHÆA OFFICINALIS. L. Marshmallow.

Stated by Bellew to be used about Kandahár, &c., as greens.

A. ROSEA. Cav. Hollyhock.

Vernacular. *gul-khaira, khatmí,* root, *rísha khatmí.*

Commonly grown as a garden-flower. Its seeds are officinal, being mucilaginous and demulcent, diuretic and febrifuge, and the flowers are reckoned cooling and diuretic, and given in rheumatism. Of the former it would appear from Davies' Trade Report that 5 maunds, and of the latter 10 maunds, are annually imported from Affghánistán *viâ* Peshawar. The root is considered astringent, and given in fever and dysentery. Of it also Davies' Trade Report gives 10 maunds as annually imported from Affghánistán *viâ* Peshawar.

GOSSYPIUM HERBACEUM. L.

Vernacular. K. *kappas, kapá.* C. *kapá.* Plains, *kapás, kapá, bárí.* S. P. *vár.* Clean cotton, *rúí;* seeds, *binaula, barúngí.*

Commonly grown in many places all over the Punjab as a hot-weather crop, ripening up to Christmas. It is cultivated up to the Kashmír Valley (5,000 feet), but the quality does not appear first-rate. It is most frequent in places which are not the best and moistest, nor yet too dry, yet in some rather arid places, (*e. g.*, Shahpúr), it is raised in quantity without irrigation. Is rare in Northern Trans-Indus, though abundant in places up to near Attock. Is frequently treated as a biennial or even triennial crop (Agri-Horticultual Society Selections). The Punjab probably furnishes a considerable supply for Affghánistán, but the distance from the sea as yet restricts the export by the Indus. The seeds are officinal, being esteemed diaphoretic.

HIBISCUS CANNABINUS. L.

Vernacular. J. *shan.* Plains, *san, sankokla, patsan.*

Not uncommon throughout, except in the extreme north-west. But Bellew states that it is grown at Ghuzní (about 7,000 feet), and it is not uncommon to 3,000 feet in the N. W. Himalaya. It is generally raised in narrow strips along the edges of fields of cotton or pulse, being sown either about April, and irrigated up to the rains, or sown during the latter, the former giving much the best results (Edgeworth). Its fibre is used for the manufacture of ropes, twine and sacking. In Sind its fibre is considered the best for nets and ropes, but it is rarely used for cloth. The seeds are officinal.

H. MUTABILIS. L.

Vernacular. *gul-i-ajáib.*

Commonly cultivated in flower-gardens.

H. SABDARIFFA. L.

Vernacular. *patwa.*

Said to have been introduced from the West Indies. Is cultivated for its succulent acid calyces, which make excellent jelly. These come to maturity in the Punjab, but even at Lahore the seeds hardly ever ripen.

H. sp. ?

Vernacular. *janglí sankokra, janglí binda.*

A plant growing wild in the Siwálik tract, the fruit of which is used as a pot-herb.

LAVATERA CACHEMIRIANA. Camb. (?)

Vernacular. J. *gul khair.* C. *sazposh.*

A handsome plant like hollyhock, growing in parts of the basins of the Jhelum and Chenáb at from 5,000 to 10,000 feet. Of no known use.

MALVA PARVIFLORA. L.
M. ROTUNDIFOLIA. L.
M. SYLVESTRIS. L.

Vernacular. S. *narr.* T. I. *panírak, súpra.* S. R. *sonchal, gogí ság.*

There is some confusion as to these species. The first, however, and probably the second, grow in the hills to 8,000 or 9,000 feet, and are common cold-weather weeds in the plains. The third also appears to occur in the hills from 5,000 to 9,000 feet. They are frequently eaten as pot-herbs, especially in time of dearth. And the seeds, being demulcent, are used in coughs and ulceration of the bladder (Honigberger). In Kanáwar, women clean their hair with (an infusion of ?) the root, and woollen cloth is washed by its aid. Bellew states that the root is used as *rísha khatmí ?*—(see Althæa rosea).

SIDA CORDIFOLIA. L. ?

Vernacular. *kharentí;* Bazár, seeds, *bíjband, chúka, hamáz kowár, simák.*

A common small wild plant of the plains, which is used in fevers. The seeds are reckoned aphrodisiac, and are administered in gonorrhœa. Bellew states that they are given for colic and tenesmus. For other seeds, &c., used under some of the Bazár names given above (each of which was applied to specimens of this seed sent to the Punjab Exhibition) see Rumex acutus, Oxalis corniculata, and Rhus parviflora.

THESPESIA POPULNEA. Corr.

Vernacular. *páras pípal* (corrupted into *pahárí pípal*).

Two trees only are known to grow in the Punjab, at Khángarh in the Mozaffargarh district. These were raised from seed brought from the south by a fakír about forty years ago. The larger is about four feet girth and thirty-five in height, but their seed does not ripen. The Hindús carry off their leaves to be used in *púja* at deaths.

N. O. BOMBACEÆ.

ADANSONIA DIGITATA. L.

Vernacular. *imlí Khorasání.*

This tree, of which some specimens are stated to exist in the N. W. Provinces, and which is common in parts of Central India and Bombay, has never been grown in the Punjab, although seeds were tried at Lahore so far back as 1853.

BOMBAX HEPTAPHYLLUM. Cav.

Vernacular. J. *sum*; Plains, &c., *sembal, simbal, simmal;* Bazár, gum, *mochras, sembalgond*; root, *musalí sembal.*

This tree grows to a very large size, and, about March, is a striking object with its immense buttressed trunks, and its large showy red flowers, six inches in breadth, clustered on the leafless branches. The latter generally leave the trunk by six or seven radiating from about one level. The tree occurs wild in the Siwálik tract, occasionally to 3,500 feet, and perhaps to beyond the Indus, as Bellew mentions it in Chinglái. It may sometimes be seen as high as 6,000 feet near the Rávi, and is not uncommonly planted in the plains as far as Múltán. Curious discussions occasionally take place as to whether the prevailing wind or what other cause leads to the formation of the buttresses on particular aspects of the trunk. The tree furnishes a whitish, coarse-grained, weak, brittle wood, which is very subject to the attacks of white ants. It is thus for the most part used only for planks, doors, boxes, &c., and is said not even to be good fuel. But curious enough, like some other woods of similar texture, moisture seems to render it more durable, and it is a favourite for well-curbs *(nímchaks)*, water conduits, troughs, and bridges. It is also made into scabbards in Kángra and Yúsafzái. In some places, *e. g.*, near Kángra, the leaves and twigs of the tree are severely lopped, probably for fodder. The flower buds are eaten as a pot-herb, and the cotton of the pods is occasionally used to stuff pillows; it is too short-stapled and smooth to be applicable to textile purposes. The gum, which exudes from the bark, is given often with Ægle (q. v.) for dysentery and diarrhœa. The root furnishes one of the kinds of *musalí*, being considered cooling, astringent, and aphrodisiac, and is given in gonorrhœa, &c.

N. O. BYTTNERIACEÆ.

KYDIA CALYCINA. ROX.

Vernacular. C. *púllí*. R. *púlá*. *B. polá*. V. *pulá*. S. R. *púlí*.

A tree which is common wild in many parts of the Siwálik tract to 3,000 feet, up to the Indus, and occasionally seen planted in the plains. The wood is used for building, charcoal, and fuel. I do not know that the bark is used in the Punjab as in the N. W. Provinces for clarifying sugar.

PENTAPETES PHŒNICEA. L.

Vernacular. *gul dupaharia*.

Commonly cultivated as a garden flower. Its fruit is officinal.

N. O. STERCULIACEÆ.

HELICTERES ISORA. L.

Vernacular. *marorphalí, kupásí*. Bazár, fruit, *marorphalí*.

A large shrub which is found wild in the Siwálik tract for some distance into the Punjab. Its fruit is spirally twisted, and on "the doctrine of signatures," which prevails in India as it was universally held in Europe some centuries ago, is esteemed as efficacious in colic (and dysentery) being given in powder. It is sometimes applied externally also (Honigberger).

STERCULIA.

There is some confusion about the species of this.

S. VILLOSA. ROX.

Vernacular. C. *gulkandar, kúrí*. S. *oshá*. U. *godgudála*. S. R. *massú*.

Sometimes a tree, but often seen very small, is common in many places in the outer hills to 3,500 feet or more, up to the Indus, and occurs in the Salt Range. Its bark is frequently made into ropes of some strength; in Southern India, elephant ropes and in Bombay bagging are made of it. In Dehra Doon *good* paper has been made from it.

S. WALICHII.

Vernacular. C. *kúrí*. R. *úlán*. B. *wulena*.

A shrub, occasional to 3,500 feet in similar places, and with similar qualities to the last, but apparently less widely distributed.

N. O TILIACEÆ.

CORCHORUS CAPSULARIS. L.

Vernacular. Bengál, *pat*.

Occasional wild in the Punjab. Cultivated largely in Bengál for its fibre, called jute in commerce.

C. DEPRESSUS. L.

Vernacular. *baphallí, kúrand*.

Common wild in the Southern Punjab. The plant is rubbed down and given as a cooling medicine.

C. OLITORIUS. L.

Vernacular. Bengál, *banpat*.

Found wild in the Punjab. Is cultivated in Bengál for its fibre.

C. TRILOCULARIS. L. (C. ACUTANGULUS. Lam.)

Vernacular. *báphallí*. Bazár, seeds, *isband ?*

Not uncommon wild. The plant is officinal, and may furnish the officinal seeds, *isband*, which are given in rheumatism.

GREWIA ASIATICA. L.

Vernacular. *phálsa*.

A small tree commonly cultivated in the plains for its pleasantly acid small fruit. The appearance of its leaves has caused Europeans to mistake it for the Hazel. The leaves and buds are officinal.

G. BETULÆFOLIA. Juss.

Vernacular. T. I. *gangí, inzarre, khírcha.* S. R. and S. S. D., *ganger*.

A small shrub common on the low hills, Trans-Indus, in the Salt Range up to 3,000 feet, and in the more arid tracts of the Western, Southern, and Eastern Punjab as far as Delhí. The natives eat the small fruit and, as usual, call it "sweet," but it has neither substance nor flavour.

G. ELASTICA. Royle. (?)

Vernacular. S. R. *farrí, dhamman.* J. D. *dhamman.*

In the Salt Range, and Siwálik tract below Kángra. The timber is said to be very strong and elastic. The fruit is eaten.

G. OPPOSITIFOLIA. Buch.

Vernacular. J. C. and R. *thamman, dhamman.* R. and B. *dhamman, biúl, bahul.* U. *dhámun.* T. I. *pastúwanna.* S. R. *dhamman.*

A small tree common in all the lower hills, Cis and Trans-Indus, and in the Salt Range, up to 4,500 feet. Lowther mentions trees as thriving at Kháí near Ferozepúr; but these were probably Celtis (q. v.), which distantly resembles this in appearance. The wood is tough and elastic, and is valued for handles, shafts, bangy-sticks, &c., the ring for supporting the seat of the single-rope bridge, &c. And Vigne states that in the Súlimán range bows are made of it (though no other authority seems to mention bows as being used by any of the tribes in that tract). The chief value of the tree is on account of the leaves, which largely serve as fodder, wherever it is common, and are said to increase the quantity of milk. The bark is made into sandals, &c., and after being steeped for 10 or 15 days in water, makes a fair rope, which, however, is stated not to be durable. Under European supervision a fair paper has been manufactured from the bark in the Kángra Valley and elsewhere.

G. ROTHII. DC.

Vernacular. S. R. *bather, nikkí bekkar.*

G. VILLOSA. Roth.

Vernacular. T. I. *inzarra, pastuwanne.* S. R. *jalidar, kaskúsrí, thamther.*

Both species occur in the lower hills, Trans-Indus, and in the Salt Range. The fruit of both is eaten, but is very poor.

Triumfetta angulata. Lam.?

Vernacular. ?

Occurs in the Punjab plains; has been eaten as a pot-herb in times of famine.

N. O. DIPTEROCARPACEÆ.

Shorea robusta.

Vernacular. *sál.* Resin, *rál zard; r. sufēd; r. kála, dhúná.*

West of the Jumna there is only one considerable tract of this valuable tree, close to that river at 1,500 to 2,000 feet, and even there it does not attain any considerable size. While in two small patches in the Siwálik region below Kángra, the climate is so unfavorable that the trees as a rule remain quite small and crooked. This tree is very difficult to raise even close to its natural habitat; and outside of the hills in the Punjab I only know of a very few specimens. In Saharunpúr Botanic Gardens, a tree of 35 years old is 7½ feet in girth. The timber is hard and heavy and durable, and is one of the best possible for all purposes where great strength is required and weight is no objection. The resin which exudes from the tree is officinal, and is used in the arts.

N. O. AURANTIACEÆ.

Ægle Marmelos. Corr. Bengál Quince.

Vernacular. *bil, bel.* Fruit pulp, *bel giri.*

This small tree, which is not uncommon at different places below Simla to about 4,000 feet, extends sparingly up to near the Indus, and is said by Bellew and others to be found beyond that river. It is occasionally seen planted in the plains up to 2 or 3 feet in girth. The wood is whitish, clean-grained, hard and strong, and is valued for building and making charcoal, but is not often used (in Kángra at least), as the Hindús venerate the tree and offer its leaves on the shrines of Síva. The pulp of the fruit, fresh or dried, is undoubtedly of use in affections of the bowels, nor do I see any reason to place credit in a newspaper statement, that from the trees of these hills it is less efficacious than from those growing further east. The pulp is also used in lime cement. In Peshawar, large numbers of snuff-boxes for Affgháns are made from the shell of the fruit, which is prettily carved over, and fitted with a small bone-plug for the opening in the end which serves as entrance and exit for the snuff.

BERGERA KÖNIGII. L.

Vernacular. R. *gándla*. B. *gandla, gándalí*.

A common shrub in the outer low hills reaching to 4,000 feet or more up to the Rávi at least. It is large enough for fuel only. Its leaves are applied to blows (Lake).

CITRUS.

I know of no species wild in the Punjab, although some are found in the Siwálik tract and outer hills further east. The usual species and varieties are grown, comprized for the most part under the following. Some of them are cultivated up to 4,000 feet, but it is doubtful if the fruit ripens at that elevation.

CITRUS ACIDA.	Sour lime.	*Nímbú.*
C. AURANTIUM. Risso.	Orange.	*Narangí.*
C. DECUMANA. L.	Pumelo.	*Chakotra.*
C. LUNETTA. Risso.	Sweet lime.	*Mítha nímbú.*
C. MEDICA. Risso.	Citron.	*Bajaurí nímbú.*

FERONIA ELEPHANTUM. Corr. Wood apple.

Vernacular. *kait, bilin*.

I have not seen this tree wild in the Punjab except sparingly in the Siwálik tract above Hoshyarpúr. It is occasionally seen planted in the eastern part of the Province. Its timber is not valued, and its fruit and gum do not appear to be used in the Punjab as elsewhere in India.

SKIMMIA LAUREOLA. Zucc. (LIMONIA. Wall.)

Vernacular. J. *ner*. R. *barrú, shalanglí*. (?)

A common small shrub in many parts of the Punjab Himalaya from 5,000 to 9,000 feet up to the Indus. In Hazára the leaves, which have an orange-like smell when crushed, are burned near smallpox patients, with a view to curative effects. As the leaves are dotted, this may have arisen from "the doctrine of signatures." Jameson states that the hill-people assert that the musk-deer gets its musk by feeding on the leaves of this plant. Madden comments on Ogilby's statement in Royle's Illustrations, that the same animal is supposed to get its musk from the roots dug up by its teeth! (It is, however, a "kind of ground nut" which Ogilby mentions in this connection).

N. O. HYPERICINEÆ.

Hypericum perforatum. L. St. John's wort.

Vernacular. R. *bassant.* B. *dendlú.*

A small plant common (with several others of the same genus) in many parts of the Himalaya from 2,500 to 10,000 feet. Honigberger states that it is not officinal, but is recommended in Arabic medicine for a vermifuge, &c.

N. O. MALPIGHIACEÆ.

Hiptage Madablota. Gært.

Vernacular. C. *endra.* R. *chopar.* B. *benkar, khúmb.* Plains, *chábuk chúrí.*

A fine large climber with handsome flowers found at low elevations (generally under 3,000 feet) in many places of the outer hills up to near the Indus. Cultivated at Lahore.

N. O. ACERINEÆ.

Acer Creticum. L. (?)

Vernacular names multitudinous, the following are a selection:—J. *tilkhan, trekhana, kukandra.* K. *serán, tilpattar.* C. *kitlá, kákrái, mandar, kángla.* R. *mandar.* S. *tían.*

A small tree, which strongly resembles the description of the above species, is not uncommon at places on most of the great rivers from the Rávi westward from 3,500 up to 6,000 feet. Of no special use.

A. cultratum. Wall. Maple.
A. sterculiaceum. Wall. Maple.

Vernacular. J. *trekan, tilpattar, killú.* K. *tilpattar, kilpattar, kanur.* C. *hanzal, kanzaa, kanzrú, kákrá, mandar.* R. *mandar, chírindí.* B. *mandar, kaura.* S. *mandar, kánjar, kalindra, jarimú, laur.*

It is not attempted to separate these two species of maple as they much resemble each other, often grow in similar or the same places, and are frequently confused. They are found on all the rivers up to near the Indus at from 4,000 to 10,000 feet, the latter generally growing at somewhat greater elevations than the former. They are handsome trees, and attain a considerable size; (I have frequently seen specimens of the latter up to 12 feet girth), but the timber is not particularly valued. It is, however, close-grained and tolerably strong, and in Kángra is used for making ploughs, bedsteads, and *jámpán*-poles. From Bissahir, &c., there is a considerable export of drinking-cups of maple-wood, to Tibet, where they are much used and often set in silver. Gerard states that they are made of juniper, and Moorcroft says horse-chesnut—(see Pavia)—but J. D. Cunningham mentions the knots or excrescences of these two maples (by native names) as giving the best kinds. The juice of the leaves is in Kanáwar said to be so acrid as to hurt the hands, but the leaves and twigs are in places, high in Hazára especially, much lopped for fodder.

N. O. SAPINDACEÆ.

Cardiospermum Halicacabum. L.

Vernacular. Bazár, seed, *habo ul kulkul.*

A pretty, slender climber found wild in the lower hills, and occasionally cultivated in gardens. Its seeds are officinal.

Dodonæa Burmanniana. DC.

Vernacular. J. *sanattha.* C. *sánthá.* R *ban mendú.* B. *mendrú.* T. I. *ghuráske, veravena, shumshád.* S. R. *sanatha.* Plains, *aliár.*

A handsome small evergreen shrub, well suited for hedges, for which it is often used, and generally called "bog myrtle," why I know not. It is common in the lower hills, Trans-Indus, and east of that river extends to Umb, Cis-Biás, in the outer hills, and it occurs frequently in the Salt Range. Its branches are tough, and used by natives in the last to put under the earth of their roofs. The leaves are hard and dry, and only eaten by cattle when very hungry. Jameson and others consider this a distinct species from D. Burmanniana, and he calls it D. Mackesonii; and it is probably the indigenous species "with small leaves," which Firininger names D. dioica. Our plant is certainly diœcious, and as certainly not a scandent shrub as the Bombay Flora states that D. Burmanniana is.

Pavia Indica. Wall. Himalayan Horse-chesnut.

Vernacular. J. *bankhor.* K. *háne, hanúdún.* C. *gúgú, gún.* R. *gún.* B. *kanor.* S. *kanúr.* T. I. *torjaga.* Bazár, fruit, *jauz mukaddam.*

A fine tree frequently seen up to 10 and occasionally 15 feet girth, very like the European horse-chesnut; grows in most of the higher hills Cis and Trans-Indus from 4,000 to 9,000 feet.

The bark peels off in long strips upward on the trunk, as was remarked by Jacquemont; and compared to that of North American hickory by Vigne. The wood is light-colored and easily worked, but is not much valued, being for the most part only used for ordinary building purposes, for packing cases, water troughs, tubs, platters, &c. It is sometimes employed for furniture, and makes nice-looking tea-boxes. Part of the drinking-cups, so largely used by the Tibetans, are made from the wood of this tree, but not the best kind—(see Acer cultratum). Mr. Watson, Madhopúr Workshops, states that it does well for rough pattern-making. The leaves are much lopped for winter fodder in the Himalaya, as in Káffiristán (Griffith), and the fruit is collected for feeding cattle and goats. The latter is in some parts also used as food for man, especially in times of scarcity, after being steeped in water for many days, and is generally mixed with flour, as, when taken alone, it is very bitter and apt to produce colic. The fruit is officinal likewise, being applied externally in rheumatism (Honigberger).

SAPINDUS DETERGENS. Royle. (?) Soapnut tree.

Vernacular. R. B. and S. *dodan*; fruit, *rítha*.

A handsome smallish tree, not uncommon planted up to 3,500 feet in the valleys as far as the Rávi. The largest tree noted by me was 8½ feet in girth. The timber is white, soft, and weak, and is in no repute. In Kángra the leaves are used as fodder. The large seed is used for washing woollen and silk (Honigberger), and is also employed for cleaning the hair, though Vigne is mistaken in saying a decoction of it is applied to cause the hair to grow! The seeds are also officinal, being given in cases of salivation, in epilepsy, and as expectorant.

SCHLEICHERA TRIJUGA. Willd.

Vernacular. B. *samma.?* U. *jamoa.?* Plains, &c., *gausam*.

This valuable timber tree occurs rarely wild in the Siwálik tract up to the Biás, and is seen planted occasionally in the plains; but it is much too unfrequent in the Province to require more than a passing notice here.

N. O. MELIACEÆ.

AZADIRACHTA INDICA. Ad. de Juss.

Vernacular. *ním*.

Is common planted in the more eastern part of the Province (Cis-Sutlej) where it is often seen of 6 or 7 and up to 8 or 9 feet in girth. West of the Sutlej it is comparatively rare, and is not often seen of more than 2 or 3 feet in girth. Beyond the Jhelam it speedily disappears altogether, and I do not know that a single specimen exists Trans-Indus. It is stated not to grow from cuttings, but to graft readily on the next mentioned tree. The wood is said to be ant-proof. The leaves are good fodder for camels, an infusion of them is given medicinally, and they are applied to boils, &c. From incisions in the bark, some very old trees discharge a large quantity of juice which is reputed to have medicinal powers. In Sind, "the aromatic seeds are used for the hair by women," and an oil, which is applied to sores, is extracted from them. This oil appears to be largely extracted and exported from Southern India. Honigberger mentions that the bark likewise and a "gum" of this tree are officinal. The gum is likewise mentioned in Southern India as medicinal.

MELIA AZEDARACH. L. (M. SEMPERVIRENS. Swartz. M. COMPOSITA. Willd.) Bead-tree.

Vernacular. B. *kachen, jek*. Plains, &c., generally, *drek, bakáin*. Bazár, seed, *habb ul bán*.

In the Punjab this tree (in which I can see no specific difference, although two or three species are made out by some) replaces the last, being rare in the east, and abundant in the centre and west. With its bunches of light colored fruit hanging on the bare arms for some months of the year, it is not a favourite tree with Europeans, although it was frequently planted along roads, &c., in the rudimentary stage of arboriculture after annexation of the Province. But it is liked by natives for its pleasant shade and verdure in the hot weather, and is generally planted by them at wells, &c. Griffith mentions that it is common planted at villages in the less elevated parts of Affghánistán. In the Himalaya it is seen to 5,000, and occasionally to 6,000 feet; but I am not aware that I have ever observed it truly wild anywhere. Below Chumba, &c., at about 2,800 feet, trees of 12 or 14 feet girth may occasionally be seen. In the plains I have never seen any at all approaching this size. The wood is yellowish, soft, brittle, and weak, but is bitter and not subject to the attacks of insects. In Bengál it is used for making idols, and in Sind well-curbs are constructed of it. The leaves are said by Honigberger to be officinal. The fruit is greedily eaten by goats and sheep (Aitchison). The seeds are considered hot and are given in rheumatism, and in Kángra pounded and mixed with apricots they are rubbed in for the same disease.

N. O. CEDRELACEÆ.

Cedrela toona. Rox.

Vernacular. *tún*. Bazár. flowers, *gúl tún*.

This fine tree does not, as a rule, seem to grow much over 2,500 feet, though many trees of 7 or 8 feet girth, and some to 10, may be seen at 3,000 near Chumba, one at the bridge there exceeding 12 feet girth, and I have noted one fine tree at 4,800 feet. It is indigenous in the outer hills, and at one time there have been large numbers wild and planted in the Siwálik tract between Kángra and the plains, where it was formerly a "royal tree," *i. e.*, preserved for the use of the rulers. Out in the plains it is grown throughout the Province, Cis-Indus, though more uncommon west of the Jhelam. In its earliest stage it is not very easily raised from seed; recently some trials of growing it from cuttings have succeeded. Its growth is fairly rapid, and as its darkish wood is not subject to worm or warp, and looks well when properly polished, it is a favourite for cabinet work, which has led to most of the best trees being cut down. Unless some means are taken for extending its cultivation, the wood will by and bye be exceedingly scarce and dear. From the flowers a fleeting *bassanti* (yellow) dye is got, and they are officinal, being considered emmenagogue and abortive.

C. toona. var. serratta. Royle.

Vernacular. J., K. *drawí, drab, túní*. C. *derí, chíti sirín*. R. *der, dorí, bíurú, gúldar*. B. *daral*. S. *daral, khíshing, khanam*.

Is considered to be only a variety of the last, the chief difference being that the leaves of this are always serrate or saw-edged. It is found in most of the valleys from 4,000 to 8,000 feet, up to near the Indus. The wood is often very red, and it has a strong fœtid smell when fresh. It is lighter and more open in texture than the last (for which it is at times sold), and is in Kanáwar said to be well suited for bridges. It appears to be pretty tough, as in some places the hoops of sieves are made from it.

Swietenia Mahogani. L. Mahogany.

I know of no tree of this in the Punjab. At Saharanpúr a tree of 35 years is 8 feet in girth.

N. O. AMPELIDEÆ.

CISSUS CARNOSA. Lam. (VITIS. Wall). (C. CAPREOLATA. ?)

Vernacular. C. *kárik, ámal bel.* R. *gídardák.* B. *drúkrí.* B. D. *vallúr.*

A pretty climber (perhaps two species ?) which is found in several of the valleys from 2,000 to 8,000 feet, and occurs in parts of the plains. It is eaten by camels in the latter, and in Jummoo the root ground with black pepper, is applied to boils.

LEEA ASPERA. Wall.

Vernacular. B. *holma.*

Occasional up to the Bíás at from 4,000 to 6,000 feet. The fruit is eaten.

VITIS INDICA. L. } Vine.
V. LANATA. Rox.
V. VINIFERA. L.

Vernacular. Plains and hills generally, *dákh.* J *búrí.* K. *tanaur, talor dach, newala.* C. *dakkí, dehla.* R. *gandelí, mámre.* S. *láning.* Bázar, currants, *zirishk mítha.* Lad. *básho.*

I have not distinguished between these three species. That with velvety, white or red-backed leaves (V. lanata), which is only found wild, appears to run into the glabrous-leaved wild one; these are generally found at from 3,000 to 6,000 feet, and appear to give both purple and green fruit; cultivated, the vine is generally seen at 5—6,000 in Kashmír, &c., to 6,500 or more on the Upper Chenáb, to 9,000 (at Sungnam) on the Sutlej, and from 6,500 to more than 9,000 feet in Tibet. The fruit is of either color, and the crop is very precarious, especially in Kanáwar on the Sutlej. Grapes of varying quality are raised at most places in the Punjab plains, those of Peshawar being the best; currants are made from a small grape in Kanáwar, as well as in Western Tibet and Yárkand. Cayley mentions that 15 maunds of currants were imported into Lêh from Kashmír in 1867. In Kanáwar a spirit prepared from the juice is compared to grape-brandy by Hoffmeister. This spirit is, according to Longden, called *rak* or *arrak,* and he mentions that a wine also *(sheo)* is made there. The circumstance that the Hindú name is applied to this and the barley brandy of Lahoul—(see Hordeum)—would seem to imply that the art of distillation has been introduced into these countries from below. In Affghánistán, Bellew states that a grape wine is prepared, which is consumed by well-to-do Mussalmáns, and a raisin wine for Hindús. Several attempts have been made to manufacture wine in the Punjab on European principles. And a correspondent has recently informed the Agri-Herticultural Society of India, that sparkling and good wine was made at Peshawar about 1861, and he states that since then still better results have been attained.

N. O. GERANIACEÆ.

Erodium and Geranium.

A good many species grow in the Himalaya, and some in the plains of the Western Punjab. Only one of the latter genus needs mention here.

Geranium nodosum. L. (G. Napaulense. Sw. ?)

Vernacular. Bazár, root, *rowíl, bhánd.*

The root of a species of G. is brought from the hills. (G. Napaulense appears to grow at from 3,500 to nearly 12,000 feet), and sold as a red dye. In appearance it resembles *rattanjot*—(see Onosma).

N. O. BALSAMINEÆ.

Impatiens var. sp. Balsam.

Vernacular. J. *bantil.* K. *bantil, tatúra, trúal.* R. *pallú, tílphar.* S. *hálú, júk.*

The seeds of some of the numerous Himalayan species are eaten in Chumba, &c., and the oil expressed from them is on the Sutlej both eaten and burned. The occurrence of *til* in the names of some of them points perhaps to this. or more probably to the resemblance of the flower to that of the Sesamum. Madden states that I. Balsamina flowers (?) are in Gurhwál used for a dye, whence it is called *majíti*—(see Rubia).

I. sulcata. Wall.

Vernacular. (?)

Aitchison states that in Lahoul the husks of the seeds of this species are eaten raw.

I. tingens. Edge.

Vernacular. (?)

This species, so named by Edgeworth from its coloring his herbarium paper yellow, is a common weed in Lahoul, where

Aitchison states that an oil is expressed from the seeds, only to be used, however, for polishing the cups, &c., made by the inhabitants from the knots of chiefly Acer (q. v.) perhaps imported from further down, as on the Sutlej.

N. O. OXALIDEÆ.

Averrhoa Carambola. L.

Vernacular. *kamrakh.*

This tree is very rare in the Punjab. It produces fruit at Hoshyarpúr, and there is at least one tree in Lahore.

Oxalis acetosella. L. Wood sorrel.

Has been found by myself and others in various parts of the N. W. Himalaya at from 3,500 to 9,000 feet.

O. corniculata. L.

Vernacular. S. *súrchí.* T. I. *trawuke.* S. R. *khatta mítha.* Bazár, plant, *chúkhá.*

Common in the plains and in the hills up to 8,000 feet. In Kanáwar it is eaten raw, and cooked as a pot-herb. The plant is officinal.

N. O. ZYGOPHYLLEÆ.

Fagonia Cretica. L.

Vernacular. T. I. *spalaghzái.* B. D., &c., &c., *dhamá, damiyá.*

A small spinous weed common in most parts of the Punjab plains, and occurring in Affghánistán to about 3,500 feet (Bellew). The plant is given as a febrifuge and tonic, and Bellew states that in the Peshawar Valley it is administered to children as a prophylactic against smallpox.

Tribulus alatus. Del.
T. lanuginosus. L.
T. terrestris L.

Vernacular. T. I. *krúnda.* S. S. D. *lotak.* B. D. &c., *bakhra, bhúkrí.* Lad. *rásha, kokullak.* Bazár, *gokhrú desí.*

One or other species common in the plains in most parts of the Province. Some of them occur to from 3,000 to 5,000 feet in the Himalaya, and one is found to 10,500 feet in Tibet. The young plant is in some places eaten as a pot-herb, and the seeds are used as food, especially in times of scarcity. They are also officinal, being considered diuretic and astringent, and Bellew states that in the Peshawar Valley they are taken by women to ensure fecundity, and that water, viscidified by the fresh plant, is drunk for impotence, and an infusion of the stems taken for gonorrhœa.

ZYGOPHYLLUM SIMPLEX. L.

Vernacular. *alethi.*

In Múltán, where the plant occurs, Edgeworth states that the seeds are swept up off the ground by the poor to be used as food.

N. O. RUTACEÆ.

PEGANUM HARMALA. L.

Vernacular. T. I. *spelane.* Plains generally, *harmal.* Bazar, seeds, *isband Lahouri.*

Abundant in many parts of the Punjab plains from the Sutlej westward, is more rare to the east. It also occurs in the N. W. Himalaya up to Kashmír (5,000 feet), and in Tibet at 8,300 feet (Thomson). Has a strong, nauseous smell, was remarked by Elphinstone (*en route* to Kábul) near Peshawar, and compared to "Devil in the bush," so was supposed by Royle to be NIGELLA. The burned seeds are in some places applied to the cut navel-string and other wounds. The seeds are officinal and considered narcotic, being given in fevers and colic, and Bellew states that in the Peshawar Valley they are burnt near the sick to keep off evil spirits at night, and to avert the evil eye, that a decoction of the leaves is given for rheumatism, and the powdered root with mustard oil is applied to the hair to destroy vermin. The seeds of this plant are (or were) imported into England from the Crimea, &c., as a red dye, and three years ago enquiries were made with a view to sending some for trial from the Punjab. But it was found that they would not have a chance, chiefly owing to the discovery of the cheap coal-tar dyes.

RUTA AUGUSTIFOLIA. Pers. (R. GRAVEOLENS. L.) Rul.

Vernacular. Basár, seeds, *sudáb.*

I am not aware that this plant is cultivated in the Punjab (as in some parts of India), for the seeds, which are officinal, and found in the Bazár, those of EUPHORBIA DRACUNCULOIDES? (q. v.) being sometimes substituted. They are given for colic, &c.

N. O. SIMARUBEÆ.

Nima quassioides. Ham.

Vernacular. C. *puthorin, bera, máthú, mont.* R. *bering.* S. *pesho, khashbar, birgo.*

A tall straggling plant common in places in the Punjab Himalaya at from 3,000 to (occasionally) 9,000 feet from the Sutlej to the Chenáb. It is browsed by goats and sheep, and in Chumba the leaves are applied to itch. In some parts the red fruit is eaten.

N. O. XANTHOXYLLACEÆ.

Xanthoxylon hostile. Wall.

Vernacular. J. *timbúr.* K. *timbrú timbar.* C. *timbrú, tirmal.* R. *timbar.* B. *tirmar, tezmal.* S. *timrú, timar.* Bazár, seeds and bark, *tezbal, kabába.*

A very prickly large shrub common in many parts of the hills up to near the Indus from 2,000 to 6,000 feet. The stems are made into walking-sticks and clubs, and Honigberger states that they are often used in preference to bruise *bhang*—(see CANNABIS), as the wood gives it a pepper-like flavour. The twigs are employed as tooth-sticks. The aromatic pungent fruit, though turpentiny, is exported to be used as a condiment. It, as well as the bark, is officinal, the former being given for digestion, the latter as astringent. The latter is in some places said to be employed to kill fish (Brandis); a gum is mentioned as obtained from the plant. In Kumaon a prickle is pushed under the tooth for toothache.

N. O. ?

Coriaria Nepalensis. Wall.

Vernacular. J. *gúch.* K. *tadrelú, balel.* C. *shálú, baulú.* R. *kande, shalá, rau.* B. *ratsahara, armúra, phapharchor.* S. *árchálwa, shere, lichakhro.*

A straggling small shrub found sparingly in many places in the Himalaya up to near the Indus at from 2,500 to 7,500 feet. The branches are browsed by sheep. The fruit is very insipid, but is frequently eaten, although at times it is said to cause thirst or colic, and at one place on the Chenáb was called deadly poison! As is well known, the fruit of certain species in other countries is poisonous.

N. O. STAPHYLEACEÆ.

STAPHYLEA EMODI. Royle. Serpent-stick.

Vernacular. T. I. *márchob.* J. K. *chitra, kúrkni.* C. *chúal, ban shágalí, ban bakhurú.* R. *thanárí.* B. *gúldar.* S. *nágdaun, kaghanía.*

A small tree, the bark of whose branches is speckled, whence, on the "doctrine of signatures," arises the belief that a branch or stick of it kept by one will drive away snakes. It is often found in the Himalaya from 6,000 to 9,000 feet, up to the Indus, and beyond it.

N. O. ILICINEÆ.

ILEX DIPYRENA. Wall. Himalayan holly.

Vernacular. C. *shangala.* R. *kanjrú, karelú, drúnda.* B. *dodrú, dinsa, krúcho.* S. *kalúcho.*

A moderate sized tree not uncommon in the Punjab Himalaya up to near the Indus at from 5,000 to 9,500 feet. The wood is not esteemed. On the Biás, the leaves an occasionally given as fodder to sheep.

N. O. CELASTRINEÆ.

CELASTRUS PANICULATA. Willd.

Vernacular. C. *málkangni, sankhú.* R. *sankhír.* Basár, seeds, *mál kangní.* Leaves, *kotaj, kuter.*

A large scrambling shrub common in parts of the outer Punjab Himalaya at from 2,000 to 4,000 feet. The red seeds are given to cattle and are officinal, being considered hot and administered for rheumatism. An oil is extracted from them, which is rubbed and given internally in rheumatism. The leaves also are officinal.

ELÆODENDRON ROXBURGHII. W. and A. (NERIJA DICHOTOMA. Rox). ?

Vernacular. R. *padriún, merandú.* B. *merandú.* U. *jamoá.*

A small tree not uncommon in the eastern part of the Siwálik tract up to the Rávi. The timber is white, soft, and brittle, and is used only for small wood-work by the natives and for fuel.

EUONYMUS FIMBRIATA. Wall.
E. HAMILTONII. Wall.

Vernacular. J. *síkí, battal, barphalí.* K. *síkí, pakúá, chúál.* C. *wattal, dúdhápar, hanchú, mará, pápar. pásh.* R. *banchor, randi, trithú.* B. *kárún, chíkan.* S *sidhera, kioch, rang-chúl.*

These two trees are common in many places in the Punjab Himalaya up to near the Indus, the former at from 6,000 to 10,500 feet, and the latter at from 3,800 to 8,500 feet. They do not grow to a great size, and are not valued for construction, but the wood is close-grained and tough, and spoons are made of it. The leaves are eaten by goats, and on the Sutlej the red seeds are strung into ornaments for the head.

GYMNOSPORIA SPINOSA. Hf.

Vernacular. J. *kandiárí.* K. *láp, patákí.* C. *lí, kamla.* R. *parmíaun.* B. *badlo.* S. *kadewar.* T. I. *súrayhzái, kharazza, kandazera, zaral.* S. R. *kander, patákí, phúpárí.*

A shrub with strong spines, common Trans-Indus, in the Salt Range, to 5,000 feet, and to 3,500 feet in the low valleys of the outer Himalaya, along which I am doubtful as to how far it extends to the east. In the Salt Range the smoke of the seeds is said to be good for toothache.

N. O. RHAMNEÆ.

BERCHEMIA Sp. or PALIURUS Sp. ?

Vernacular. C. *brinkol, shonfol, karúr, phámphlí.* R. *drángú.* B. *katrain, cháunsh.* S. *kánda, thum.*

A shrub which is not uncommon from the Sutlej to the Chenáb at from 3,000 to 7,500 feet. In most places the small black fruit is only eaten by goats, in a few men also eat it. P. aculeatus is common in the Holy Land, and is called Christ's thorn from the tradition that the platted crown of thorns was made from its twigs.

RHAMNUS PERSICA. Boiss.

Vernacular. T. I. *kúkai, wúrák.* S. R. *nikkí kander, jalidar, kúchní.*

A shrub which is common at from 2,000 to 5,000 feet on the Salt Range, and the low hills, Trans-Indus, and may extend to some distance along the outer Himalaya, but has been somewhat confused with R. VIRGATUS. The small black fruit is said to be sweet, but to affect the head when eaten in excess.

R. PURPUREUS. Royle.

Vernacular. J. *bal sinjal.* C. *kári, memarárí, tadrú.* R. *kúnjí, túndhe, tunána madána.* S. *chaterní.*

This tree is common up to near the Indus at from 4,500 to 9,500 feet. In Hazára the fruit is used as a purgative. The fruit of some of the European species is powerfully purgative.

R. VIRGATUS. Rox. (?)

Vernacular. J. *phipní, dadrú, tadúr, seta pajja.* K. *nár, tadrú, dadúr.* C. *mamrál.* R. *kánjí.* B. *reteon, sindrol.* S. *múttú, romusk, niar, chattr.*

A small tree common on all the rivers up to near the Indus at from 4,000 to 9,500 feet. The fruit is said to be bitter even when ripe, and to cause diarrhœa when eaten.

SAGERETIA BRANDRETHIANA. Aitch.

Vernacular. J. *ganger, kanger.* K. *bhándí bajan, ganger.* T. I. *múmání.* S. R. *koher.*

A large shrub which was first collected by Griffith (" Maimanna of the Affgháns"), and has been named by Dr. J. E. T. Aitchison, after Mr. A. Brandreth, C. S. It abounds in places Trans-Indus from 2,000 to 3,500 feet, and in the Salt Range, and occurs low in the Jhelam basin. The fruit, which is well known in the Bazárs of Peshawar and Affghánistán, is small and black, and is very pleasant eating when fresh and in sufficient quantity, the flavour being not unlike that of the bilberry. In the Salt Range, a *chatní* is made of the fruit.

S. OPPOSITIFOLIA. Brongn. (?)

Vernacular. K. *kanak, gídardák.* R. *drange.* B. *girthan.*

A shrub which appears in some measure to replace the last to the eastward at from 2,000 to 3,000 feet in the outer hills. Its fruit also is eaten.

ZIZYPHUS FLEXUOSA. Wall.

Vernacular. J. *sínjlí.* K. *sínjlí, símli, bárj, bán.* C. *berí.* R. *ber, relnú.*

A large shrub or small tree which is not uncommon at places from 2,400 to 6,500 feet, from the Rávi to near the Indus. It has glossy green leaves, and is the handsomest of these Zizyphi, and when planted (as near Chumba) and taken care of, grows to a considerable size. I have noted specimens of 5 or 6 feet in girth, and 25 or 30 high. The fruit is well-flavoured.

Z. Jujuba. L.

Vernacular. T. I. *berra.* Plains generally, *ber;* cultivated var. *peuandi.* Bazár, fruit, *unnáb.*

Several varieties (and perhaps species ?) are included here, particularly Var. hortensis, the cultivated kind, and Edgeworth's Hysudricus, which he states to be the most abundant of all in the Punjab. With him, I am in great doubt as to the tree being found truly wild in the Province, although it is common all over up to 3,000 and occasionally 4,000 feet, but less frequent in the east. The cultivated kind is said to be most affected by Mussalmáns, and is not unfrequently seen of over 10 feet in girth (at the gate of Shálimár near Lahore there is a specimen almost this size). The excellence of the fruit of those about Pák Pattan and Depálpúr is spoken of far to the east of the Sutlej, a hundred miles off. The fruit was called Pomum Adami by Marco Polo, and Sir Henry Elliot identified it with the lotus of the ancients; but although the large juicy product of the garden Zizyphus is by no means bad, yet, as Madden quaintly remarks, one might eat any quantity of it without danger of forgetting home and friends.

The wood is tough, and tolerably strong and durable, and is used in ordinary constructive work, for well-curbs, well-wheels, ploughs, &c., and for charcoal. The bark is employed by tanners. Bellew states that near Peshawar the lather (?) formed by the leaves in water, is used by women to wash the head. It is not certain that part at least of the *unnáb* fruit of the Bazár is not imported from the west. It is given as a medicine in bronchitis, &c., and natives say that a few of the ordinary fruit after meals help digestion. In Kángra, Jhelam, &c., *lákh* for dyeing is collected from the tree in the rains, being generally found on Var. Hysudricus (Edgeworth). For some years it has been known that in Kángra the cocoon of a wild silk worm is found on this tree, but apparently in no very great quantity. This silk was or is generally used for tying the barrel on the stock of the matchlock, being found better for the purpose than sinews or leathern thongs.

Z. nummularia. W. and A.

Vernacular. J. *jand, ber.* B. *birár.* T. I. *karkana* S. R. *ber, birota.* Plains generally, *mallá, kokní ber, mara ber, jharberí, zarí.*

A small shrub abundant in many parts of the plains, though less common in the Southern Punjab, and ascending occasionally to 3,500 feet in the outer hills. It is sometimes called "camelthorn" erroneously—(see ALHAGI). The fruit though small is eaten, and at times is fairly well-flavoured. The bush is of value, and is largely cut each year to make heaped fences, and at times a very good and neat fence is made by sticking the branches upright and binding them with straw ropes. The leaves are beaten from the prickly branches, and largely used as *bhúsa*, fodder.

Z. VULGARIS. Lam.

Vernacular. J. K. *phitní, kokan ber*. C. *ganyerí*. B. *kándika, kandíarí, bararí*. S. *shamor*. T. I. *karkan ber*. S. R. *amlái, anmiá*.

A large shrub, common at many places in the Punjab Himalaya, especially towards the west at from 2,000 to 4,000 feet, and in Kashmír to 6,000 feet. It also occurs in the Salt Range, and is occasional in gardens in the Punjab (Edgeworth). The fruit is small and sour, but is eaten.

N. O. SAMYDEÆ.

CASEARIA TOMENTOSA. Rox.

Vernacular. *chíla, chílla*.

A small tree not uncommon in the Siwálik region at from 2,000 to 3,000 feet, up to near the Indus. The timber is whitish, soft, and brittle, and is only used for small wood-work by natives, but is said to furnish good fuel. In some places the fruit is used for poisoning fish.

N. O. AMYRIDEÆ.

BALANITES ÆGYPTIACA. Del.

Vernacular. *hingot, híngol*.

This is cultivated in Egypt under the name *soum*, its sour leaves being used as anthelmintic, and a recent traveller states that the turners of Jerusalem, near which it grows, often make use of its straight yellow wands for walking sticks, on which they inscribe "Jordan" in Hebrew characters. So far as I know, it is found in the Punjab only from Dehlí westward to Rohtuk, where it reaches 18 inches in girth. The wood is soft, and shoe-makers' boards are made from it. The young twigs, &c., seem to be browsed by cattle. The hard shell of the orange-sized fruit is used for *ándrs* in native pyrotechny, and the seeds are given for coughs.

Boswellia glabra Rox.

Vernacular. *sálhe.*

This tree is found just to the west of the Jumna in the Siwálik tract within the Punjab, but not in numbers sufficient to render it of much economic interest.

Garuga pinnata. Rox.

Vernacular. *kharpat.*

This also only extends sparingly within our limits, just to west of the Jumna. The wood is of no great value, the bark is used by tanners, and the leaves for fodder.

N. O. TEREBINTHACEÆ.

Buchanania latifolia. Rox.

Vernacular. *chiraulí.*

It is doubtful if this tree extends in any numbers far into the Punjab, in the Siwálik tract. The wood is worthless, the leaves are used for dishes, and the bark by tanners, and the oily kernels of the fruit are put in confectionery.

Mangifera Indica. L.

Vernacular. *ám, amb.* Bazár, unripe fruit, *ámchúr*; seeds, *ám-ki-gúthlí.*

This valuable tree, so common in the N. W. Provinces, extends to Lahore in some numbers, being most common towards the hills and nearer the south, *e. g.*, in Harriána; is abundant in parts of the Gúrdaspúr district and the Kángra Valley, &c., to the north, and common at Múltán to the south; westward from the line of the Rávi it almost disappears, except at one or two places in Mozaffargarh and about Seálkôt. At Peshawar there are only a few small trees with indifferent fruit, and it is very rare further down Trans and Cis-Indus, except in the extreme south. It grows to 3,500 feet, but at such elevations is said to give fruit only each second year. Even the largest trees rarely exceed 10 or 12 feet girth in the Punjab. Its wood is coarse-grained, and prone to be insect-eaten and not very strong or durable, and is only used for ordinary work, packing cases, &c. Early flowering is said to portend much heat, and a productive season of the fruit is believed by natives to indicate an unhealthy season. According to Edgeworth the fruit of some of the Múltán trees is notably good, and similar to that of the grafted Bombay kind, the best being the *Sháh-pasand,* with a thin skin and smooth velvety flat stone, the fruit of which in former times was kept for the reigning sovereign. This tree is inserted among those yielding gum in Kángra. Even the kernels are eaten in times of famine; the unripe fruit and the seeds are officinal, the former being used in ophthalmia and eruptions, and the latter in asthma.

ODINA WODIER. Rox.

Vernacular. J. *klámil.* C. *kambal, batrín, kimlú.* R. *kembal.* B. *dhauntika, kemal, koamla, sulámbra.* S. *pichka, lidra.* S. R. *dila, kamlái.* Bazár, gum, *jingna* or *kaní gond.*

A tree which attains a considerable size in the Siwálik region, and to 3,500 and occasionally 4,000 feet up to near the Indus, and in the Salt Range. In some parts it is called the male of RHUS BUCKIAMELA. The outer wood is very subject to worms, the inner is dark colored and tolerably durable when well-seasoned, being used for door-frames, &c. In some places it is lopped for fodder (?). The gum is used in cloth-printing, and is officinal, being given in asthma, and as a cordial to women.

PISTACIA.

Several species growing to the west and south of the Punjab seem to merit notice here.

P. ATLANTICA. Desf.

Vernacular. *tagho* of Affghánistán.

Yields mastic called *Rúmí mastigí, kúndar Rúmí* in the Bazárs, of which Davies' Trade Report states that 5 maunds are annually imported viâ Peshawar. It is given for asthma and mixed in ointments, &c.

P. LENTISCUS. L

Of the Mediterranean region, also yields a mastic, and is said in books to yield the officinal seeds *tantarik* (see RHUS PARVIFLORA).

P. CABULICA. Stocks.

Was found by Stocks to yield a resin like mastic in Sind.

P. vera. L.

Of Persia and Turkistán yields the *pista* or pistachio nut, an oily small seed which is imported into Northern India in considerable quantities, being eaten with relish by natives, though probably indigestible. Davies' Trade Report gives 40 maunds as annually brought through the Bolán pass. It also (probably) yields the gall of native druggists called *gúli pista* or *bazghanj (bozaghanj)*, which is used as an astringent and dye for silk. Davies' Trade Report gives the quantity of this annually imported viâ Peshawar as 50 maunds, and 100 maunds as brought down by the Bolán. And the officinal *post bírúní pista* are the shells of its fruit. They are given for digestion.

P. integerrima. Hf. and T. (Rhus integerrima. Wall).

Vernacular. J. *khakkar, kangar.* K. *kakkar, drek, gurgú.* C. *kakkrei, tanhárí, kákrá.* R. *kakkeran, kákrá, túngú.* B. *kakráin.* S. *kakla, kakkar, kakkrangche.* T. I. *shne, sarawán, masna.* S. R. *kakkra, khangar.* Bazár, excrescence, *kakkra singí;* fruit, *sumák.*

Not uncommon in many places from 1,500 to 5,500 feet, from the Sutlej to the Indus, and occasionally beyond that river, and in the Salt Range. Is most common of all in parts of Hazára. It may be the *shne* of Affghánistán called "xanthoxylon?" by Griffith, but this Pushtú name appears to be applied by the Affgháns to several species of Rhus and Pistacia (see next species). Trees of over 10 feet girth are now but rarely seen (I have noted only two of 12 feet and one of 15), as its zebra wood makes handsome chairs, cabinets, &c., and much of it has been felled for the use of Europeans. In Kángra the wood is said at times to be used for sugar-mills. There the tree was reserved for the ruler's use in former times. Of late years it has been introduced into gardens at various places in the plains, and does fairly well. It is ornamental, especially in spring when the young red leaves are coming out. In Hazára particularly the twigs and leaves are lopped off, to serve for fodder, and I have seen them browsed by camels. An excrescence which forms on the leaf-bud, dark and horn-like, sometimes grows to 6 or 7 inches long and as thick as a finger. I have found a spider with young nestled in one, and the natives said "it is always so," but I doubt if it is not caused by some other insect. Stocks found a similar excrescence on a Pistacia (Cabulica or Atlantica?) in Belúchistán. This Punjab excrescence is officinal, and is given for cough, &c. The officinal *sumák* found in the Bazárs appears to be the fruit of this tree. It is administered for strengthening digestion.

P. Terebinthus. L.

Vernacular. Aff. *khinjak ?* T. I. *shne.*

Bellew states that this tree is common over the hills of eastern Affghánistán, and I found a single tree of what appears to be this in Wazíristán on the eastern skirts of the Súlimán Range. According to Bellew the fruit is in Affghánistán considered warm, stimulating, and stomachic, and is given in colic and dyspepsia, and the gum (the *aluk ul-umbat* of the native pharmacopeia, and according to Stocks yielded in Sind also by this tree) is used as a masticatory and in various ointments. The books state that this tree yields *elk ul butm,* " Chian turpentine," and to it is attributed the source of *tantarík,* which appears in the Punjab to be generally the fruit of Rhus parviflora q. v.

Rhus.

There is confusion among the native names of the species, and as to the identity of some, but I have made the best I could of those I have got.

Rhus acuminata. DC.

Vernacular. J. *arkhar.* K. *arkhol.* C. *arkhol, lakhar, títar.* R. *arkhar, títri.* B. *arkhar, ríkhúl.* Bazár, fruit, *habat ul khizra.*

This tree is not uncommon in the Kashmír Valley, and occurs more sparingly to the eastward from 4,000 to 7,000 or 8,000 feet. Vigne states that the juice of the fresh leaves blisters the skin, and the Kashmírians said the same to me, but on my showing that it had not blistered mine, they declared it only affected those who feared it ! The wood is not valued. Bears are said to eat its fruit, which seems to be the officinal *habat ul khizra* administered in phthisis.

R. Buckiamela. Rox. (R. semialata. Murr.)

Vernacular. J. *arkhar, tatrí, tetar, thissa.* K. *tetar, títrí, chechar.* C. *titrí, arkol, kakkarí.* R. *titrí, kakkaran.* B. *vrásh, títrí, knítrí.* S. *títrí, káshín, hulashing, wásho.*

A tree common on all the rivers up to near the Indus, from 2,500 up to 7,000 feet or more. In some places this is called the female of the Odina. The timber is valueless, except for fuel. The fruit is said to be sometimes eaten, and is given for colic.

R. Cotinus. L.

Vernacular. J. *páán, bhán*. K. *phán, bhán, bana, manú*. C. *baura, túng, tittrí*. R. *túng*. S. R. *largá*.

A large shrub common in places Trans-Indus and eastward in the Himalaya to at least the Rávi, from 2,300 occasionally to 6,000 feet, as well as in the Salt Range. The largest I have noted was about 3 feet in girth, but the usual size is very much under that. The wood is yellowish, resembling that of Pistacia integerrima, but small. The twigs are used for baskets. The leaves have a pleasant balsamic odour when bruised, and they as well as the bark are used for tanning.

R. parviflora. Rox.

Vernacular. S., &c. *túng, túngla*. Bazár, seed, *tantarík, túng*.

It is doubtful if this shrub, which resembles the last, comes further west than the Sutlej. The wood is hard and yellowish like that of the last. The *tantarík* of the Bazár (generally attributed in books to Pistacia lentiscus (q. v.) and P. Terebinthus) appears in the Punjab to be the fruit of this. It is used in Hindú medicine, and, mixed with salt, is said to act like tamarinds.

R. succedanea. L.

Vernacular. J. *títar, tatrí*. C. *choklú, holáshí*. R. *halá, haláí*. S. *kakkrín, húlashing*.

This tree appears to be found on most of the great rivers from 3,000 up to 8,000 feet. It does not grow to a great size, nor does its wood seem to be valued. The juice of its leaves is stated to blister the skin. In Bombay, a varnish is said to be yielded by this species.

R. vernicifera. DC.

Vernacular. C. *gudámbal*. B. *ríkhalí, arkhar*. S. *arkol, urkúr, hulása, ríkhúl*.

In Bombay, this tree is stated to yield a varnish. Its wood is not esteemed. Corrosive properties are attributed to the juice of the leaves, which in some places is rubbed on thread to strengthen it.

Semecarpus Anacardium. L. Marking nut.

Vernacular. *bhiláwa*.

I have not seen this tree much to the west of the Sutlej in the Siwálik tract. But its fruit is found in all Bazárs, being used to prepare a wash for salivation, and its smoke is reckoned efficacious for impotency. It is also employed instead of ink.

SPONDIAS MANGIFERA. Pers. Hog-Plum.

Vernacular. C. *báhamb.* B., &c., *ambára.*

Extends sparingly as far west as the Chenáb in the Siwálik tract. The timber of this tree (which is entered as producing gum in Kángra) is worthless, being soft and brittle. The fruit is like a particularly bad mango; and Firminger, who implies that it is cultivated (?) at Calcutta, hardly does justice to its poorness. Unripe it is used for *chatní,* and ripe for pickles.

N. O. LEGUMINOSÆ.

ABRUS PRECATORIUS. L.

Vernacular. *ghúnchí.*

A small slender climber growing in the outer hills, and in the plains in the east of the Province. Its red (and occasionally white) seeds are well known as goldsmiths' weights (*rattí*). They are also officinal, being applied for fistula in Hindú medicine. Eaten they are stated to prevent fecundity. They are said to be used as food in Egypt, which disposes of the assertion of their poisonous qualities, attributed by some to the white kind only. The roots of this are used and sold as liquorice (see GLYCIRRHIZA) and an extract is made from them as from it.

ACACIA ARABICA. Willd.

Vernacular. *kikkar* (*babúl* in N. W. P.) Bazár, bark, *kikkar kíchal,* gum, *kikkar-ke-gond.* Extract? *ákákia.*

This tree, which is rare in Rohilkund, becomes more frequent about Dehlí, though not attaining the same luxuriance as in the west, and is profuse over the Central and Southern Punjab. In the tracts north of the Salt Range and Trans-Indus, it is rare or unknown, commencing to flourish about the line of the Jhelum and Chenáb, and it is not common in Harriána. Stunted trees may occasionally be seen up to 3,000 or 4,000 feet in the Himalaya. But the attempt of Goláb Sing (mentioned by Lowther as in progress in 1851 ?) to grow *kikkar* in Kashmír for gun-carriages was hopeless. I have seen it nowhere indigenous except in Sind, where to the south of Sukkur there are considerable natural forests of the tree ranging to over 6 feet girth. In the Punjab it will, under tolerably favorable circumstances, reach 30 inches in girth in 10 or 12 years, and trees of 9 and 10 feet girth are not uncommon. Of several over 9 feet girth close to Lahore, one at a Mussalmán shrine, which is said to be one hundred years old, and has been dying for 20 years, only one bough being now alive, is said to have shed blood when the sacrilegious Sikhs attempted to fell it. Edgeworth mentions one of 16 feet 4 inches near Múltán; very old trees are frequently hollow. In the upper parts of the Gangetic Doáb I find it is raised from cuttings, but elsewhere it is grown from seed. It germinates easily, and its chief enemies are rats and frost. The former are fond of its sweet roots, the latter nips the tender seedlings often to the ground, or the young shoots of larger plants. In Sind and more rarely in the Punjab (notably in winter 1867-68), the effects of the frost are much more severe, young trees to 12 and 15 feet high having many of their branches nipped or even the trunks killed. And at times some of the smaller plants are killed down to the ground for several years running.

The lighter-colored sap-wood of this tree is subject to be attacked by white ants, the heart wood much less so if properly seasoned. The latter is dark-colored, reddish, hard, strong, and heavy, weighing 70 ℔s. a cubic foot green, 40 ℔s. dry. It is said that even seasoned wood will only float for a few days. For particular work the wood is generally water-seasoned. It is much used for parts of boats, well-curbs, cart-axles, and wheels, sugar-rollers, the portion of the plough above the share, Persian wheels, &c. The wood is an excellent fuel, and the tree is being largely raised in the Railway fuel plantations. The bark is extensively used in tanning (and in Sind for dyeing a reddish brown), and in some parts the large branches are cruelly lopped to get the bark. The latter (especially from the roots ?) is also put into native spirits. It is likewise officinal, being reckoned demulcent. (?) The leaves are eaten by goats and sheep. In Sind much *lákh* is collected from this tree, but only below Sukkur where the climate is less arid than in Upper Sind and the Southern Punjab. The gum is used for the ordinary purposes of Gum Arabic, and in Yunání medicine is given in cough, &c. The *ákákia* appears to be an extract, and may be from this tree or may be imported from the west. It is given as a purgative to children.

The variety A. A. SPINA-ALBIDA, mentioned by Griffith, Jameson, Aitchison, &c., is conceived by myself and others to be no true variety, most strong shoots springing after a young tree has been cut down, &c., having very large long spines.

A. A. Var. Cupressiformis.

Vernacular. *Kábulí kikkar.*

This is a well-marked variety, which grows like a cypress, with the branches closing up to the trunk. The Darwinian reason has been assigned for this peculiarity, that it has ensued from ages of ruthless lopping of the side-boughs! This variety is found in Bombay, where it is called *rám babúl,* and in Sind where it has the Punjab prefix *Kábulí (bubbúr).* In the Punjab it is most abundant and most typical in the upper part of the Jech Doáb, between Goojrát and Jhelam. It is rather common also to the south of this near Jhang, and is seen, though in small numbers, and generally of less typical form, at some places Trans-Indus and at Lahore, and many other places east as far as Dehlí. At Saharanpúr, there are two trees of 17 years old, 12 or 15 inches in girth, and about 25 feet high. Edgeworth states that near Múltán this is sometimes seen on the same tree with the ordinary form. I am inclined to think there must be some mistake here in the wording of the statement at least. The timber of this variety is *said* to be less sound and durable than that of the ordinary *kikkar.*

A. Catechu. Willd.

Vernacular. T. I. *khwarech.* Elsewhere, *kháir, kheir, kher.* Bazár, extract, *kath, kattha.*

A small tree found along the Siwálik tract to 3,000 and occasionally to 4,000 feet up to the Indus, and sparingly beyond it. One of the best tracts I know in the Punjab is below Trêt, where for miles it is the chief tree, running up to 5 or 6 feet in girth. The timber is dark-colored, hard, heavy, and not subject to the attacks of insects, and though somewhat brittle is much valued for all purposes where strength is required and weight is no objection, and it is carried for sale to fairs, &c., many miles from the place of growth. It is valued for pestles, sugar-crushers, cotton-rollers, weavers' beams, shafts of ploughs, axles, &c. The extract, catechu, is used in dyeing, and in medicine as an astringent, and for gonorrhœa, and externally in ointment, &c., for itch, syphilis, and burns.

A. eburnea. Willd.

Vernacular. T. I. *babúlí.* S. R. *kikkarí, dadda.*

A small shrub very like a miniature *kikkar,* found abundantly in the Salt Range, and more sparingly Trans-Indus up to 3,000 and occasionally to 5,000 feet. Is of no special use.

A. elata. Wall. Dhoon Siris.

Vernacular. *sufêd siris; (kareo* N. W. P.)

A very handsome large tree with greenish-white bark, nowhere wild in the Province, but occasionally cultivated, although less so than it should be, as it is a much finer tree and grows quicker than the common *siris* (A. SPECIOSA q. v.), and its timber, in the parts where it is common, is said to be about as good. Has a great capacity for growing from cuttings, quite large poles used to support climbers sometimes shoot and grow.

A. FARNESIANA. Willd.

Vernacular. *babúl wiláyatí kikkar, paháran kikkar, Kábul kikkar.*

A large shrub nowhere wild in the Province, though occasionally naturalized, as at places on the Western Jumna Canal. I have seen plants of it up to nearly 5,000 feet in the Himalaya. It is usually grown as a fence, for which purpose it answers well if planted close. It is in flower in the cold weather, the blossoms having a fine scent; and in Europe they are said to yield a perfume.

A. JACQUEMONTI. Bth.

Vernacular. J. *kandiárí.* T. I. *hanza.* S. S. D. *babbil.* B. D. *babúrí.* H. *bambúl.* D. *ár.*

A small shrub with immense white spines, which grows in clumps from 6 or 7 up to 10 feet high, common on sandy knolls and ridges in many parts of the arid tract from Dehlí westward by Harriána, Sirsa, Montgomery, &c., to Trans-Indus, to about 2,000 feet. The flowers are yellow, and the seeds ripen about May. Its spines prevent it from being much browsed by cattle, but its leaves are thrashed out to feed them. The flowers have a delicious odour which scents the whole air near. The bark of the root is put into native spirits "to render them stronger," in the same way as that of the *kikkar* (A. ARABICA q. v.)

A. LEUCOPHLÆA. Willd.

Vernacular. B. D. *rerú.* J. D. *karír, jand.* H. *raunj, nímbar.* D. *raunj, jand.*

This tree extends in some numbers from about Lahore along the arid tract to Dehlí. It has a greenish-white bark, whence the name, and the young spines are dark brown, otherwise the tree is in appearance not unlike A. ARABICA. It does not, however, reach the same size; one of the largest I know is about 6 feet girth, hanging over Bába Attal's tank at Umritsur, old, crooked, and gnarled. But I am told of one of 15 feet girth, and 80 or 90 feet high, at the Kasíl chaukí on a cut of the Bárí Doáb Canal south of Umritsur. This is rarely planted, but the natives often spare it "for its shade," in some of the more treeless tracts. It flowers during and after the rains, the fruit ripening at the beginning of the hot weather. The wood is said to be very subject to the attacks of insects, and is not valued except for fuel. A good many trees stood on some of the land recently cleared for Railway fuel near Lahore, and it is said to be the best of all now in use there. The fruit appears to be largely collected for fodder in places where the tree is common. On the twigs of some trees a woody excrescence is very common, similar to, but softer than that of PROSOPIS (q. v).

A. MODESTA. Wall.

Vernacular. T. I. *palosa.* Elsewhere, *phalá, phuláí.*

This tree, which in its natural state does not often reach or get a chance of reaching a large size, is indigenous in the Salt Range and all the low hills east to the Sutlej at least, in the plains Trans-Indus, and in the extreme north-west of the Province, as well as the most northern portion of the Bárí and Jalandar Doábs, and the north-western corner of that of Ambála. Planted trees may occasionally be seen in other localities. It ordinarily prefers rough, rocky, arid ground, but in some places, markedly in the Bíás *Khádir* near Kanowán, it may be seen growing in numbers in almost marshy places, so much so that an early observer states that the tree "only grows in moist places." These are, however, mostly tall and weedy as if under unnatural conditions, and their timber would seem to be less good than of trees grown elsewhere. In the Múltán Division, Edgeworth states that it "only grows towards the north," where I have seen it on the *hills* close to Chiniot, and do not think it exists on the level plain near that. The largest specimens are generally those which have been preserved, near houses, &c. I have noted several of 10 feet and one or two of 12 feet girth, and in some places many wild trees may be seen of 5 or 6 feet girth and 25 feet high. There is one of 9 feet in the station of Ambála. In Saharanpúr garden, a tree of about 30 years old is 5½ feet girth and 30 in height.

As a tree it is not often planted, for it is of slow growth, but it is frequently grown by Europeans as a fence, for which purpose it answers well. Edgeworth aptly notes the delicate green of the foliage mingled with the white spikes of blossoms, and the delightful perfume of the latter in spring, and the rapid passing away of both, as the flowers soon fade, and the leaves become grey. The seed ripens in the cold weather. The wood of an old tree is very dark brown, or nearly black, hard, strong, and heavy. Green it weighs 69½ lbs., and dry 53½ a cubic foot. It is very durable, and is a favourite for cart-wheels, sugar-mills, plough-stocks and shares (? Bellew), Persian wheels, the mallets for cleaning cotton, &c. I have been informed by a friend who was through the second Punjab campaign, that after Chilianwála many of the elephants were affected by a disease in which the "hoofs dropped off," which was attributed to their browsing this tree (?), but have no means of verifying this. In some parts the fallen blossoms, mixed with some leaves, are swept up and given to cattle, goats, &c. The tree yields sparingly a gum similar to gum Arabic, which Bellew states the people of the Peshawar Valley consider to be restorative.

A. SPECIOSA. (A. SIRISSA. Buch. ALBIZZIA LEBBEK. Bth. A. MOLLIS. var. JULIBRISSIN. Bth.)

Vernacular. J. *lasrín, lasrian.* C. *sirín, kálí sirín.* R. *sirín, shúrúngrú.* B. *shírs, shírí, mathírshí.* S. *shírsh, mathírsh.* Plains generally, *siris, sírí.*

Under this head are probably included several species which grow wild in the Himalaya from the Indus eastward from 2,200 to 5,000 feet. Cultivated the *siris* is common in most parts of the plains, except the most arid tracts about Harriána and Sirsa, and in some of the western Doábs where it is rare, short-trunked, and scraggy. But it was probably very much less common at annexation, for in 1851 we find a good authority recommending to the Agri-Horticultural Society its introduction into the Punjab. It is easily raised from seed, (occasionally from cuttings, and poles stuck in as supports readily shoot) is tolerably hardy, except against great drought, and grows with notable rapidity, perhaps quicker by a fourth or fifth than DALBERGIA (q. v.) In Sind, the rapidity of growth of this tree is remarkable. Specimens of 6 and 7 feet in girth are not very uncommon in the Punjab—one of about 12 feet stands near the Anarkullee Dispensary. It requires a large space in order to grow freely, and in groves, &c., is apt to be overborne by other trees, and its branches are frequently broken by wind and other accidents. The natives in some parts call it a *bárah mási* tree, but although it flowers for weeks, the period does not by any means extend the whole year. The blossoms have an agreeable odour which diffuses itself to some distance. The seeds ripen in the cold weather. The heart-wood of an old tree is dark-colored, hard, heavy, and strong, and, if properly seasoned, is not subject to warp or crack, but it is said to be less lasting than DALBERGIA. It is stated in Mysore to be equal in strength to teak. It is used for ordinary constructive purposes (the Hindús in Kángra, however, consider it unlucky), and for mortars for oil-mills, for well-curbs, and for parts of boats, and the heart-wood makes good charcoal. The leaves and twigs are gathered as fodder for camels and other animals. The bark is stated to be applied to hurts of the eye (Madden), and the seed is officinal, forming part of an *anjan* for ophthalmic disease. The gum is similar in quality to gum Arabic, but I do not know of its being collected or sold in quantity. The name of the Julibrissin is a curious instance of how names become altered when transferred to another language, it being an altered state of *gul abresham,* "the silky-flowered."

A. STIPULATA. DC. (A. KANGRAENSIS. Jameson).

Vernacular. J. *lasren*. C. *súrangrú, kasír, ban drenkh*. R. *ola*. B. *ohí, durgárí*.

There is some little doubt as to the identity of this tree on the various rivers, where it grows at from 3,000 to 4,000 and up to 6,000 feet occasionally. It is handsome in appearance, resembling somewhat POINCIANA REGIA, and is seen in great abundance and luxuriance in portions of the Kángra Valley, where it reaches 7 and 8 and occasionally 9 feet in girth. It has been sometimes grown in the plains, though more rarely than it deserves. In Saharanpúr Botanic Garden there is a specimen of 7 feet in girth said to be only about 17 years old. If so, the growth is extremely rapid, even for India. The wood of the old tree in Kángra is stated to be brownish, soft, brittle, and light, and it is not valued, being used only for planks and other ordinary purposes.

ÆSCHYNOMENE CANNABINA. Roxb. (Æ. INDICA. L.)

Vernacular. B. D. *jhijan, jhanjhan*.

A plant of dubious species which grows tall and rank (to 6 or 8 feet high) in waste land. A pretty strong rope for home use is made from its fibre, which is also said to be used to adulterate other kinds of tow. This may be Roxburgh's plant, which he states to be cultivated in parts of Bengál for its fibre.

ALBIZZIA ODORATISSIMA. Bth.

Vernacular. C. *sírí, lasre, polách, drek, tandáí*. B. *karmrú, karámbrú*. U. *sirí*.

This tree grows sparingly in valleys at from 2,500 to more than 5,000 feet, up to the Chenáb. Its timber is valued in some parts of India as being hard, light, and strong, but in Kángra is said to be soft and only used for fuel. The tree produces a gum, and the leaves, &c., are used for fodder.

ALHAGI MAURORUM. Tourn. Camel-thorn.

Vernacular. T. I. *zoz, zozán* (*jojh* Per.?) S. R. *tamrya.* Plains, generally, *jawá, jawása, jawán.* Bazár, manna, *anj bín.*

This is the *shútar khár* (camel-thorn) of the Persians, camels delighting in it above most other plants, and it abounds in many of the arid parts of the Punjab plains. In parts of the Southern Punjab where the usual grass for making *tatties*—(see ANATHERUM)—is scarce, these are made of this, and in Sind all appear to be constructed of it. The officinal manna of this, which is used as a purgative, does not appear to be found in the Punjab; but we know from Griffith, Bellew, and Irvine, that near Kandahár and Herát it is found on the bushes at the flowering time, "just after the spring rains," and is shaken off them and collected. Davies' Trade Report gives 25 maunds as the quantity yearly brought from Affghánistán to Peshawar.

ALYSICARPUS NUMMULARIFOLIUS. DC.

Bazár, plant, *nág bala.*

This, which grows wild, may be the officinal plant so called.

ARACHIS HYPOGÆA Rox.

Vernacular. *múng phallí.*

Not very commonly cultivated in the Punjab, except towards the east. Is largely grown, and the nut and oil exported from parts of India. The nut is a favourite food of the Hindús on fasts, in Bombay.

ASTRAGALUS HAMOSUS. L.

Vernacular. Bazár, pods, *aklíl-ul-malik.*

A small prostrate plant occasional in the central Punjab. The pods are officinal, and are ground to be mixed with plasters.

A. MULTICEPS. Wall.

Vernacular. C. *kandiara kandei, much kánta gágarkand, bramatsa, kátarkanda.* Lad. *písar.* P. *kiútú.* T. I. *spínaghzái, sarmúl, pishkan, bízú da khwan.* S. R. *tinání, diddani, jandí.* Aff., ? *butá-i-miswák.* Bazár, plant, ? *áthníl.*

This is a very spinous plant with yellow flowers, somewhat resembling gorse. It may at times have been confused with some of the other spinous ASTRAGALI, of which a good many are found in the Himalaya, but appears to be common Trans-Indus, in the Salt Range, and in parts of the western outer Himalaya up to 5,000 feet. It also grows in Lahoul and Pítí up to 10,000 feet, and in Ladák to 16,500 feet. It is at times browsed by cattle, and in the Salt Range the calyces, which have a sweetish pleasant taste, are eaten; on the Chenáb the seeds are given for colic. It appears to be this species which is found in the Bazárs under the name *úthníl,* and used for leprosy. This or a very similar plant is called by the name given above in Affghánistán (Bellew), but I know not if it is used for tooth-sticks *(miswák).* Several other similar species grow on the eastern skirts of the Súlimán Range, and others in Ladák.

A. SP.

Vernacular. S. *niamcho, raskiách.*

Strongly resembling the previous plant, grows in Kanáwar at 9,000 to 10,500 feet. Is occasionally browsed by horses, goats, &c., and is burned so as to remove the spines, and then used as winter-fodder.

A. TRIBULOIDES. Del.

Vernacular. T. I. *ogái.*

The seeds of this, which grows in the western and central parts of the Punjab plains, appear to be used medicinally.

BAUHINIA PARVIFLORA. Vahl.

Vernacular. J. D. *kosúndra.*

A great climber, which is found in the eastern part of the Punjab Siwálik tract. Its gum is used medicinally in Southern India.

B. RACEMOSA. Vahl. (B. VAHLII. W. and A.)

Vernacular. C. *marwár.* B. *taur.* U. *máljan.*

An immense climber with very large leaves and great flowers and pods which grows in the Siwálik tract as far west at least as the Chenáb. The branches are used as ties for fences, &c., and a strong and durable rope is manufactured from the bark, without steeping. The leaves are eaten by buffaloes, &c., and are used for packing and for making umbrellas (being put between strips of bamboo, so as to overlap each other). They are also favourite leaves for plates, used at the marriages of Bráhmins, &c., for which purpose they are at times brought from some distance. The seeds are eaten in various places.

B. VARIEGATA. L. var. PURPUREA. (PHANERA P. Bth.)

Vernacular. J. *kolár, karál.* C. *koliár, padriár.* R. *karár.* B. *karálli, angurí.* Aff. *arghawán.* S. R. *kolár.* Plains, generally, *kachnár.*

A small tree which occurs in the Salt Range, and is common wild in the outer hills to near the Indus, and perhaps beyond it, up to 4,000 and occasionally 5,000 feet. It is often planted in the plains for its fine purplish lilac and white flower blossoming in March. It is evidently the red *arghawán*—(see EDWARDSIA for the yellow), mentioned by Masson, Griffith, &c., as still growing at Baber's tomb at Kábul, where it was introduced by that Monarch. Irvine calls it the "anemone shrub," and mentions that it grows there (and in Badakshán?) to 20 feet in height, that its wood is used for making spear shafts, and that it is "most remarkable for the beauty of its flowers." This tree sometimes has an upright cupressiform shape. The wood is red, light, soft, decays quickly, and is subject to insects, and is little used except for fuel. The flower buds are used as a pot-herb in curries and pickles, and the leaves are given as fodder. The bark ("the leaves" by mistake, Irvine) is used by tanners.

BUTEA FRONDOSA. ROX.

Vernacular. C. *sarúra.* R. *plá.* Plains, generally, *palás, plá, chichra, dhak.* Bazár, flowers, *kesú*; gum, *kamarkas.*

Ordinarily seen as a shrub, but when preserved grows to a considerable tree, reaching 10 or 12 feet in girth and 40 high, with a large handsome red flower, blossoming in March, April. Is common south-east of Ambála, and more rare to the west, except in patches or over somewhat isolated tracts in the Jalandar and Bári Doábs, &c. Is rare to the south of Lahore a few planted trees only occurring in the extreme south, but is more common along near the hills, and to a little way within them, as far as Jhelam. Trans-Indus, in the Peshawar Valley, I have seen trees, but doubt if they were wild, for the natural habitat appears to finish suddenly near Bukrála, in the eastern Salt Range. The natives in some parts have a very good opinion of the soil where the tree flourishes, but may have put the cart before the horse in the statement that its leaves destroy *kallar.* The wood is fibrous and rather tough, but not strong or durable. Here the only special use it is put to is for well-curbs, and it is sometimes burned for gunpowder charcoal. In parts of Southern India it appears to be used for building, &c. It is a fair domestic fuel, but is only poor food for the locomotive, though it has perforce to be used at times.

From the root-bark a kind of rope is occasionally made, and it is said to be employed for matches, and is stated to be useful for the same purpose as oakum by Jameson, who correctly notes that Griffith must have been mistaken in the remark that paper is made from the tree. The trees are often mercilessly lopped and stripped of the leaves, which are used for elephant's fodder, for bedding cattle, for plates, and for wrapping up, &c. The flowers are used in dyeing *basanti*, a fleeting yellow, in preparing the *Holi* powder, and are used as a poultice to orchitis, &c., in Yúnání medicine. According to Bellew they are given in decoction to puerperal women, in cases of diarrhæa, and to sheep for hæmaturia (on "the doctrine of signatures"?), and are applied to bruises and sprains. One of the books mentions an officinal *zard gopí*, which consists of the yellowed fæces of cows which have been fed on *kesú!* The seeds are given as purgative, mostly in veterinary medicine. The bark is in some places extensively incised for the gum, which is a kind of kino. It is used in dyeing blue, in tanning (? Aitchison), and in medicine as an astringent. In Hindústán, *lákh* is formed on this tree, and in 1861 some of the insects were transplanted into some Butea preserves in the Jalandar Doáb. They were spreading up to 1864, since which time I have no information.

CÆSALPINIA SAPPAN. L.

Vernacular. *bakkam, patang.*

Erroneously stated by Irvine to grow in the mountains of Kashmír. Is indigenous nowhere near the Punjab.

C. SEPIARIA. Rox.

Vernacular. J *phulwáí, úran.* K. *kando, úrí.* C. *relú, dodúr.* R. *relmi, didrián, dhár-ki-karer.* B. *ándí, arleí, dughaurí.* S. *ongwá.*

A large, straggling, prickly climber with fine yellow flowers, which grows wild in the outer Punjab Himalaya to 5,000 and occasionally 6,000 feet. It is called "Mysore thorn" in the south, and is said to have been grown by Hyder Ali round his forts, &c., as a defence. In Chumba the bruised leaves are applied to burns.

CAJANUS INDICUS. Sprengel. (C. FLAVUS. DC. and C. BICOLOR. DC.?)

Vernacular. *arhar, dinger, tohar.*

The yellow and parti-colored kinds are not uncommon, the one as a cold weather, the other as a hot weather crop, in the eastern and central Punjab, and extend sparingly to Trans-Indus. They are rarely cultivated in fields by themselves, but generally in narrow strips round other crops. The pulse is said to be easily digested, and suitable for invalids.

CANAVALIA GLADIATA. DC.

Vernacular. *sem.*

A kind of bean cultivated in gardens, for its unripe pod as well as its seed.

CARAGANA PYGMÆA. DC. (VERSICOLOR. Royle).

Vernacular. Lad. *táma, tráma, dáma.*

A small prickly shrub, somewhat resembling furze. Common in Tibet and the drier parts of the inner Himalaya from 12,000 to 16,000 and occasionally to 16,500 feet. It is at times browsed by goats, and although it burns very fast, it is much valued for fuel in these treeless, shrubless parts. Bellew found it at 8,000 to 9,000 feet near the Sufêd Koh, Trans-Indus.

C. TRAGACANTHOIDES. Poir.

Vernacular. J. *sat bargí.* K. *drob, burkundú.*

A largish prickly shrub, which occurs in Kashmir and Hazára at about 5,000 feet, and near the Sufêd Koh. I am not sure that it is of any use.

CASSIA ABSUS. L.

Vernacular. Bazár, seed, *cháksú.*

A small plant with an orange flower growing in the eastern part of the Punjab plains. Its seeds are officinal, being powdered and blown into the eye, or applied in ointment, for ophthalmia.

C. ACUTIFOLIA. Del. (C. LANCEOLATA. Forsk.)

Vernacular. *sanna Makkí.*

Cultivated for senna-leaves in various parts of India, and said by Aitchison to be so in the Punjab, where I have not observed it.

C. OBOVATA. Wall.

Vernacular. T. I. *jíjun, san búti, saríndiga.* S. R. *sanna.*

A small prostrate species found in the Salt Range and Trans-Indus up to 2,500 feet; its leaves are used as senna, and collected for native druggists in some places.

C. OCCIDENTALIS. L. (C. SOPHORA L. ?)

Vernacular. Bazár, seed, *kasaunda, ponwár.*

A tall weed not uncommon in the Punjab plains, the seeds of which are officinal, being given and applied for eruptions, &c. From the second native name, it would appear to be sometimes confused with the next.

C. TORA. L.

Vernacular. C. *hírú.* Bazár, seeds, *ponwár*; leaves, *chakaunda.*

Smaller than the last, and more common. Its seeds are stated to be eaten in times of dearth, and are likewise officinal. The leaves also appear to be officinal under the above name.

CATHARTOCARPUS FISTULA. Pers. (CASSIA. L.)

Vernacular. C. *karangal.* R. *kiár.* B. *áli, kaniár.* U. *karwála.* Plains generally, *amaltás.* Bazár, bark, *kamarkas.*

A small tree common in the Siwálik tract up to 4,000 feet to near the Indus, and said by Bellew to grow in the hills north of the Peshawar Valley. Is frequently planted in the plains for its handsome yellow flowers, which cause it to be sometimes called Indian Laburnum. Aitchison states that it generally flowers and fruits twice a year, but flowering again in a mild autumn is only occasional. The wood is worthless, being brittle and very liable to insects. The bark is used by tanners and dyers, and is officinal under the above name (and see BUTEA). The dried pulp of the long fruit (the sound of the seeds in which cause the tree to be called *chimkaní,* the "rattler" in Sind) is officinal, being used as a purgative. Bellew mentions that the root is given as a tonic and febrifuge.

CERATONIA SILIQUA. L. Carob tree.

Vernacular. Bazár, pod, *kharnúb núbtí.*

This tree grows in the Mediterranean region, and is supposed by some to have furnished the "locusts" of St. John. For some years it has been introduced into the Punjab, in parts of which it thrives and is spreading somewhat, though it does not grow rapidly, and does not yet ripen its seed, or indeed produce pods, except in rare instances. One or two female trees existed in one of the Lahore gardens, and were cut down by the owner, Vandal-like, probably because he did not care to be bothered by questions from the Agri-Horticultural Society as to their progress. It is curious that in the Bazárs the pods are sold as an astringent medicine under the name above given, probably finding their way from Syria by devious routes. In those parts of southern Europe where the tree is common, the pods are given as fodder to horses.

CICER ARIETINUM. L. Chick-pea; *gram* of Europeans.

Vernacular. *channa, chola.*

Commonly cultivated as a cold weather crop throughout the Punjab plains, alone, or mixed with cereals; when reaped is sometimes pulled up, but generally cut; needs no irrigation (indeed dislikes moisture, and after much rain is subject to weevil, *súndí*), and wants but little cultivation, and is very largely grown in the high tract between Rawul Pindí and the Punjab Salt Range. It is extensively exported to Sind, &c., is the chief grain given to horses, and is much eaten parched *(chabena)* by men. Masson states that made into bread it is sweet, and was a favourite of the Sikh *Sirdárs*, and it is still frequently eaten thus in parts of the Punjab. The leaves have often a sour moisture (oxalic acid) on them, and are occasionally eaten. The stalks and leaves, after the seed is thrashed out, constitute one of the most valued kinds of *bhúsa* for fodder.

CICER SOONGARICUM. Steph.

Vernacular. C. *tízhú, jawáne, banyarts.* Lad. *sárrí, serrí.*

A small plant somewhat resembling the last, which grows wild on the Upper Sutlej and Chenáb, in the Jhelam basin and in Ladák, at from 8,500 to 15,000 feet. It is said to fatten cattle quickly. Its seeds were sent to the Agri-Horticultural Society many years ago (having been first found in the Himalaya by Captain Munro about 1844-45), with information that the grain is eaten by the people, the young shoots are prepared as a pickle by "the Chinese," and a vinegar is made from the leaves. The latter are often covered by a viscid exudation, with a strong aromatic odour. Aitchison states that in Lahoul they are used as a pot-herb, and that the peas are eaten there as they are, both raw and cooked in parts of Ladák.

Clitorea ternatea. L.

Vernacular. *dhanattar.*

A garden flower, the leaves and seeds of which are officinal; the former being given in infusion for eruptions, and the latter being aperient.

Colutea arborescens. L. Bladder Senna.

Vernacular. Lad. *bráa.*

This plant grows in the south of Europe where its purgative leaves are employed to adulterate officinal Senna. It was found by Bellew in Affghánistán; but I am not aware that it is used there. A species, perhaps this, grows in Ladák at 10,500 feet on the Sutlej and further east, in the Himalaya.

Crotalaria Burhia. Ham.

Vernacular. T. I. *sís, sissái, meíní, pola.* S. R. *khippí.* S. S. D. *búta, khep.* B. D. *khip, bhata, búí.* H. *láthia, kharsan.* D. *kauriála.*

A naked-looking, bushy plant common in all the more arid parts of the Punjab from Dehlí to Trans-Indus, up to Peshawar. It is browsed by cattle. It has a very tough bark, and with exactly the smell of broom when bruised, which probably gets it the name *búí,* "smeller." Years before I knew it was used for ropes, I suggested that it seemed a likely material for such purpose. Ropes are in many parts made from it by the dry process, (and apparently sometimes after two or three days steeping) but notably not so in places near Dehlí, where the *khip* used for this is a very different plant, Orthanthera (q. v.) The rope is not strong, and is probably only used on account of the cheapness of the material. In Sind also no rope is made from it. I presume the plant has some coagulant power, as a bunch of it is sometimes used to stir milk. The branches and leaves are in the east used as a cooling medicine.

C. juncea. L.

Vernacular. *sanní.*

Commonly cultivated for its fibre in the plains, except in the extreme north-west, generally in strips round other crops, but at times in patches alone. It is sometimes called the female of *san*—(Hibiscus cannabinus q. v.) The fibre is used for ropes, cordage, strong packing-cloth, &c.

C. MEDICAGINEA. Lam.?

Vernacular. Bazár, plant, *guládbí*.

This appears to be the small officinal plant sold under the above name.

C. SERICEA. Retz.

Vernacular. *sanní*.

A plant resembling C. JUNCEA, which is cultivated as a garden flower.

CYAMOPSIS PSORALOIDES. DC.

Vernacular. *kaurí, phalíguár*. Bazár, plant, *bhedmangí*.

A tall plant occasionally cultivated as a hot weather crop for its pulse, west to the Rávi at least. Its stem and leaves appear to be officinal under the above name.

DALBERGIA SISSOO. Rox.

Vernacular. J. *tálí*. K. *safedar*. C. *tálí, shíshái, shín, nelkar*. B. *tálí, shíá*. T. I. *shewa*. Plains generally, *tálí, shísham, sissú*. Bazár, raspings, *búra-de-shísham*.

In the Himalaya I have generally seen this tree indigenous at about 2,000 to 3,500 and occasionally 4,500 feet, where it is seen in many places scattered over steepish slopes in considerable numbers, but short-trunked and rarely exceeding 2 feet in girth. But planted trees, even at some height in the hills, often do well; I have noted several of 8 feet girth and 50 high at about 3,000 feet. In the Punjab plains the only place I know where this tree seems certainly indigenous is the Kachhí Forest on islands in the Indus opposite Bunnoo, where there are many thousands of trees, and have been more, some of considerable size, but generally much less symmetrical than trees grown by man. In similar situations on the Surdah and the Oudh rivers the tree is common. In some places the natives say that this tree was formerly much more abundant than now; but I agree with Aitchison that what with our planting, &c., there are now in most districts more *tálí* than at any former period. Still there is no doubt that handsome black old wood has often to be brought from great distances, and in some places very many fine trees have been cleared within the traditional period, *e. g.*, on the Indus above Attock, where thousands are said to have been destroyed by the cataclysm of 1839; and in the tract on the Chenáb south of Jhang, where very many trees were cut for Sáwan Mull at Múltán, the natives tell of one thousand (?) trees from the lands of a certain village. In the excessively arid tract of the Sind Ságur Doáb to the west of this, the tree is raised with *very* great difficulty, and specimens are very rare, although fine trees up to 10 feet in girth stand at Bakkar near the Indus, on the western edge of the tract, and the Kachhí itself is not far off to the north. In the southern parts of Múltán and Mozaffargarh, on either side the Chenáb (Trimáb) trees of *táli* are exceedingly numerous and fine. Aitchison recommends for zemindars the *ber* and *kikkar*, as the *táli* is slow of growth. But from the average of actual measurements of many trees it is known under fair conditions to grow to about 30 inches girth in 10 or 11 years; and at Shêkhopúra, near Lahore, there is a tree 33 years old of 6 feet in girth. Specimens of 6 or 7 feet girth are not uncommon in the Punjab, and in the station of Anarkullie there is one upwards of 8 feet; the largest I know of, being one at Mozaffargarh, 13½ feet girth. In this Province *táli* is generally raised from seed; but in Jhang, Mozaffargarh, and Múltán, it is often or always grown from cuttings. In Sind, where the tree gets very rare to the south, it is invariably propagated in the latter way. The natives there say that the seed of these trees is never fertile, and it may be so in Sind where seedlings are stated never to spring up under the old trees as in the Punjab; but I believe that at Lahore, Sind seed, sent up for this experiment, was found by Dr. Henderson to germinate and grow like any other. The young trees are very subject to be browsed by cattle, goats, and camels; the last especially preferring them to most others. They are not very subject to be nipped by frost. The timber of this tree is hard, strong, and heavy, a cubic foot weighing 68 lbs. green and 48 (?) dry. It is also very durable, and said not to be attacked by white ants, even when green. It is much valued, and the tree was in Kángra a *padsháhi* one, (*i. e.*, preserved for the ruler's use). The wood is one of the best for gun-carriages, and in some parts of India is said to be largely used in dockyards. It is also employed for furniture, building, boxes, camel-saddles, &c. On especially the western rivers, where it is more easily got, it is much used for boat-building, and a boat built of it is stated to last 20 years. The wood is likely to be a valuable fuel (hitherto it has not been cheap enough to be largely tried), and will be extensively grown in the Fuel Plantations. Possibly, when it is available of sufficient size and in sufficient quantity, it may come into use as Railway sleepers. The raspings of the wood are officinal, being considered alterative.

Desmodium argenteum. Wall.

Vernacular. C. *sambar*. R. *prí*. S. *múse, chíti mort, martan*.

A shrub of some size which is found on several of the rivers, where the climate is somewhat dry, at from 3,500 to 9,000 feet. In Kanáwar its bark is used for ropes after steeping in water. These are not lasting, but very strong, and on the Hindústán and Tibet Road, when platted as thick as the wrist, were found to stand under a heavy temporary strain when English ropes snapped. Cleghorn states that in Kanáwar the bark is used for making paper. Aitchison notes that in Lahoul paper is occasionally made from a D., and, although he says that several species are met with there, none appear to have been sent to England with the collections on which his paper is founded, nor did I see any so far up the Chenáb.

D. tiliæfolium. Don.

Vernacular. J. *chamyár, chamrá, chamkát*. K. *chamkát, marára*. C. *gúr kats, dúd shambar, gúr shágal*. R. *pírhí, pri*. B *kathí*. S. *laber, káli mort*. Bazár, leaves? *shál purní*.

A shrub of much wider distribution than the former, being found abundantly in many places on all the rivers at from 2,800 to 8,000 feet. It is browsed by cattle, the twigs are used for tying loads together, and Cleghorn recommends the tough bark as a paper-making and textile material. The leaves appear to be the *shál purní* of the Bazárs (which, however, may be those of D. Gangeticum, Wall., as given by Jameson).

Dolichos lablab. L. (Lablab vulgaris. Savi.)

Vernacular. *catjang, kála lobia*.

Cultivated for its unripe pod as well as its seed in gardens in the plains.

D. Sinensis. L.

Vernacular. *lobia*.

Commonly cultivated as a hot weather crop, the seeds being eaten, parched and otherwise, and the leaves cooked as a pot-herb

D. UNIFLORUS. Lam.

Vernacular. J. *kalatt, kúlat.* C. *kúlt, kolt.* R. *roíong ráwan.* B. *kolth, gáglí.* S. *barát, botang, guár kúlatt.* Bazár, seed, *gulattí.*

There is some doubt as to the native names of this, but it is commonly cultivated for its pulse in the Himalaya up to 7,000 feet or more. Occasionally grown outside near the base of the hills, Ambála (Edgeworth). The seeds appear to be officinal in the plains.

EDWARDSIA HYDASPICA. Edge.

Vernacular. S. R. *kún, kohen, málan.*

A small shrub with a fine yellow flower, somewhat resembling broom, which is common at many places in the Salt Range and Trans-Indus from 2,000 to 5,000 feet. Goats occasionally browse on it, but it is said to be fatal to other animals.

E. MOLLIS. Royle. ?

Vernacular. J. *buná,* K. *jangli kits, bankeintí.* C. *tilún, tarní, kathí.* R. *brisarí.* Aff. *arghawán.* T. I. *gojár, ghwareja.*

There is some doubt as to whether these are all the same species or whether some of the western specimens may not belong to the last. This is a larger shrub than the latter, and grows at a good many places in the hills at from 2,500 to 8,000 feet, generally in rather arid parts. It appears to be the species found by Bellew on the Súlimán Range at 8,000 feet, and is doubtless the second kind of *arghawán*—(see BAUHINIA VARIEGATA)—mentioned by Baber or his translator as growing at Baber's tomb at Kábul, as Bellew gives his plant that name. No special property is assigned to it, except the beauty of its flowers. I have seen it cultivated in Kashmir.

ERVUM LENS. L. Lentil.

Vernacular. Plains and hills generally, *masúr.* Lad. *chanching, kerge.* S. P. *maurí.*

Commonly cultivated in the cold weather for its pulse, but not generally in the more arid tracts. I believe I have seen it grown as high as 5,500 feet on the Chenáb, and it is cultivated in parts of Ladák to 11,500 feet. Its pulse is said to be heating, and apt to cause eruptions.

ERYTHRINA ARBORESCENS. ROX.? (E. STRICTA. ROX.?) Coraltree.

Vernacular. C. *thab*. R. *gilerú, gaderwa*. B. *pariála*. S. *pūdárá*. U. *dhaul dhák*. Plains generally, *gul násar, gul nashtar*.

A tree with large prickles growing from the young stem and branches, which is commen wild in the Siwálik tract, and occurs further in, at least to the Chenáb, up to 4,500 feet. It is also seen occasionally planted in the plains. It grows to 50 feet high in its natural habitats, and has a striking appearance with its handsome red flowers which blossom before the leaves show. Its wood is white, soft, and tough, and sieve hoops and scabbards are made of it, and it is occasionally employed for the short planks of roofs.

FABA VULGARIS. Mænch. (VICIA FABA. L).

Vernacular. K. *káiún*. S. *chástang*. Lad. *nákshan, nakhthan*. Plains, *bákla*.

Probably not grown in the plains except by Europeans, but commonly cultivated in Kashmír, 5,000, and Kanáwar, Spiti, and Tibet, 8,000 to 12,000 feet. The beans are ground into flour for food, and are, on the Sutlej, given to cattle (Hugel).

GLYCIRRHIZA TRIPHYLLA. F. and M.
G. SP.

Vernacular. Aff. *zaisí*. Bazár, root, *aslasús, jetimadh, muleti*; inspissated juice, *rabísús*.

Several species, possibly including that of Europe, G. GLABRA L., are common wild in Affghánistán, where they are mentioned by Griffith, and where Bellew collected two as above at 5,000 to 6,000 feet. Davies' Trade Report gives 10 maunds of the root (?) as annually imported from Kábul *viâ* Peshawar. The root and extract are both officinal, and are given mixed with purgatives and for colds, &c. Honigberger is probably mistaken when he states that those are imported from Tibet also. And Bellew's Glycirrhiza, found in the Peshawar Valley, is probably ABRUS PRECATORIUS (q. v.)

GUILANDINA BONDUC. L. (CÆSALPINIA B. ROX.)

Vernacular. *katkaranj*.

A great thorny climber with yellow flowers rarely seen cultivated in the Punjab. Its seeds are sold in the Bazárs, being tonic and antiperiodic.

INDIGOFERA HETERANTHA. Wall.

Vernacular. J. *khenti.* K. *kütz.* C. *shágali, kátsú, kuts.* R. *káthi, kâthú, mattá.* B. *káti, kathi.* S. *kathi, kathewat.* T. I. *kaskei.*

The commonest of the Himalayan species, a shrub which is abundant in many places in the hills and the eastern skirts of the Súlimán Range from 2,500' to 8,000 feet. In Kashmír and elsewhere the twigs are largely used for making baskets, &c., and in some cases they form part of the twig-bridges—(see PARROTIA). In Kángra the flowers are used as a pot-herb.

INDIGOFERA LINIFOLIA. Retz.

Vernacular. *torki.*

A small prostrate plant common in the plains up to near the Indus. Honigberger states that it is given medicinally in febrile eruptions.

I. TINCTORIA. L. Indigo.

Vernacular. *níl.* Bazár, extract, *nílbari.*

Is not very commonly cultivated in the Punjab, although indigo from the Indus is said to be mentioned in Arrian's Periplus, and many traces of an export of it by the same river to Europe are found in the historical records as early as the middle of the 17th century. At present the chief tracts for its cultivation are in the Southern Punjab near Múltán, &c., about Hánsí, and in portions of the upper parts of the Jalandar and Bárí Doábs. It is very rarely grown in the extreme N. W. Punjab. In some parts Hindús are said to have a prejudice against cultivating it. Considerable quantities are exported from the Southern Punjab to Affghánistán; and in 1863 a company of Europeans and Natives was formed at Múltán for growing and preparing it, but it appears to have been unsuccessful. Locally indigo is used to dye cloth, and to colour the hair and beard. Cayley states that a few maunds were, in 1867, exported to Lê thence to be carried into eastern Tibet and Túrkistán. The extract is officinal, being administered in epilepsy and nervous disorders.

LATHYENS APHACA. L.

Vernacular. *rawan, rawári.*

A common field-weed all over in the plains, and in some places pulled up and collected as fodder for cattle. Said to be cultivated near the Jumna, the seeds at times lying dormant in the ground for a year.

L. SATIVUS. L.

Vernacular. *kisári, mattar, churál.* Lad. *karas, karil.*

Often cultivated in the plains as a cold weather field crop for its pulse, and grown to 12,000 feet in Tibet. Edgeworth states that in Ambála he never saw it cultivated, though it was common as a weed in fields with pulse or cereals. It is also common as a weed in parts of the Himalaya to 9,500 feet. I have never heard of its producing paralysis in the Punjab, as it is said to do at times in the N. W. Provinces; but Thomson suggests it may have had something to do with a paralysed village he visited at 11,000 feet in Tibet.

MEDICAGO DENTICULATA. Willd.

Vernacular. *mainá.*

Abundant as a weed in fields in the central Punjab, and said to be cultivated also. Is largely gathered for fodder, being considered good for milk.

M. LUPULINA. L.

Vernacular. ?

Common as a weed in part of the plains, in many parts of the hills, and to 12,000 feet in Zanskar (Thomson). Collected for fodder.

M. SATIVA. L. (?) Lucerne.

Vernacular. Aff. *rishka, dureshta.* Lad. *hol.*

Is found wild in the N. W. Himalaya from 5,000 to 12,000 feet, and is cultivated extensively in Affghánistán, where it is used as fodder for horses, &c. Moorcroft says that it also grows wild, and it is cultivated in Ladák for the same purpose, and he states that fields of it continue to be regularly cut for several, up to "50 or 60 years."

MELILOTUS LEUCANTHA. Koch. (M. ALBA. Lam. ?)

Vernacular. *chita sinji.*

Occurs wild in several parts of the Punjab plains, and to 8,500 feet or more in the Himalaya. In the former it is said to produce swelling of the belly in cattle which browse it.

M. PARVIFLORA. Desf.

Vernacular. *sínjí.*

Is extensively cultivated for fodder in parts of the central Punjab, and said to be good for milk. Also occurs wild in the plains and hills, and is perhaps the MELILOT mentioned by Thomson at 13,000 feet in Zanskar.

M. SP.?

Vernacular. ?

A tall yellow-flowered species grows in the outer hills, where it is said to be browsed by camels only.

MIMOSA RUBICAULIS. Lam.

Vernacular. J., K., and C. *rál, riaul.* R. *didriár.* B. *arlú.* S. R. *allá.* B. D. *kikkrí.* Bazár, fruit, *deo khádir.*

A very prickly shrub of some size which grows in the outer hills to 3,000 and occasionally 4,000 feet, up to near the Indus, and is at times found on the banks of rivers or canals, some way into the plains. In Chumba the bruised leaves are applied to burns, and the fruit appears to be officinal under the above name.

MUCUNA SP.

Vernacular. ?

Found in the Salt Range, where its seeds are used as a purgative.

OUGEINIA DALBERGIOIDES. Bth. (DALBERGIA OUGEINENSIS. Rox).

Vernacular. J. to U. *sannan, sándan.*

A smallish, somewhat crooked tree, from which in Bombay a kind of kino is said to be obtained, grows sparingly throughout the Siwálik tract to 4,000 feet occasionally, up to the Jhelam. The timber is hard and strong, resembling that of DALBERGIA, and is said to be very durable, and not subject to warping or to worms. It is much valued for ploughs, wheels, sugar and cotton-rollers, combs, &c.

OXYTROPIS SP.?

Vernacular. ?

Moorcroft says that in Ladák a kind of "sainfoin" is much eaten by sheep, and that its inner bark is there the only material for paper.

Parkinsonia aculeata. DC.

Vernacular. *wiláyáti kikkar.*

Since annexation this has spread largely throughout the Punjab, but as it only becomes a scraggy small tree, is not much valued by Europeans except for hedges, for which it answers well if sown close and well cropped, and it needs but little water. It is subject to be severely lopped of its smaller branches, &c., to be given as fodder to goats, as may at any time be seen on the Lahore roads.

Phaseolus aconitifolius. Jacq.

Vernacular. *moth* (sometimes applied to other pulses in the hills).

Commonly cultivated as a hot weather crop, for its pulse, all over the Punjab plains, but chiefly in the arid parts with light soil. The pulse is not much valued, and is thought to be heating.

P. Mungo. L.

Vernacular. *múng, múngi, múji.*

Commonly cultivated in the plains, and to 3,500 feet in the hills, for its pulse, which is considered nutritious and digestible.

P. radiatus. Rox. (P. Roxburghii. W. and A.)

Vernacular. in plains and hills, *másh, máh, (úrad).*

Cultivated as a hot weather crop, for its pulse, in the plains, and to 6,500 feet in the hills. This is considered the most heating, and apt to give colic, of all the pulses.

Pisum sativum. L.

Vernacular. B. *sen*. B. D. *mattar, khandú*. Lad. *shánmá ahandil.*

Cultivated for Europeans' use in the plains by natives in parts of the central Punjab, and in the outer hills near Kángra, &c., as well as in Kanáwar, Spiti, Lahoul, and Ladák, up to 13,000 or 14,000 feet. At the latter height it does not ripen its seeds, but is chiefly used as fodder. Masson also mentions "peas" at Bamean, in Affghánistán, at a considerable elevation.

Pongamia glabra. Vent.

Vernacular. *sukh chein.* Bazár, pod, *bara karanj.*

A handsome tree occurring in the Siwálik tract up to near the Rávi, and not uncommon planted out in the plains, but not growing to a large size in the Punjab. Its leaves and pods are officinal.

Prosopis spicigera. L.

Vernacular. T. I. *aghzakái*. S. R. *seh*. H. *khár*. Plains generally, *jhand, jandí, jand*: pod, *sangar, sankhrí, shángar*. Bazár, galls, *kharnúb Hindí*.

Abounds generally as a large shrub (from lopping, &c.,) in the central Punjab, and occurs more sparingly to either side. Is also common in Sind, and in Bikanír is said to be the chief plant of any size. The natives in some parts say that it especially favours a heavy soil which needs much irrigation. About Mozaffargarh they state that the best land is where it grows small but abundant. When protected in villages, &c., the tree attains a respectable size, the bark being often furrowed into large divisions, resembling the scales of a reptile, and the finely drooping branches with light green foliage and yellow spikes of flowers look pretty about the latter part of April. Trees of 5 feet girth are not uncommon; the largest I have seen being (one of 9 feet girth at Gúmbaz in Sind) one of 9 feet girth and 60 feet high at Bhowání, north of Jhang, one of 8 feet girth near the same place, one of 8 feet girth and 35 feet high near Dehra Ghází Khan, one of 8 feet girth and 25 feet high, and another very fine tree of 6 feet and 45 feet at Sirsa, and one of 6 feet and 40 feet at Bilot, Trans-Indus. At Sánpla near Rohtuk there is a well-preserved plot of hundreds which range up to 6 feet girth and 40 in height. The trees occasionally assume a cupressiform appearance, a fine specimen of 4½ feet girth and 50 high standing at Mittankôt. But these are *rari nantes*, for by far the greater part of the Prosopis seen in the Punjab are lopped, browsed, and hacked into dwarfhood and deformity, many with their trunks hollow from the constant deprivations they have undergone. The growth of the tree is slow, probably not to more than 15 inches in girth in 15 years. One in Saharanpúr Botanic Gardens, said to be 30 years old, is 3 feet in girth. The wood is soft and open-grained, and subject to be eaten by white ants. A cubic foot dry weighs 51 lbs. It is used as timber only for the commonest purposes, except for well-curbs, and in Sind where much furniture is made of it. But it is a good fuel either for domestic or Railway use, and burns fairly well even when recently felled. In the central Punjab this is the chief plant used for fuel on the large scale.

The pods, which ripen before and during the rains, contain, when scarcely ripe, a considerable quantity of a sweetish farinaceous substance, which in many places is largely consumed as food, in some parts by all classes, in others only by the poor or in times of scarcity. It is eaten green or dry, raw and alone, or boiled with salt, onions, *ghí*, &c., and eaten with bread, or mixed with *dahí*. The quantity which may be consumed at once by a man has been variously put to me from a *chitták* to a *ser*. I am not certain that the pod is not sometimes used medicinally. On many trees a spongy wooden gall is produced, sometimes in great quantities. It is probably inert, but is officinal under the above name, being reckoned astringent. From the stumps of pruned branches and other scars, a gum exudes similar to gum Arabic, but I do not know that it is collected or used.

PSORALEA CORYLIFOLIA. L.

Vernacular. Bazár, seed, *bábehí*.

An herb which occasionally occurs in the drier tracts of the plains and in the Salt Range. Its seeds are officinal, being used in ointments, and internally as a vermifuge.

P. PLICATA. Del.

Vernacular. *bakhtmal*.

Resembles the preceding; is common in some arid tracts in the plains up to the Indus. Edgeworth states that camels delight in it.

PUERARIA TUBEROSA. DC.

Vernacular. C. *siálí, badár*. R. *siáli, saloha*. Bazár, tuber, *bilái kand, bidárí kand*.

A great climber, common in some parts of the Siwálik tract up to near the Indus. The very large tuberous yam-like roots are eaten, and said to be sweet, and are exported to the plains, where they are officinal as a cooling medicine, and are used as poultices.

SESBANIA ÆGYPTIACA. Pers. (ÆSCHYNOMENE SESBAN. L.)

Vernacular. *jait, jaintar*. Bazár, seed, *riwásan, jel*.

A straggling large shrub commonly cultivated in gardens as a hedge, and for its bunches of flowers, particoloured, yellow, and occasionally white. It is a ready and quick grower, but has nothing special to recommend it, nor is the wood of any use, although it sometimes attains 2 feet in girth. The seeds are officinal, being applied in ointment for eruptions, for which also the juice of the bark is given internally.

Soja hispida. W. and A.

Vernacular. *bhut.*

A patch of this pulse was seen by Cleghorn at 6,000 feet in Bissahir.

Tamarindus Indica. L.

Vernacular. *imlí.* Bazár. fruit, *tamar Hindí.*

This fine tree which is common in the N. W. Provinces, and whose wood being hard, heavy, and strong, is very valuable for naves, sugar and oil-mills, &c., &c.; is rare in the Punjab oncept about Dehlí. A few trees are found as far west as Múltán, Jhelam, and towards Rajaorí, but even so far east as Ambála the fruit is said not to ripen. Its pulp is valuable as food and as a laxative medicine, and the powdered seeds are given for rheumatism in the Hindú system, and for herpes by the Yúnanís.

Tephrosia purpurea. Pers.

Vernacular. H. *bánsa.* D. *jhojhrú, sarphonka.* Bazár, plant, *sarphonka.*

This or a closely allied species is not uncommon in the plains from Dehlí west as far as the Jhelam, and in the Salt Range, but is rare or unknown in most parts to the south and in the extreme north-west. In Harriána the twigs are used for making baskets. The plant is officinal, being considered depurative and cordial, and in some places an infusion of the seeds is considered cooling.

Trifolium pratense. L. (T. fragiferum. L.?)

Vernacular. J. *trepattra.* K. *chit batto.*

Not uncommon in parts of the N. W. Himalaya from 3,500 to 8,000 feet up to the Indus, and to 8,600 feet in Tibet (Thomson). It is eaten by cattle.

T. repens. L.

Vernacular. T. I. *shaftal, shotul.*

Common in many parts of the Himalaya up to 10,000 feet, and in the plains of the extreme N. W. Punjab. It is eaten by cattle, and does well for turfing lawns in the hills.

T. SP.

Vernacular. Aff. *shaftal, shotul.*

Stated by Irvine to be wild in Affghánistán where it is abundantly cultivated as fodder for horses, &c., much of it being twisted into long cables to be dried for winter use. Moorcroft says that he "never saw ground so covered with hay of any kind" as with this at Kábul. Bellew mentions that it is grown in Swát, and I have seen a kind cultivated under the above namis in Hazára at 3,000 feet, which is probably the same plant.

TRIGONELLA FÆNUM GRÆCUM. L.

Vernacular. *methí.*

Commonly cultivated in the plains in the cold weather, the leaves, &c., being used as a vegetable. If eaten by cows, is said to be heating and to dry up the milk. The seeds are officinal, being used in fomentations, and given for colic and flatulency, and in the Arabian system for dysentery.

T. POLYSERRATA. L.

Vernacular. *mainí.*

A common field weed in the central Punjab. Is said to cause swelling of the belly in cattle which eat it.

URARIA CHETKUBRA. Jameson. (HEDYSARUM ALOPECUROIDES. Royle).

Vernacular. Bazár, leaves, *chitkabra Hindí, pusht barní.*

The identity is uncertain of the plant whose leaves are officinal under the above names. They are supposed to increase the flow of bile.

U. PICTA. Desv. (?)

Vernacular. Bazár, seed, *deterdáne.*

Occasionally grown in gardens. Fruit is found in the Bazárs, and used officinally under the above name, being applied to the sore mouths of children.

N. O. ROSACEÆ.

AMYGDALUS COMMUNIS. L. Almond.

Vernacular. *badám.*

Sometimes cultivated in the Punjab plains, but rarely bears fruit, and still more rarely ripens it. Vigne states that in

Kashmír (?) it furnishes much oil, but he probably refers to the kernel of the Apricot—(see PRUNUS ARMENIACA). Large quantities of sweet, and some bitter almonds, are imported from the west.

A. PERSICA. L. Peach.

Vernacular. J. *árú.* K. *súnnú, tsúnú.* C. *arúí, chinannú.* R. *árúí.* B. *árú.* S. *bem beimi.* T. I. *ghwareshtaí, ghargashtáí.*

Cultivated in the plains, the fruit being generally very poor, but very good at Peshawar. I believe I have seen it wild at several places from 3,000 to 6,000 feet with miserably small poor fruit in the Himalaya, where it is cultivated to 10,000 feet in Kanáwar, and to 9,000 feet in Lahoul, but fruit not good at the higher limit, and not worth much below. In Ladák it is possibly cultivated at higher elevations than these, but Vigne says the fruit is generally small. In Kashmír some of the fruit is said to be excellent. One of the kinds grown at Kandahár, Bellew states to be the best peach he knows. Vigne states that in Ladák the foot rot in sheep is treated by a decoction of the leaves.

AMYGDALUS PERSICA. L. VAR. LÆVIS. Nectarine.

Vernacular. *shoftálú, múndla árú.*

Rarely cultivated in the Punjab plains (but not very successfully) and frequently in Affghánistán. Dr. Cayley states that trees occur in at least one village near Lê, and ripen fruit. The fruit is said by the natives to have the property of killing the intestinal parasite *kenchwa*—(Ascaris lumbricoides).

A. SP.

Vernacular. Aff. *badám talkh.*

A small species found wild by Bellew near the Sufêd Koh, of which the thin outer bark is used as a covering for pipe-stems, is probably the A. mentioned by Griffith under the above native name.

CERASUS VULGARIS. Mill. Cherry.

Vernacular. K. *gilás.* Aff. *álú bálú.*

The cherry is not cultivated by natives, and has always failed with Europeans in the plains of the Punjab. In Kashmír the tree is commonly cultivated, and some of the kinds are good, both sweet and bitter, the latter excellent for cherry-brandy. One tree of the latter kind, planted in Pangí on the Upper Chenáb, has done well, and bears abundant fruit. Cherries are cultivated at Kandahár (Bellew) and at Kábul. Masson states that three varieties were introduced by Baber as recorded in his Memoirs. The wild tree is said also to be a favourite at Kábul and Kandahár, being planted for the sake of its white blossoms.

COTONEASTER OBTUSA. Wall.
C. ROTUNDIFOLIA. Wall.

Vernacular. J. *lúní*. K. *lehan, lín, khárix*. C. *riú, rau, linú, lillún*. R. *riú, rísh*. S. *reús, rí*. T. I. *kheroa, kheraba*. S. R. *sichú*.

Of several species of COTONEASTER, these two, which are apt to be confused, are most common, from 4,000 to 10,500 feet in the Punjab Himalaya. Their wood, though small, is tough and strong, and is much used for the secondary supports of roofs, axe-handles, and walking-sticks, and it is said for *jámpán*-poles (?) In Kashmír the twigs are extensively employed for basket-making, and are frequently mixed with PARROTIA (q. v.) for the twig-bridges.

CRATÆGUS CRENULATA. Rox.

Vernacular. *gíngárú*.

I have not seen this shrub except to the east of Punjab limits, but Cleghorn states that on the Sutlej it is used for staves, &c.

C. OXYACANTHA. L. Hawthorn.

Vernacular. J. *ban-sanjlí, súr sínjlí*. K. *ringo, ríng*. C. *píngyát, ramnia, ring*. R. *phindák, patákhen*. T. I. *ghwanza*. Aff. *durána*.

Not uncommon from the Rávi westward, from 6,000 to 9,000 feet, and found in the Súlimán Range up to 9,000 feet by Bellew near the Sufêd Koh. Griffith and Masson mention it at Kábul, and the latter states that it was brought thither from the hills. In the Himalaya trees may be seen 5 feet in girth and 25 feet high, but I do not know that its timber is applied to any special purpose. On the Chenáb particularly the fruit is large and really decent eating, much better than I recollect of at home.

Cydonia vulgaris. Pers. Quince.

Vernacular. K. *bam tsúntú.* Plains, &c., generally, *bihí.* Bazár, seed, *bihí dána.*

Cultivated in the plains in many places, but not of particularly good quality, and grown in the Himalaya to 5,500 feet. Common in Kashmír, where the fruit is said by Vigne to be very fine. Cayley states that a small quantity is exported from Kashmír into Tibet. Abundant in Affghánistán, whence fruit and seed are largely imported into the Punjab (Davies' Trade Report gives two maunds of the latter as annually imported viâ Peshawar), and where, according to Bellew, the fruit is eaten fresh, candied or dried. Irvine states that that of Affghánistán excels all other quinces in quality (but that except them, "there is no other fruit of remarkable goodness.") The seed is officinal, being demulcent and cooling.

Fragaria vesca. L. Strawberry.

Vernacular. J. *kanzars.* K. *ingrách, yang tash.* C. *palfor.* R. *búnún, musriní.* S. *bana phal.* T. I. *tawái.*

Found wild in most parts of the Punjab Himalaya from 4,000 to 12,000 feet. Adams states that the brown bear is *very* fond of its roots. The fruit, though small, is excellent when gathered dry, and has been proved by various trials to be improved by cultivation in a garden. The strawberry is only cultivated in the gardens of Europeans, and very good and abundant fruit is raised in some stations even in the plains.

F. Indica. Andr.

Vernacular.

Is common in the Himalaya, and has a small tasteless fruit; is sometimes mistaken for the other by Europeans.

Potentilla discolor. Jacq.

Vernacular.

Appears to be frequent in Kanáwar, Spiti, and Ladák, from 11,500 to 15,000 feet. The under-surface of the leaves is covered with a fine dust, which, when the plant is shaken, causes violent sneezing.

P. Inglisii. Royle. (P. fruticosa. L. var.)

Vernacular. C. *spang jhá, merino.* Lad. *pinjúng, penmá.*

Is not uncommon in the higher parts of the Chenáb basin, where Aitchison and Longden state that its fragrant leaves, &c., are used as a substitute for tea. It also grows in Spiti and Ladák, occurring in the latter up to over 10,000 feet. Is browsed by sheep.

P. nepalensis. Hook.

Vernacular. S. *rattanjot.*

Not uncommon in the Punjab Himalaya at 6,000 or 7,000 feet. The reddish root is exported to the plains under the above name from some parts. There are, however, several other roots sold under the same name—(see Onosma). They are employed in dyeing wool, and are officinal, being considered depurative, and they are used externally in the Yúnání system, the ashes being applied with oil to burns.

P. Salesovii Steph.

Vernacular. Lad. *shour.*

Grows in Lahoul, Spiti, and Ladák, at 11,000—12,000 feet. Is browsed by sheep.

Prinsiepia utilis. Royle.

Vernacular. J. *gurinda, chamba, arund.* C. *tatúa, phúlwára, rári, jínti.* R. *bekklí, karngúra.* B. *behkul.* S. *bhekkal, bekkar, bekhúl, bekhwa, bekling.*

A common shrub throughout the Punjab Himalaya from 2,500 to 8,000 feet, up to near the Indus. Its wood is said to be used for walking-sticks. The fruit yields an oil, which is eaten or burned, or both, except in the extreme north-west where the shrub is more rare.

Prunus Armeniaca. L. Apricot.

Vernacular. J. *hárí, harian.* K. *gurdálú, cherkúsh.* C. *chirolí, tser-kují, chúlí, chír, sárí.* R. *chír, chiran, sárí.* B. *shári.* S. *jaldárú chúlí.* Lad. *chúlí.* T. I. *mandata,* dried, *khubání,* moist, *khista.*

I believe I have seen the apricot wild in many places from 4,000 to 6,000 feet, in the Punjab Himalaya. It is commonly cultivated all over up to 10,000 or perhaps 10,500 feet (and not 11,200 as stated by Hoffmeister) in some places in the arid climates of the Upper Sutlej and the Upper Chenáb, and even to 11,500 or 12,000 feet in parts of Tibet. A great deal of the fruit, especially at the higher elevations, is very inferior, and in Tibet particularly Vigne mentions that it is generally small, which would seem to be corroborated by the fact that 200 maunds were imported into Lê from Kashmír in 1867 (Cayley). Yet Aitchison states that the dried apricots are imported into Lahoul from Tibet. But very fair fruit is grown in many parts, and in some of especially the Kanáwar villages, the trees constitute a chief form of the wealth of the inhabitants, and yellow heaps of it may be seen drying in thousands on the roof of almost every house. A considerable quantity (Davies' Trade Report puts it at 100 maunds viâ Peshawar) of dried apricots are annually imported into the Punjab from Affghánistán where the tree is largely grown. The fruit is eaten green or dried, and the kernels are sometimes eaten separately, or more frequently pounded with the pulp to lessen the sourness of the latter. Hoffmeister states that mixed these are considered an antidote to hill sickness. Wherever the tree is common the kernels are pounded, and their oil expressed by hand. It is stated to have a pleasant taste with a bitter almond flavour, and is largely consumed as food and burned. It is also used for the hair, though probably not specially as a perfume, as Moorcroft states. In various parts the half ripe fruit dried are used by goldsmiths to remove the black oxide from silver, or as in Affghánistán, a decoction is employed for this purpose (Bellew). In Tibet an apricot is applied after mastication to ophthalmia, and Bellew mentions that the dried fruit is in Affghánistán used as a laxative and refrigerant in fevers, &c. A gum, similar to gum Arabic, exudes from wounds in the bark of the tree. The wood does not appear to be used for any special purpose, except occasionally for making the Tibetan drinking-cups, as stated by J. D. Cunningham—(see ACER).

P. BOKHARIENSIS. Royle. Bokhára Plum.

Vernacular. *álú Bokhára.*

The fruit is imported from Affghánistán, and the tree thrives in the Upper Provinces (Firminger). It grows well at places near Lahore, producing a deep red fruit.

P. DOMESTICA. L. Plum.

Vernacular. K. *olchí, er, aor* (?) Plains, &c., *alúcha.*

Appears to be common wild and cultivated in Kashmír, and is cultivated in Affghánistán, &c. (Moorcroft mentions some from Yárkand as "infinitely preferable to the best French plums.") It is also cultivated in the Punjab plains, yielding a waxy yellowish fruit. In Kashmír the wood is used for making the skeletons of the "papier maché" boxes.

P. Padus. L. (Cerasus cornuta. Royle). Bird cherry.

Vernacular. J. *páras, kála kát, gídar dák, bart.* K. *zamb chule.* C. *jamún, krún.* R. *dúdla, jamú.* S. *krún, jámú, jammú.*

A fine tree, with handsome bunches of white flowers in April, which grows in many parts of the Punjab Himalaya from 4,000 to 10,500 feet, up to the Indus. The wood is not much valued, but is used for ploughs, railings, &c., and for spoons. The fruit is eaten by the natives, but has a mawkish astringent taste, not peculiarly attractive to Europeans. The specific name given to this tree by Royle arose from the fact, that from the puncture of some insect the fruit frequently grows into a horn-like dark excrescence up to 3 inches in length. These are occasionally seen in most seasons, and were exceedingly common on many trees in parts of Hazára in 1867.

P. prostrata. Labill.

Vernacular. *paltú.*

Stated by Aitchison to occur at one village in Lahoul 9,500 feet, and to be common in Kanáwar (but there would appear here to have been some confusion with Pyrus Kumaonensis q. v.)

P. Puddum. Lind.

Vernacular. J. *chamiárí, amalgúch.* B. *pajja, paddam* S. *pajja, pája.*

A small tree which occurs in the Punjab Himalaya from 3,000 to 5,000 feet, up to near the Indus. The fruit is eaten by the natives, though it is always somewhat bitter. The wood is coarse-grained, light, soft, apt to split, and to be attacked by insects. It is used in building, and occasionally for implements.

Pyrus Aucuparia. Gært. P. ursina. Wall. Mountain ash, Rowan.

Vernacular. J. *battal.* C. *ránthúl wámpú litsi.* S. *rangrek.*

A small tree which occurs occasionally from 8,500 to 11,500 feet in the Punjab Himalaya, up to near the Indus. It has red fruit (sometimes white, according to Madden), which resembles those of P. AUCUPARIA of Europe in flavour. They are not eaten.

P. BACCATA. Wall.

Vernacular. *liú, liwár, lhíjo, lítsí.*

A small tree which is common wild, and I think cultivated on the Upper Chenáb from 8,200 to 10,000 feet. Its fruit is very small and very sour, but has the true apple flavour, and Aitchison states that it is much eaten by the Lahoulís.

P. COMMUNIS. L. (P. SINENSIS. Lindl. ?) Pear.

Vernacular. J. and K. *tang, batang, batank.* C. *nák.* Plains, &c., *náshpátí, nák.*

The pear tree is occasionally cultivated in the Punjab plains, producing a wretched fruit, and appears to be quasi-indigenous in Kashmír. It is also cultivated there and in Affghánistán, and according to Vigne in Tibet, but this is doubtful. Some of the fruit, which is imported into the Punjab (Davies' Trade Report puts it at ten camel loads annually viâ Peshawar) is juicy and tolerably good—much of it indifferent. Aitchison states that it is quite unknown in Lahoul, but further down on the Chenáb at 8,000 to 8,500 feet, a pear tree, sometimes wild and sometimes apparently cultivated, is not uncommon. Irvine states that in Kashmír a spirit is manufactured from the fruit, but this is unlikely.

P. FOLIOLOSA.

Vernacular.

Stated by Madden to grow on the Sutlej, but with no notice of its fruit or uses.

P. KUMAONENSIS. Wall. (P. ARIA. Ehrh.)

Vernacular. J. *doda, chota.* K. *chitana, máil tang.* C. *máil, mahaul, lítsí.* R. *maul, kanglú.* B. *ban pála.* S. *marphol, pálú, bisír.* T. I. *gún palos.*

A small tree common in many parts of the Punjab Himalaya from 6,000 to 10,500 feet, up to the Indus, and doubtless beyond that river from there being a Pushtú name for the tree. The smallish fruit ripens about October and looks well, but is very indifferent eating even when half rotten, in which state it is generally consumed by the natives.

P. Malus. L.

Vernacular. J. *sher*. K. *tsúnt, (amrú) sun*. C. *tsûnt, chung, seu, kashú*. R. *khajú, seu, cho*. S. *lí*. Lad. *kúshú*. T. I. *mána*. Plains generally, *seu*.

Is cultivated in parts of the Punjab Himalaya, and is apparently wild in places with a miserable fruit from 5,000 to 9,000 feet on the Chenáb and Sutlej; is also grown in Ladák to 11,500 feet, and in Affghánistán, whence Davies' Trade Report says that 75 maunds are imported annually viâ Peshawar. In some parts, especially towards the west, the fruit is juicy and pleasant, though not to be compared with English apples. Some years ago an European was got out by the Maharaja of Kashmír to initiate the manufacture of cyder, but the attempt broke down. Vigne says the apples of Tibet are excellent, and they are really very palatable. Apples are also cultivated in the plains, but of very inferior quality.

P. variolosa. Wall.

Vernacular. J. *batangí*. K. *shindar, tang, tángí*. C. *keint, kithú, gádkújí*. R. *keint, kiat*. B. *keitha, kent*. S. *keint, shegúl*.

A moderate sized tree, occasionally reaching 6 feet in girth, and found in most parts of the Punjab Himalaya from 2,500 to 7,000 feet, up to the Indus. The timber is tolerably strong, and is used for implements, walking-sticks, &c. The fruit is harsh and bitter until half rotten, like a medlar, when it is *eatable*.

Rosa Brunonis. L.

Vernacular. J. *phúliári, chal*. K. *phúl wári, krür*. C. *karer*. R. *karír, kajei*. B. *kújo, kújí, phuliári, gúngári*. S. *kúí, kahí*. T. I. *gulob ghurei*.

A fine wild white rose climbing luxuriantly over bushes and even tall trees. Is common in the outer Himalaya from 2,400 to 7,000 feet, up to and probably beyond the Indus.

R. centifolia. L.
R. Damascena. Mill.
R. Indica. J.
R. moschata. Mill.

Vernacular. *guláb, sewti*, &c. Bazár, stamens, *zíreh guláb*.

All of these appear to be cultivated in the plains. From the first especially, and perhaps others, rosewater and *attar* of roses are prepared in many places. The flowers are officinal, being considered aperient and cordial, and the stamens are used as a cooling aperient in inflammations.

R. EGLANTERIA. L.

One or more wild yellow roses are found in Kashmír, Lahoul, Tibet, &c. Lowther states that they are sometimes double, and Thomson mentions double yellow roses at 11,000 feet in Ladak. Masson speaks of a Kábul rose, the petals of which are yellow externally (perhaps variety PUNICEA of R. EGLANTERIA).

R. MACROPHYLLA. Lindl.

Vernacular. J. *shingárí*. C. *guláb, jikjik*. R. *banguláb, akhiárí*. S. *bankújrú, yal, trind, túmbí*.

There is some confusion as to this species, but it seems to grow over a wide range up to the Indus, from 4,500 to 10,500 feet. Its fruit is eaten, and is stated by Madden to become very sweet when black and rotten. In Kanáwar a perfume is said to be extracted from the flowers for export towards the plains.

R. WEBBIANA. Wall.

Vernacular. J. *kantián*. C. *sikanda, manyar, shádwalí chúa*. S. *ríngyál, kugína*. Lad. *sía, sea*.

This rose is found chiefly in the rather arid tracts of the Punjab Himalaya from 5,000 to 9,500 feet, up to near the Indus, and in Ladák it reaches 13,500 feet. Its fruit is eaten, and in parts of Spiti the stems are largely used for fuel.

RUBUS.

The native names are inextricably confused. I have made the best possible of them and of the species.

RUBUS BIFLORUS. Sm.

Vernacular. J. *akhrerí*. C. *kantanch, khariára*. R. *karer*. B. *ankren*. S. *bumbal, ínsra, bátang, kalkalín*.

A red fruited species which appear to be common in many places in the Punjab Himalaya from 5,000 to 10,500 feet, up to the Indus.

R. FLAVUS. Ham.

Vernacular. J. *pukána, gurácha*. R. *ákhí, kunáchí, gurácha*.

Yellow fruited, not very common from 2,500 to 7,000 feet, up to near the Indus.

R. FRUTICOSUS. L. (R. FLORIBUNDUS. H. B. K.?)

Vernacular. K. *álish, sháli dag gánch.* B. *akhi.* T. I. *karwárei.*

With dark purple fruit is not uncommon at rather low elevations (up to 5,000 feet occasionally), and found at the foot of the hills in the extreme N. W. Punjab.

R. LASIOCARPUS. Sm.

Vernacular. J. *gunácha, pagúnai, pakána.* K. *pakáni, gurácha, kandiára, kharmach, surgauch.* C. *tulanch, oche.* T. I. *manzakhta.*

A black fruited species one of the commonest of all, from 3,000 to 8,000 feet, up to and beyond the Indus.

R. PURPUREUS. Bunge.

Vernacular. ?

Mentioned by Aitchison as growing in Lahoul at, say, 10,000 feet.

R. ROTUNDIFOLIUS.?

Vernacular. J. *kanachi, krora.* K. *chench, kanáchi, pukána.* R. *úkhra, kharen.* B. *ánkhi.* S. *esar.*

With yellow fruit, not uncommon at rather low elevations (from 2,300 to 6,000 feet) up to the Indus. The identity of this species is very doubtful.

R. TILIACEUS. Sm.

Vernacular. K. *púlla.*

A black fruited species not uncommon from 4,500 to 8,500 feet, up to the Indus. The fruit is not much prized.

Of the fruit of the Himalayan RUBI, Moorcroft says that the red is nearly equal to English, but the light and dark yellow are not so good.

SPIRÆA KAMTSCHATIKA. Pall.

Vernacular. K. *angrásha.* S. *zhúk.*

A small and pretty species resembling the meadow-sweet of Europe, one of the less common kinds, grows from 6,000 to 10,000 feet. Is of no use so far as I know.

S. LINDLEYANA. Wall.

Vernacular. J. *kíhrí.* K. *dor, bat pís.* C. *káprú, kurkní, ránthúl.* R. *dodal, kírne, amrethí.* S. *kangtar, búglí, krúst, kanúrí.* T. I. *sarlakhtei.*

A shrub with fine white flowers the handsomest and one of the commonest of the Himalayan species of SPIRÆA, grows from 4,000 to 10,500 feet, up to and beyond the Indus. Is of no special use.

N. O. COMBRETACEÆ.

CONOCARPUS LATIFOLIA. ROX.

Vernacular. *dhan, chál.*

A large and handsome tree common in the Siwálik tract up to the Rávi. In some parts of India the timber is much valued for beams, naves, and in ship-building, &c. Here it is reckoned strong and durable, and is used for implements, beams, &c. It also furnishes a very good charcoal. The leaves are employed for tanning, and in some parts are exported to the plains for this purpose. The gum, which exudes from incisions made in the bark, is used in cloth-printing.

PENTAPTERA TOMENTOSA. ROX; and P. GLABRA. ROX. (TERMINALIA. W. and A.)

Vernacular. *ásan, sein.*

Grows to a large tree, and is found in the Siwálik tract up to near the Rávi, but is not common within Punjab bounds, except in the extreme east. Its wood is of fair quality, and is employed for ordinary purposes, and for making charcoal.

TERMINALIA ARJUNA. W. and A. (PENTAPTERA. ROX.)

Vernacular. B. *árjan.* Plains, *jumla.*

A tree which occurs scantily in the Siwálik tract up to the Rávi. The dark heart-wood is said to be heavy, hard, and strong, but to be apt to split and liable to the attacks of white ants. In Kángra the bark is applied medicinally to sores, &c.

T. Bellerica. Rox. Belleric Myrobalans.

Vernacular. *bahera.*

A large tree which grows in the eastern part of the Siwálik tract, and occurs planted, attaining a considerable size, in some places in the plains up to the Indus, and in the hills north of the Peshawar Valley (Bellew). Its yellowish wood is coarse-grained, and subject to the attacks of white ants and other insects. It is used in building, but in Kángra is considered unlucky when thus employed. In Kángra also the leaves are considered the best fodder for milch cows. They are likewise used in tanning. The fruit is employed as a mordant in dyeing and in tanning, and for making ink. Halfi ripe they are purgative, and ripe they are astringent, and are used medicinally in mucous discharges from the lungs and bowels.

T. chebula. Retz. Chebulic Myrobalans.

Vernacular. *har, harrar.* Bazár, fruit, *har* of three or four kinds according to ripeness and size.

Grows to be a large tree, but mostly planted, in the Siwálik tract, up to the Peshawar Valley (Bellew). The wood is yellowish, hard, and heavy, and is used for agricultural implements, &c., but is not valued. The fruit is employed by dyers as a mordant, and in various stages, under different names, is used medicinally, mostly in diseases of the bowels.

N. O. HALORAGEÆ.

Trapa bispinosa. Rox. Water caltrops.

Vernacular. K. *gaúnri.* Plains, &c., *singhárá.*

Not uncommon in pools and tanks (probably always introduced) in parts of the Punjab plains up to Peshawar, and in Kashmír (5,000 feet). The fruit, which in flavour resembles a chesnut, is eaten both raw and cooked, especially by the Hindús, as it is *phaláhar, i. e.,* may be eaten in their fasts. In Kashmír miles of the lakes and marshes, &c., are covered with this plant. Moorcroft states that in the valley it furnishes almost the only food of at least 30,000 people for five months of the year, and that from the Wúlar lake ninety-six to one hundred thousand ass-loads are taken annually, the Government drawing 90,000 rupees duty on it. And within the last few years it has been stated on good authority that the Maharaja gets more than a lákh of Company's rupees annually from this source.

N. O. LYTHRARIEÆ.

AMMANNIA AURICULATA. Willd.} ?
A. VESICATORIA. Rox.

Vernacular. *janglí mehndí.* Bazár, plant, *dádmárí.*

It seems probable that blisters are prepared from both of these plants in the Punjab. They grow in wet places; the former apparently at least to some little elevation (4,000 or 5,000 feet) in the hills. The plant is officinal for blistering purposes, in parts of India.

GRISLEA TOMENTOSA. Rox.

Vernacular. J. *táwí.* K. *táwí, thái.* R. *táwí, tau.* B. *daháí, dháwí khúrd.* U. *dhá.* S. R. *táwí, dáwí.*

A shrub with a fine red flower, which grows abundantly in many parts of the Siwálik tract, and in the Salt Range, up to 4,000 feet, and occasionally still higher. The wood is only used for fuel, being small. The flowers are employed in dyeing, and in medicine are considered astringent, and applied in plaster for headache, &c. The leaves also are officinal in the Punjab. In Kángra, part of the plant is stated to be used in the preparation of spirits. (?)

LAGERSTRŒMIA PARVIFLORA. Rox.

Vernacular. *báklí, dháu, dhaura.*

This, which grows to be a large tree, is not common in the Punjab Siwálik tract. Its timber is yellowish, elastic, and tough, and is valued for agricultural implements, &c. In the N. W. Provinces it is reckoned one of the best woods for buggy-shafts, &c.

LAWSONIA INERMIS. L.

Vernacular. T. I. *nakríze.* Plains generally, *mehndí, hinna.*

A small shrub cultivated throughout the Punjab plains for its leaves, which are used to dye cloth, the feet and hands, and beard. There is a detailed account of the method of cultivation by Edgeworth in the *Journal As. Soc.* for September 1838. From Davies' Trade Report 50 maunds would appear to be annually imported into Peshawar from Jalálabád, and curiously enough 2,000 maunds as exported to Affghánistán by the Bolán. (?)

N. O. TAMARISCINEÆ.

Myricaria elegans. Royle.

Vernacular. S. *húmbú. (?)* Lad. *úmbú, húmbú.*

There is some confusion as to these two species, but I believe I have found this at 9,000 feet sparingly on the Sutlej, and it grows from 10,000 feet on the Upper Chenáb to 15,000 in Ladák. Aitchison states that in Lahoul its leaves are applied to bruises, &c. The leaves are often covered with a saline efflorescence. The twigs are in Ladák browsed by sheep and goats.

M. Germanica. Desv. (?)

Vernacular. J. *bís.* K. *shúlakát.* C. *hambúkh, kathí.* S. *humbú.* Lad. *úmbú, joaraktse.*

Not uncommon in various parts of the basins of the Jhelam, Chenáb, and Sutlej, and in Spiti and Ladák, from 6,000 to 14,000 and occasional specimens up to over 16,000 feet. Is smaller and less handsome than the other, and of no use so far as I know.

Tamarix dioica. Rox. Tamarisk.
T. Gallica. L. (T. Indica. Rox.)

Vernacular. *jhaú, lái, kachlei, ghazlei, pilchí, rúkh, koán.* Lad. *rgelta.* Bazár, twigs, *hásha.*

I shall not attempt here to distinguish between these two species. The former, with sometimes the latter, is common along much of the banks of the great rivers, by small streams and in other moist sandy places. The latter is found to 10,600 feet on the Sháyokk in Ladák. The former is generally small, but the latter reaches 3 feet in girth and 30 high, and furnishes much of the steamer fuel in the Southern Punjab, and still more in Sind. There also the wood, which is coarse-grained and often very red, is used for Persian wheels, in turning, &c., as well as occasionally in the Southern Punjab. In Ladák where wood is scarce, this is used for the handles of the sticks for *polo,* hockey on horseback. For manna and galls, said sometimes to be produced by the latter of these, see the next species. The twigs are used in medicine as astringent.

T. ORIENTALIS. L. Tamarisk.

Vernacular. *ghwá, ghuz*. Plains generally, *farwá (farás) úkhán, rukh, kharlei, narlei*. Bazár, galls, *mái bari, mái chhoti*; manna, *gazanj bín, misrí leí*; flowers, *búr*.

A tree, sometimes mistaken by Europeans for a fir, which grows commonly in the Punjab plains, chiefly from Dehlí westward, along the more arid tracts up as far as Peshawar, flowering after the rains. A proportion of the trees grow with their branches rather upright and close to the trunk, somewhat like ACACIA ARABICA CUPRESSINA q. v. Elphinstone remarked its extremely sombre cypress-like shade, but the twigs, with small scale-like leaves, are so fine that it furnishes a very insufficient guard from the sun. It grows very rapidly, and to a large size, and I have frequently seen trees of 10 or 12 feet girth (there is one of 12 feet at the tomb close to the Agri-Horticultural Society's garden, Lahore) and 60 or 70 high; but it speedily decays at the heart, and most of the larger specimens are hollow. Edgeworth states that he has seen trees of six or seven years as much as 5 feet in girth, and that they often fall of old age at 20 years. It mostly grows where the soil is saline, but not too light. The small light downy seeds would be extremely difficult to collect, but it is raised very readily from cuttings, and it is stated that a branch or log will shoot when lying on the ground. The cuttings to be put in about June may be a foot long, and the upper end should be covered with cowdung to prevent rotting; they are frequently merely buried lengthwise in the ground. The timber is coarse-grained, and weighs 92 lbs. per cubic foot green, and 60 lbs. dry. In the Southern Punjab it is used for ploughs, Persian wheels, and small rafters, being often cut as coppice for the last purpose. In Sind the wood is employed in turnery. When the green wood is used for fuel, it is said to give out a most offensive odour, rendering it intolerable in a room, whence the European soldiers at Peshawar gave it a ludicrous nickname. But when dry it burns without smell, and makes a tolerable fuel for ordinary purposes, although by the Railway people only the SALVADORA (q. v.) is reckoned worse for the locomotive. The galls appear mostly or altogether to be derived from this species, and the two names seem to me to indicate merely difference of size, not of origin. They are employed as a mordant in dyeing, and in medicine are reckoned astringent, being used in gargles, &c.; Trans-Indus the bark is stated to be used for tanning. The manna of the Tamarisk is said to be very accurately described by Diodorus Siculus. Near Sinai it is stated to be produced by the borings of an insect. Aitchison notes that he never saw it on the tree in the Punjab, nor have I observed anything nearer it than a white caterpillar-looking larva, with which I have repeatedly seen trees infested. It is, however, said to be produced largely in parts of the Punjab, *e. g.*, near Jhang, but I have been unable to get detailed information. Masson states that in Brahuistán it is produced on the white flowered kind only (in the Punjab some few trees have whitish, instead of reddish flowers), and in alternate years with the galls, but this hardly seems probable. The twigs have often or always a saline taste from a very minute efflorescence of salt, and Edgeworth mentions that poor people near Múltán dip them in water in order to season bread. In parts of the Punjab the flowers are said to be used in dyeing.

N. O. ALANGIACEÆ.

Marlea begonifolia. Rox.

Vernacular. J. *tilpattra, chit pattra, kúrkni.* K. *prot.* C. *siálú.* R. *padlú.* B. *bodará, mandrá.*

A handsome small tree with maple-like leaves, occurring from about 3,200 occasionally to 6,000 feet, up to near the Indus. Its leaves are eaten by sheep.

N. O. PHILADELPHEÆ.

Philadelphus Sp.?

Vernacular. S. *búzrú, múdnú, zhbang.*

On the Sutlej at least, what appears to be a species of P., occurs at from 8,000 to 9,500 feet, and is stated to be used for ropes.

N. O. MYRTACEÆ.

Eucalyptus Sp. var. Gum tree.

These Australian trees have as yet not been found easy to raise in the Punjab, although improvement is taking place in that respect. But several of the trees, which have succeeded at Lahore and Madhopúr, when they were first introduced in 1860, by seed obtained from Dr. Chalmers, have grown at least twice as rapidly as the ordinary Punjab trees.

Myrtus communis. L.

Vernacular. *viláyatí mehndí, múrad.* Bazár, leaves, *múrad;* fruit, *habb al ás, habhúl.*

Occasionally grown in the Punjab, by Natives and Europeans. The leaves, however, seem also to be brought from the west, and are officinal, being given in cerebral affections, and for flatulence, &c. The *habb ul ás*, though nominally always the fruit of the myrtle, appears at times to be the small fruit of some other plants not yet identified with certainty. It is given in cases of diarrhœa and internal ulcerations, as an emetic, and in cases of rheumatism.

Psidium Guajava. Guava.

Vernacular. *amrút. amrúd.*

Not very commonly cultivated except in the east of the Punjab, and probably introduced by Europeans.

Púnica granatum. L. Pomegranate.

Vernacular. J. *dárú, darúní, dariún.* C. *darûní, danú, dáán.* R. *jaman.* B. *dárú, dáran.* T. I. *anor.* Plains generally, *ánár.* Bazár, rind, *náspál;* seeds, *ánár dána.*

Is common wild in the N. W. Punjab Himalaya at from about 2,500 to 6,000 feet, from the Biás up to and beyond the Indus. It is commonly cultivated in the plains. The wood is used by the natives for roofs, &c. Though the fruit of the Punjab is immensely inferior to what comes from the west, (Davies' Trade Report puts the quantity annually imported viâ Peshawar at 2,250 maunds), yet curiously enough, Masson says that the Affghánistán fruit is not so much esteemed as that of warmer regions. The Punjab fruit, such as it is, is eaten by the natives, and Moorcroft mentions that its juice is boiled with Capsicums to make a sauce. The rind is extensively used in tanning and dyeing, and the seeds are reckoned astringent, and given for coughs. The root bark is an excellent vermifuge, deserving attention even from European practitioners, and is said to be useful in diarrhœa.

Sizygium Jambolanum. DC.

Vernacular. *jáman, jaman.*

A tree commonly cultivated in the Punjab, though less frequent towards the north-west. One authority states that it will succeed in the most alkaline soil. It grows to a large size, and even in the Punjab, trees of 8 and 9 feet girth, and 70 or 80 feet high, are not uncommon. There is one of 11 feet girth at the Chiniot ferry on the Chenáb, one of 15 feet below Dhunêra at 3,000 feet near the Rávi, and another of 15 feet at 3,200 feet elevation, on the top of Tilla in the Salt Range. The heart-wood is reddish and strong, and not subject to worms, but is apt to warp, and is said not to last well in air, although it is a favourite for well-work. Agricultural implements, sugar-mills, &c., are sometimes made of it. The astringent fruit is eaten by natives, and is said to be employed for making spirits. Even the kernels are eaten in time of famine; they are used in medicine as astringent, and a decoction of the bark is employed as a gargle in sore mouth.

N. O. BARRINGTONIACEÆ.

Careya arborea. Rox.

Vernacular. U. *kúmbhí.* Bazár, flowers, *vakhúmba.*

As this tree appears just to cross the Jumna into the Punjab in the Siwálik region, it is necessary only to mention it here. Its flowers are officinal, being given by Hindús after child-birth.

N. O. CUCURBITACEÆ.

Bryonia umbellata. Willd.

Vernacular. J. *gwál kakrí.* S. *mohakrí.*

Not uncommon at from 2,500 to 7,500 feet in the Punjab Himalaya. The fruit is eaten, and on the Sutlej the root is said to be given for spermatorrhea.

Benincasa cerifera. Savi.

Vernacular. *petha, chál kumra, gol kaddú.*

Cultivated for its fruit, a large pumpkin.

Citrullus vulgaris. Schrad. var. Cucurbita citrullus. L. (Cucumis citrullus. Ser.) Water-melon.

Vernacular. H. *mathíra.* Plains, generally, *tarbúz, hindwána.*

Commonly cultivated throughout the Punjab plains. If not really wild, it is apparently so and covers the ground for miles in sandy deserts near Sirsa, and in the Sind Ságur Doáb, ripening in the cold weather. It grows also over immense tracts on the low ground along some of the rivers, *e. g.*, the Biás, in Gúrdaspúr, &c. Its fruit is a favourite with natives, and in some parts (*e. g.*, Shahpúr) the seeds are eaten parched, with other grain.

C. VULGARIS. Schrad. var. C. FISTULOSUS. Stocks.

Vernacular. *tind, albínda, dilpasand.*

A small round gourd commonly cultivated (in Sind where it was first described by Stocks and) near Múltán and Lahore, and it is said much further east. It is sown about April, and ripens in July; is cooked as a gourd, and has a pleasant flavour when young, but the seeds are troublesome as it gets old. A French authority maintains that this and the last, unlike as they are, are only varieties produced by long-continued cultivation.

COCCINEA INDICA. W. and A.

Vernacular. *kandúrí, ghol, kúndrú.*

Not uncommon wild in the Punjab plains, except perhaps in the western parts. Its fruit is eaten, generally uncooked.

CUCUMIS COLOCYNTHIS. L. (CITRULLUS COLOCYNTHIS. Schrad.) Colocynth gourd.

Vernacular. T. I. *maraghúne, khartúma.* S. R. *ghúrúmba.* S. S. D. *kúrtamma.* B. D. *khartúma, túmbí.* H. *ghorúmba.* Bazár, fruit, *hanzal, indráyan;* seeds, *tukhm túmma.*

This plant, which furnishes the colocynth of the European pharmacopeias, grows abundantly in most of the arid sandy tracts of the Punjab, from Dehlí up to Peshawar (as it does in the deserts by the Jordan and near Sinai). Its fruit is extensively used as a purgative for horses, &c., and the pulp is officinal, being given to men, in preference when fresh, in warm water, or when dried with *ajwáin*—(see PTYCHOTIS) &c., and it is reckoned especially valuable in cholera, which smacks of homæopathy. The seeds also are officinal. The fresh root is used as a tooth brush, and dried and powdered is given as a purgative (Bellew).

C. MELO. L. Musk melon.

Vernacular. *kharbúza.* Lad. *zaghún.* Aff. *sarda, palíz.*

Cultivated all over the Punjab plains, some of the kinds being excellent, especially some of those of Múltán and Jhang. Those of the latter have been compared to the best Egyptian. Those of Kashmír are stated to be rather watery; but Moorcroft declares the people fatten on them, "as horses are said to do at Bokhára." Vigne states that the melons of Tibet, where they are grown to 10,500 feet, are small but good. In reality those of

Ladák are very similar to those of the plains, &c., but with less flavour. In Affghánistán (where *palíz* appears to mean the CUCURBITACEÆ generally, and not melon-*fields* as Masson puts it) several varieties of melon are extensively grown, and Davies' Trade Report states that 300 mule loads are annually imported thence viâ Peshawar. The best known and most valued of these is the *sarda*, which by express reaches the N. W. Punjab in good condition. It has been frequently raised in the Punjab, but is said speedily to degenerate to the ordinary standard.

C. MOMORDICA. Rox.

Vernacular. *kachrá, phúnt.*

Cultivated throughout the Punjab plains for its fruit.

C. PUBESCENS. Willd.

Vernacular. *kachrí.*

Occurs wild in the Punjab plains. The small fruit is eaten.

C. SATIVUS. L. Cucumber.

Vernacular. *khíra.* Bazár, seeds, *tukhmí khiyárain.*

Commonly cultivated throughout the Punjab plains. The seeds of this and the next are officinal, being considered cooling. May be the *balam khíra*, or hill cucumber, mentioned by Lowther.

C. UTILISSIMUS. Rox.

Vernacular. *kakrí.*

Cultivated throughout the Punjab plains, and to a considerable elevation (I believe I have seen it at 6,000 feet on the Rávi) in the hills. This gourd attains 2 or 2½ feet, and is stated to reach the extraordinary length of 5 feet.

CUCURBITA MAXIMA. W. and A. C. PEPO. L. (C. MELOPEPO. Willd.) ? Squash.

Vernacular. K. *al ?* Lad. *daghan, kaddú sufêd, mítha kaddú, halwa kaddú.*

There is a confusion as to this species, but it is cultivated throughout the plains, and apparently in Kashmír, to 6,000 feet, or possibly to 9,000 in other parts of the Himalaya, and at 10,500 feet in Ladák, for its fruit, a large pumpkin.

LAGENARIA VULGARIS. Ser.

Vernacular. *kaddú, Kábulí kaddú, laukí, túmba.*

A large gourd cultivated throughout the Punjab plains. Its seeds are used medicinally, being given in headache, &c.

LUFFA ACUTANGULA. Rox.

Vernacular. *kálí torí, turál, jhinga (?)*

L. PENTANDRA. Rox.

Vernacular. *ghía torí, ghí turái.*

Both of these appear to be cultivated throughout the Punjab plains for their fruit, which is cooked and eaten as a vegetable. Bellew states that in the Peshawar Valley the seeds of one or both are given, with black pepper in warm water, as emetic and cathartic.

MOMORDICA CHARANTIA. L.

Vernacular. *karela.*

Cultivated in the plains for its bitter fruit, which requires steeping ere being used. Edgeworth mentions that it is wild on sand-hills in the Southern Punjab.

M. DIOICA. Rox.

Vernacular. C. *dhár karela.* S. R. *kirara.*

Wild in various places in the outer hills, Salt Range, and plains. (?) I am not aware that it is used.

M. MURICATA. Willd.

Vernacular. *kakora.*

Wild in parts of the Punjab plains. The fruit is cooked and eaten, and is also said to be officinal. The root likewise is used medicinally, being given as an astringent and warm medicine, and in Hindústan is applied to hæmorrhoids, &c. (Honigberger).

MUKIA SCABRELLA. Cern. (BRYONIA SCABRELLA. L.)

Vernacular.

Grows wild in the Southern Punjab (Edgeworth).

TRICHOSANTHES ANGUINA. L. Snake gourd.

Vernacular. *gálar torí, pandol, chichinda.* (Hí.)

Cultivated extensively throughout the plains for its fruit, cooked and eaten as a vegetable.

T. DIOICA. Rox.

Vernacular. *palwal.*

Wild in the eastern and central parts of the Punjab. Its fruit is cooked and eaten.

The identity of each of the following CUCURBITS is doubtful:—

1. S. S. D. *banga* or *danga,* a cucumber said to be peculiar to Jhang; may be a variety of CUCUMIS UTILISSIMUS (q. v.)

2. F. *kekra,* a sweet fruited wild gourd growing near Ferozepúr, and much eaten by natives; perhaps MOMORDICA MURICATA (q. v.)

3. B. D. *khora,* a kind of pumpkin, resembling a vegetable marrow, cultivated in the plains; may be CUCURBITA PEPO (q. v.)

4. F. *kuchsa,* grows wild near Ferozepúr, its acid fruit used for flavouring, and used by goldsmiths to clean metals.

5. J. *tribrí* with a smallish fruit, which is eaten; grows wild in fields at about 6,000 feet in Hazára; may be a variety of CUCUMIS UTILISSIMUS (q. v.)

6. With a small oval eatable fruit like CUCUMIS PUBESCENES (q. v.) common wild in fields, &c., at 8,500 to 4,500 feet in parts of the Jhelam basin.

N. O. PAPAYACEÆ.

CARICA PAPAYA. L.

Vernacular. *arand kharbúza, and-kharbúza.* (?)

Of this tree, which is occasionally seen in gardens in the N. W. Provinces, I have remarked or know of none further west than Dehlí, where there are a few specimens.

N. O. PORTULACEÆ.

PORTULACA OLERACEA. L.

Vernacular. *lonak.* Bazar, seeds, *dhamni.* (?)

A common garden and field weed in the plains, and apparently to 7,000 feet in the Punjab Himalaya. Often eaten as a pot-herb, especially in times of scarcity. The seeds may be the officinal *dhamní*. This and P. SATIVA seem at times to be used indifferently.

P. QUADRIFIDA. L.

Vernacular. *lúnak, haksha.*

Not uncommon in the Salt Range, and low hills, Cis and Trans-Indus, to 3,000 and at times 4,000 feet. It is used as a vegetable, and is considered cooling.

P. SATIVA. L.

Vernacular. *khúrfa.* Bazár, seed, *dhamní.*

Cultivated as a pot-herb in the plains. Bellew states that the fresh leaves of this or P. OLERACEA are used as a cataplasm in erysipelas. The seeds of one or both are considered cooling and astringent, and given as demulcent in internal inflammations, &c.

TRIANTHEMA CRYSTALLINA. Vahl.

Vernacular. *alethí.*

Very common in some of the desert tracts of the Punjab, and found up to Peshawar. Edgeworth mentions that near Múltán its seeds are swept up in times of famine and eaten.

T. PENTANDRA. L.

Vernacular. *biskhapra, itsit, narma.*

A common weed in waste ground in the plains. Eaten as a pot-herb in times of scarcity, but apt to produced diarrhœa and paralysis. The plant is officinal, being considered astringent in abdominal diseases, and is also stated to be used to produce abortion (Edgeworth).

KALANCHOE VARIANS. Haw.?

Vernacular. R. B. *talára.* S. *rungrú.* Plains, *haiza-ka-patta.*

A fleshy-leaved, yellow-flowered plant; apparently this species is found growing in places up to 5,000 feet in the outer hills as far as the Rávi. It is poisonous to goats, and the leaves are, at Lahore, where it is grown in some native gardens, reckoned a specific for cholera. In Kángra they are burned and applied to abscesses.

SEDUM RHODIOLA. DC.

Vernacular. *shrolo.*

S. TIBETICUM. Hf. and T.

Vernacular. ?

Both of these are stated by Aitchison to grow in Lahoul (10,000 feet), and to be eaten as pot-herbs.

N. O. MESEMBRYACEÆ.

GLINUS LOTOIDES. L.

Vernacular. B. D. *gandí bútí, porprang.* Bazár, plant, *zakhmí haiyát.*

Not uncommon wild in the eastern and central Punjab plains. It is officinal, and is given in the Punjab as a purgative in diseases of the abdomen under the name of *zakhmí haiyát,* which is generally ascribed to SPHŒRANTHUS HIRTUS (q. v.) CISSAMPELOS PAREIRA (q. v.) is also occasionally so called.

N. O. CACTEÆ.

CACTUS INDICUS. ROX.

Vernacular. *kábúlí tsúí, gángi sho, kánghí chü.*

This plant, which Roxburgh supposed to be indigenous in India, and later writers conceive to have been introduced from America, is not uncommonly grown as a hedge in the outer hills to 4,000 and occasionally to more than 5,000 feet, as far up as the Jhelam, and is sometimes seen in the plains at least as far south as Lahore and Jalandar. Griffith mentions his having seen a specimen in a garden in Kaffiristán said to be brought from Bajaur to the eastward. Previous to annexation, this plant would appear to have so abounded at places from Ambála to Goojrát that the Sikhs prohibited its extension as a nuisance. In 1844 it is stated to have "dried up," or have been so destroyed by an influx of the cochineal insect, which feeds on it, that in 1852 only one hedge remained near Loodiana where it formerly abounded. Jameson about 1840 stated that the CACTUS abounded near Goojrat; but it is mentioned that it almost disappeared in that tract in the rains of 1849, from an irruption of the insect. Purdon mentions that in 1851 he saw the latter on this plant to the west of Goojrát. No experiment on the dye appears to have been made in the Punjab. But the wild kind of cochineal insect, *grana sylvestra*, was introduced from Mexico into the country near Calcutta before the end of last century, and the experiment of its propagation continued for twelve years. And, although from 1796 to 1807 as much as 90,000 lbs. of the dye were sent to Europe, it appears that the operations did not pay, so they were discontinued; and a reward of two thousand pounds sterling, offered by Government with sanction of the Court of Directors for the introduction of the *grana fina*, seems to have led to no result.

N. O. GROSSULARIEÆ.

RIBES GROSSULARIA. L. (R. HIMALENSIS. Royle.) Gooseberry.

Vernacular. C. *amlánch, kánsí, pílsa, teila.* S. *súr-ka-chúp.*

Is not uncommon wild in the arid parts on the Upper Sutlej, Chenáb, and Jhelam, and in Tibet, from 8,000 to 12,000 feet or more. It was also found by Bellew near the Sufêd Koh at about 10,000 feet. The fruit is small and intensely sour, and hardly ever eaten even by the natives. The European gooseberry grows, but does not thrive or give much fruit in the Himalaya.

R. LEPTOSTACHYUM. Dne. (R. VILLOSUM. Wall.) Yellow currant.

R. NIGRUM. L. Black currant.

Vernacular. J. *gwáldakh.* C. *murádh, nábar, kadash niangna.* R. *mandrí.* B. *hádar, belí.* S. *shaktekas.* Lad. *askúta.*

These are not uncommon from 7,000 to 14,000 feet in the Himalaya, and the former at least grows in Tibet, and was found by Bellew at about 10,000 feet near the Sufêd Koh. The fruit of the latter is very like the cultivated black currant, and very fair eating.

R. RUBRUM. L. (R. HIMALIENSE. Dne.) Red currant.

Vernacular. J. *dák, kagh dák.* C. *ráde, áns, phulánch, nangke.* B. *hádar, khádrí.* T. I. *wara wane.*

This appears to be the red-fruited species, which frequently occurs in the Punjab Himalaya from 5,800 to 11,000 feet, up to the Indus, and probably beyond it. But it may partly be R. GLACIALE, Wall. Its fruit is nearly worthless, so far as I have seen or tried it. Aitchison calls it a sweetish acid, and I should say the latter predominates.

N. O. SAXIFRAGACEÆ.

SAXIFRAGA LIGULATA. Wall.

Vernacular. J. *bat pia.* K. *popal, wat phúta.* C. *shaprocht, kúrgotar, dharposh, banpatrak.* R. *saprotri, til kachálá.* B. *shiblách makhán bed.* S. *dakachrú.* T. I. *kamarghwal.* Bazár, root, *pakhán bed, jintiána, maslún.*

A large species with great leaves and handsome flowers, often found growing on rocks, &c., from 4,500 to 13,000 feet, in the Punjab Himalaya up to the Indus, and got by myself at 7,000 and Bellew at 10,000 Trans-Indus. The leaves are frequently used as plates, and the root is bruised and applied to boils or to ophthalmia in some of the places where the plant grows. The root is also officinal generally under the first, occasionally under the second Bazár name given, and I have once heard it called by the third name—(see POLYGONUM BISTORTUM). It is reckoned absorbent, and given in dysentery and cough, &c.

N. O. HYDRANGEACEÆ.

HYDRANGEA. SP.

Vernacular. ?

A scandent species is mentioned by Thomson as growing at 5,500 feet on the Sutlej, the loose bark of which is used for paper.

N. O. UMBELLIFERÆ.

It may be noted that, although a considerable number of this family are cultivated as condiments, &c., in the plains, and a great many grow wild in the hills, the products of some of which are used, yet almost none are cultivated in the latter.

ANETHUM SOWA. Rox. Dill.

Vernacular. *soya.*

Cultivated in the plains, the plant used as a vegetable. The seeds are officinal, being considered emmenagogue.

ANGELICA GLAUCA. Edge.

Vernacular. *churá.*

A plant under the above native appellation, and named as above by Edgeworth as growing at 8,000 to 10,000 feet on

Hattú, &c., near the Sutlej; is found also in the Dhaula Ḍhúr Range above the Kángra Valley. Its aromatic root is added to food to give it "a celery flavour" (Cleghorn).

APIUM GRAVEOLENS. L. Celery.

Vernacular. *ajmod*. Bazár, root, *karafsh, bekh-karafsh, bhút jhata*; seeds, *ajmod, karafsh.*

This is cultivated by Europeans in the usual way, and by natives in the Punjab for the officinal root, which is considered alterative and diuretic, and given in anasarca and colic, and for which that of FŒNICULUM (q. v.) may sometimes be substituted. The seeds also are given as stimulant and cordial.

ASTRANTIA SP.

Vernacular. B. *losur*. S. *lasser.*

An aromatic root of the Himalaya is mentioned by Hoffmeister under the names *lasser* and ASTRANTIUM—(see FERULA). Longden notes in Kúllú at 11,000 a plant called *losur,* which is highly scented, and eaten as a stimulant.

BUPLEURUM MARGINATUM. Wall.

Vernacular. K. *kálí zewar*. S. *sípil, zíra. (?)*

This and allied species are abundant in many parts of the Punjab Himalaya, from 2,500 to 11,500 feet. In Kanáwar the root is stated to be eaten raw, and the seeds to be exported as *zíra*—(see CARUM).

CARUM CARUI. L. (C. GRACILE. Bth. C. NIGRUM. Royle.) Carraway.

Vernacular. C. *yúnyún*. Lad. *úmbú*. Bazár, seed, *zíra síyah.*

CARUM CARUI (as well as C. GRACILE, if it is distinct) grows in profusion in many of the more arid tracts on the Sutlej and Chenáb, &c., and in Kashmír and western Tibet, from 9,000 to 145,000 feet. It would also appear to grow in Affghánistán, as Davies' Trade Report gives an annual import viâ Peshawar of no less than 100 maunds (but there may be some mistake, as the same authority gives 50 maunds as exported by the same route).

The carraway seeds are used to season vegetables, and are largely exported to the plains from some of the parts where the plant grows, to be used as a condiment, and in medicine as a stimulant.

Coriandrum sativum. L. Coriander.

Vernacular. *dhania.* Bazár, seeds, *dhania, kashníz.*

Abundantly cultivated throughout the plains, and frequently seen (quasi) wild in fields as noted by Edgeworth. The plant is eaten as a vegetable, and the seeds as a condiment. The latter are also imported from Affghánistán (25 maunds per annum according to Davies' Trade Report), and are also used medicinally, being given in decoction for colic, and on the Yúnání system for cerebral diseases.

Cuminum Cyminum. L.

Vernacular. C. *zíra.* Bazár, seed, *zíra sufêd.*

Bellew mentions this as being wild in the hills north of the Peshawar Valley, and Aitchison states that it is common wild in Lahoul (10,000 feet), whence the seeds are largely exported towards the plains. Davies' Trade Report gives 500 maunds as annually imported from Affghánistán through the Bolán Pass, but 1st, the name *zíra* has probably caused Carum (q. v.) to be mistaken for this; and 2nd, the quantity seems enormous. The same authority also gives 25 maunds as *exported* by the same route. The seeds are officinal, being considered diuretic and lactagogue.

Daucus carota. L.

Vernacular. K. *mor múj, bal múj, kách.* Plains, *gájar.*

Cultivated extensively for the root in many parts of the Punjab plains, and towards the west often given to horses, whose coat it is said to improve very much. It is also common wild from 3,200 to 5,000 feet in Kashmír and some of the neighbouring tracts, where I was once only told that its root is eaten. Dr. Adams, in his "Wanderings of a Naturalist," mentions that in Kashmír the brown bear is fond of a small white wild carrot, but this must apply to some Umbellifer growing at a greater elevation than this. The seeds are officinal, being considered aphrodisiac, and also given in uterine pains.

Eryngium planum. L. or E. dichotomum. Desf.

Vernacular. J. *polí, mittúa* (Cleghorn). K. *kandú.* Bazár, root, *shakákul misrí, pahári gájar.* Aff., seeds, *núrálam.*

An Eryngium grows wild in Kashmír and the neighbouring tracts up to 5,000 feet, as well as in the Peshawar plain, and in the Salt Range. On the spot it is not said to be of any use, but

Royle, I know not on what grounds, assigns to ERYNGIUM (CAMPESTRE), the origin of the officinal root called as above, the true source of which is still unknown, Honigberger having assigned it to "PASTINACA SECACUL," and some previous writers to SIUM. Davies' Trade Report estimates the annual quantity of this imported from Affghánistán viâ Peshawar at as much as 25 maunds. It is considered tonic and aphrodisiac possibly on the "doctrine of signatures." In Kandahár the seeds are stated to be officinal under the above name.

FERULA ASSAFŒTIDA. L. (NARTHEX. Falc.) Assafœtida.

Vernacular. Aff. *angúza*. Bazár, gum resin, *hing*. Kashmír, *yang*.

I got this plant in Khágán (Jhelam basin) at about 6,000 feet, and Cleghorn mentions specimens of it as being brought to him on the Upper Chenáb at over 8,000 feet. (It is also given by Aitchison as growing in Lahoul (10,000 feet), not much further up the Chenáb, but I find from Mr. Jaeschke that this was a DOREMA). Cleghorn also states that Dr. Falconer sent seeds of the plant from Iskardo to Mussooree and England (where it thrives in the open air). Dr. Adams states that he saw the plant in Kashmír, and that loads of it are taken to Sirínuggur, but Dr. Elmslie assures me that the plant is not known there. And it is hardly likely to be common or its product known as derived from it, Cis-Indus, for what ASSAFŒTIDA is used in the Punjab Himalaya is imported from Affghánistán viâ the plains. In Affghánistán the plant grows wild abundantly on the plains to the west of Kiláti-Ghilzi (7,000 feet), and the chief supply is obtained from the hills to the north of the Bolán Pass, and about the Halmand (perhaps 3,500 feet) according to Bellew. He states that in April and May incisions (chiefly long cuts which produce lumps, sometimes pricks which yield tears) are made across or round the crown of the root. Gum exudes and is collected for a fortnight from these, to the amount of from one ounce to two pounds (?) from a single plant. Bellew also mentions that in Affghánistán the leaves, which likewise have the alliaceous smell, are used as a vegetable, and the succulent part of the young stem is eaten after roasting with salt and butter. The Affgháns only use the gum medicinally, but very large quantities of it are annually imported into India to be used as a condiment by natives. In some parts, *e. g.*, Kashmír, only Hindús eat it. Davies estimates the yearly import viâ Peshawar at 200 maunds. It is also officinal, being considered absorbent, and given in colic, &c. This has been conjectured to have produced the *lasser* of the ancients—(see ASTRANTIA)—which, however, is now ascribed to a THAPSIA.

Fœniculum vulgare. Gært. Fennel.

Vernacular. *saunf.* Bazár, root, *bekh karafsh.* (?)

Cultivated commonly in the Punjab plains as a pot-herb. Its seeds are officinal, being considered carminative, and the root appears to be occasionally used under the above name for that of Apium (q. v.), being considered alterative and diuretic, and given in anasarca, and likewise in colic.

Heracleum sp.?

Vernacular. R. *padálli.* S. *porál.*

This (one of several Himalayan) species is common in parts of the hills from 8,500 to 11,000 feet. In Bissahir and Chumba it is collected for winter fodder, and Cleghorn mentions that it is believed to increase the milk of goats fed with it.

Ligusticum ajowan. L. (Ptychotis ajowan. DC.) Lovage.

Vernacular. *ajwain.*

Cultivated in the Punjab plains for its seeds, which are give. in colic, strangury, &c.

Petroselinum sativum. Hoff. Parsley.

Vernacular. *pítar salerí.*

Cultivated in the plains, but probably only for Europeans, as the native name is merely a corruption.

Pimpinella anisum. L. (P. involucrata. W. and A).

Vernacular. *anísún.*

I have not seen this cultivated for use as a pot-herb in the Punjab, but Bellew states that in the Peshawar Valley the plant is used as a vegetable. About Lahore, &c., it is grown for the seeds, which are officinal, being carminative.

P. crinita. Boiss.

Vernacular. S. R. *bal ajwáin.*

A small plant common in the Salt Range up to about 2,000 feet, and in several of the more arid tracts of the Punjab, Cis and Trans-Indus. In some parts the seeds are given for colic, but they are not identical with the *bal ajwáin* of the Lahore drug-sellers, which has not yet been identified with certainty, but may be a species of P.—(see Ptychotis).

Pleurospermuni Govanianum. DC.

Vernacular. ?

Grows at from 10,000 to 15,000 (?) feet in parts of the Himalaya. Mr. Jaeschke informs me that the natives in some places attribute the pass-headache to this plant.

Prangos pabularia. Lindl.

Vernacular. Lad. *prangos.* (?) Aff. *komal, komál.* Bazár, seed, *fitrasúliún.*

This plant grows south from Iskardo in western Ladák at 10,000 feet, in parts of Kashmír at 5,000 to 6,000 feet (I found it above Vernág, where Moorcroft also says he saw it), and in Affghánistán, in the high land round Ghuzní, about 7,000 or 8,000 feet (Bellew), and near Maidán, close to Kábul, at 6,000 feet, and towards Hájiguk, perhaps 12,000 feet (Moorcroft, who calls it *komai*). Bellew brought at least one other species of P. from Affghánistán. In Ladák and Affghánistán it is collected (with most other plants, as in these countries vegetation is scarce) for winter fodder for cattle, sheep, and goats, horses taking to it less readily, and no animal browsing more than its flower while it is growing. In Affghánistán it would appear to grow much shorter than Cis-Indus, where its seed ripens about August. Moorcroft wrote that it is "one of the most valuable fodder plants in Ladák, and perhaps of any country whatever," and considered that its use accounted for the absence of liver fluke in the sheep of that country. He also reported to a Member of the Court of Directors, that its "probable utility is unrivalled in the history of agricultural productions." And since then a strong desire has at various times arisen that other countries might reap the advantage of its being introduced as a fodder-plant; quite recently an urgent request for its seeds came to the Punjab from Madras, and a large supply has just been got through Dr. Cayley. But it would appear that Moorcroft unintentionally very much exaggerated the virtues of the *prangos.* He himself states that the peasants of Kashmír (where vegetation is much more abundant than in Ladák) were ignorant of these supposed virtues, and Vigne in Ladák itself apparently heard no great accounts of its reputation. In Kashmír and Affghánistán (?) Falconer also found it nowhere highly prized, and Griffith says that in Affghánistán so great is the dearth of herbage that the people cut almost every plant of any size for fodder. (Falconer's statement is difficult to reconcile with the curious remark of—I think—Burnes, that he found it eaten even by his fellow-travellers on account of its supposed fattening powers). Moorcroft's editor mentions that the plant raised from the seeds, sent to England by the former in 1822, had died, and none had been got since. But within the last few months, a writer in the *Gardener's Chronicle* mentioned that it had been raised in England, and that there is no reason to suppose that the belief in its virtues as to liver fluke are aught but illusory. It was raised at Mussooree from Falconer's seeds, and is said still to grow there. Moorcroft states that the water in which the plant is steeped "destroys snails," and that its root rubbed on itch will cure the disease. The *fitrasúliún* (a term corrupted from the Greek) found in the Lahore Bazárs, and used as an aphrodisiac, is the seed of this or some nearly allied species of PRANGOS.

PTYCHOTIS COPTICA. DC.

Vernacular. S. R. *bal ajwain.*

Is stated by Edgeworth to be cultivated in the N. W. Provinces (for its seeds ?), and is not uncommon wild in the Salt Range up to 2,000 feet. In the latter its seeds are given medicinally—(see PIMPINELLA CRINITA). Several dubious UMBELLIFERÆ may be noted here for what the information is worth—

1. R. *Budkes*—(see CORYDALIS). B. *gúdú músalí.* S. *spogú.* One (or more) species growing to 12,000 feet in Chumba, Kúllú, &c., of which the bitter roots and young leaves are put into the fermented liquor of those parts to "make it strong." This may be one of the species of OREOCOME of Edgeworth. I think it is the leaves of the same plant, which in Kanáwar (growing also about 9—12,500 feet) are stuck by the men in their caps as ornaments, and on account of their odour.

2. S. *Magózíra* grows near moisture at about 9,500 feet in Kanáwar, of which the seeds are eaten, and some exported.

3. J. *Morchar,* a fine plant, one of the largest of the UMBELLIFERS that I know, growing with a very thick stem, &c., to 5 or 6 feet high in moist places at 8,000 to 9,500 feet in Khágán. Its very large root, redundant with yellow juice, has a pleasant odour, and is pounded and mixed with snuff, which is said to be good for headache.

4. R. *Tilla, Singo* (apparently a generic name) a slender tallish plant growing at 6,800 to 13,300 feet in Chumba. The tuber is eaten, both raw and cooked. This may be a BUNIUM "Earth-nut," of which several species are found in the Punjab Himalaya, particularly B. (CARUM Koch) BULBOCASTANUM L., a British species which occurs above 6,000 feet.

5. S. A white flowered UMBELLIFER (which I did not have pointed out to me on the spot, and it may be the same as the last) grows high in Kanáwar, of which the tuber is eaten, its flavour being compared to that of chesnuts by Europeans. Its seeds are said to be exported to the plains as *zíra*—(see CARUM).

6. About 1851 (?) the seeds of an UMBELLIFER were sent to the Agri-Horticultural Society at Lahore from Nuggur in Kúllú. Plants had there been raised from seed got from Lahoul, where the plant grows wild. Its root was praised as a vegetable, and said to resemble "PARSNIP OR SCORZONERA."

N. O. ARALIACEÆ.

ARALIA CACHEMIRICA. Dne.

Vernacular. *banakhor, chúriál.* C. *dúnúk, chandurí, rárar, salod.* ?

A rank plant growing to 6 or 8 feet high, which is abundant in some places in the Jhelam and Chenáb basins at 5,200 to 9,000 feet. It is said to be eaten by goats.

HEDERA HELIX. L. Ivy.

Vernacular. J. *halbambar, arbambal.* K. *karmora, mandiá.* C. *kurol.* R. *kurie, karúr.* B. *brúmbrúm, dakárí.* S. *karbárú, kaniúrí.* T. I. *parwattí.*

Is common in the Punjab Himalaya at places from 3,200 to 8,000 feet, and occurs in the Salt Range and Trans-Indus. Bellew got it at 9,000 feet near the Sufêd Koh. It is stated to be a favourite food of goats, and in Kúllú the leaves are said to be added to the beer of the country to make it strong.

N. O. HAMAMELIDEÆ.

PARROTIA JACQUEMONTIANA. Dne. Wych hazel.

Vernacular. J. *psher, pishor.* K. *páhú, po.* C. *killar, kirrú, páre.* R. *killar.* S. *shá.* T. I. *spilecha.*

A shrub of some size which grows abundantly in many places on most of the rivers up to the Indus (as well as more sparingly beyond it) from 2,800 to 8,000 feet. It is generally seen in clusters and thickets, the stems ranging up to 12 or 15 inches girth, and 15 or 20 feet high. The leaf resembles that of the hazel, for which this plant has frequently been taken by Europeans, although the fruit is very different. In some places its leaves are said to be browsed by cattle. The wood is hard and strong, and makes good pegs, native bedsteads, rice-pestles, walking-sticks, &c., and Vigne states that he had an excellent flute made of its wood in England. The twigs are also used for binding loads, making baskets, &c. But the chief use of the plant is for the twig-bridges. These are in most places made of PARROTIA twigs, either in whole, or mostly (COTONEASTER, OLEA and INDIGOFERA HETERANTHA q. v., being sometimes mixed with these), and in some cases it must be read for the "birch-bark" of travellers. For the bridges, &c., PARROTIA is cut at all seasons, and is not very lasting, requiring frequent piece-meal renewal. Longden mentions a birchen *jhúla* at Koksar now replaced by a bridge, and willow is stated to be employed in Spiti, Zanskar, Ladák, &c. Near Mozaffarabád there are several bridges of the same construction, (viz., one longitudinal rope to walk on, and two lateral ones to hold by connected with the former by thinner ropes), but made of twisted hide, and one is mentioned by Hutton in Kanáwar made of Yak's hair.

N. O. CORNEÆ.

BENTHAMIA FRAGIFERA. Lindl.

Vernacular. B. *tharwar*. S. *thesi*.

A small tree which occurs in the Punjab Himalaya at from 4,500 to 7,000 feet, as far west only as the Biás. The ripe fruit is sweetish, and eaten by the natives, and Cleghorn states that it is made into a preserve.

CORNUS MACROPHYLLA. Wall.

Vernacular. J. *kandar, kandrú*. K. *kasír*. C. *haddú, harrú*. R. *hariú, haleo, nang*. B. *kochan, kchúr*. S. *kaksh, kágash, shka*.

A tree which grows to a considerable size, and is common in many parts of the Punjab Himalaya from 3,000 to 8,000 feet, up to near the Indus. Its wood is used for making gunpowder charcoal, goats feed on its leaves, and the natives are stated to eat the fruit.

C. OBLONGA. Wall.

Vernacular. J. *ban kúkúr*. U. *bakar*.

A smallish tree which occurs sparingly in the Siwálik tract occasionally to 4,000 feet up to near the Indus. Its timber is of no special use.

N. O. LORANTHACEÆ.

ARCEUTHOBIUM OXYCEDRI. Bieb.

Vernacular. C. *shúksár.*

A pretty little species of misletoe, common on JUNIPERUS EXCELSA, at some places, 9,000 to 9,500 feet in Lahoul. It frequently kills the trees which it attacks. It is said to flower generally in winter. One of the Lahoul Missionaries had an idea that only plants of one sex of this would be found on a single tree, but this was found not to be the case.

LORANTHUS LONGIFLORUS. Desv.

Vernacular. K. *pand.* R. *parand.* B. *parand, pand.* S. *amút.* U. *banda.*

A handsome parasite with branches sometimes 6 or 7 feet long, large broad leaves and orange-coloured flowers, which is found in the Punjab Himalaya, chiefly on the eastern rivers, from 1,500 to 3,000 feet, and occasionally higher. I have seen what I conceive to be this species on FICUS RELIGIOSA, PLATANUS, MORUS, MELIA, SALIX, oak, ROTTLERA, Peach, Pear, and ACACIA ELATA, and A. MODESTA. (?)

L. SP.

Vernacular. *phágrí.*

A similar but smaller species with scaly calyces, which I have seen on the Rávi and Biás at 2,500 to 4,500 feet, growing on OUGEINIA and OLEA.

VISCUM ALBUM. L. Misletoe.

Vernacular. J. *bambal.* K. *wahal, ahalú.* S. *kakbang, ríngí.* T. I. *túra pání.* Generally, *bhángrá, bándá.*

This parasite occurs in many places at from 3,500 to 9,000 feet, in the Punjab Himalaya up to the Indus, and in the Súlimán Range. I have noted it frequently on the apricot, peach, and walnut, repeatedly on the pear, LOMBARDY POPLAR, OLEA, and ULMUS CAMPESTRIS, and at least once on each of PAVIA, ALNUS, QUERCUS, MORUS SERRATUS, and CRATÆGUS CRENULATA. As is now well known, the "baleful mistleto" is rare on the oak in England, and is supposed to have been so even in the time of the Druids, who held the oak-mistleto in such high regard. In England it most frequently occurs on the apple-tree, on which it can readily be propagated by rubbing the viscid seeds on the bark until they adhere. It is occasionally found on some twenty other kinds of trees in England. I have only seen it once on an oak in the Himalaya—(see next species)—but Griffith appears to have met with it on QUERCUS ILEX (as well as the olive at 3,600 to 4,000 feet) in Affgháníštán, where he says it is used "for fodder." (?) I know of no use to which it is put in the Himalaya; but Honigberger states that it is given in enlargement of the spleen, in cases of wound, tumour, diseases of the ear, &c.

V. ATTENUATUM. DC.
V. DICHOTOMUM. Don.

Vernacular. R. *búdú*. B. *pand*.

One (or both?) of these occurs, but more rarely than the last, at from 4,000 to 7,500 feet, up to near the Indus. I have repeatedly noted it on QUERCUS ILEX, and Q. INCANA, and occasionally on Q. DILATATA, DIOSPYROS, and Apricot.

N. O. CAPRIFOLIACEÆ.

ABELIA TRIFLORA. Br. in Wall.

Vernacular. J. *chetí búta*. C. *ban bakhurú, salauker*. R. *dalúng, kút, sái*. S. *zbam, matz'bang, pení, nagdaun. (?)* T. I. *adei, pakhtáwar*.

A shrub which grows abundantly in many places from 4,000 to 9,500 feet in the Punjab Himalaya, and was found in the Sufêd Koh and Súlimán Range at 10,000 and 6,000 feet by Bellew and myself. It has a pretty scented flower, and is browsed by goats, but appears to be of no special use

LONICERA AUGUSTIFOLIA. Wall. (?)

Vernacular. C. *míthíga*. R. *jinjrú*. S. *pílrú*.

What appears to be this species is a small shrub, which is not uncommon in the Punjab Himalaya from 7,500 to 13,000 feet, up to near the Indus. Its small, red, sweet fruit is eaten.

L. GLAUCA. Hf. and T.

Vernacular. Lad. *shing tík, shea, shewa*.

A shrubby species found up to 14,000 feet in Ladák, in parts of which its seeds are given to horses for colic.

L. HYPOLEUCA. Dne.?

Vernacular. C. *kharmo, kodí.* S. *zhíko, rapesho.*

A small shrub which is common in the arid tracts in part of the Jhelam basin, and on the Upper Chenab and Sutlej, at from 8,400 to 11,200 feet. Goats are said to fatten on its leaves, &c.

L. QUINQUELOCULARIS. Hardw. Himalayan Honeysuckle.

Vernacular. J. *phút.* K. *títa baterí, pákhur.* C. *bakhrú.* R. *khúm, sái.* B. *dendrú.* S. *klíúntí, zbang, razbam, bijgái.* T. I. *jarlangei, adei.*

A shrub which grows most abundantly of all this genus at from 2,500 to 9,000 feet in the Punjab Himalaya, and was found Trans-Indus at 9,000 feet near the Sufēd Koh, and 6,000 feet in the Súlimán Range by Bellew and myself. It is browsed by and given as fodder to cattle, &c.

SAMBUCUS EBULUS. L. Dwarf Elder.

Vernacular. J. *ríchh kas, mushkiára, ganhúla.* C. *gándal, gwándish, siske, tásar.*

Found abundantly at many places in the upper parts of the basins of the Chenáb and Jhelam at from 4,500 to 11,200 feet. Its smell, especially when bruised, is most fœtid, resembling that of burnt flesh. Tinder is said to be made from its bark (?) on the Chenáb.

VIBURNUM COTINIFOLIUM. Don.

Vernacular. J. *ríchh úklú, bankúnch.* K. *ríchhábí kilmích, gúch.* C. *bathor, pápat kalam, khímor, rájal, túmma.* R. *kátonda.* S. *jáwa, khatip, túštús, sússú.* T. I. *marghwalawa.*

A shrub which grows abundantly from 4,000 to 11,000 feet in the Punjab Himalaya, and in various parts of the Súlimán Range, Trans-Indus. Its ripe fruit is sweetish, and is eaten in many places.

V. FŒTENS. Dne.

Vernacular. J. *gúch, úklú, kúnch.* K. *kílmích, gúch, kwíllim, kulára, jamára.* C. *tiaulandhá, púlmú, tiláts, túin.* R. *talhang, tandei, túndhe, tanání zanání.* B. *kíllur, grúštú, talháná.* S. *talena, nagdaun.*

A common shrub in the Punjab Himalaya at from 5,000 to 10,800 feet, and found near the Sufēd Koh by Bellew. The fruit when ripe is sweetish, and is eaten in most places where it grows. In Kanáwar it is said to be put into the beer locally made by natives. As Madden remarks, the flowers have a delicious scent, the name being derived from the stench emitted when the branches are bruised, &c.

V. NERVOSUM. Don. (V. CYLINDRICUM. Ham. ?)

Vernacular. R. *ámbre, amrola, árí.* B. *rís, dáb.*

A shrub occasionally found in the Punjab Himalaya at from 5,000 to 7,000 feet. Its pretty red fruit is eaten.

V. STELLULATUM. Wall. (V. MULLAHA. Ham.)

Vernacular. J. *jal bágú.* K. *amliácha, phulsel.*

A shrub frequently found at from 4,500 to 10,000 feet on some of the rivers of the Punjab Himalaya. The ripe fruit though sour is eaten.

N. O. RUBIACEÆ.

HAMILTONIA SUAVEOLENS. Rox.

Vernacular. C. *muskei, kantálú, fisáúni.* R. *niggí, tulenni phúl, gohinla.* B. *kanera, pudárí.* S. *phillú.*

A shrub which is common at places in the Punjab Himalaya from 2,500 to 6,000 feet, up to near the Indus. Its wood is very small, but in Chumba it is said to be used for making gunpowder charcoal.

HYMENODICTYON EXCELSUM. Wall. (?)

Vernacular. R. *thab (?), barthoa.*

There is some doubt as to the identity of this, which grows to be a large tree, and appears to extend up to the Rávi low in the Siwálik region. Its timber is white, soft, and light, and used for inside work, yokes of ploughs, and especially scabbards. The leaves are given as fodder (and in Southern India the bark is employed in tanning).

MORINDA CITRIFOLIA. L.

Vernacular. *ál.*

Irvine states that this tree grows wild in Bajaur, &c., to the north of the Peshawar Valley, and that the root is used, not in dyeing (as in general), but as a cathartic. But there is no probability that the tree grows within Punjab limits.

NAUCLEA CORDIFOLIA. Rox.

Vernacular. U. *haldú.*

I have only seen this (which in the N. W. Provinces is common, and grows to be a very large tree) sparingly in the eastern part of the Punjab Siwálik tract near the Jumna. It yields a poor wood, which is used for planks, &c., and is said to decay quickly when exposed to moisture.

N. PARVIFOLIA. Willd.

Vernacular. C. *kám.* R. B. *kalham.* U. D. *keim.*

A tree which grows to a considerable size, seen in some numbers in the Siwálik tract up to the Biás, and occasional specimens (probably planted) to the Chenáb. It is rarely seen out in the plains even in the central Punjab; but at Sánpla, west from Dehlí, there are some hundreds of trees up to 10 feet (one about 13) in girth, and 50 or 60 feet high. The wood is white, light, and soft, and said to be subject to the attacks of worms. It is used for agricultural implements, beams, &c., of native houses, and combs are made of it. The leaves are given as fodder.

RANDIA DUMETORUM. Lam.

Vernacular. U. *míndhal.* Bazár, fruit, *mendphal.*

A small tree, probably this species, extends some little way into the Punjab in the Siwálik tract, and I have seen specimens up to 4 feet in girth in the plains in the east of the Province. The wood is not much valued. The bark is applied with cowdung to bruises, and the fruit is officinal, being used as an emetic, and on the Hindí system used externally as an anodyne in rheumatism.

RUBIA CORDIFOLIA. L. Willd. Madder.

Vernacular. J. *kúkarphalí, tiúrú.* K. *dandú, faharghás.* C. *manjít, khúrí, shení, rúna.* R. *mítú.* B. *majít.* S. *múnzat, rúnang.*

This plant grows abundantly in many parts of the Punjab Himalaya from 3,200 to 10,000 feet, and occurs in the Súlimán Range. In one part of Kashmír territory, low in the Chenáb basin, I was told distinctly that it is sometimes cultivated (but it may have been the next species which was meant), and its root is certainly used as a dye in many places, although in some parts where it is common wild, it is not, but other substances are used for dyeing reddish brown. The published notices do not clearly distinguish between this and the next species, but it is probably this with which Moorcroft says that the Bhotias in Kumaon and the Ladákis dye woollen cloth after a bath of alum. Madden (?) also refers to a similar practice of the Bhotias in Garhwál. On the Sutlej the people say it is collected for export, and give details of the prices they get, &c. It may be this or the next species which Cleghorn states to be sold in the Simla Bazár. He mentions that from the Nilgherries a bale of roots, not nearly so fine as to size and colour as those of the Punjab Himalaya, was sent to England, and that the report of a dye chemist on the former was very favourable.

R. TINCTORUM. L. (?) Madder.

Vernacular. Aff. *rodang, manjít.*

Resembles the preceding, and is probably identical with the European plant. It is only known in its cultivated state in Asia. Dr. Brandis first found it being grown in small quantity on the Sutlej at about 8,000 to 8,500 feet for home consumption, to dye wool red, but I have not observed it in the Punjab Himalaya elsewhere than in Kanáwar. Beyond the Indus, Irvine mentions that a little is collected in Gandáva, Belúchistán, and parts of Túrkistán, but that the chief tract for its cultivation is from Kábul to near Kandahár. In that tract Bellew mentions seeing it at Khúshí and Ghuzní (7,000 feet), while Masson notices it at Mastung to the south (3,500 feet ?) near Quetta, where Griffith refers to it at length. He states that it is occasionally dug up after two years, but usually is allowed to remain in the ground for five or six seasons. There it is probably propagated by buds or sets from the rhizomes, as was found to be the case in Kanáwar. Griffith also mentions that the herb is used as camel-fodder, and that the young shoots have a pleasant salad-like flavour. Davies' Trade Report states that 250 maunds are annually imported from Affghánistán viâ Peshawar. But there must be some mistake in the statement by the same authority that 6,000 maunds (?) are imported by the Bolán. From the Punjab, part is again exported; Cayley mentions a small quantity as carried beyond Lê to the east. According to Cleghorn, madder has been grown in the Punjab from French seed, I know not with what permanent results.

WENDLANDIA EXSERTA. DC. ? (W. CINEREA. Wall.)

Vernacular. R. and B. *pansíra.*

There is some doubt about this species, but it appears to grow as a large shrub in the Siwálik tract, up to the Rávi at least.

Edgeworth found two specimens far down in the Punjab plains, whither they or the seeds had been carried by the rivers. The wood is small and soft, and is not valued or used except for fuel. The leaves are stated to be given as fodder in Kángra. The flowers have a strong scent.

N. O. VALERIANEÆ.

Nardostachys Jatamansi. DC.

Vernacular. R. *matthúsal.* Bazar, root, *bál char, sambal ul tíb, jatamási, indurlatib ?*

I have been unfortunate as to this plant, and can say but little as to its habitats in the Punjab Himalaya, where it ranges from 10,000 (?) feet upwards. In Chumba its root is said to be added to the beer of that tract, and it is exported to the plains to be used in medicine, being considered cordial. The *indurlatíb,* of which Davies' Trade Report states that five maunds are imported from Persia viâ Kábul and Peshawar annually, has been dubiously identified with this drug.

Valeriana Hardwickii. Wall. Valerian.

Vernacular. R. and B. *nahání.* T. I. *char.* Bazár, root, *ásárun, bála, taggar.*

Is not uncommon in various parts of the Punjab Himalaya apparently at from 6,000 to 12,000 feet, and seems to occur beyond the Indus. The root of this and the next (and probably other) species is exported largely to the plains, where it is officinal, its properties being similar to those of the Valerians of Europe. By some of the books *asárún* is ascribed to Asarum Europœum, but probably only from similarity of name. In the hills the root is also put among clothes to keep off insects.

V. Wallichii. DC.

Vernacular. J. *mushkwálí, bála.* Bazár, root, as last.

Grows in the hills apparently from 5,000 to 11,000 feet, up to the Indus. Its roots are exported to the plains to be used medicinally, as the last.

N. O. DIPSACEÆ.

Morina breviflora. Edge.

Vernacular. ?

First found by Edgeworth at 10,000 to 11,000 feet near the Nítí Pass, in Kumaon; is stated by Aitchison to be thrown on the fire as an incense, by the Buddhists in Lahoul, giving an agreeable perfume.

N. O. COMPOSITÆ.

Achillea millefolium. L.

Vernacular. K. *momádrú, chopándiga.* Aff. *búí mádarán.*

This plant is common in many parts of the Punjab Himalaya from 3,500 to 12,000 feet. The officinal *búí mádarán*—(see Artemisia Indica)—of India has in the books generally been assigned to Artemisia absinthium, or other species of A. But Bellew, who probably saw the plant growing, says it is "yarrow." It consists of flower-heads, &c., which are used medicinally as an aromatic stimulant.

Antennaria contorta. DC.

Vernacular. *jhúla, bokla, gúfa.*

Madden mentions that several species are used for tinder and moxas on the Sutlej, &c.—(see Oreoseris). Jameson gives the specific and native names as above.

A. sp.

Vernacular. (Kumaon *máshí, gúgula*).

A species which also grows at 11—12,000 feet in the Punjab Himalaya, I found was used in Kumaon as an offering at shrines.

Aplotaxis candicans. DC.

Vernacular. J. *batúla.* S. R., T. I. *kálí zírí.*

This is not uncommon in the outer hills from 1,800 to 6,500 feet, in the Salt Range, and on the skirts of the Súlimán Range, &c., Trans-Indus. The seeds are in some places said to be collected for the drug-sellers, and the name would indicate a connection with one of the *zíras,* so that it is probably sometimes gathered, and used for the true *kálí zírí*—(see Serratula anthelmintica).

A. gossypina. DC. (Saussurea gossypina. Wall.)

Vernacular. S. *kasbál, bút pesh.*

Madden mentions that this plant is offered at shrines on the Sutlej.

Artemisia elegans. Rox. (A. scoparia. W. and K.)

Vernacular. K. *jhau, lasaj.* C. *píla jau.* R. *jhau.* S. *bíur, kingkhak.* T. I. *durunga, lawange.* S. R. *lawange.* Hí. *doná, marúa.* Bazár, plant, *chúrí saroj, dantí.*

This plant has a very wide range of growth, being found up to 9,000 feet in the Himalaya, and abounding in many parts of the Punjab plains, especially in the arid desert tracts. Edgeworth alludes to its "most delicious fragrance," and the odour in brushing through masses of it is at times very powerful, and not unpleasant. The branches appear to be officinal in the Punjab, their smoke being considered good for burns, and their infusion is given as depurative.

A. Indica. Willd.
A. vestita. Wall.

Vernacular. K. *tataur, púnjan, banjírú.* R. *chambra.* S. *úbúsha.* T. I. *tarkha.* Bazár, plant, *búí mádarán, afsuntín.*

These two species have got into confusion in my hands. One (or both) of them is common in parts of the plains of the western Punjab, and in the Himalaya up to 12,000 feet; also Trans-Indus. Bellew states that in Affghánistán a strong decoction is given as a vermifuge, and a weak one to children in measles. He also mentions that infusion of any of the Artemisias is given as a tonic. The officinal *afsuntín,* used as a febrifuge, appears to be one of these or some similar species. For another *búí mádarán,* see Achillea.

A. parviflora. Rox.

Vernacular. C. *kanyúrts.* Lad. *búrmar, basna tashang.*

A species, apparently this, is common from 10,000 feet upwards in Lahoul and Ladák, occasionally attaining nearly 17,000 feet in the latter. Browsed by goats and sheep, not much liked by *yaks.*

A. Persica. Boiss.

Vernacular. ?

Bellew collected this species in Affghánistán, where he states that it is very abundant, the plant being used as a tonic, febrifuge, and vermifuge.

A. SACRORUM. Led.

Vernacular. K. *tatwen.* C. *munyú, niurtsi, jau.* B. *chúmbar.* S. *zbiir.* Lad. *búrnak.*

A short absinthoid species resembling A. PERSICA (q. v.), which grows to considerable heights in the drier tracts on several of the rivers up to near the Indus. It is browsed by cattle, sheep, &c., and in Chumba is said to be given medicinally to horses in affections of the head. In Ladák its thick roots are at times used as fuel.

A. VULGARIS. L.

Vernacular. *tatwen.*

This is found in the Jhelam and Chenáb basins, &c., from 3,000 to 11,500 feet. It is stated by Honigberger to be given in fevers, &c.

A. SP.

Vernacular. J. *chau.*

This is a species resembling the last with broad leaves white on under-surface, and growing from 9,000 to 12,000 feet, which in Khágán is said to cause the nausea and faintness sometimes felt at considerable heights. With a view to prevent these, the people stick some of the leaves of the plant into each ear.

A. SPP.

Vernacular. ?

Mr. Jaeschke informs me that in Lahoul the leaves of several species of ARTEMISIA are boiled to a paste and applied to the cheek for toothache.

ASTER SP. (?)

Vernacular. S. *gulbás.*

A white-flowered species in gardens in Kanáwar at 8,000 feet.

AUCKLANDIA COSTUS. Falc.

Vernacular. *kút, kot.* Bazár, root, *kút* or *kúst talkh.* Bengal, *pachak.*

This plant, whose root excited attention for long before its true source was made known, and the plant named by Dr. Falconer, has probably for ages been exported from the tracts near Kashmír. It grows at from 10,500 to 13,000 feet in parts of the basins of the Jhelam and Chenáb. Bears are said to be fond of the young shoots. The Sanscrit name, *Kashmirja*, of the root indicates the chief place whence it was brought. Cleghorn states that it is also exported from Pangí on the Upper Chenáb to the plains. 'The loads of it, when passing, scent the air to some distance. It is used locally for hair powder, and to protect shawls from insects.' It is also officinal in the Punjab, being applied in powder to ulcers, for worms in wounds, &c., and for toothache, and also given in rheumatism. But great part of it passes on through the Punjab to be sent to China, where it is used as incense. Davies' Trade Report gives 20 maunds as exported to Affghánistán viâ the Bolán. Royle mentions that in one year (1837-38), 6,697 maunds of this root (called *pachak* in Calcutta), valued at Rs. 99,000, were exported from Calcutta to China; and I find that in the official year 1867-68, 347 cwt., nearly 10,000 maunds, were exported from Calcutta to China. In Kashmír territory the Maharaja is said to take it over from the collectors at half the price at which he sells it again. In 1864 his income from this source was put by what ought to have been good authority at 3,00,000 *chilkí* equal to nearly 1,90,000 Company's rupees, but this is hardly credible. It is said by Kashmírís to be apt to be adulterated with five or six other kinds of roots—(see LIGULARIA). Dr. Johnstone had live roots brought from the hills to Goojrát, where I saw them shooting the succeeding year. (Up to that time they had not had a very good chance, being exposed to the full sun of the plains). I do not know if they are still alive. I may note here that the source of *kút shirín*, another officinal root, is still quite unknown. It has by some been assigned to COSTUS q. v. It is considered depurative and aphrodisiac.

BERTHELOTIA LANCEOLATA. DC.

Vernacular. *reshamí, resham-bútí.* T. I. *sármei.* Bazár, leaves, *rásanna.* (Sind, *kúra sanna*).

An annual plant which grows abundantly in many parts of the plains up to Peshawar, in places forming thickets up to 4 and 5 feet high. Its roots extend to several yards, sending up other shoots as they go. And although it is not considered particularly troublesome by Punjab agriculturists, it is said to be one of the chief evils with which cultivators near Agra, Jounpúr, &c., have to contend. (Specimens of it were on this account sent to Lahore for identification by J. H. Batten, C. S., when Commissioner, Agra Division). Almost every specimen of Bazár *rásanna* I have seen consists of the leaves of this plant, and in Sind also it is said to be used to adulterate, or rather, instead of *sanna*—(see CASSIA ACUTIFOLIA) as a purgative.

CALENDULA OFFICINALIS. L.

Vernacular. T. I. *zergul*. (Gardens, *sadbarg*).

Is common wild in some parts of the plains and low hills Trans-Indus. Bellew states that, when browsed by cows, it is considered to increase the quantity of milk. For *sadbarg* see CARPESIUM SP.

CARDUUS NUTANS. L.

Vernacular. R. *kanchhári*. S. *tiso*. Bazár, flowers, *bádáward*.

Not uncommon from 5,000 to 11,000 feet in the Punjab Himalaya up to the Indus, and got at 7,000 feet in the Súlimán Range. It is greedily eaten by camels when they get a chance. Its flowers, &c., are officinal as a febrifuge in the Lahore Bazár, under the above name, which is by some of the books attributed to CRATÆGUS.

CARPESIUM RACEMOSUM. Wall.

Vernacular. Bazár, plant, *hukmandáz*.

This plant is given by Honigberger for Kashmir, where he says it is used medicinally.

C. SP.

Vernacular. *wotlángil*.

A species which is common in and near Kashmír at 2,500 to 5,000 feet. As mentioned by Vigne, the plant is used in Sirínaggar in dyeing silk yellow.

C. SP.

Vernacular. Bazár, plant, *sadbarg*.

The plant of one species is officinal at Lahore; as mentioned under CALENDULA; the latter is called *sadbarg* (by gardeners).

CARTHAMUS OXYACANTHA. Bieb.

Vernacular. *kantiári, kandiára, poli*. T. I. *kháreza*.

Abundant in many of the more arid tracts of the Punjab from Ambála up to Peshawar. In many places the seeds are eaten parched alone, or with wheat, or ground and mixed with wheaten flower for bread (as are said to be those of C. or ONOBROMA PERSICUS). Near Peshawar and elsewhere an oil extracted from the seeds, is burned and eaten. Bellew states that it is also used medicinally.

C. TINCTORIUS. Rox. Safflower.

Vernacular. *kúsam, kúrtam.* Bazár, seed, *khar, polian.*

Cultivated to some extent in most parts of the Punjab plains, and rarely in the hills, occasionally to 5,500 feet, and more sparingly towards the north-west (oddly enough, Irvine states that it is mostly grown in Kashmír, &c., in the hills, and not in warmer parts). Moorcroft and Masson mention it at Kábul, and the former says that what is raised there gives more colour than that of India, to which the flowers are exported, but this seems unlikely. Davies' Trade Report gives 150 maunds as imported from Affghánistán viâ Peshawar and 28 viâ the Bolán. The flowers are largely used as a dye, and are also given medicinally in diseases of the tonsils. I do not find that in the Punjab the seeds are eaten or have the oil extracted as in the (last) wild species, but they are officinal, being considered diuretic and tonic.

CHRYSANTHEMUM INDICUM. Rox. (?)

Vernacular. *gendi.* C. *bágáur.* Lad. *kalzang.*

Commonly cultivated in gardens in the plains, in Kashmír (yellow, white, and pink, according to Hugel), on the Upper Chenáb, &c., to 9,200 feet, and in Ladák at 11,300 feet. Masson mentions a C. at Kábul.

CICHORIUM INTYBUS. L.

Vernacular. K. *hand, gúl.* C. *suchal, hand.* Plains, *kásni.*

The pilose variety is not uncommon wild in the plains of the N. W. Punjab and in Kashmír, &c., to 5,500 feet, and Aitchison mentions it in Lahoul 9,500 feet, but without specimens, and it does not appear to grow there. The young plant is in some places used as a vegetable. Davies' Trade Report gives 20 maunds of the seed as imported from Affghánistán viâ Peshawar. The seeds of both appear to be officinal, being considered carminative and cordial. The root also is used medicinally.

CIRSIUM ARGYRACANTHUM. DC.

Vernacular. ?

Not uncommon in the Punjab Himalaya from 1,000 (?) to 10,000 feet. Aitchison states that in Lahoul the plants are left standing in the reaped fields as amulets.

COTULA ANTHEMOIDES. L.

Vernacular. Bazár, flowers, &c., *babúna.*

This plant would appear to grow wild in the eastern part of the Punjab plains, and probably furnishes part of the officinal *babúna*—(see MATRICARIA)—which is heated with oil and applied in rheumatism, &c.

COUSINIA CALCITRAPÆFORMIS. DC.

Vernacular. T. I. *lakhtei.* S. R. *polí, kandiárí.*

Is not uncommon wild in the plains Trans-Indus, and in the Salt Range to 2,000 feet. In the latter the young plant is used as a vegetable.

C. SP.

Vernacular. K. *kritz.* C. *trutsa, búsh, tsuk.* P. *túse.*

Much larger than the last. Grows in Kashmír at 5,000 and on the Upper Chenáb and in Spiti from 8,500 to 12,000 feet. Its leaves are bruised and used for tinder—(see OREOSERIS)—and it is browsed by goats.

CYNARA SCOLYMUS. L. Artichoke.

Vernacular. *hátí chuk.*

Only cultivated by or for Europeans. There is no probability in a recent newspaper statement that a wild variety had been found near Simla. The next plant may possibly be the one meant.

DOLOMIÆA MACROCEPHALA. DC.

Vernacular. J. R. *dhup.* C. *dhúpa.* K. B. *dhúp, gúgal.* S. *zhangar, dhup, gúgal.* Bazár, root, *dhúp, pokhar-múl.* ?

Not uncommon from the Sutlej up to the Indus at from 10,500 to 13,000 feet, often growing as noted by Aitchison on the crests of ridges. The odorous root is locally used as incense offered at shrines and to Rájas (Madden), and the flowers also are placed in temples on the Sutlej. The bruised root is likewise applied to eruptions, and a decoction of it is taken in colic, &c. Aitchison also remarks that some part of the plant is used medicinally. The root is from many places exported to the plains, sometimes after being pounded and made up into cakes with its own juice, as I was informed in Khágán. And it appears to be officinal in the Punjab Bazárs under both of the above names. It is considered cordial, and given in puerperal fever, &c. This is probably the *jarí* (root) *dhúp*, of which nearly seven maunds from Bissahir were exposed for sale at the Rampúr fair in 1867, according to the Official Report.

Echinops nivea. Royle.

Vernacular. R *brúgh, laura brúsh*. B. *bush*. S. *tso, púr-cho-bachá*.

A large spinous annual plant with tomentose leaves, which is not uncommon in the drier tracts of the Punjab Himalaya from 5,500 to 10,000 feet, up to near the Indus. In various parts the leaves are used for making tinder (for which *bacha* appears to be the Kanáwarí word)—(see Oreoseris).

Eclipta erecta. L.

Vernacular. *búkan, bhangra*. Bazár, plant, *bhangra, muk-and bábrí*.

Abundant all over in the plains at moist places, and occasional to 5,000 feet in the hills. The plant is officinal, under both the above names, being considered cooling.

Francœuria crispa. Cass.

Vernacular. *búí, gídí*. T. I. *sutei*. S. R. *phatmer*.

Common all over in the Punjab plains, &c. In the Salt Range the dried plant is bruised and applied as a vulnerary to bruises, &c., of bullocks.

Gnaphalium sp.

Vernacular. ?

Madden states that one species is used on the Sutlej for tinder and moxas—(see Oreoseris).

G. sp.?

Vernacular. Bazár, leaves, &c., *bál raksha.*

These are officinal in the Bazárs, and appear to be from a Gnaphalium.

Lactuca sativa. L. Lettuce.

Vernacular. *káhú.*

Cultivated in the plains for its seeds, which are officinal, being considered diuretic and purgative. Masson mentions the lettuce as abundant at Kábul, and Davies' Trade Report gives 10 maunds of the seed as imported thence viâ Peshawar.

Ligularia sp. (Senecillis Jacquemontiana. Dne.)

Vernacular. K *poshkar.*

A tall yellow-flowered plant which grows at 7,500 to 11,000 feet on the Pír Punjál, and various other parts as far east as the Rávi at least. Birdwood states (but does not mention his authority) that the root of a plant with this native name is used for adulterating *kút*—(see Aucklandia)—and Kashmírís at Lahore make the same statement, so there must be some foundation for it. But it may not be *this* plant, as in Kashmírí *poshkar* appears merely to signify a large herb with showy flowers. Jacquemont's plant seems to be the same as mine, and was found near the same locality as some of my specimens.

Matricaria Chamomila. L. Chamomile.
M. disciformis. DC.
M. præcox. DC.

Vernacular. *babúna.* T. I. *suteigul.*

The first is cultivated and wild in the plains of the eastern Punjab. The two others are found wild Trans-Indus. The flowers of all are probably at times sold and used as *babúna*—(see Cotula)—either of the two last may be Bellew's "Anthemis," of which he states that in Affghánistán it is wild "all over the country," and that a weak infusion is given as tonic and febrifuge, and a strong infusion as an emetic, and that an oil from the flowers is used as a liniment for rheumatism.

Microrhynchus nudicaulis. Less.

Vernacular. *batthal, dúdhlak.* T. I. *tarízha, spúdukei.*

A common weed throughout in the plains and up to 6,000 feet occasionally in the hills. In the Southern Punjab the plant is used medicinally, in *sharbat.*

MULGEDIUM TATARICUM. DC.

Vernacular. Lad. *kháwe.*

Common in Ladák from 11,000 to 14,500 feet. It is occasionally browsed by sheep, but is said at times to produce bad effects.

MYRIOGYNE MINUTA. Less.

Vernacular. *nakhchhinkní.*

A common weed in the plains of the eastern and central Punjab. The plant is officinal, as it excites sneezing (whence the native name), and is powdered and snuffed up in cerebral affections. It is also said to be used in *kimia* (alchemy).

OREOSERIS LANUGINOSA. DC. (CHAPTALIA GOSSYPINA. Royle.)

Vernacular. J. *patpatúla.* K. *kho.* C. *búr, buzlí, kapfí.* R. *púrjlú, bújlo, kapfí, tsar.* B. *kafí.* S. *kúfra.* T. I. *kharebútí.*

Common in the Himalaya up to the Indus, (and found in the hills beyond it) from 3,200 to 7,000 feet. Wherever it grows in any quantity, tinder and occasionally moxas appear to be made from it, sometimes by beating up the body of the leaf with the tomentum on its under surface (as is done with some other plants), but generally by breaking through the former and tearing off the latter to be used alone. (For other plants used for tinder, see ANTENNARIA CONTORTUM, COUSINIA SP., ECHINOPS, GNAPHALIUM SP., and COMPOSITÆ DUBIA 1 and 2). Several newspaper writers and others have stated that cloth is made from this, but I have nowhere found this to be the case in the Punjab Himalaya. Still more have recommended it for such purposes, but the practical objections to doing this on the large scale (apart from the probability that the fibre is not strong enough) are these—1st, the plant is quite small, and does not grow closely, so that a wide area would need to be searched to get any considerable quantity of the tomentum; and 2nd, the process of removing the latter is a tedious one, and would probably be costly.

PHÆNOPUS. SP.?

Vernacular. S. R. *ganhúlí.*

A small herb which grows at from 2,000 to 2,500 feet in the Salt Range, where it is given for colic.

Pluchea sp. ?

Vernacular. T. I. *dingrí*. Bazár plant, *mujní*. (?)

A herbaceous plant found Trans-Indus and in the Salt Range to 1,500 feet. It is eaten by goats, and appears to be the officinal *mujní* of the Lahore Bazárs.

Prenanthes quinqueloba. Wall. ?

Vernacular. S. *morta*.

Several species are common in many parts of the Punjab Himalaya from 3,200 to 8,500 feet. In Kanáwar the seeds of what appears to be this species are given for colic.

Pyrethrum sp.

Vernacular. *akarkara, zoenil.*

Honigberger mentions under the above native names a species which grows in Kashmír, the root of which, when given for salivation, cures it, and in excess produces salivation. *Akarkara* is a common drug applied for toothace, and assigned by Jameson to Spilanthes oleracea. It is probably derived from different plants in different places.

Saussurea obvallata. Edge. (Aplotaxis. DC.)
S. sacra. Edge.

Vernacular. *kanwal.*

Edgeworth mentions that these two species (which probably grow in the Punjab Himalaya also) are offered up at the shrines of Budrinath, &c.

S. sorocephala. Schr.

Vernacular. R. B. *gúgí*.

Grows at from 9,000 to 14,500 feet on the Chenáb, Rávi, and Biás. In Chumba it is offered up at shrines.

Senecio angulosus. Wall. ?

Vernacular. J. *chitawála.*

A tall species growing at 6,000 feet in Hazára, where its leaves (large with white under surface) are applied

S. LACINIOSUS. Wall. Ragwort.

Vernacular. C. *sanggye, mentog*. Bazár, flowers, &c., *nímbar*.

This species appears to be common in many parts of the Punjab Himalaya from 5,000 to 13,200 feet. Honigberger states that it is officinal in Kashmír. In Lahoul it is held as sacred to Buddha. It is probably the *nímbar* of Lahore drug-sellers, which is a SENECIO.

SONCHUS OLERACEUS. L.? Sow thistle.

Vernacular. Plains, *dodak*.

A common weed from the plains to 8,500 feet in the Punjab Himalaya. The Kashmíris are said to use it as a vegetable, and it is probably the "dwarf sow thistle," the shoots of which the Ladákis use in a similar way, according to Moorcroft, though this may be the TRAGOPOGON (q. v.)

SPHÆRANTHUS HIRTUS. Willd. (INDICUS. L. MOLLIS. Rox.)

Vernacular. *múndí bútí*. Bazár, plant, *khamádrús, múndí, ghúndí, zakhmí haiyát*.

This plant is common in the eastern and central Punjab, and seems to yield the officinal flowers, &c., sold under the above names, and which are highly esteemed, being used as alterative, depurative, cooling, and tonic. Honigberger states that the root is anthelmintic.

TAGETES ERECTA. Willd. African marigold.
T. PATULA. L. French marigold.

Vernacular. S. *tangla*. Lad. *mentok*. Plains, *génda*.

Both are grown by natives in the Punjab plains, and one is commonly cultivated for its flower in Kashmír 5,000 feet, on the Upper Chenáb to 6,400 feet, on the Sutlej (red and yellow, Hoffmeister) to 8,000 feet, and in Ladák 11,300 feet. Masson mentions French and African marigolds at Kábul. Lowther states that the flower of the latter was a favorite of the late Maharaja of Kashmír, and strings of them are often hung up at shrines, &c.

TANACETUM TENUIFOLIUM. Jacq. Tansy.

Vernacular.

Cleghorn states that this, growing at 10,000 feet on the Sutlej, is useful for flavoring puddings.

T. tomentosum. DC.

Vernacular. Lad. *púrkar.*

Common in Ladák from 14,000 to 17,000 feet. It is at times browsed by goats, and its thick roots are occasionally used as fuel.

T. vulgare. L.

Vernacular. *peilmundí.*

Mentioned by Honigberger under the above names as being officinal in Kashmír.

Taraxacum officinale. Wigg. Dandelion.

Vernacular. K. *dúdal.* C. *baran.* B. *kanphúl, dúdlí.* S. *radam.* Lad. *yamaghí khá, rasúk.* T. I. *shamukei.* S. R. *dúdh batthal.*

A common weed from the level of the plains in the N. W. Punjab to 13,300 feet in the Punjab Himalaya, and occasionally to 17,500 feet in Ladák. In many places the young plant is eaten as a vegetable, and Honigberger mentions that it is officinal in Kashmír. The leaves are found in the Himalaya as in Europe to be excellent food for tame rabbits.

Tragopogon major. Jacq.

Vernacular. ?

The young root is eaten as a vegetable in Lahoul, where the plant is common wild at 10,000 to 12,000 feet. It is also said to be cultivated, but this appears doubtful.

Tussilago Farfara. L. Coltsfoot.

Vernacular. C. *wátpan.*

Not uncommon in many places in the Punjab Himalaya from 5,000 to 11,000 feet. Its leaves are sometimes applied to wounds.

Vernonia anthelmintica. Willd.
(Serratula anthelmintica Rox).

Vernacular. Basár, seed, *kálíjírí.*

The seeds are officinal, being given in anasarca, and used in plasters for abscesses.

WALDHEIMIA TRIDACTYLITES. Kar. and Kir.

Vernacular. Lad. *pallo.*

A small plant with a pretty lilac flower, common in Lahoul and Ladák. In the latter it attains 18,500 feet, being the greatest elevation reached in the N. W. Himalaya by any flowering plant known to me. It is browsed by goats and sheep when under stress of hunger.

XANTHIUM STRUMARIUM. L.

Vernacular. K. *tsúr, láne tsúrú.* C. *wangan tsúrú, chírrú, kúrí, jojre.* B. *súngtú.* S. *gúdal.* T. I. *baggiári.* Bazar, fruit, *gokhrú kalán.*

Not uncommon locally in the plains of the N. W. Punjab, and in many parts of the Himalaya up to 6,500 feet, and in the Súlimán Range at 5,000 feet. The fruit is officinal, being considered cooling, and given in small-pox (on the "doctrine of signatures" from the appearance of the fruit ?). In some parts it is burnt and applied to diseases of the mouth.

The following COMPOSITÆ must be left among the DUBIÆ in the meantime :—

1. *Kúfra, posha,* a plant of 2 feet high, which grows at 6,000 feet on the Sutlej. Its tomentum is used for tinder—(see OREOSERIS)—and the stems are said to be used for making paper.

2. *Damang-bacha,* a tall plant growing at 9,000 feet on the Sutlej, the dried leaves of which are rubbed up for tinder—(see OREOSERIS).

N. O. CAMPANULACEÆ.

CODONOPSIS OVATA. Benth.

Vernacular. C. *lúdút.*

Occurs from 9,000 to 11,000 feet in several parts of the Punjab Himalaya, and was got in Affghánistán by Griffith. Aitchison states that in Lahoul its large tap-root is ground into flour and eaten, and is applied as an emollient to bruises, and swollen joints, &c.

CYANANTHUS SP. ?

Vernacular. R. *murra.*

With a pretty blue flower growing at 10,000 to 12,000 feet in Chumba. The calyces are eaten, being mawkish-sweet, and are said to be good for asthma.

N. O. ERICACEÆ.

Andromeda ovalifolia. Don.

Vernacular. J. K. *rattankát*. C. *rattankát, arur*. R. *eilan, eilaur*. B. *eran, ellal, bhel*. S. *erana, ayatta*. T. I. *sarlakhtei*.

A small tree abundant in many parts of the outer Punjab Himalaya, often growing along with Rhododendron arboreum, at from 4,000 to 7,000 feet. The seeds and young leaves are poisonous to cattle, goats, &c., (*rattankát* means blood-cutter) in the spring months only. One man told me that they produce cerebral symptoms, and that his herd recovered by the use of *lassí* (sour milk). Madden states that the honey, got from the flower, is poisonous also. The wood is soft and weak, and used for fuel and charcoal only.

A. fastigiata. Wall. (Cassiope. Don.)

Vernacular. B. *chhota lewar*.

Occasional in the Punjab Himalaya at from 10,500 to 13,000 feet. It strongly resembles heather, and is the "Himalayan heather" of some travellers.

Rhododendron anthopogon. D. Don. (Osmothamnus fragrans. DC.

R. lepidotum. Wall.

Vernacular. J. *níchní, rattankát, nera*. K. *tázak-tsun*. R. *kát zabán, morúa, talísa*. B. *talísrí*. Bazár, leaves, *talísfar*.

These two small bushy species often grow together, and are apt to be confused as they strongly resemble each other, the chief easily observable difference being that the flowers of the former are yellowish white, and of the latter reddish or lilac. The leaves of both are very aromatic, and their smoke is considered useful externally in some diseases. The leaves are officinal in the plains, being considered stimulant.

R. arboreum. Sm.

Vernacular. J. *ardáwal*. C. *mandál*. R. *chiú, árú*. B. *brás, brod, chacheon*. S. *brás*.— T. I. *tríkh gandere*.

A small tree common at many places in the outer Himalaya (often in the Quercus incana tract, along with Andromeda ovalifolia) from 3,000 to 6,000 feet or occasionally to 8,000 feet, and also found Trans-Indus. The gorgeous flush of crimson flowers adorns some of our hill-stations about March, but occasionally trees will flower as early as 1st February (Masson), with snow on the ground. In 1867 again, the newspapers reported that hardly a tree flowered till the middle of June. The seed is said to ripen about Christmas. Dishes, &c., are sometimes made of the wood, but it is soft and weak, and mostly only used for charcoal, and for native houses. Madden states that the young leaves of this also—(see ANDROMEDA)—are poisonous. The flowers have a sweet-sour taste, and are said to make a good sub-acid jelly. They are in some parts of the Himalaya eaten by natives, who, according to Madden, get intoxicated if they consume a large number. It is also stated that they are medicinal, and they are applied to the forehead for headache on the Biás. Hoffmeister mentions that in Nepál they are offered in temples. He also notes that a snuff, made from the bark of the tree, is excellent.

R. CAMPANULATUM. D. Don.

Vernacular. K. *gaggar yurmí*. R. *sarngar, shinwala*. B. *shargar*. S. *simrung*. Bazár, leaves, *tamáku* or *hulás* or *patti Kashmírí, bargí Tibet*.

A shrub which is not very common in the Punjab Himalaya at from 9,500 to 14,000 feet, up to near the Indus. The whitish or lilac flowers (Honigberger mentions rose-coloured and yellow flowers as rare) appear from May to July, and the seed ripens in October. It seems certain that the leaves of this likewise—(see last species)—sometimes are poisonous to goats. Vigne states that bees are very fond of the buff-coloured under-surface of the leaf, and that a few of the latter are therefore put into or near hives. The leaves are exported to the plains, where they are officinal under the above names, being errhine and ground to be mixed with tobacco for a medicinal snuff used in hemicrania. The smoke of this, when used as fuel, is the most acrid and irritant of any I have ever experienced.

N. O. PRIMULACEÆ.

ANAGALLIS ARVENSIS. L.

Vernacular. S. R. *dhabbar*.

A common weed throughout the plains and in the Himalaya up to 6,000 and occasionally 9,000 feet. All the plants I have ever seen in the plains are of the blue-flowered variety, which is rare in Great Britain (but occurs with the other in Sydney). On the other hand, all those I have seen in Kashmír are the ordinary red-flowered variety of England. Madden mentions that the triturated plant is used to poison fish, and to expel leeches from the nostrils.

N. O. MYRSINACEÆ.

Myrsine Africana. L.

Vernacular. J. *bebrang, kokhúr.* C. *gúgul, bránsh, prátshú, bránti.* R. *chachrí, jutrú.* B. *ban-dárú.* S. *átúlgán, bínsín.* T. I. *shamshád.* S. R. *paprí, vávarang.* Bazár, fruit, *bebrang.*

A smallish shrub common in many places in the Himalaya from 2,500 to occasionally 8,500 feet, as well as in the Salt Range and Trans-Indus. In the Punjab Bazárs the officinal *bebrang,* used as an anthelmintic for small intestinal worms, appears always to be the fruit of this, although generally ascribed to Embelia ribes, which does not seem to grow within our limits. This plant is well worth trying as a hedge in our hill-stations, as it would look neat, and would probably stand trimming.

Reptonia buxifolia. A. DC. (Edgeworthia. Falconer.)

Vernacular. T. I. *gúrgúra.* S. R. *garar.*

A small tree common in the Trans-Indus hills from 2,000 to 3,000 feet, and occasional in the western part of the Salt Range. Its wood, though small, is hard, strong, and fine-grained. The fruit, which is mentioned among those of Affgháuistán by Elphinstone, &c., is collected in April and eaten by the natives, but to European tastes is very poor. Dr. Falconer first described this plant, and named it after Mr. Edgeworth, B. C. S., but the name appears to have been pre-occupied.

N. O. SAPOTACEÆ.

Bassia latifolia. Rox.

Vernacular. *mahwá, mawwa.*

This tree does not appear to be indigenous in the Punjab, but planted trees (from seed) are not uncommon in and near the Siwálik tract, up to the Rávi, and single specimens may be seen as far from the hills as Ambála and Batála. The wood is said to be cinnamon-coloured, close, hard, heavy, and durable, and is used for building in Kángra, &c. An oil is extracted from the seed, which is eaten and burned, and "used to adulterate ghí," and spirits are extracted from the flowers.

MIMUSOPS ELENGI. L.

Vernacular. *maulsarí.*

A handsome tree occasionally planted in the east of the Punjab for its "appearance and the fine smell of the flowers," though even near Dehlí I was told that the fruit does not ripen. There are one or two small specimens about Lahore and Umritsur, and one tree in the Hazúrí bagh, Múltán, is mentioned by Vigne and Edgeworth as traditionally stated to have been brought by a late Nawáb from Mecca, which may perhaps be doubted, especially as it seems unlikely that the tree grows there at all. The bark is officinal at Lahore.

M. KAUKI. L.

Vernacular. *khirní.* Bazár, root, *khirní lodh.*

A tree occasionally planted as far west as Hoshiárpúr, Múltán, Lahore, and Eminabád, near Goojanwála. The seeds are applied powdered in ophthalmia, and the root is also officinal at Lahore.

N. O. EBENACEÆ.

DIOSPYROS EMBRYOPTERIS. Pers. (EMBRYOPTERIS GLUTINIFERA. Rox.)

Vernacular. *gáb.*

I have no knowledge of this tree growing in the Punjab, but Honigberger states that it grows at Lahore, and that the bark has been used in intermittent fevers.

D. LOTUS. L.?

Vernacular. J. *amlok, malúk,* (male) *gwalidar.* B. *Bissahrí pála.*

A tree which is not uncommon in the western part of the Jhelam basin from 2,500 to 6,000 feet, and appears to be common in some parts of the northern Trans-Indus hills; and one or two specimens were grown at Peshawar. It is a handsome little tree, growing generally to 3 or 4 feet in girth, the largest I have seen in its usual habitats being one of 6 feet girth and 35 feet high at

Jared in Khágán, and another about the same size on the Kishenganga. But curiously enough, there are three trees (probably introduced by fakirs) at Juggatsúkh (6,000 feet) in Kúllú, and there called *Bissahrí púla*, the largest of which is a remarkably fine tree of 12 feet girth. These were first noted by His Honor the present Lieutenant Governor of the Punjab, when Commissioner of Jalandar Division, and are the trees mentioned by Cleghorn as D. TOMENTOSA (q. v.) I do not know that the wood is specially valued, but I have nowhere seen the tree so common that much of it could be got. As Griffith remarks, the fruit is "not worthy of any notice," but when fresh or even carefully dried it is sweet and pleasant enough, and the Affgháns, &c., prize it, large quantities being brought to the Peshawar Bazárs from Swát, &c. Bellew mentions that it is eaten plain or with rice, or is used in *sharbats*. I presume Irvine was mistaken in stating that spirits are in the Punjab distilled from the fruit.

D. MONTANA. Rox.?

Vernacular. B. *kendú, hirek*. D. *kendú, pasendú*.

A small handsome tree whose bright green spring foliage looks pleasant. Is not uncommon along the Siwálik tract up to near the Rávi, and occasional out in the plains westward from Dehlí to near Sirsa. I remarked one tree in central Sind. It ordinarily grows to about 3 feet girth. I have seen two trees of 7 feet. The wood is used for native roofs, &c. The fruit is not eaten, and I have heard it called "poisonous." In some places it is applied to the hands for boils, to which *bhístis* are said to be subject.

D. TOMENTOSA. Poir.

Vernacular. B. *kinnú*. U. *kendú, tindú*. Bazar, raspings, *búra de abnús*.

Occasional, in some places common, in the Siwálik tract westward near to the Rávi. I have almost never seen a decent unlopped tree of 2 feet girth within Punjab bounds. Many years ago, Sir Donald McLeod (then Commissioner of Jalandar) wrote that he had great difficulty in getting good specimens of the timber; and in 1866 it took 15 days searching in Hoshiárpúr to find a fair specimen to send to Europe for the Secretary of State. The heart-wood of a good tree is generally called *ábnús*, "ebony," and is fine, black, hard, and somewhat brittle. It carves well, and insects are said not to touch it. Mr. Watson, Madhopúr Workshops, informs me it is good for cogs if it could be got, though hardly so strong as OLEA (q. v.) In and near the Rohilkund Siwálik tract, where the tree is more common or better looked to, handsome work-boxes, &c., are made from the wood. Combs are made from it in the Ambála district. In Kángra, &c., it is used for ploughs, in house-building and for small boxes. The fruit, which is said to ripen in June with the mango, is eaten, being sweetish and astringent, and not unpleasant. But I find one authority reports its pulp as bitter, fœtid, and emetic. Raspings of the wood are officinal, being given as alterative.

N. O. STYRACACEÆ.

Symplocos cratægoides. Don.

Vernacular. C. *lodar*. R. *lú, laudar*. B. *loj, losh*. Bazár, bark, *lodh Patháni*.

It appears to me to be the same species, which, as a small tree, is found in the Punjab Himalaya at from 3,000 to 7,000 feet, up to near the Indus, though very scarce towards the north-west. The wood does not seem to be specially valued; an oil is said to be extracted from the seeds, and the leaves are stated to be used in dyeing. Cleghorn mentions that the bark is employed for dyeing with madder, and it is officinal, being considered tonic in the Hindú system of medicine, and also used in ophthalmia.

N. O. OLEACEÆ.

Chionanthus sp.?

Vernacular. R. B. *rabán*. B. *síra*.

A small tree probably belonging to this genus, is occasionally seen in the outer Punjab Himalaya from 4,000 to 6,000 feet, up to the Rávi at least. Its wood is white, soft, and light, and is used for native houses and implements in Kángra, where also the bark is said to be medicinal, and the leaves to be used as fodder.

Fraxinus floribunda. Wall.? Ash.

Vernacular. J. *sum*. K. *húm, hamú*. C. *sinnú, shúnnú*. R. *súnnú*. T. I. *úgái, shing, banaush*.

A handsome tree with a deeply furrowed bark, growing occasionally to upwards of 12 and at times to 15 feet in girth and 120 feet high, the finest specimens being those planted at villages and temples, &c. It is found sparingly wild, and rarely seen planted in one or two places on the Rávi, more abundantly in parts of the basin of the Chenáb, and rarely on the Jhelam, at from

4,000 to 8,500 feet. It also grows Trans-Indus in the hills, having been collected by Bellew. The wood is excellent, possessing most of the qualities of European ash, though at times it has been spoken lightly of, possibly from the trees having been felled at the wrong season. It is valued for *jámpán*-poles, ploughs, platters, spinning-wheels, &c., and in Kashmír is reckoned by far the best wood for oars. A supply of it was, on one occasion, taken from Hazára as far as Peshawar for a special purpose.

F. XANTHOXYLLOIDES. Wall. (F. MOORCROFTIANA. Wall.)

Vernacular. J. *núch, hanúz, shílli.* K. *chíjla, chúj, síjú.* C. *bútrú, sandal, shangal, chúm.* S. *chúm, thúm.* T. I. *shang.*

A small tree, or as generally seen, a large shrub common in the arid tracts on the Sutlej and Chenáb, and in the Jhelam basin, from 3,500 to 9,000 feet, and in Tibet to 12,000 feet. It also occurs on the eastern skirts of the Súlimán Range at 5,000 feet. It very rarely reaches 5 feet in girth and 25 feet high. Its wood is hard, heavy, and strong, but, being small, is mostly only used for handles, &c., and for fuel. Cleghorn states that it is at times used for *jámpán*-poles. The leaves vary remarkably in size on the same tree, the upper being often three or four times the size of the lower. They are used as fodder.

F. SP.

Vernacular. Aff. *síyáh chob.* Bazar, manna, *shír khist.*

Masson mentions that the tree with the above native name grows in the mountains to the north of Kábul, and was seen by him as a good sized bush on the mountain Chehal thán (10,000 feet?) north of the Bolán Pass. It may possibly be the species first mentioned above (F. FLORIBUNDA), and is known to yield the officinal *shír khist* (as a manna is yielded by an ORNUS, flowering ash, in Italy, &c.) This is imported into the Punjab from Affghánistán, and is used as a laxative. Davies' Trade Report gives the annual quantity imported by each of Peshawar and the Bolán as one maund.

OLEA EUROPÆA. L. var. CUSPIDATA. Wall.
O. FERRUGINEA. Royle. Olive.

Vernacular. *kau, khan, ko, kohú, (bankau).* S. *ki.* T. I. *khwan, ..hwan, shwawan.* Aff. (Per.) *záitún.*

A smallish tree abundant Trans-Indus from the plains level, and in the Salt Range, common in the western part of the Siwálik tract, and over a considerable part of Hazára (where it is remarkably fine, *e. g.*, below Trêt), and found on the Chenáb, Rávi, and Sutlej, reaching 6,000 feet on that river. (It is also found in the Jumna basin to the eastward). Its foliage looks more dense than it really is, and gives a rather checquered shade. The tree grows to 6 feet in girth when well preserved, and I have seen a few trees of 10 or 12 feet girth. I think there must be some error in Jameson's statement of "several trees in lower Hazára of upwards of 8 feet diameter at 3 feet from the ground." The wood is hard, strong, and close-grained, and Mr. Watson states that it is the best he knows for cogs of wheels. It is also used for agricultural implements, cotton-wheels, walking-sticks, in turning, and for combs. The crooked timbers are largely used for the knees of boats on the Indus near Attock. On the Chenáb at one place, I found that the twigs are used for the short suspending rope of the *jhúla*—(see PARROTIA)—for which purpose, however, the people said it did not answer well. The leaves are bitter, and are considered one of the best kinds for fodder for goats. The fruit ripens in October, but I think that, as a rule, most of the trees do not yield every year. Elphinstone says that the Sheráwanís eat the fruit, both fresh and dry, but there must be some mistake here, for there is but little fleshy pericarp to eat, even were it pleasant to the taste, which it is not. Oil is nowhere extracted from the fruit so far as I know, but Irvine states it is used for medicine, as does Bellew. In the Agri-Horticultural Society's records is an account of an experiment on a sufficient scale made by bruising the fruit in a common *kolhú* after fermentation, at Kohát (in 1851?). The oil is reported to have been very like European olive oil, burning and tasting well, but the success was hardly sufficient to justify extension of the experiment, as only one gallon of oil was got from a maund of dry fruit. One or two European olive trees were imported into the Punjab long ago, and a good many have been got within the last eighteen months, in order to test the effect of grafting on the Punjab variety, as suggested by Lowther as far back as 1850, which it is to be hoped will be successful. Firminger mentions that the European olive had been introduced into the Calcutta Botanical gardens in 1800, but up to 1864 had not borne fruit. I may note that the native name *ban-kau*, used in parts of Hazára, puzzled me for long, but I have recently found that it is applied to the variety, or rather those specimens in which the under-surface of the leaf is rust-coloured (whence the name proposed by Royle, who considered this a distinct species).

SYRINGA EMODI. Wall.

Vernacular. C. *bán phúnt, ban dákhúr, júarí.* R. *kármar, banchír.* B. *chímú. (?)* S. *sháfrí, dúdla, loltí, rang chúl.*

A shrub occurring at many places in the Punjab Himalaya at 7,000 to 11,000 feet up to the Indus, and collected by Bellew at

9,000 feet near the Sufêd Koh. The wood is white and close-grained, and carves well. The leaves are eaten by goats.

S. PERSICA. L. var. B. LACINIATA. Vahl.?

Vernacular. K. *hídsmín.*

A shrub cultivated in some of the gardens on the Kashmír lake seems to be var. LACINIATA of this. I found what I think is var. INTEGRIFOLIA of the same species, growing wild in Wazíristán on the eastern skirts of the Súlimán Range at 8,000 feet.

N. O. JASMINEÆ.

JASMINUM GRANDIFLORUM. L.
J. PUBESCENS. Willd.
J. SAMBAC. Ait., &c.

Vernacular. *chamba, chambelí, múgra,* &c.

Cultivated in the plains for their flowers. From these and those of the other species a perfumed water is prepared in a similar way to rosewater.

J. OFFICINALE. L.
J. REVOLUTUM. Sims; and var. PUBIGERUM.

Vernacular. J. K. *chamba.* C. *sím, rí.* S. *shíng, púring, martí.* T. I. *naugei.* Plains, *jái.*

Both are cultivated in gardens, and grow wild in the Himalaya, the former from 3,500 to 8,500 feet, the latter to 6,000 feet, and they are found Trans-Indus. Honigberger states that the root of the former is believed to be useful in ringworm.

NYCTANTHES ARBOR TRISTIS. L.

Vernacular. C. *ladúrí.* R. *pakúra.* B. U. *kúrí.* Gardens, *harsinghár.*

A tall shrub which grows wild in the Siwálik tract up to the Chenáb, and is occasionally cultivated in the plains. The wood is only used for fuel; the flowers give a transient yellow dye.

N. O. APOCYNACEÆ.

CARISSA CARANDAS. L.

Vernacular. *karaunda.*

A large shrub which is not much cultivated in the Punjab plains. Its fruit is made into pickle by natives (and makes a very good jelly).

C. DIFFUSA. Rox.

Vernacular. *gan, garna, garinda.*

A shrub which is common along the Siwálik tract and in the outer hills to 2,500 feet up to the Indus, and in the eastern Punjab extends into the plains to the south of Dehlí and Ambála. The small flowers vary from white to pinkish, and have a fine scent, which about April perfumes the air around. Goats and sheep eat the leaves. The cut bushes are employed for fences, and the wood is used for combs, in turning, &c., and as fuel. A Kángra authority states that the very old wood gets quite black and fragrant, and is sold at a high price as *aggar*, or *úd Hindí*, an officinal wood generally referred to ALOEXYLON AGGALOCHUM, which is given as a tonic and cholagogue.

HOLARRHENA ANTIDYSENTERICA. Wall. (WRIGHTEA. R. Br.)

Vernacular. C. *kogar*. R. B. *kawar*. U. *kúra*. Bazár, seed, *indarjáu*.

A milky-juiced large shrub or small tree which is common in parts of the Siwálik tract up to the Chenáb. The leaves appear to be used as fodder (or litter)? The wood is white, light, and close-grained, and is cut into spoons, combs, &c. The seeds are officinal, being considered febrifuge, and in some parts of India (but not in the Punjab so far as I know) the bark also is given for fever.

NERIUM ODORUM. Soland.

Vernacular. C. *kanira*. R. *ganhíra*. B. *kanira*. T. I. *gandere*. Per., *kharzahra*. S. R. *kanira, ganira*. Plains generally, *kaner*.

Commonly cultivated in gardens for its flowers, and grows wild in the plains Trans-Indus, in the Salt Range, along the Siwálik tract, and in the outer hills, up to 3,500 feet. The stalks are in some places said to make hookah tubes. The leaves are considered poisonous (whence the Persian name ass-poisoner), but are said to be eaten by goats. In some parts they are given dried for colic, and Bellew states that in powder they are used as an errhine in neuralgia, &c.; the root is poisonous. In Kángra I am informed that the bark and root of this plant furnish the poison most frequently used by suicides. From the bark a wash is made for curing itch and destroying vermin.

Rhazya stricta. Dne.

Vernacular. S. R. *vena*. T. I. *gandera*. Bazár, fruit, *sanwár*.

A small shrub somewhat resembling the last (whence the Pushtú name), which grows abundantly in many places Trans-Indus, and occurs in the Salt Range at low elevations. The dried branches are used as fuel. The leaves are given as food to goats after steeping for some days. They are also bruised and given with milk to children for eruptions, and an infusion of them is stated to be good for sore throat. The fruit and upper leaves were sent as officinal to the Punjab Exhibition in 1863, being considered efficacious in cases of boils and eruptions.

Vinca rosea. L.

Vernacular. *rattanjot*.

This species is cultivated in the plains. It is mentioned as *rattanjot*—(see Onosma)—under the name of V. minor by Honigberger, and certain medical properties attributed to it.

Wrightea mollissima. Wall.

Vernacular. B. *kiláwa*.

A large shrub occasional in the Siwálik tract, sometimes to 3,500 feet, up to near the Indus, though very rare west of the Biás. The wood is a yellowish white, light, and soft, and does well for turning, carving, &c. For combs it is taken as far as Umritsur.

N. O. ASCLEPIADEÆ.

Boucerosia Aucheri. Dne.

Vernacular. *charúnglí, chúngí*. T. I. *pawanne, pamanke, panjangusht* (Per.)

This is doubtless the "stapelioides eaten as a vegetable," mentioned by Griffith as found in the Khyber, and Masson's medicinal "lichen" got Trans-Indus (page 80, Volume 2). It is found in the western part of the outer Himalaya, in the Salt Range, and Trans-Indus, to 3,000 feet. Its juicy stems, about 4 or 5 inches long, are in bunches somewhat resembling fingers (whence some of its names), and have a very bitter taste like *karela*—(see Momordica). They are said to be sometimes cooked like it, but are generally eaten raw, being considered stomachic, carminative, and tonic. Bellew states that Trans-Indus they are also used as vermifuge, and Masson mentions that dried and powdered they are taken as stimulants.

B. EDULIS. Edge.

Vernacular. S. S. D., &c., *chúng, pippú, pippá.* S. P. *sitún.*

I have not seen live specimens of this, but it is not uncommon in the arid tract from the Salt Range southward to the boundary of the Punjab (and in Sind, Edgeworth). Its stems are longer and thinner than those of the former, and the natives say they are less bitter and somewhat saline tasted, but more powerful. Coldstream states that they have a pleasant sub-acid taste. They are largely eaten by the poorer classes as a relish to farinaceous food, and may sometimes be seen for sale in the Bazárs of the southern Punjab.

CALOTROPIS PROCERA. R. Br. (C. HAMILTONII. Wight.)

Vernacular. *ak.* (Hi. *ák, mudár*). T. I. *spulmei, spalmak, pashkand.* Bazár, manna, *shakar ul ashar, shakar al tighál.*

This plant, which is Masson's "milky EUPHORBIA," is found also in Palestine, Arabia, &c., and in Abyssinia. It is common in many places throughout the Punjab plains up to Peshawar, and occurs to 3,500 feet Trans-Indus. In the extreme east it does not appear to reach the same size as near Sirsa, north of Dehra Ismail Khan, and in parts of Montgomery and Múltán, where it is often seen in quantity, of 15 inches girth and 10 or 12 feet high, "quite arboreous," as Edgeworth remarks, mentioning that it reaches 18 inches girth. In Central Sind, however, it grows still larger, and I have there seen trunks of 4 and 5 feet girth, though not taller than the largest Punjab specimens. If the plant was less common, the flowers would be considered both handsome and curious; they exhale a strong and not unpleasant scent at times. In Sind the bark of the plant is stripped off, and by the dry process is made into halters for cattle, painters for boats, nets, and fishing lines, which are said to be very durable. In 1854, a sample of this textile material was sent to the Bombay Chamber of Commerce, which reported favorably of its strength and fineness, but nothing further appears to have been done. At Leia and Jhang, experiments were made on it about the year 1852, (?) and the twine produced was reported very strong. The silky floss of the seeds is in some parts used to stuff pillows, and hopes of its becoming an important textile material have at various times arisen. The fibre, however, is very short, and, under the microscope, quite smooth, so that it is not likely to prove of much value, and experience has confirmed this. In 1863, seven hundred pounds of this floss were sent from the Punjab to England to a mercantile firm, for whom it was spun into thread and worked up. But it was reported on as unsuited for ordinary machinery, and very weak, so as to be worth only 3¾ pence per ℔. in England, whereas it had cost for collecting and carriage to Sukkur nearly 5 pence per ℔., so that thus far there is no chance for it. All parts of the plant abound with an acrid milky juice, which is stated to be used by the Rájpúts to destroy their surplus daughters. It is rubbed on leather to "remove its odour" and to clean it, and Bellew mentions that in the Peshawar Valley it is employed in the preparation of catgut, and used for raising blisters and discussing chronic tumours. He also states that the fresh root, used as a tooth-brush, is considered by Patháns to cure toothache. Irvine mentions that some part of the plant is employed in dyeing, but I have no further information as to this. He also notes that charcoal is made from the stems. The bark of the root is used by natives in medicine, and has frequently been tested by European practitioners, who find that its effects are very similar to those of ipecacuan. The manna, which I have never seen on the plant, and which is said to be brought from the east, is officinal, and used in medicine like other kinds of manna.

Ceropegia esculenta. Edge.

Vernacular. *galot.*

This plant, I believe I have not met with, but Edgeworth mentions that its tubers and acid leaves are used as a vegetable in Múltán (and Sind).

Dæmia extensa. R. Br.

Vernacular. *karíal, siáli, trotú.*

A climber occasionally found in the Salt Range and Trans-Indus. It is browsed by goats.

Marsdenia Roylii. Wight.

Vernacular. C. *pathor.* S. R. *tar, verí.*

A climber found in the outer hills and in the Salt Range at 2,000 to 4,000 and occasionally to 8,000 feet. The unripe fruit is in some places powdered and given as a cooling medicine, and Madden and Jameson mention that excellent fishing lines are made from the fibre of the plant.

ORTHANTHERA VIMINEA. Wight.

Vernacular. B. *mattí.* T. I. *mowá, lánebar.* D. *khip.* (Sind, *kip*).

A twiggy leafless plant not uncommon about Dehlí, and I think in some other parts Cis-Indus, occasional in the Siwálik tract, and Trans-Indus. Jameson mentions that the fibres are well fitted for cordage, and near Dehlí, after four or five days steeping, its fibre is extracted for making rope. In Sind also it appears to be this plant of which the unsteeped stalks are made into ropes for Persian wheels, which are said to be very durable, as they do not readily rot from moisture.

OXYSTELMA ESCULENTA. R. Br.

Vernacular. R. D. *gharot, ganí.*

A slender climber not uncommon in the arid tracts of the central and southern Punjab. The fruit is eaten.

PENTATROPIS SPIRALIS. Dne. (P. MICROPHYLLA. W. and A.)

Vernacular. T. I. *ambarvel.* B. D. *van verí.* Bazár, flower, *ark pushpí.*

A slender climber found in the central Punjab. In spring the people state that tubers, which grow on its root to a couple of ounces each, are peeled and eaten, being "sweet" and filling. (There may here have been some confusion with CEROPEGIA q. v.) The flowers of this apparently are officinal in the Punjab under the above name.

PERIPLOCA APHYLLA. Dne.

Vernacular. J. C. *báta.* T. I. S. S. D. *barrarra, barre.*

A plant with leafless erect stems, common in many places Trans-Indus, and in the Salt Range, and occurring in the outer hills east to the Chenáb, occasionally up to 3,500 feet. In parts of the Peshawar Valley it is so common as to be used for fuel. It is eaten by goats. In various places the buds are eaten raw, or cooked as a vegetable; and, on one occasion, I was informed that as food they are considered to have a beneficial effect on wounds!

VINCETOXICUM CANESCENS. Dne. (V. VULGARE. Rœm. and Sch.?)

Vernacular. R. *tranna.*

Not uncommon in parts of the western Punjab Himalaya from 5,000 to 9,500 feet. In some places the natives commend its *khúshbo* (perfume), which is really a rank heavy smell given out when it is bruised.

V. OFFICINALE. MŒNCH. (V. VULGARE. R. and S.)

Vernacular.

V. VULGARE is stated by Honigberger to be officinal in Kashmír. It may be this or the preceding, as both grow there.

N. O. GENTIANACEÆ.

AGATHOTES SP.
OPHELIA ALATA. Griseb. O. AUGUSTIFOLIA. Don., and O. CHIRATA. Griseb.
SWERTIA SP.

Vernacular. K. *búí*. Bazár, plant, *chirreta, kasb ul zaríra, hátmúl, harúntútia.*

I shall not attempt to distinguish between these, which are slender plants of the Gentian order, many of which grow at moderate heights in the Punjab Himalaya, several of them being exported to the plains for use in medicine. *Chiretta* has undoubtedly tonic and febrifuge properties, is largely used by natives, and occasionally by Europeans. Honigberger supposes *harúntútíya* to be from one of these—(see COLCHICUM SP.)

GENTIANA DECUMBENS. L.

Vernacular. ?

Common at considerable elevations in the various parts of the Punjab Himalaya. A tincture of it has been used as a stomachic by the Lahoul Missionaries.

G. KURROO. Wall.

Vernacular. J. *nílkant.* C. *nílkant, kamal phul.* B. *nílakil.* Bazár, root, *karrú.*

This, which has a handsome blue flower, is common on rather sunny slopes in many places in the Punjab Himalaya at from 8,000 to 9,000 feet. Locally its root is used as a toric and febrifuge, or given to cattle in inflammations, and it is exvorted to the plains in some quantity, constituting part of the oficinal *karrú*—(see PICRORRHIZA)—which is given in ascites, &c., and also applied externally.

G. TENELLA FRIES.

Vernacular. Lad. *títa.*

Found in various parts of the Punjab Himalaya up to 15,000 feet in Ladák. Aitchison states that in Lahoul a decoction of the leaves and stems of this and other species is given in fevers. In Ladák its root is put into spirits.

VILLARSIA NYMPHOIDES. Vent. (LIMNANTHEMUM. Link.)

Vernacular. K. *kúrú, khair posh, gul jafari purnka.*

Common in the lakes of Kashmír, where it is very largely used for fodder. Honigberger states that the milk of cows is increased by feeding on it.

N. O. BIGNONIACEÆ.

AMPHICOME ARGUTA. Royle. (INCARVILLEA. Royle.)
A. EMODI. Royle. (INCARVILLEA. Wall.)

Vernacular. S. *chalí.*

These probably constitute one species which occurs locally Trans-Indus, in the Siwálik tract, and in the valleys of some of the rivers from 2,000 up to 5,000 feet, and on the Sutlej to 8,000 feet. It is of no use that I know of, but has perhaps the finest flower of our Punjab herbs, and generally occupies striking habitats, hanging with its handsome green leaves and pinkish trumpet flowers from the face of perpendicular cliffs.

BIGNONIA INDICA. L. (CALOSANTHES. Blume.)

Vernacular. C. *mulín, sorí.* R. B. *tát moráng, tát palang.* Bazár, leaves, *síonak. ?*

A small tree growing in the Siwálik tract up to the Chenáb. The timber is said to be soft, spongy, and useless. It has an enormous flat pod-like fruit resembling a scimetar, filled with seeds having very broad membranaceous wings. These are in some places applied to abscesses, and elsewhere are said to be given in hemicrania. The officinal *síonak* of the Punjab Bazárs appears to be the leaves of this tree.

B. SUAVEOLENS. Rox. (STEREOSPERMUM. DC.)

Vernacular. R. *pádal, kaltháun, summe.*

This, which, under favorable circumstances, grows to be a large tree with an useful timber, extends sparingly in the Siwálik tract up to the Rávi. Its wood is used for charcoal.

TECOMA UNDULATA. G. Don. (BIGNONIA. Rox.)

Vernacular. *rohíra, lahúra, lúár.* T. I. *regdáwan, reodán, rebdún.*

A small stiff-looking tree occurring locally, chiefly in the arid tracts from Dehlí westward through Harriána, and the central Punjab to the Salt Range and Trans-Indus, where it occurs up to 2,500 or 3,000 feet. Edgeworth also mentions it in the Siwálik tract opposite Ambála, and Dr. Jameson found a specimen close to the Biás below Kángra (and Hardwicke first found it near Cawnpúr). This has perhaps the handsomest flower of any indigenous Punjab tree, and its gorgeous orange blossoms make quite a show in some parts in the west of the Province about April; in the east their colour appears to be much more faint. Trees of 4 and 5 feet girth are not uncommon; and in Sirsa, near the Sutlej, I saw a group of a score up to 7 or 8 feet girth and 40 feet high. The leaves vary greatly in size, upon which circumstance chiefly Dr. Henderson is inclined to make two varieties of the tree. The foliage is browsed by cattle. The wood is hard, close-grained, and strong, but is rarely large or abundant enough to be much used except for natives' ordinary work.

N. O. SESAMEÆ.

MARTYNIA DIANDRA. Glox.

Vernacular. *bíchú?* Bazár, fruit, &c., *hathajorí.*

This plant is only known in gardens in the Punjab (but is naturalized in several places in and near the Siwálik tract of Rohilkund). Its fruit is officinal in the Punjab Bazárs.

SESAMUM INDICUM. L.

Vernacular. *til.*

Is grown alone (or sometimes mixed) as a hot-weather crop, but rarely in the western Punjab, except in the hills, where I have frequently seen it at 2,500 and occasionally at 5,000 feet. Thomson observed it in Kashmír at the latter elevation. The seeds are sometimes eaten parched, and are put in sweetmeats, but are mostly used for the oil, which is sweet and largely consumed in food. The oil-cake is given to cattle, and sometimes used by the poor as food when mixed with flour. The seeds are also officinal, being considered diuretic, but are said to injure digestion.

N. O. CONVOLVULACEÆ.

BATATAS EDULIS. Chois. (CONVOLVULUS BATATAS. L.)

Vernacular. *shakarkand.*

Is commonly cultivated (in the cold weather) in the eastern part of the Punjab plains. The root is eaten as a vegetable.

CONVOLVULUS ARVENSIS. L.

Vernacular. *verí ?* Bazár, plant, *hiranpadí.*

An abundant weed all over the plains of the Punjab, and to 10,000 feet in the Punjab Himalaya. The officinal *hiranpadí* (deer's foot) appears to be this plant.

C. PLURICAULIS. Chois.

Vernacular. *porprang, gorakh pánw, baphallí, dodak.*

A common plant in many places throughout the Punjab plains. It is eaten by cattle, and is reckoned cooling, and used as a vegetable or given in *sharbat.*

EVOLVULUS ALSINOIDES. L.

Vernacular. Bazár, plant, *sankh pushpí.*

Common in many parts of the Punjab plains. The plant appears to be the officinal *sankh pushpí* of the Bazárs.

IPOMŒA REPTANS. Poir.

Vernacular. C. *ganthian.* B. D. *nárí, nálí.*

An aquatic plant, common in parts of the eastern and central Punjab. It is frequently eaten as a vegetable by the poorer classes, and in places its root also appears to be eaten.

I. SESSILIFLORA. Roth.

Vernacular. *bhánwar.*

Occurs sparingly in the plains up to the western frontier. It is one of the plants which in Indian famines is eaten.

I. TURPETHUM. Br.

Vernacular. *chita bánsa ?* Bazár, root, *turbud, nisot.*

Bellew states that this is indigenous in the Peshawar Valley, but I have no knowledge of it nearly so far west. He mentions that the stems are considered demulcent and laxative. The root is officinal, and considered beneficial in diseases of the mucous membrane, in leprosy and paralysis.

PHARBITIS NIL. Chois.

Vernacular. J. *bildí, ker.* C. *kirpáwa.* B. *phaprú ság.* Bazár, seed, *káládána.*

Not uncommon in the Siwálik tract and outer hills occasionally to 5,000 feet, up to near the Indus. The seeds are purgative, and are found in all Bazárs. This appears to be the plant which, when young, is used on the Biás as a pot-herb.

CUSCUTA MACRANTHA. Don. (C. REFLEXA var. GRANDIFLORA. Wall. ?)

Vernacular. J. *níla thárí.* C. *ámil.*

I have allowed my species of CUSCUTA to get into confusion, but this appears to be common in the Punjab Himalaya from 6,000 to 9,000 feet, up to the Indus. It is found on POPULUS, SALIX, SPIRÆA, LONICERA, DESMODIUM, URTICA, and POLYGONUM. Like some of the other species it exhales a very strong scent at times. It is eaten by cattle and goats. Edgeworth mentions that the mountaineers believe that crows pluck sprigs of this (and C. ANGUINA, Edge.) to drop into water, when they become snakes, and so furnish food for them. Madden states that the natives promise boundless wealth to him who finds the root of it, while others again believe that the possession of its root will confer the gift of invisibility.

C. PEDICELLATA. Led.

Vernacular. K. *kwiklapot, zránd.* C. *amlú.*

This is found on MORUS, LEPTOPUS, PLECTRANTHUS, POLYGONUM, ARTEMISIA, &c., in Kashmír, &c., from 4,000 to 5,000 feet, and was got in Affghánistán by Bellew on TAMARISK, ALHAGI, and PEGANUM.

C. PLANIFLORA. Ten.

Vernacular. ?

Edgeworth found this in fields of Kashmír lucerne, at Googaira, in Montgomery, and it is common in Lahoul and Ladák up to 11,000 feet, growing on CARUM, ARTEMISIA CINEREA, and A. PARVIFLORA, SOLENANTHUS, and PEROWSKIA.

C. REFLEXA. Rox.

Vernacular. J. *andal.* K. *midasat.* C. *andal, baunde.* B. *ghásvel, mínjrí, satrawala, alellú.* T. I. *zarbútei, banausha, parwattí.* S. R. *níra tár.* Plains generally, *níla tárí, níradhár.* Bazár, seed, *ákás bel, áftimún, kasús.*

This is common in the Punjab plains, generally on ZIZYPHUS or ADHATODA VASICA, and less often on DALBERGIA, POPULUS EUPHRATICA, or FICUS CARICOIDES. In the hills it appears to grow to 9,000 feet on SPIRÆA, SAMBUCUS, INDIGOFERA, CARDUUS, SALVIA, and NEPETA, &c. The flowers have a pleasant and powerful scent. In various parts the seeds are boiled and put over the stomach as a carminative, and bruised for washing the head, or bruised or burned they are applied as anodyne. They are also officinal as *ákásbel* or *aftímún,* which is given in cold infusion as a depurative, and they constitute part at least of the *kasús* of drug-sellers, given as a purgative and cholagogue.

N. O. BORAGINEÆ.

ARNEBIA ECHIOIDES. A. DC.

Vernacular. *paighambarí phúl* or *gúl, sparlei gúl, mumanní.*

This plant is mentioned by Burnes as "a violet" under its most common native name "prophet's flower," "probably so called on account of its fine odour." I have only seen it in the northern Trans-Indus, where it is common, but to no great elevation. It is liked by the Patháns on account of its delightful scent, and is also held in veneration by them, as the five dark marks on the corolla are said to be those of Mahomed's fingers.

A. HISPIDISSIMA. DC.

Vernacular.

This small plant is chiefly remarkable for its great range. It is common in the plains of the central and eastern Punjab and N. W. Provinces, and a species found in Lahoul 9,500 and Tibet 16,000 feet appears to be the same.

CORDIA MYXA. L. (C. LATIFOLIA. ROX.)

Vernacular. *lasora, lasiára.*

A tree which grows wild in the Siwálik tract up to the Rávi, and is commonly planted in the plains and outer hills up to 3,500 or 4,000 feet. The wood in Kángra is said to be white and soft, and is mostly used for fuel. The leaves are used for fodder and for plates. The astringent viscous fruit is eaten by natives, and is used for the marking nut (SEMECARPUS q. v.), though its colour is transient. It is also officinal, being given for coughs, &c., and in Sind is employed in the distillation of spirits. In Sind also fuse is prepared from the bark of this tree.

C. ROTHII. R. and S. (C. AUGUSTIFOLIA. Rox.)

Vernacular. *gondní, gondí.*

This small tree with a small viscous fruit and worthless wood is common planted in the central and eastern Punjab plains, and occurs up to the Indus.

C. VESTITA. Hf. and T. (C. INCANA. Royle.) (GYNAION VESTITUM. DC.)

Vernacular. B. *kúmbí.* S. R. *karúk.*

A small tree, rare in the Siwálik tract nearly as far as the Jhelam. One or two trees (probably planted) are seen on Tilla in the Salt Range to 3,000 feet. Where the tree is common (N. W. Provinces Siwáliks, &c.,) the wood is valued for wheel-work. The fruit is eaten, and said to be sweet.

CYNOGLOSSUM MICRANTHUM. Desf.

Vernacular. Bazár, plant, *nílakrái.*

This officinal plant appears to be the above, which grows in and near the plains in the N. W. Punjab, and to 7,000 feet in the hills.

EHRETIA ASPERA. Rox.

Vernacular. R. *gín.* B. *chamarr.* T. I. *maraghúne, kharawúne, khabarra, tutíri, lor.* S. R. *saggar, ganger, barí kander.* S. S. D. *chambal.* Plains generally, *chamror.*

A small tree not uncommon in the Siwálik tract, Salt Range, and Trans-Indus, to 2,500 feet, and occasional in the plains throughout. Edgeworth states that the timber is much valued for its hardness, but I have not heard this from natives. The bark is said to be ground and mixed with flour and eaten in times of dearth.

E. SERRATA. Rox.

Vernacular. J. *súm.* R. *kálthaun.* Generally, *púnná.*

A small tree frequent in parts of the Punjab Siwálik tract and in the outer hills, occasionally to 5,000 feet, up to near the Indus. Its timber is said to be tolerably strong and durable, and to be used for house-building, implements, &c.

HELIOTROPIUM BREVIFOLIUM. Wall.

Vernacular. T. I. *kharai, tindu.* S. R. *sufêd bhangra.* Bazar, plant, *chiti phúl, gorakh pánw.*

A small plant common in many parts of the Punjab plains. It is officinal under the above names.

H. EUROPÆUM. L.

Vernacular. T. I. *níl kattei.* S. S. D. *bîthúa.* B. D. *atwîn, popat búti.* Generally, *gidar tamákú.*

Not uncommon throughout the Punjab plains. A yellow-flowered variety (?) grows in parts of the Peshawar Valley. The plant bruised is emetic, and is also given after snake-bite.

H. RAMOSISSIMUM. Sieb.
H. STRIGOSUM. Willd.
H. UNDULATUM. Vahl.

Vernacular. *pîpat-buti.* Bazar, plant, *jati misák.*

These are found in several places of the Punjab plains, &c., and one or other is in some places given after snake-bite, and with tobacco oil is applied to the bite itself. Is also officinal under the above name.

MACROTOMIA BENTHAMI. DC.??

Vernacular. ?

Found at 10—12,000 feet on the Pír Punjal and elsewhere. It is collected as medicine, being considered useful in diseases of the tongue and throat.

M. EUCHROMA. Hf. and T. (LITHOSPERMUM EUCHROMON. Royle.)

ONOSMA ECHIODES. L.

Vernacular. C. *rattanjot, koame, moghst.* R. *ratmundî.* S. *khomiye, kháme, bocho.* Bazar, root, *rattanjot ;* leaves, *gaozabán ;* flowers, *gul gaozubán.*

I have unfortunately confused these very different plants, which grow in the more arid regions of the Himalaya to 10,000 and in Tibet to 16,000 feet, and the latter at least occurs down to near the plains level Trans-Indus. The bruised root of one or other or both is locally applied to eruptions, and is sent to the plains as the officinal *rattanjot*—(see POTENTILLA NEPALENSIS)—which is also used in dyeing wool. Royle assigned *rattanjot* to LITHOSPERMUM VESTITUM (and see GERANIUM NODOSUM). In Lahoul, Spiti, and Kanáwar, it is used by the Lambas to stain images, and as a red dye for cloth, being applied with *ghí* or the acid of apricots. The seeds were many years ago sent as those of an ANCHUSA to the Agri-Horticultural Society, Lahore, for trial, but apparently without result. The leaves of the latter appear to be most of the officinal *gauzabán*—(see TRICHODESMA SP.)—used as an alterative, and its flowers are apparently those sold by the drug-sellers under the same name, as stimulant and cardiac. Davies' Trade Report states that 25 maunds of *gauzabán*, and one maund of *guligauzabán*, are annually imported viâ Peshawar from Affghánistán.

SOLENANTHUS SP.

Vernacular. J. *lendí*. C. *lenwa*; root, *mutín*. Lad. *shomá*, *dimmuk*.

Found in parts of the basins of the Chenab and Jhelam at 4,000 to 10,000 and in Ladák up to 16,000 feet. The pounded root is applied to abscesses, and appears to be exported to the plains, although I have not identified it with any drug from the Bazárs.

TRICHODESMA INDICUM. R. Br.

Vernacular. J. *andusí*. S. R. *kaurí búti*. Bazar, leaves, *ratmúndí*.

Common in many parts of the Punjab plains and occasionally found to 4,500 feet in the hills. Locally it is used as a cooling medicine, and its leaves are officinal under the above name, a cold infusion being considered depurative.

T. SP.

Vernacular. T. I. *parbúr pání*.

Four species, two from Affghánistán about 6,000 or 7,000 feet, by Bellew, and two I found on the rocky mounts at Chiniot on the Chenáb, resemble each other very strongly, especially in their extremely harsh leaves. Part of the officinal *gauzabán*—(see ONOSMA)—consists in the Punjab of the leaves of one or other of these.

N. O. SOLANACEÆ.

ATROPA BELLADONNA. L.

Vernacular. S. *súchí*.

A plant found wild in Kanáwar at 8,500 feet appears to be this. There it is stated to be burned in order to kill fleas.

CAPSICUM ANNUUM. L. Red pepper.

Vernacular. K. *matitsa wángrú*. C. and plains, &c., *lál mirch, marcha*.

Commonly cultivated for its fruit, used as a condiment, in the plains throughout, in Kashmír, &c., and on the Chenáb to 6,500 feet. When grown at the greater altitudes, it is said to be more pungent than that of the plains. The fruit is also used medicinally in plasters; and taken in cholera, and to counteract bad climate.

DATURA STRAMONIUM. L. (D. ALBA. Nees.)

Vernacular. K. *tattúr, dattúr*. Plains, &c., generally, *dhatúra*.

Not uncommon in waste ground near houses in the plains throughout, and up to 9,000 feet in the Himalayas, and mentioned by Griffith in Affghánistán. Its seeds are used in poisoning, and are given medicinally in asthmatic complaints, being sometimes smoked with tobacco thus, and for vicious indulgence. The leaves are applied to boils and ulcers, and are also smoked with tobacco for asthma.

HYOSCYAMUS NIGER. L.

Vernacular. C. *dandúra, bazrbang*. R. *dentúrú*. S. *datúra, súra*. T. I. *damtúra, bangidiwána*. Bazár, seed, *bazr ul banj*.

Frequent in waste ground near houses, from 5,000 to 10,000 feet in the Punjab Himalaya, where it is stated on first-rate authority to be eaten by cattle. The seeds are on the Sutlej said to be poisonous, and are officinal in the plains for their narcotic effects.

LYCIUM EUROPÆUM. L.

Vernacular. B. D. *kangú, kúngú, ganger*. H. *mrál*. D. *chirchitta*.

A small thorny shrub not uncommon in the drier tracts of the Punjab plains from Dehlí west to the Súlimán Range. The plant is browsed by camels, goats, &c., and is used for fuel and wattling. The berries are eaten in some places, and are used medicinally as aphrodisiac.

L. Ruthenicum. Marr.

Vernacular. Lad. *khíchar, kitsarma.*

Resembles the last, and is common in parts of Ladák from 10,000 to 14,000 feet. The fruit is eaten, but is very mawkish.

Nicotiana rustica. L. Latakia tobacco.

Vernacular. J. *Chilási tamákú.* C. *kakkar t.* Lad. *tamákú.* Plains, *kakkar t., Kandahári t., Kalkatti t.*

The existence of this species in India appears not to have been suspected till in the spring of 1865 I discovered that it is grown in considerable quantities about Lahore, sometimes equal in area to the ordinary kind. Subsequent enquiries have elicited, that, under various names, it is cultivated at many other places in the Punjab, Múltán, Hoshiárpúr, Dehlí, Harriána, &c.; also in the Gangetic Doáb, Oudh, &c., and quite recently what appears to be this species is reported to the Agri-Horticultural Society of India, as grown to some extent in Cooch Bahar, Rungpúr, and Assam. I have also seen it cultivated in some quantity in Pangí on the Upper Chenáb from 7,500 to 9,400 feet, in Khágán and on the Kishenganga in the Jhelam basin from 3,300 to 4,500 feet, and in Ladák at 10,500 feet. I have not certainly identified it in Kashmír, but there is some evidence that it is grown in parts of the valley (5,000 feet) about Islámabád, &c. The accounts in most of these localities agree that more of it than of the ordinary kind can be grown per acre, especially as in many places the flowers of it are not plucked off, but are mixed with the leaves for smoking, and that it brings a larger price than the ordinary species. It is said to be much stronger than the latter, and to be generally smoked mixed with a large proportion of it. Its qualities, when smoked in the European pipe, give assurance that, if properly cured, it would rival Turkish tobacco. I have hitherto failed to discover how it reached India. At Sahâranpur, where it was known as N. quadrivalvis, there are two statements given—one, that its seed had been brought from Kábul by a Captain Lawson or by Affghán merchants for Falconer, another, that it had been got from Calcutta in Griffith's time; nor can I get any definite information as to its source from the Agri-Horticultural Society, Calcutta. Towards the east its name would indicate a Calcutta origin; towards the west the names Kandahári and Chilási would suggest that it came from the other direction.

Whencesoever it spread it would appear to have reached the Punjab very long ago, or it could hardly have penetrated to near the centre of the Himalaya in Lahoul; and yet it must still be spreading, for in one district a complaint was made to the Magistrate that a plant was being sold for tobacco which was something quite different.

N. Tabacum. Tobacco.

Vernacular. *támákú.*

This is the common species which is largely cultivated, in good soil and with plenty of water and manure, all over the plains, in the Himalaya up to 7,400 feet at least on the Chenáb, to 11,000 feet on the Sutlej (Hoffmeister), and in Affghánistán. Aitchison states that none is grown in Lahoul, and I certainly saw none so far up. Moorcroft mentions that tobacco is cultivated in a few gardens in Ladák—(see N. rustica)—but a good deal is probably imported thither, as Cayley gives 32 maunds as taken to Lê from Kashmír in 1867. Davies' Trade Report states that 7,500 maunds of tobacco are annually brought from Affghánistán viâ Peshawar, and 440 maunds, as well as 50 maunds of snuff, by the Bolán. But in return, the Peshawar snuff being famous, Bellew mentions that much of it is carried to Kábul, &c. In the plains the chief harvest of it takes place in spring, but in some places, under favorable conditions, it is cultivated all the year. It may be noted that among the Patháns, as well as in Kanáwar (Hoffmeister notes this), and in Ladák, it is not uncommon in default of a pipe to improvise one by two small holes formed in the ground and connected by a little tunnel.

Physalis Indica. Lam. (Nicandra Indica. R. and S. N. physalodes. Gært.)

Vernacular. Bazár, fruit, *habbí káknaj.*

So far as I am aware, this is not cultivated in the Punjab, but the fruit is officinal in the Bazárs, being considered tonic, diuretic, and purgative. It is probable that Honigberger is wrong in attributing this to P. alkekengi L. So far as the Punjab is concerned, Birdwood is quite mistaken in ascribing *káknaj* to Withania coagulans (q. v.)

P. sp.

Vernacular. *rangolí.*

With a large inflated, coloured calyx, not uncommon wild in parts of the Jhelam basin, where its fruit is eaten.

SCOPOLIA PRÆALTA. Dun. (BELENIA P. Dne.)

Vernacular. C. *sholar, bajar bang, lang tang, nandrú. dandorwa.* Lad. *lang thang.* T. I. *khardag.*

Common in waste ground in parts of the Chenab basin from 6,800 to 9,500 feet, in Zanskar and Spiti, and to 16,000 feet in Tibet, and apparently found sparingly Trans-Indus in the plains, and perhaps the same plant in one place near Lahore. In the hills the leaves are applied to boils, and are also said to be poison, the mouth swelling from their touch, and the head and throat being affected when they are eaten. A man was poisonously affected by eating the plant gathered in the Lahore habitat, and the Negí of Lahoul, when at Lê in 1867, suffered from its narcotic effects for two or three days, some of its leaves having been gathered by mistake with his *ság.* At the same time they can hardly be very poisonous to all animals, for in Lahoul they are browsed by cattle. In a recent communication to the Agri-Horticultural Society of India, Dr. Christison of Edinburgh states that this has the same property of dilating the pupils as Belladonna.

SOLANUM DULCAMARA. L.

Vernacular. Bazár, leaves, &c., *rúba barík.*

This occurs in the Punjab Himalaya at 7,000 to 7,500 feet. Its leaves, &c., (or those of S. NIGRUM q. v.) are officinal under the above name.

S. GRACILIPES. Dne.

Vernacular. T. I. *howá, marghí pal.* S. R. *kaurí bútí, kandiárí.* S. S. D. *pílak.* B. D. *valúr, patrawála damá.* Bazár, leaves, *gákra.*

A slender straggling thorny plant found Trans-Indus, in the Salt Range, and as far east as Lahore and Montgomery. In some places the small fruit is eaten; in others it is said to be collected by *hakíms* to be applied in otitis. The leaves, &c., are officinal under the above name.

S. LYCOPERSICUM. L. (L. ESCULENTUM. Mill. Tomato.

Vernacular. *wilayatí bengan.*

I am informed that one kind of this, which is generally supposed to have been introduced from America, has for long been cultivated by the natives. It is said to have clustered or much tuberculated fruit, and to have come from Kashmír (? ?)

S. MELONGENA. L.

Vernacular. *bengan.*

Cultivated abundantly in the plains for the large fruit, which is eaten as a vegetable. It is a favourite with natives, but is considered heating and apt to lead to dyspepsia and constipation.

S. NIGRUM. L.

Vernacular. K. *kámbeí.* T. I. *kwan saf safei.* Plains, &c., generally, *káchmách, riaungí.* Bazár, leaves, &c., *rúbabarík?* Fruit, *anbúsálib, mako.*

A common weed throughout the plains and to 9,000 feet in the Himalaya, a pilose variety being not unfrequent. The fruit is commonly eaten, without bad effects, as it is stated to be by children in Sydney, New South Wales. It is also officinal, being given in anasarca, &c. The leaves also of this or S. DULCAMARA (q. v.) are kept by drug-sellers under the above name.

S. SANCTUM. L.

Vernacular. T. I. *maraghúne.* S. R. *barí mauharí, mahorí.* Generally, *tíngí.*

Seen occasionally Trans-Indus, and in the Salt Range, &c., to 4,500 feet. In some places the fruit is eaten fresh and in pickle.

S. TUBEROSUM. L. Potato.

Vernacular. *álú.*

Is now cultivated at a good many places in the plains as a cold weather crop, and abundantly and with still greater success in parts of the hills up to 9,000 feet, but mostly only for Europeans. Khatris, &c., occasionally use them as food, but most classes of natives think they tend to indigestion and flatulence. In some parts of the hills, however, they are largely consumed by natives, being cooked and eaten with buckwheat, &c.

S. VERBASCIFOLIUM. L.

Vernacular. J. *kala mewa.* C. *tiárí.* R. B. *olá.* T. I. *kharawúne.*

A shrub of some size occasional in the Siwálik tract and outer hills to 4,000 feet, and also found Trans-Indus. I do not know of its being used in the Punjab, though in southern India it is cultivated for the fruit, which is used in curries.

S. XANTHOCARPUM. SCHRADER. (S. JACQUINI. Willd.)

Vernacular. *warúmba, kharián maraghúne.* S. R. *chhotí mauharí, mahorí.* S. S. D. *harndulí.* B. D. &c., *kandiárí, mamolí, pílak.* Bazár, fruit, *katela, bat kateya.*

Common throughout the Punjab plains and occasional to 5,000 feet in the outer hills. In some places the seeds are eaten. They are also applied for bruises and in otitis. The fruit likewise is officinal, being bruised and applied for pain.

WITHANIA COAGULANS. Dun.

Vernacular. T. I. *spín bajja, shápiang, khúmazare, makhazura, panír.* S. R. *khamjíra, kútílána.* S. P. *panír.* Bazár, fruit, *akrí, panír.*

A small shrub with light-coloured leathery leaves, which is common Trans-Indus and along the Salt Range (to 4,500 feet), and occurs in the southern Punjab, generally near houses or fields, seldom in the real desert. Griffith and Bellew state that the Affgháns use it for curdling milk to make cheese, whence its Persian name *panírbád* and some of those used in the Punjab. The seeds are considered stomachic about Peshawar, as was first remarked by Masson, and they probably possess anodyne or sedative properties like those of the next species. In home practice they are given to children for colic, and are used in veterinary medicine, and are sold in most Bazárs. Honigberger states that the bitter leaves of this plant are given as a febrifuge by the Lohánís.

W. SOMNIFERA. Dun.

Vernacular. C. *ak.* T. I. *kútílál, sin.* S. R. *aksan.* Bazár, root, *asgand Nagaurí, vaman.*

Is not uncommon in waste ground up to the Súlimán Range, and in the outer hills to 3,500 feet. The plant is browsed by goats, so the leaves, &c., can hardly be dangerously narcotic. In many places the root is given in veterinary practice. It is also officinal, being considered aphrodisiac, and given for lumbar pains, &c. At least one case has occurred in the Punjab in which the root was used with a view to effect criminal abortion, and I learned that in Sind this practice is not uncommon. The second name, under which this is sold, seems to be a corruption of *behman,* with regard to the origin of both red and white kinds of which, as usually sold, we are still quite in the dark. Davies' Trade Report gives 25 maunds as the quantity of both *behmans* annually brought from Affghánistán viâ Peshawar.

DUBIA. *palhára.*

A fine herbaceous plant, reaching 5 or 6 feet in height, found in various places in the Jhelam basin at from 7,000 to 7,500 feet. Goats eat it, but in several places, where its fruit had been by mistake included among pot-herbs, delirium for several days had ensued.

N. O. SCROPHULARIACEÆ.

LANCEA TIBETICA. Hf. and T.

Vernacular. ?

With a blue flower, one of the prettiest of the herbaceous plants of Ladák, where it occurs up to 16,000 feet.

PEDICULARIS HOOKERIANA. Wall.

Vernacular. ?

Aitchison mentions that this grows in Lahoul (9,500 feet) where some part of it is used in medicine.

P. PECTINATA. Wall. (?)

Vernacular. S. *míchren.*

Common in the Punjab Himalaya from 5,000 to 12,000 feet. In Kanáwar the pounded leaves are given for hæmoptysis. This is probably the species which Honigberger says is officinal in Kashmír.

P. TUBIFLORA. Fisch.

Vernacular. ?

A small almost stemless species with a handsome long yellow corolla, which is seen carpeting the ground in places by streams in Ladák up to 15,000 feet.

P. SP.

Vernacular. (?)

Aitchison mentions an unnamed species of Lahoul (9,500 feet) as often having a scent of musk like that of DELPHINIUM BRUNONIANUM (q. v.)

PICRORHIZA KURROOA. Royle.

Vernacular. R. *karrú*. Bazar, root, *karrú, káli kútki*.

Common in the Punjab Himalaya at from 5,500 to 14,000 feet. Honigberger states that it is more frequently used in veterinary than in human medicine, but in the latter its root is one of the regular febrifuges, and is given for ascites and applied in plaster. It must be used in considerable quantity, as 36 maunds of *karrú* are reported as exposed for sale from Kúllú at the Rampúr fair in Bissahir in 1867. Part of the *karrú* sold is the root of GENTIANA KURROO (q. v.), and some of it is possibly produced by other plants. Davies' Trade Report gives 20 maunds of *kútki* as annually exported from Peshawar to Kábul.

SCROPHULARIA KOTSCHYI. Bois.

Vernacular. Lad., *shústi*.

Common in Ladák from 14,000 up to 16,500 feet. It is browsed by goats. but not by *yaks*.

VERBASCUM THAPSUS. L. Mullein.

Vernacular. K. *vúlr, phúl*. C. *ban tamákú, phasrúk, bhún ke dúm*. S. *eklbír, kadanda, phúntar, kwíspre*. T. I. *khargosh, kharkharnár, spín kharnár*. S. R. *gúrganna, karáthrí, rewand chíní*. B. D. *gídar tamákú*.

Not uncommon in the plains, and grows in the Himalaya to 11,000 feet, a white-flowered variety occasionally occurring at the higher elevations. It is eaten by camels, goats, &c. In Bissahir the root is given as a febrifuge. The name *rewand chíní* would seem to indicate that the root is at times used to adulterate or employed for rhubarb—(see RHEUM).

VERONICA BECCABUNGA. L.

Vernacular. (?)

Frequent in the Himalaya at from 5,000 to 9,000 feet. Honigberger states that the plant is officinal in Kashmír.

N. O. OROBANCHACEÆ.

PHELIPÆA CALOTROPIDIS. Walp.

Vernacular. T. I. *khíza, kharlanne, sharíd* (Per.) S. R. *khalátrí, khúrjín*. S. P. *bhúmphor, bhoiphúl*. H. *músal*. (Sind, *bhonphor*).

This was first found near Ambála by Edgeworth, and named from the circumstance that he considers (and the natives sometimes say so also) that it grows only on CALOTROPIS. There is, however, some reason to doubt this. Dr. Henderson and I believe that we have frequently seen it where there was no CALOTROPIS near. At the same time it probably affects that plant most. It grows in sandy places Trans-Indus, in the Salt Range (not over 1,500 feet) in the southern Punjab, and parts of Ambála, Sirsa, &c., east of the Sutlej. Its stem is very succulent and juicy, dry though its habitats are, and it presents a curious appearance with its stem covered with fine flowers an inch and a quarter long bursting through sand (*bhúmphor*, means "earth-splitter") often below bushes. It attains a girth of 6 or 8 inches and a height of 2 or 2½ feet above the surface, and sometimes even exceeds these dimensions. The bruised stem is applied to sores in horses, and in Mozaffargarh the upper part of it is given as fodder to oxen and goats, and less frequently to camels.

N. O. ACANTHACEÆ.

ADHATODA VASICA. Nees.

Vernacular. J. *bhekkar*. K. *pekkar*. C. R. *basúti, basoti*. B. *báshí, basúti*. T. I. *tora bujja*. S. R. *bekkar*. Bazár, leaves, *bánsa sabz*.

A small shrub with a large white flower, common in all the outer hills, occasionally to 4,000 feet, and sometimes even higher in the Salt Range, and east of the Sutlej often seen far out in the plains. Has a strong smell when bruised, whence several of the native names from *bás*, odour. Most animals do not browse on it, and even goats only crop a few leaves. It is frequently used for making the friable charcoal employed for gunpowder. There was a case of suspected poisoning by this plant at Hoshiárpúr within the last two years, but there is no reason to suppose that it *is* poisonous. Bellew states that the leaves are given as a cattle medicine, and to men for rheumatism, and that the fresh flowers are bound over the eyes for ophthalmia. The leaves are officinal at Lahore, being given for coughs, &c.

ÆCHMANTHERA WALLICHII. N. ab E. var. b. GOSSYPINA.

Vernacular. R. *patrang, ban marud*.

There is some doubt about this plant, but it appears to be not uncommon in the Punjab Himalaya from 3,000 to 6,000 feet. Madden states that bees are particularly fond of its flowers, and Jameson mentions that a kind of cloth is made from the tomentum of the leaf.

ASTERACANTHA LONGIFOLIA. Nees.

Vernacular. Bazár, seed, *tal makhána.*

Not uncommon in moist places in the eastern and central parts of the Punjab plains. The seeds are officinal, being given for gonorrhœa.

BARLERIA CRISTATA. L.

Vernacular. J. *tadrelú.* Bazár, leaves, *bánsá siyáh.*

Occurs in the outer hills to 4,000 and occasionally to 5,000 feet, and is found at times Trans-Indus. Madden states that the seeds of this or a similar species are administered for snake-bite. The leaves (apparently of this) are officinal at Lahore, being given for coughs, &c.

DICLIPTERA ROXBURGHII. N. ab E.

Vernacular. J. *kírch.* B. *somní.* Bazár, plant, *lakshmana.*

Not uncommon Trans-Indus, in the Salt Range, in the Siwálik tract, and in the outer Punjab Himalaya occasionally to 6,500 feet. The plant is officinal.

N. O. VERBENACEÆ.

CALLICARPA INCANA. Rox.

Vernacular. J. *pattharman, bá-pattra, baunú.* C. *súmálí.* R. *denthar, drúss.*

A shrub frequent in the outer Himalaya to 4,500 feet. In Hazára the leaves heated are applied to rheumatic joints (whence the name *bá-pattra* from *bá* rheumatism).

CLERODENDRON INFORTUNATUM. L.?

Vernacular. B. *kálí básútí.*

A species, apparently this, occurs in the Siwálik tract and occasionally out in the plains, and it is probably the one that Edgeworth mentions as being used to give fire by friction in the Ambála tract.

C. SIPHONANTHUS. Spr.

Vernacular. B. D. *arní.* Bazár, root, &c., *dawái mubárik.*

Occasionally seen in gardens. Its root and leaves are officinal.

Gmelina arborea. Rox.

Vernacular. *kúmhár, gúmhár.* Bazár, fruit, *kákódúmbarí.*

A tree which occurs wild in the easternmost part of the Punjab Siwálik tract, and is occasionally seen planted in the plains, up to the Chenáb at least. In parts of India, where the tree is common, its wood is reckoned strong and durable, and is much used. The fruit is officinal in the Punjab.

Lippia nodiflora. Rich.

Vernacular. S. R. B. D. *mokna, búkan, jalním,* &c. Bazár, plant, *gorakh mundí.*

Common in and near water all over the Punjab plains, and to 2,000 feet in the hills. The plant is officinal, being considered cooling.

Premna mucronata. Rox.

Vernacular. C. *ganhíla.* R. *gían, bankár.* B. *bankár.*

A tree which occurs in the Siwálik tract to 3,000 feet up to the Rávi. In parts of India where it is common, the timber is found good and useful, and the juice of the bark is employed medicinally. The wood is said to be good fuel.

Tectona grandis. L.

Vernacular. *ságún.*

This valuable tree is extremely difficult to raise in the Punjab, and only a few specimens exist as far west as Lahore.

Verbena officinalis. L.

Vernacular. K. *pámúkh.* Bazar, plant, *karáita.*

Common in moist places all over the Punjab plains and at places to 7,000 feet in the hills. Bellew states that the fresh leaves are used as febrifuge and tonic, and the plant is officinal at Lahore, being considered depurative and febrifuge.

Vitex Negundo. L.

Vernacular. J. *tórbanna, morann, marwan.* C. *binna.* R. *banna.* B. *banna, sanáke.* S. *shwárí.* T. I. *marwande. warmande.* S. R. *marwan, maura.* Bazár, root and leaves, *samálú;* fruit, *filfil barí.*

A common shrub in the Siwálik tract and up to 8,500 feet in the outer hills and occasional in the Salt Range and out in the plains. The branches are used for wattle-work. The leaves are in Chumba given for colic; they are also officinal and used in poultices. The root and fruit likewise are officinal.

N. O. LABIATÆ.

Many of the members of this family being odorous or with a strong taste from the presence of essential oils, a considerable proportion are used in native medicines.

Ajuga bracteata. Wall.?

Vernacular. J. *kaurí búti*. B. *karkú*. S. *nílkanthí*. T. I. *khúrbánei*. S. R. *wadí búti*. Bazár, plant, *jániadam*—(see Salvia lanata)—*múkand bábrí, nílkanthí* (Royle.)

This and several other species resembling it, occur in the Punjab Himalaya from 1,000 to 8,500 feet, and in the Salt Range. In the latter it is used to kill lice. The plant is also officinal under the above names, being considered depurative.

Ballota limbata. Benth.

Vernacular. J. *búi, phútkanda*. K. *phút* (?) *jandí*. C. *kandiárí, lána*. T. I. *aghzan, spínaghzái*. S. R. *awúní búti*

A small prickly shrub with yellow flowers, which occurs in the Salt Range, Trans-Indus, and in the Jhelam basin, at times to 4,000 feet. It is browsed by goats, and the juice of the leaves is applied to children's gums, and to ophthalmia in man and beast.

Calamintha umbrosa. Benth. (Melissa. Bieb.)

Vernacular. Bazar, seed, *faranj mushk*.

This is common in the Punjab Himalaya from 2,500 to 9,500 feet. It is probably the Melissa calamintha, whose seeds Honigberger says he found all the Bazar *faranj mushk* to be—(see Ocimum Basilicum).

Colebrookia oppositifolia. Sm.

Vernacular. J. *dúss, sampní*. C. *súálí*. R. *dúss*. B. *bridlí, basúti*. S. *barmera*. T. I. *shakardána*. S. R. *phís bekkar*.

A large shrub which occurs in the Siwalik tract to 4,000 feet, and in the Salt Range and Trans-Indus. Gunpowder charcoal is made from it, and its leaves are applied to wounds and bruises.

DRACOCEPHALUM HETEROPHYLLUM. Benth.

Vernacular. Lad., *zánda, shankú karamm.*

Grows from 13,000 to 16,000 and even to 17,000 feet in Ladák, where its root appears to be used as a vegetable. It is also browsed by goats and sheep.

ELSHOLTZIA POLYSTACHYA. Benth.

Vernacular. J. *rangcharí, mehndí.* C. *garúdar, tappaddar.* R. *dúss.* S. *pothí.*

A shrub found in the Punjab Himalaya at 6,000 to 10,000 feet. To the south of Kashmír it is said to be used as a dye.

EREMOSTACHYS VICARYI. Benth.

Vernacular. S. R. *gurganna, khalátra, rewand chíní.*

A fine yellow-flowered plant common in the Salt Range to 2,500 feet (and Trans-Indus?). The seeds are given as cooling medicine, and in a statement for the Punjab Exhibition it is mentioned that the plant is used for poisoning fish in the Eusufzai near Peshawar.

LALLEMANTIA ROYLEANA. Benth. (DRACOCEPHALUM. Wall.)

Vernacular. T. I. *gharei kashmálú.* S. R. *tukhm-malanga.* Bazár, seed, *tukhm bálangú.*

Is common wild in many places in the Salt Range and Trans-Indus to 5,000 feet. Its seeds are officinal, being considered cooling and sedative.

LEUCAS CEPHALOTIS. Spr.
L. ASPERA. Bth.

Vernacular. K. *phúman.* Bazár, plant, *sisalíús, maldoda, guldoda, chatra.*

One or both common in the western Punjab plains, and to 4,000 feet in the hills. The plant is stirred in milk "for its odour," and is officinal, being reckoned stimulant.

LYCOPUS EUROPÆUS. L. Gipsywort.

Vernacular. K. *gandamgúndú.* Bazár, leaves, &c., *jalním.*

Occurs wild Trans-Indus and in Kashmír to 7,000 feet. Part of this plant appears to be officinal under the above name, as a cooling drug.

MARRUBIUM VULGARE. L. White Horehound.

Vernacular. ?

This species (apparently) I have found in some eight or nine different places in and near Kashmír, on the Chenáb, in the Salt Range and Trans-Indus, at elevations varying from 2,000 to 7,000 feet. I have only seen it growing locally and scantily near habitations, but have no occasion to think that it is cultivated, nor could I learn that it is used for any purpose.

MENTHA INCANA. Willd. "Persian mint."
M. ROYLEANA. Benth.

Vernacular. J. *babúrí.* K. *vien.* C. *yúra, púdna.* B. *kúshma.* S. *koshú.* T. I. *velanne.* Bazár, leaves, *mushk tara mushí.*

The former of these is common in the plains Trans-Indus, and one or other in the Himalaya and Tibet, to 11,000 or 12,000 feet. The former is also occasionally cultivated in gardens, and its leaves are officinal as astringent

M. SATIVA. L. (var. of M. ARVENSIS. L. ?) Marsh whorled mint.

Vernacular. *podína.*

Grown in gardens in the plains. Honigberger states that its leaves are officinal at Lahore. M. ARVENSIS is found wild in Kashmír from 5,000 to 9,000 feet.

M. VIRIDIS. L. Spearmint.

Vernacular. *pahárí podína.* Bazár, leaves, *podína.*

Cultivated in gardens in the plains. Probably constitutes with the last, the *podína* of the drug-sellers, which is stimulant and given in cholera, &c.

MICROMERIA BIFLORA. Benth.

Vernacular. ?

Abundant in most parts of the Punjab Himalaya from 2,000 occasionally to 9,500 feet, and found Trans-Indus. It has a weak odour of thyme, which it somewhat resembles in appearance, and is often mistaken by Europeans for it.

NEPETA CILIARIS. Benth. (N. LEUCOPHYLLA. Bl.)

Vernacular. Bazár, plant, *zúfa yábis.*

Occurs in the Punjab Himalaya at from 4,000 to 8,000 feet. This or some very similar species seems to be the *zúfa yábis* of the Lahore drug-sellers, which, however, is brought from Affghánistán (to the large extent of 50 maunds in a year, according to Davies' Trade Report), and is by the books connected with hyssop, probably from a resemblance of the names. It is given in *sharbat* for fever and cough.

N. ELLIPTICA. Royle.

Vernacular. S. R. *takht malanga.*

What appears to be this species is found in the Salt Range and in the Punjab Himalaya from 3,000 to 9,000 feet. In the former its seeds are said to be medicine, but my informant may have confused it with LALLEMANTIA (q. v.)

N. FLOCCOSA. Benth.

Vernacular. Lad., *chongmongo.*

This appears to be the species which is found at from 10,000 to 16,500 feet in Ladák, where it is browsed by goats and sheep.

N. RUDERALIS. Ham.

Vernacular. Bazár, leaves, *billí lotan, búdranj boya, bebrang Khatái.*

What is apparently this plant grows in the Siwálik tract and Salt Range to 3,000 feet. It seems to be part at least of the officinal *billí lotan*, which has been assigned to various LABIATE plants, and is probably obtained from several. It is considered cardiac.

N. SP. ?

Vernacular. Bazár, plant, *gordil.*

This, which is sold as medicine, appears to be a species of NEPETA.

OCIMUM BASILICUM. L.
O. SANCTUM. L.

Vernacular. *túlsí, babúrí.* Bazár, seed, &c., *faranj-mushk, túlsí* or *rehán;* plant, *nigand bábri, nigand (páur).*

These species are cultivated in the plains, and the latter at least in Kashmír (5,000 feet). The latter is also found wild in the

Salt Range at 1,500 feet. The seeds of these probably constitute the chief part of the officinal leaves, flowers, and seeds, called *faranj-mushk*, &c., which are attributed to various species of OCIMUM and other LABIATÆ (*e. g.*, CALAMINTHA q. v.) The seeds and flowers are reckoned stimulant, diuretic, and demulcent, and are much used. The leaves are ground and applied to scorpion-stings. Part of the officinal *nigand bâbri* also appears to be one of these; it is considered to be febrifuge. Curiously enough, Davies' Trade Report gives 25 maunds of *rehán* as annually imported, and the same quantity as exported viâ Peshawar. The former is probably correct.

O. GRATISSIMUM. L.

Vernacular. S. *banjere.*

This, which is cultivated in the plains of parts of India, seems to be a species found in gardens in Kanáwar at 6,800 feet, where the seeds are eaten mixed in ordinary bread.

ORIGANUM NORMALE. Don. (O. VULGARE. L.) Marjoram.

Vernacular. Bazár, plant, *mirzanjosh.*

This herb grows commonly in the Punjab Himalaya from 2,500 to 10,500 feet, and appears to be the officinal plant above named. Aitchison states that in Lahoul it is eaten as a pot-herb. I do not know what may be the "sweet marjoram" of Lahore gardens mentioned by Honigberger, but O. MARJORANA is said to be cultivated in southern India for its seeds, which are there officinal, being considered astringent.

PLECTRANTHUS RUGOSUS. Benth

Vernacular. J. *búi.* K. *solei.* C. *piúmár.* (Flea-killer), *chúgú, solá, solei.* R. *kot, síríngrí.* S. *pek, rosbang, chichrí, tsarbs.* T. I. *khwangere.* S. R. *itsit.*

A small, rather slender, shrubby plant, abundant in the Punjab Himalaya from 3,000 to 9,000 feet, and occurring in the Salt Range. In places it is used as bedding to keep off fleas. In a recent paper in the Journal of the Linnæan Society on the plants of the tract near Sinai, I see an allusion to the fact that powerful smelling herbs keep off such insects.

PRUNELLA VULGARIS. L.

Vernacular. Bazár, flowers, &c., *aústakhadús.*

Common in many parts of the Punjab Himalaya from 3,500 to 10,500 feet. It constitutes the chief part of the officinal substance above named, which is considered expectorant and antispasmodic, and has been attributed to various LABIATÆ (*e. g.*, STŒCHAS, probably from the similarity of name).

ROYLEA ELEGANS. Wall.

Vernacular. R. *kaur*. B. *kaurí*.

Occasional in the outer hills up to the Rávi about 3,000 feet. An infusion of the leaves is drunk for blows (and further east in the Himalaya it is used as a bitter tonic).

SALVIA LANATA. Rox.
S. MOORCROFTIANA. Wall.

Vernacular. J. *kálí jarrí*. C. *sholrí*. R. *thút*. S. *potú-kanang, hálú*. S. R. *gúrganna, khalátrí, laphra, pápra*. Bazár, leaves, *farásiún, jániadam* (Lowther); seed, *kanocha, kalauncha, shorlí* (Honigberger).

These two species have been confused in my hands, and must be treated together, though it is certain that most of the medicinal properties are ascribed to the latter of the two. Either (or both) is common wild in the plains of the N. W. Punjab, in the Salt Range, and in the Himalaya to 9,000 feet, the latter having the wider range as to elevation. In the Salt Range the stalks of the latter are peeled and eaten, being mawkish-sweet in taste, and there the root is given for coughs, the seeds for vomiting, and the leaves are applied to guinea-worm. In Hazára the leaves are applied to itch. The leaves are also officinal as *farásiún,* and Lowther states that poultices of them, under the name of *jániadam*—(see AJUGA)—are applied to wounds. The seeds are the officinal *kanocha,* which Bellew states to be taken for hæmorrhoids. At Lahore they are given in colic and dysentery, and are applied to boils.

S. PLEBEIA. R. Br.

Vernacular. B. D. *sathí*. S. P. *samúndar sok*. Bazár, seed, *samúndar sok*.

Common as a field weed in the plains and to 5,000 feet in the Punjab Himalaya. The seeds are officinal, and are much used in the Hindú system, as mustard, and for gonorrhæa and menorrhagia.

S. PUMILA. Benth.

Vernacular. S. R. *tukhm malanga*.

A small half-shrubby plant common in the Salt Range and Trans-Indus to 2,500 feet. Goats and sheep are said to be very fond of it. The seeds are used in diarrhœa, but from the vernacular name it would seem to be confused with *bálangú*—(see LALLEMANTIA).

SCUTELLARIA LINEARIS. Benth.

Vernacular. S. R. *mastiára.*

Not uncommon in the Salt Range and Jhelam basin to 4,000 feet. In the former the plant, which is very bitter, is eaten.

STACHYS PARVIFLORA. Benth.

Vernacular. S. R. *kírimár,* (worm-killer) *baggí-búti.*

Common in many places, Hazára, the Salt Range and Trans-Indus, and found by Bellew in Affghánistán from Kandahár to Ghuzní (3,500 to 7,000 feet). In the Salt Range the bruised stems are applied to guinea-worm.

THYMUS SERPYLLUM. L. Thyme.

Vernacular. C. *másho.* S. *rángsbúr.* T. I. *marízha, shakei.* Bazár, *kalandar zatar ?*

Common in the Punjab Himalaya and Tibet from 5,000 to 15,000 feet, and in the Súlimán Range. On the Chenáb the seeds are given as a "warm" medicine, and Honigberger states that the plant is officinal in diseases of the eyes and stomach, under the name given above, but I have not met with it.

N. O. PLUMBAGINACEÆ.

PLUMBAGO ZEYLANICA. L.

Vernacular. Bazár, root, *lál chitra.*

This plant is occasionally cultivated in gardens in the plains, and is not uncommon wild in the lower hills to 3,000 feet. The root is officinal, being used as a vesicant, and is employed locally to produce abortion.

N. O. PLANTAGINACEÆ.

PLANTAGO AMPLEXICAULIS. Cav.
P. CILIATA. Desf.
P. DECUMBENS. Forsk.

Vernacular. T. I. *spíghwol.* S. R. *isafghol.*

These species are common wild Trans-Indus, and in the Salt Range, &c., under 2,000 feet.

P. ISPAGHULA. Rox.

Vernacular. Bazár, seeds, *isafghol, bártang ?*

Edgeworth states that this is cultivated at Múltán. I have never seen it cultivated in the Punjab, but understand it is grown sparingly at Lahore. It is probable that the seeds of all these, and of the following, and it may be of others of the wild species, at times are collected and sold as the officinal seeds known under the two names given. These are considered cooling and emollient, and given in diarrhæa and fever, &c.

P. MAJOR. L. var. ASIATICA.

Vernacular. K. *gúl, isafgol.* C. *karet.* T. I. *ghuzhbe.* Bazár, fruit, *gaz pípal.*

Common wild in the Siwálik tract and Punjab Himalaya to 11,000 feet, and occurs in the plains at Peshawar, &c. The fruit forms in the Punjab part of the officinal *gaz pípal*—(see ABIES)—which is generally ascribed in books to POTHOS. In Lahoul the leaves are applied to bruises.

N. O. SALVADORACEÆ.

SALVADORA INDICA. Wight. (S. PERSICA. Rox.)

Vernacular. S. P. T. I., &c., *jit, kaurí ván, kaurijál, chhotí ván.* D. and N. W. P., *jál.*

Differs from the next species in being taller, with very white branches, which are more graceful and less stiff; the leaf is larger, and the fruit is bitter. It grows over a much smaller area in the Punjab than the other species. I have only seen it in quantity from Rájanpúr south towards the Sind border (and in Sind itself). Edgeworth states that it is rare in Múltán. I have been told that it grows in the south of Mozaffargarh (but saw none there), and also that it is found to the east of Jhang. I observed one or two trees at Dehlí and the Kutab, and was told of one near Ferozepúr. I have also seen it planted in Rohilkund. Edgeworth mentions a tree of 14 feet 9 inches in girth; I have noted none at all approaching this. It is said to flower in the hot weather. The wood of the tree is useless, "even for burning;" the leaves are eaten by camels, and Edgeworth states that they are used as salad. Pieces of the wood are carried to long distances for sale, as it is much favored for tooth-sticks, "*miswák,*" by Mussalmáns, who use theirs for a number of times (Hindús using theirs only once). The employment of it thus is said to be good for the digestion, and speedily to cure bleeding gums.

S. oleoides. Dne. (S. Persica. L.)

Vernacular. *jál, van, váni (míthiván*; fruit, *pílú, píl)*, and dried fruit, *khokar*. T. I. *plewane;* fruit, *ták*.

A more stiff-looking tree than the former, and with greyer foliage, except for a short time in spring; when with Tamarisk, &c., it gives some appearance of verdure to parts, which, from aridity and saline soil, would otherwise be hideous. In the black *kallar*, however, *i. e.,* where there is probably more common salt in the soil which looks dark and damp, even this tree does not flourish as it does where there is the ordinary saline impregnation. This species grows in Palestine, &c., and has by some been identified with the "mustard tree" of scripture, perhaps on insufficient grounds. It occurs as far east as the Jumna, and is not uncommon at the Kutab near Dehlí, extending thence westward through Harriána, and probably reaching its maximum of luxuriance in the central and southern Punjab, Cis and Trans-Indus, where in many parts it forms almost the only vegetation of any size over miles of country. It is also common in parts of Sind. I have seen a tree of 12 feet girth (at the ground), a few miles east of the Sutlej. Edgeworth mentions one of 11 feet 4 inches and another of 12 feet girth near Múltán, and Coldstream at Mozaffargarh measured one of 14 feet girth, several feet from the ground. These very large trees, however, are rare, and are generally hollow. This species flowers about April, and the fruit ripens at the beginning of the hot weather. It is sweetish, and is largely eaten by the natives, immense numbers of whom go out to collect it in the season, and so much do they depend on it that Coldstream states that a bad crop is reckoned as a calamity. Trans-Indus, aphrodisiac qualities have been attributed to the fruit, but the phenomena leading to this theory are probably rather to be attributed to the fact of crowds of both sexes wandering in the wilds at the ripening time. A Subordinate Medical Officer at Sirsa states that there the people say, if the fruit are eaten singly, they cause tingling and small ulcers of the mouth, therefore they prefer to eat them by handfuls, seeds, and all, and the latter are apt to accumulate in masses in the sigmoid flexure of the intestines, &c., leading to disagreeable results. Coldstream states that in Mozaffargarh the fruit is often dried for future use, and has then much the appearance and flavour of currants. The leaves are browsed by and occasionally collected as fodder for camels. In the southern Punjab the wood is at times used for rafters and Persian wheels, and in Sind it was found to answer well for the knee-timbers of boats. It furnishes a poor fuel, the worst the Railway get, as it smoulders, and has no body for burning alone even, if thoroughly dried. But, mixed with deodár and pine scrap-wood, it has been found to answer well for burning bricks, &c. When burned green, it is said to give a very bad smell. In some parts a gall, which is common on the tree, appears to be used in dyeing. In Sirsa the root is ground and used as a blister. Royle states that in the Bazárs the leaves are sometimes sold as *rásanna*—(see BERTHELOTIA)—but I have not found this to be the case in the Punjab.

N. O. PHYTOLACCACEÆ.

PHYTOLACCA DECANDRA. L. var. b. ACINOSA. (P. ACINOSA. Rox.)

Vernacular. J. *lúbar*. R. *búrgú, dentúrú, rínság*. B. *jirka*. S. *malazor, sarunga*.

Not uncommon in the Punjab Himalaya from 3,500 to 8,000 feet, and mentioned by Brandis as cultivated east of Simla. The fruit is said to be occasionally eaten, and elsewhere is stated to produce cerebral symptoms. The leaves are in some places eaten as a vegetable in curries, &c. In Kanawar a variety with dark-coloured petioles was pointed out to me as having in the presence of my informant produced delirium when eaten as a vegetable by some of the forest workmen.

N. O. SALSOLACEÆ.

ANABASIS MULTIFLORA. Moq.

Vernacular. T. I. *ghalme*. S. R., R. D. *lána*. B. D. *metra láne, gora láne*. Fe., *dána, short lána*.

Occurs sparingly to a short distance east of the Sutlej; in the central and especially the southern Punjab is in many places abundant and conspicuous, growing bushy to 6 or 7 feet high, with rose-coloured flowers. Is not uncommon Trans-Indus. In some places is held to indicate a good,—in others, and probably more correctly, a bad soil. Camels are fond of the plant. Aitchison states that near Jhelam it is occasionally used for the preparation of *sajji*—(see CAROXYLON GRIFFITHII)—but I have nowhere been told that it is so employed. In some parts, however, it is used for washing clothes, and it is probably this which Bellew states to be used by women in the Peshawar Valley for washing the head.

ATRIPLEX HORTENSIS. L. Orache.
A. LACINIATA. L.

Vernacular. T I. *koráke.* S. R. *surakka.*

The former has been found wild at various places in the plains Trans-Indus, and by Bellew at 3,500 feet in Affghánistán. The latter is abundant wild in many places Trans-Indus, occurs in the Salt Range, and from 12,000 to 14,000 feet in Tibet (Hf. and T.) I presume it must be the former which Bellew states to be a favorite vegetable in the Peshawar Valley, as it once was in Europe. It used to be cultivated in England.

BASELLA ALBA. L. var. RUBRA.

Vernacular. *poí.*

A conspicuous climbing plant. Rarely cultivated by natives in the Punjab, to be eaten as a pot-herb.

BETA VULGARIS. Moq. var. ORIENTALIS. (B. BENGALENSIS. ROX.) Country spinach.

Vernacular. *pálak.*

Frequently cultivated by natives, and used as a pot-herb. The seeds are officinal, being considered cooling and diaphoretic. Bellew mentions that the fresh leaves are applied to burns and bruises. It may be worth noting that many years ago an European was induced by the late Maharajah to come out to Kashmír for the purpose of growing Beet—(B. VULGARIS)—for sugar to be extracted from its root, but the scheme came to nothing.

BLITUM VIRGATUM. L.

Vernacular. J. *súndar.* C. *kúpald.*

I have found this wild at several places in the Jhelam and Chenáb and Rávi basins and Trans-Indus from 7,000 to 10,000 and in Ladák to 12,500 feet. The extremely insipid fruit is sometimes mistaken by Europeans for a kind of strawberry, which it much resembles. In Ladák the leaves are eaten as a pot-herb.

CAROXYLON FÆTIDUM. Moq.

Vernacular. *motí láne, gorá láne.*

Not uncommon in the central and southern Punjab and Trans-Indus (and Sind). Aitchison states that near Jhelam this is the plant chiefly used for *sajji*—(see C. GRIFFITHII)—though this is not the case elsewhere in the Punjab. In Sind, however, it is stated to be generally used for this purpose.

C. Griffithii. Moq. (Salsola Griffithii. ?)

Vernacular. T. I. *laghme.* Cis-Indus, *khár.*

Although many square miles of the barren clay tracts of the central and southern Punjab and southern Trans-Indus are covered almost entirely by various Salsolaceæ from any or all of which Europeans are apt at first to suppose that *sajji* is made, yet, as mentioned by Edgeworth, this, which is the chief source, is one of the more rare kinds, only extending to a little way east of the Sutlej, so far as I know in the latitude of Montgomery, nor did I observe it in Harriána. As a rule throughout the Punjab, this alone is used in making that substance, probably as giving the most abundant out-turn. Edgeworth implies that it is common in Bhuttiána to the south of Sirsa, and it is found at 10,000 to 15,000 feet in Tibet (Hf. and T.), and this is also probably one of the two plants whence *sajji* is chiefly made in Sind. *Sajji* being an impure carbonate of soda, is equivalent to the barilla of commerce manufactured in Spain, chiefly, according to Edgeworth, from Salsola soda and Salicornia herbacea, which resemble this plant, and are there cultivated for the purpose. The plant is cut about the month of November, (?) burned and lixiviated. Captain Davies gives a description of the process in his Settlement Report of Shahpúr. Great quantities of the salt are manufactured to the north of Múltán, whence it is largely exported to all parts of the Punjab, &c. It is also prepared at two or three places in the Peshawar Valley. Edgeworth states that much is sent from Bhuttiána to Europe, and considers that the plant could be profitably cultivated. It is a very favorite food of camels, and he mentions that large quantities of it are brought fresh into Múltán to be sold as fodder for them.

Chenopodium album. L.

Vernacular. C. *irr.* Lad., *em.* Plains, *bathúa, jauság, lúnak.*

A common weed throughout the Punjab plains, and apparently to 8,500 feet in parts of the Himalaya, and 13,500 feet in Ladák. It is often obnoxiously abundant in the cold weather crops in the plains. The plant is sometimes eaten as a pot-herb in Ladák and in parts of the plains.

C. murale. L.

Vernacular. *bátú, kúrúnd, kharatua.*

A common weed in the Punjab plains. It is used as a pot-herb.

C. SP.

Vernacular. K. *mustakh.* R. *gaddí shúngar, bajar banj, ratta.* B. *siriárí.* S. *bíthú, báthú, tákú.* Lad., *gniú (?)*

This possibly includes two species, and is cultivated in the Punjab Himalaya from 5,500 to 9,000 feet up to the Rávi at least, and is said to be grown in Kashmír and Ladák. It is, so far as I have seen, most common towards the east. The leaves are eaten as a pot-herb on the Sutlej, but the plant is chiefly cultivated for its grain, which is considered better than buckwheat. Within the last year, considerable stir has been made by correspondents of the Agri-Horticultural Society of India, regarding the introduction into the Himalaya of the C. QUINOA, Willd. of the Andes; and the Society made arrangements to get a supply of seed, which has arrived and been distributed. The original proposition appears to have been made in ignorance of the fact that a C. is cultivated extensively in the Himalaya, and there seems reason to doubt if very much would be gained from the introduction of the QUINOA in these mountains, where cereals are cultivated to quite as high elevations as men can occupy throughout the year.

EUROTIA CERATOIDES. C. A. M.

Vernacular. *japshan, gipshan, búrse.* P. *búrse.*

A small shrubby species which occurs in Affgháuistán, and is one of the commonest and most wide-spread plants of desert Ladák, where it is found from 12,000 to 16,000 and at times up to 17,500 feet. It is browsed by *yaks* when they are hard pressed by hunger, but its chief use is as fuel, for which its thick woody roots are largely used.

PANDERIA PILOSA. F. and M.

Vernacular. *kaura ro, búí.* Bazár, stem and leaves, *búí chhotí.*

Is abundant in many places in the central and southern Punjab and Trans-Indus, and occurs at from 8,000 to 12,000 feet in Tibet. The plant is officinal in the Bazárs.

SALSOLA KALI. L.

Vernacular. ?

Has been found sparingly in the northern Trans-Indus. This may possibly be the plant which Bellew states to be burned for *sajjí*—(see CAROXYLON GRIFFITHII)—in the Peshawar Valley, though I believe the *sajjí* used there is mostly imported from the south.

SPINACIA OLERACEA. Spr. Spinach.

Vernacular. ?

Stated by Edgeworth to be cultivated at Múltán, having been introduced not by Europeans, but by Arabs. I have not heard of its being cultivated elsewhere by natives.

SUÆDA FRUTICOSA. Moq. (S. INDICA. Moq. ?)

Vernacular. T. I. *zamái*. Cis-Indus, *lúnak, chhotí láne, phesak láne, baggí lána, dána*. Bazár, leaves, *kaskasa ?*

Abundant in many parts from Trans-Indus to east of the Sutlej on to Harriána, and grows to a considerable bush in parts of the central Punjab, where it is in perfection, covering many square miles in places, and where its growth is said to indicate a very inferior soil. It is eaten by camels. Edgeworth mentions that doubtless *sajjí*—(see CAROXYLON GRIFFITHII)—could be prepared from this, and I was told that it is so prepared in small quantities for home use in Montgomery, and Aitchison states that it is at times made from this plant near Jhelam also. It is sometimes subject to have numerous woolly excrescences on the tips of the branches. The officinal *kaskasa* of the Bazár appear to be the dried leaves of this plant, and from the Pushtú name, given by Bellew, these would appear in the Peshawár Valley to be mashed when fresh, and applied as a poultice to the eyes for ophthalmia.

N. O. AMARANTACEÆ.

ACHYRANTHES ASPERA. L.

Vernacular. T. I. *kútre*. Cis-Indus, *baggiárí, pútkanda*. Bazár, tops, *apamarg, chirchitta*.

Common in the Punjab plains, and occurs to 2,500 feet (5000 Thomson) in the Himalaya. The dried plant is locally given to children for colic, and is officinal under the above names, being given as an astringent in gonorrhœa. In Oudh, Madden states that the plant is considered protective from scorpions.

ÆRUA BOVII. Webb.
Æ. JAVANICA. Juss.
Æ. SCANDENS. Juss.

Vernacular. T. I. *azmei, spírke, sassái*. Cis-Indus, *búí, járí*. Bazár, flowers, &c., *búí kalán*.

Of several species which occur in the Punjab plains and occasionally to 3,000 or 4,000 feet in the outer hills, up to and beyond the Indus, these are probably the most common. (Edgeworth considers the first a distinct species, and not a mere variety of the second). The flowers of some of them have a sweet smell. In Sind the woolly fruit is used for stuffing pillows, and rats are probably fond of the seeds, as I have observed heaps of the wool at the mouths of their burrows. The plant is subject to woody galls. The flowering tops are officinal.

AMARANTHUS ANARDANA. Ham.
A. GANGETICUS. L.

Vernacular. J. K. *ganhár*. C. *siúl, sáwal, bhabri*. R. *káli síwal, lál síwal, siwálará*. B. *siril, saráíri, sarídra, bátú, ganhár*. S. *sarera, dankar, bíthú, chaulei, tulsia*. P. *dartú*. Plains, *lál chaulái* Bazár, seed, *síl*.

There is doubt as to the species of AMARANTH cultivated in the Himalaya, where it is common both red and green, being often grown among other crops to 9,000 feet. The second species appears to be wild also in the plains. The leaves are eaten as a pot-herb, but it is grown chiefly for the seed, used as a food grain after parching. It is considered heating. The second species at least is also cultivated in the plains to be used as a pot-herb. The seeds of one of these appears to be officinal, being considered astringent and aphrodisiac.

A. MANGOSTANUS. L.
A. OLERACEUS. Moq. (EUXOLUS CANDATUS. Moq.)
A. POLYGAMUS. L. (EUXOLUS. Moq.)

Vernacular. *chauláí, ganhár, rám-dána, marsa ?*

All of these appear to be occasionally cultivated in the plains, the leaves being used as pot-herbs.

A. POLYGONOIDES. L. (AMBLOGYNA. Rafin.)
A. SPINOSUS. L.

Vernacular. *chauláí*.

Frequent weeds in the plains, which are used as pot-herbs by the poor, and in times of scarcity.

CELOSIA ARGENTEA. L.

Vernacular. *sarwáli*.

An abundant field weed in the Punjab plains, and occasionally to 5,000 feet in the Himalaya. It is used as a pot-herb in times of scarcity. The seeds are officinal.

C. CRISTATA. Moq. Cockscomb.

Vernacular. K. *máwal.* Bazár. flower, *tāji khoros, bostán-afroz.*

Cultivated as a flower in the plains, and in parts of the Himalaya, *e. g.*, Kashmír (5,000 feet). The flowers are officinal, and Bellew states that in the Peshawar Valley the seeds are considered demulcent.

DIGERA ARVENSIS. Forsk.

Vernacular. *tartara, tandala, leswa.*

A common field weed in the Punjab plains, and to 2,500 feet in the Himalaya. Frequently eaten as a pot-herb.

N. O. NYCTAGINACEÆ.

BOERHAAVIA ELEGANS. Chois.

Vernacular. S. P. *helra.*

Occurs Trans-Indus, and appears to be abundant in the southern Punjab, where Edgeworth states that its mucilaginous seeds are collected in the desert and eaten by the natives.

B. DIFFUSA. L. (B. PROCUMBENS. Rox.)

Vernacular. J. *nákbel.* T. I. *pándarwásh.* Cis-Indus, *itsit, arsat.*

A common weed in the Punjab plains, and to 4,000 feet in the Himalaya. It is said to be browsed by animals. On the Jhelam, the plant is given as a cooling medicine.

MIRABILIS JALAPA. L.

Vernacular *gul abbás.*

Cultivated as a flower in the plains, and (as noted by Madden) naturalized in many places in the Himalaya up to near the Jhelam from 2,800 to 7,500 feet. In waste ground near villages, &c., in the hills, great beds of this plant may frequently be seen, with flowers of two or three different colours. The leaves are used as poultices, and from the root a medicinal conserve is prepared.

OXYBAPHUS HIMALAICUS. Edge.

Vernacular. S. *pumáe, báus.*

This is a scrambling viscous plant with a large carrot-like root, 2 feet long, originally found (and described) by Edgeworth at

7,800 to 8,000 feet on the Dhaulí, not far from the Sutlej, on which latter alone for a few miles in the lower part of Kanáwar at 5,000 to 9,000 feet, I have seen it. The flowers are usually reddish, but a variety has them white. It is collected by the inhabitants for winter fodder.

N. O. POLYGONACEÆ.

Calligonum polygonoides. L.

Vernacular. T. I. *balanja, berwaja, tatúke.* Cis-Indus, *phok, phog*; flowers, *phogallí.* Bazár, root, &c., *tirní?*

This, which is a moderately sized shrub, was first noted by Elphinstone *en route* to Kábul, who mentions it as abundant, and notes the use to which its flowers are put from Shekhawuttee to the Sutlej. Madden calls it an Ephedra, though oddly enough he describes the fruit, &c., correctly. He very much exaggerates the verdure of the shrub, which, however, is pleasing enough with its leafless branches and small pink flowers, which have a very strong scent as of over-ripe fruit, and about May are succeeded by the small three-cornered wigged fruit. The plant is reported on good authority to be abundant in the Bikanír desert, but I have not seen it east of the Sutlej to the northward of that. It is not uncommon to the west of Shahpúr, and for some miles north of Jhang, and is abundant in the Bárí Doáb, in places southward from 60 miles north of Múltán, and it forms great part of the jungle westward from Mozaffargarh for some miles. It is also common near the southern and eastern skirts of Shaikh Budín, and occurs near Rájanpúr in the southern Trans-Indus. I also saw it in Sind. The shoots are greedily eaten by goats and camels, and the wood is used as fuel, and in Bikanír the twigs are much used for huts, and for the linings of shallow wells. Cis-Sutlej and in the southern Punjab, the flowers, having fallen off, are swept up from the ground, and used largely as food (not, however, Trans-Indus apparently). Coldstream states that in Mozaffargarh they are made into bread, or are cooked with *ghí* and eaten as a relish. The officinal *triní* or *tirní* of the Punjab seems to me to be the root and lower part of the stem of young plants of this, but the point is very doubtful.

Fagopyrum Cymosum. Meisn.?

Vernacular. S. *banogul.*

What appears to be this species is common wild in parts of the Punjab Himalaya at from 5,500 to 8,000 feet, and probably higher. I could not find that its grain is used.

F. EMARGINATUM. Meisn. (F. VULGARIS. ?) Buckwheat.

Vernacular. C. *dardu.* C. R. *obal, phúlan ?* S. *ogal, phápphar.*

Of the two most common cultivated species (I think there are at least three in the Punjab Himalaya), this with reddish flowers is generally said to grow lower than the other, but I have seen both at the same level about 8,500 feet on the Sutlej. The leaves of this are used as a pot-herb. There is confusion as to the identification of these, and the remarks on both may be entered under the next.

F. ESCULENTUM. Mœnch. (POLYGONUM F. L.) (F. TATARICUM. Gært. ?)

Vernacular. J. *kála trúmba, chín.* K. *trúmba.* C. *karma bres, kátú, brapú drawo.* R. *bres, katú, phaphra.* B. *káthú.* S. *bras, pháphrá, ulgo úgal, tsábri.* P. *káthú tráo.* Lad., *tráo, rjao (?)* Bazár, seed, *kaspat.*

This is said to be inferior as to quality of grain to the former, but neither is considered equal to the millets even in the hills. And in the plains to which a good deal of buckwheat is brought under the name of *kotú* (to be eaten chiefly by Hindús, as it is to them *phaláhar, i. e.,* lawful to be used during their *bart* or fasts), it is considered heating, and not very palatable. Buckwheat grows at about 6,000 feet (and scattered plants are often seen much lower) on the Jhelam, 5,000 to 10,000, on the Chenáb and Rávi, 8,000 to 9,000 on the Biás, and on the Sutlej it is grown commonly to 11,500, and Gerard states he has seen it at 13,600 feet. Thomson notes it at 13,000 feet in Zanskar, and Cayley mentions it as cultivated to 14,000 in Ladák, where I have seen it to over 13,500. Bears are more fond of it than almost any other food, and commit much damage to the standing crop. In Lahoul, Aitchison states that the leaves are much used as a pot-herb in summer when other greens are not easily got.

OXYRIA RENIFORMIS. Hook

Vernacular. R. *amlú.*

Common in the Punjab Himalaya at from 10,500 to 12,500 and in Tibet to 15,000 feet. Has a pleasant sorrel taste. In Chumba is eaten raw and in *chatní,* and is considered cooling, and Cleghorn mentions that in Kanáwar it is used in medicine.

POLYGONUM AVICULARE. L.

Vernacular. R. *kesrú.* T. I. *bandúke.*

Abundant of different varieties from the plains where, in spring, with its myriads of flowers it forms masses of pink wherever water has stood, to 12,000 feet in the Himalaya generally, and considerably over that in Tibet. In Chumba it is applied externally as an anodyne, and Honigberger states that it is officinal in Kashmír.

P. BARBATUM. L.

Vernacular. S. R. *narrí.*

Not uncommon in wet places in the Punjab plains, and to 3,500 or more feet in the hills. Honigberger states that it is officinal in Kashmír.

P. BISTORTA. L.

Vernacular. J. K. C. *maslun.* C. *mamech.* S. *dorí, bajir, bilaurí.* Bazár, root, *anjabár.*

Common at places in the Punjab Himalaya from 3,500 to 12,000 feet. On the Sutlej the root is said to be applied to abscesses, and it is officinal in the plains, being very astringent.

P. NEPALENSE. Meisn.? (P. SPHÆROCEPHALUM. Wall.?)

Vernacular. B. *sat balon.*

This species appears to be common in the Punjab Himalaya from 3,000 to 9,500 feet. In Kángra its leaves are applied to swellings.

P. POLYSTACHYUM. Wall.
P. POLYMORPHUM. Led.

Vernacular. C. *amldandí, chúchí.* R. *tror.*

These are tall plants with fine flowers, one at least of them exhaling a strong honey smell at times. Both appear to be common locally in the Punjab Himalaya from 6,000 to 12,000 feet. The young leaves are used by the natives as a pot-herb, and a very good imitation of rhubarb (*chúchí* is the name of both in some parts) is got by stewing the stalks, which also, after peeling, are eaten raw by the natives in some places.

P. TORTUOSUM. Don.

Vernacular. Lad., *niála.* P. *niálo.*

This species, which grows to 15,000 feet in the Himalaya, is said to yield a yellow dye in Lahoul. In Ladák it is browsed by goats and *yaks.*

P. sp.

Vernacular. Lad., *rútsú.*

The roots of a small species with sagittate leaves, which is found to 15,500 feet in Ladák, are eaten as a vegetable.

RHEUM EMODI. Wall. (R. WEBBIANUM. Royle.)
R. MOORCROFTIANUM. Meisn. (Wall. ?) } Rhubarb.
R. SPICIFORME. Royle.

Vernacular. J. *chutiál.* C. *chotiál, pambash, átsú, artso, khabiún, lachú.* R. *chúkrí, kandául.* B. *chúchí.* S. *arts.* Lad., *lachú.* P. *láchú.* Aff., *rawásh, chúkrí.* Bazár, stalks, *ribás ;* root, *rewand chíní.*

At least two species of rhubarb are frequent in parts of the Punjab Himalaya from 6,200 to 14,000 feet, the second named occurring still higher from 15,000 to 17,000 feet, but these have got into confusion in my hands, and their separate identity is therefore not established here. In some parts of the hills, no portion of these plants is used, but in most the stalks are eaten either boiled with water or pounded and mixed with salt and pepper, and in Hazára the dried leaves are boiled with water and eaten with meat. At one place in Chumba, and also in Lahoul, I was told that the flowers are eaten. The officinal *ribás* of the drug-sellers consists of the dried stalks from Kábul, which may partly be produced by R. RIBES, Gron., a native of Carmel, &c., eastern Persia (where it is called *rivás*), and the Hindú Khúsh. In Affghánistán the plant is always wild, and appears to grow abundantly in many parts. When green, the leaf stalks are *rawásh,* and, when blanched by heaping up stones and gravel round them, are called *chúkrí ;* when fresh (in which state they are sometimes brought to Peshawar in spring), they are eaten either raw or cooked, and they are also dried for use to be eaten with other food, and are sometimes made into a preserve. The officinal root is imported into Affghánistán and India to be used as a purgative. In the former country, however, the people appear to have no idea that it is the root of a plant similar to their own *rawásh,* and the roots of the latter are, according to Bellew, spongy and tasteless. Moorcroft also mentions that the roots of the Ladák rhubarb are mostly rotten in the centre, and what roots have been brought from the Himalaya for trial at Lahore, &c., though found to be possessed of laxative properties, are by no means to be relied on. Aitchison, however, states that, although in Lahoul the R. EMODI is not used medicinally, yet its leaves, even when cultivated in a garden, had medicinal effects when eaten in salad. It is stated by Moorcroft (?) that the Bhotias of Garhwál apply the powdered root to wounds and bruises, and that they use it with *majít*—(see RUBIA)—and potash for dyeing red.

Rumex acutus. Rox. (R. Wallichii. Meisn.), or R. dentatus. Campd. ?

Vernacular. J. *húla.* K. *obúl.* T. I. *zagúkei.* B. D. *khattíkan, janglí pálak.* Bazar, seeds, *bíj band.*

Common at wet places throughout the plains, and to 12,000 feet in the Punjab Himalaya. The leaves are bruised and used as a pot-herb, and are considered cooling. Bellew states that in the Peshawar Valley they are applied to sores and burns, &c. The seeds appear to be sometimes sold as the officinal *bíj band*—(see Sida.)

R. hastatus. Don.

Vernacular. J. *khattímal, katambal.* C. R. *ámí.* B. *malorí-ghá, amla.* S. *amlora.*

Common in many parts of the Himalaya where not too moist, from 2,500 to 9,000 feet. The leaves are eaten raw having a pleasant acid taste, to which *amla* and *khatta* refer. Almora (for *aml-wára*) in Kumaon is said to get its name from the notable abundance of this plant near it.

R. vesicarius. L.

Vernacular. T. I. *triwakka, khatbírí.* Cis-Indus, *khattítan, katta mítha, salúni.*

Common in arid places in the Salt Range and Trans-Indus to 3,000 feet. Tastes like the last, but more pleasant. It is eaten raw, and in some places used as a pot-herb. It grows near Sinai, and a recent traveller there mentions that it is excellent as a salad.

N. O. LAURACEÆ.

Cinnamomum albiflorum. Nees.
C. Tamala. Fr. Nees. var. albiflora.

Vernacular. *dál chíní.* Bazár, bark, *tajkalmí ;* leaves, *tezpat.*

This tree, which is not uncommon in the Himalaya, east of the Sutlej, grows sparingly at about 5,000 feet as far as the Rávi, and probably in Hazára. Its timber does not appear to be valued. Part at least of the officinal bark and leaves above named are probably derived from this tree. The former is given for gonorrhœa, and the latter are used in rheumatism, being considered stimulant.

LITSÆA. SP.?

Vernacular. C. *chírndi.* R. *chindi, chilotu, rauli, shalanglu.* B. *charká.*

A small tree which is not unfrequent in parts of the Punjab Himalaya at 2,500 to 6,800 feet, up to the Chenáb. In some places in Chumba, an oil, expressed from the fruit, is burned, and, according to Madden, a species of LITSÆA, which may be this, yields a coarse oil in Kumaon.

MACHILUS ODORATISSIMUS. Nees.?

Vernacular. J. *kálban. chau.* C. *táura.* R. *cháu, badror, chandna, shalanglú.* B. *badror, prora, mitpattar, múkrú.* S. *bajhol, shír.*

The identity of this tree is somewhat doubtful, but it appears to occur occasionally in the Punjab Himalaya at from 4,000 to 7,000 feet, up to near the Indus. It is of no special use, and even goats do not browse its leaves, which have a pleasant orange-scent.

TETRANTHERA MONOPETALA. Rox.

Vernacular. R. *rian.* B. *gwá, harein.* Bazár, bark, *meda lakri.*

A tree of moderate size, which occurs in the Siwalik tract up to the Rávi. The wood is not valued. The bark (with that of the next) is officinal, being considered stimulant, and, after being bruised, applied fresh or dry to contusions, and sometimes mixed with milk or made into plaster.

T. ROXBURGHII. Nees.

Vernacular. S. R. *medasak.* U. *chandna.* Bazár, bark, *meda lakri.*

Is found in the Punjab Siwálik tract, and although it grows in the Salt Range to 2,500 feet, I have not seen it so far west as the last species in the former. The bark is used as that of the former.

N. O. THYMELÆACEÆ.

DAPHNE CANNABINA. Wall. (D. PAPYRACEA. Wall.)

Vernacular. R. *niggi, mahadev ka phúl.*

A laurel-like shrub which occurs sparingly, so far as I have observed, up to near the Indus in the Punjab Himalaya at from

3,500 to 8,000 feet. Cleghorn mentions that paper is made from its bark in the Punjab, but I have nowhere been told that this is the case, though in Kumaon, &c., large quantities are manufactured from it (the purple-flowered variety, Madden). In Chumba, the flowers appear to be hung up as offerings in temples.

D. OLEOIDES. Schreb. (MUCRONATA. Royle.)

Vernacular. J. *kútti lál, kanthan.* R. *gandlena, gándalún.* C. *kagsari, sind, swana, dona, mushur, shalangri.* R. *niggi, channi.* S. *zhi kak, zosho.* T. I. *laghúne.*

A shrub which is common at places on most of the rivers in the Punjab Himalaya at from 2,300 to 9,000 feet, and also occurs Trans-Indus. The latter may be D. MUCRONATA, var. b. AFFGHANICA, which in Belúchistán is said to be very hurtful to camels, but all these seem to me to be of one species. In Chumba, gunpowder charcoal is made from the wood. In Kanáwar the bark is given for colic, and it is used by women for washing their hair. It has, I believe, been tried for paper, I know not with what success. On the Chenab, the leaves or an infusion are given for gonorrhœa, and applied to abcessses. The pretty red berries are not unfrequently eaten, but are said to be apt to cause sickness.

WIKSTRŒMIA SALICIFOLIA. Dne.

Vernacular. R. *bhat niggi.* B. *thilák.*

A small shrubby plant, which occurs sparingly on some of the Punjab rivers in the Himalaya at from 5,500 to 7,000 feet, up to near the Indus. Madden states that paper (inferior to that from the DAPHNE q. v.) is made from its bark in Kumaon, and that it furnishes a strong rope at Nynee Tál.

N. O. ELÆAGNACEÆ.

ELÆAGNUS CONFERTA. (Rox.)
E. MOORCROFTII. Wall.
E. PARVIFOLIA. Royle.

Vernacular. J. K. *giwáin, kankol.* C. *gidnhan.* R. *ghin, gihen.* B. *kiáin.* S. *gikáin, rinsot.* Lad., *sarsing,* Aff., *sanjat.* Bazar, flowers, *gul sanjad, dákú phal.*

The identity of this is doubtful, but it seems to me to be the same species, which, as a considerable shrub, is frequent wild and perhaps sometimes planted in the Punjab Himalaya from 2,500 to 9,000 feet, while the species cultivated in Ladák to 10,600 feet is apparently very different, having a much larger leaf, and growing to a much larger size. I have not seen the latter in flower or fruit. E. MOORCROFTII is given by DeCandolle as growing in Ladák. Moorcroft states that there it grows to the west of the capital only, and I do not know of its being observed there out of Nuora and Baltistán. It may possibly be either the Himalayan or the Ladák species, which is common in Affghánistán, though this can hardly be, if, as Bellew mentions, the fruit there is as large as a cherry; and Moorcroft states that at Kábul a tree in good years will yield 16 or 20 lbs. of dried fruit, but I have never in the Himalaya seen one I should consider capable of anything like this. Thomson states that the tree supplies most of the winter fuel at Iskardo. The flowers have a pleasant odour. The somewhat acid fruit is eaten, and Griffith states that it is used medicinally as an astringent. The flowers at least are officinal in the Punjab, being considered cardiac and astringent. We might suppose that this is the shrub with an edible fruit noted by Vigne, as occurring below Báramúla, but elsewhere he states that from it (by name, so that he recognized it) a spirit is distilled in Yárkand. Moorcroft also mentions that a brandy is made from the fruit for the Mussalmáns and Chinese of Yárkand.

HIPPOPHAÆ RHAMNOIDES. L.

Vernacular. J. *kála bísa.* C. *bánt phút, amb, tswak, kando, tserkar, starbú.* B. *milech, miles.* S. *süts, rül.* Lad. *tsurmang, tsuk, tarrú.* P. *tsarma niechak;* fruit, *tirkú.*

A shrub which occurs in some places on most of the rivers of the Punjab Himalaya up to the Indus at from 7,500 to 10,500 feet, and is common in Lahoul, Spiti, and Tibet, to 13,000 or 14,000 feet, and even 15,500 feet in the last. It would appear that Griffith found it near Kábul (6,000 feet) in Affghánistán also. In Lahoul it is mentioned that female are much less common than male shrubs, but I have not noticed this markedly. The small fruit is so intensely sour, that in many places even the natives do not eat it. But Cleghorn states that a good jelly can be made from it, and Aitchison says it is really excellent with half its weight of sugar. The natives of Kanáwar are stated by Longden to eat it as a sort of *chatní*, but Aitchison mentions that those of Lahoul do not use it at all, although the above recipe is recommended for lung complaints in a Tibetan pharmacopia. In Lahoul and Ladák the plant often reaches 5 or 6 feet in girth and 20 or more in height; and as the wood is hard, it yields the best fuel and charcoal. In these tracts also, the spinous branches are largely used for fences, a purpose which they answer admirably.

N. O. DATISCACEÆ.

Datisca cannabina. L.

Vernacular. J. *kalbír.* C. *egilbír, drinkhari, sída atsú.* Bazár, root, *akilbír.*

This occurs on most of the great rivers in the Punjab Himalaya up to near the Indus at from 3,800 to 9,000 feet. It is a tall herbaceous plant exceedingly like hemp—(see Cannabis)—in appearance. In some of the places where it grows, the yellow root is used to aid in dyeing red, and Cleghorn states that it is exported from Pangí, Lahoul, and Kúllú, to Nadoun and Umritsur, to be used in dyeing woollen thread. Edgeworth mentions that for this purpose it is combined with *asburg*—(see Delphinium saniculæfolium). About 1853, several attempts were made to transport live roots of this plant to Lahore. (It has since been raised from seed I brought down, but appears to have died out); and about the same time enquiries were made as to the price the root would be likely to bring in Europe. But the reply was, that yellow dyes are very cheap in England. In Khágán the bruised root is applied to the head as a sedative, and Madden mentions that under the name of *bajr banga* it is used medicinally in Kumaon.

N. O. ARISTOLOCHIACEÆ.

Aristolochia sp.

Vernacular. Bazár, root, *zaráwand.*

Lowther states that he found a species growing near Púnch, in Kashmír territory, but this is extremely improbable. Some of the kinds of the officinal *zaráwand,* considered to resemble *sálib misrí* in effect—(see Eulophia)—are said to be roots of a species of A.

N. O. EUPHORBIACEÆ.

Adelia serrata.

Vernacular. C. *chopra, chiúndí.* R. *chírndí.* B. *chiraunda, drendú, thakola, katháglí.*

A small tree common in the Siwálik tract to 4,000 feet at times, up to the Chenáb. Its wood is used for fuel and charcoal.

ANDRACHNE TELEPHIOIDES. L.?

Vernacular. T. I. *tik.* B. D. *dodak.*

A small weed occasionally found in the Punjab plains Cis and Trans-Indus. In some places it appears to be mixed with corrosive sublimate previous to subliming the latter for medicinal application.

BALIOSPERMUM INDICUM. Dne. (B. MONTANUM MULLER. B. POLYANDRUM. Wt.)

Vernacular. C. *suplád, dant.* R. *nikkí japhrotí.* T. I. *tora-pána.* Bazar, seed, *jamálgota.*

A weed of considerable size, which is common at places in the Punjab Siwálik belt and near it up to 3,200 feet, Cis and Trans-Indus. Its seeds are cathartic, and probably furnish greater part of the *jamálgota* of the drug-sellers. Madden states that east of the Sutlej its leaves are in high repute for wounds, and its sap is believed to corrode iron.

BUXUS SEMPERVIRENS. L.

Vernacular. J. *chíkní.* B. *shumshád, shumáj, sufêd dháwí.* S. *páprang.* T. I. *shánda laghúne.* S. R. *páprí, pappar.* Bazár, wood, *chíkrí.*

Generally seen as a shrub from lopping, but at times grows to a tree of some girth, locally only, on the Sutlej and Biás, upon the Rattan Pír, near Púnch, above Rawul Pindí, in the Salt Range, and Trans-Indus. The flowers have a strong and not unpleasant smell. Near its places of growth, the branches are put under the earth of roofs, as they are said not to decay easily. Goats will browse a few of the leaves, but other animals will not touch them, unless in cases of dearth, and they have at times proved fatal to camels, &c. Mr. Watson, Madhopur Workshops, states that the wood is not equal to that of olive—(see OLEA)—but the specimen must have been an inferior one or badly seasoned, for, when well seasoned, this is said to be equal to that of Europe, for the uses to which the latter is generally applied. It is carried to Umritsur and other places in the plains to be made into combs, but the supply is probably getting exhausted.

CROZOPHORA PLICATA. Mull.

Vernacular. B. D. *put kanda.* Bazár, leaves, &c., *nílkhanthí.*

Occurs sparingly in the plains of the central and southern Punjab. In the Bári Doáb, the ashes of the root are given to children for cough. The leaves, &c., of this or the next species are officinal under the above name (which is applied to several other substances, *e. g.*, AJUGA q. v.) They are considered depurative.

C. TINCTORIA. L. (C. OBLONGIFOLIA).

Vernacular. B. D. *tappal búti, nílan.* Hí., *kukronda.*

Not uncommon in the central, southern, and western Punjab. So abundant on some of the low ground near Lahore that it is cut and carried into the city to be used as fuel for ovens.

EMBLICA OFFICINALIS. Gært.

Vernacular. C. *amblí.* R. *ambal.* B. *amla.* Plains, *áonla.*

A tree of some size, which grows in the Punjab Siwálik tract to 3,000 feet up to near the Indus, and is not uncommon cultivated out in the plains except in the extreme west. Specimens of 6 or 7 feet girth occur,—I have noted one of 9 feet. The wood is hard, strong, and straight-grained, but is said to be somewhat brittle. It is used for gun-stocks, door-frames, well-work, &c. The fruit is very sour (whence the native names), and is used in pickle and preserve; also in medicine as a purgative, antispasmodic, and tonic, alone or mixed with salt or black salt. It is also employed in making ink and in black dye, as well as for washing the hair. Davies' Trade Report gives the annual export viâ Peshawar to Affgháuistán at 50 maunds. In various parts of India, the leaves, bark, &c., are used medicinally.

EUPHORBIA DRACUNCULOIDES. Lam., or E. NEPALENSIS. Boiss.

Vernacular. Bazar, fruit, &c., *ríchní, sudáb;* plant, *kangi*

Both of these species are rather common field-weeds in parts of the Punjab plains, but are less frequent towards the west. The fruit of one or both is officinal under the first name, and it is often sold as *sudáb*—(see RUTA). From the first species it would appear that oil is or was extracted near Loodiana (Journal Agri-Horticultural Society, India, Vol. 2, page 91. The second appears to be officinal nnder the name *kangí.*

E. HELIOSCOPIA. L.

Vernacular. T. I. *ganda búte.* S. R. *dúdal.* B. D. *kulfadodak, chatríwal.*

A common field-weed in spring throughout the Punjab plains and the Siwálik tract, and to 7,000 feet in the outer Himalaya. The milky juice is applied to eruptions, and Honigberger states that the seeds are given with roasted pepper in cholera. It is probably this species, of which, as "common spurge," Bellew mentions that in Affghánistán the juice is used as a liniment in neuralgia and rheumatism, and the root is given as an anthelmintic.

E. HYPERICIFOLIA. L.

Vernacular. Bazár, seeds and leaves, *hazárdána.*

A small species common in many parts of the Punjab plains and the Siwálik tract. In some places it is given with milk to children for colic, and would appear to be officinal under the above name.

E. LONGIFOLIA. Don.

Vernacular.

A tall species found in the Punjab Himalaya apparently at from 4,000 to 11,000 feet. Honigberger mentions that in Kashmír its root is applied to fistulous sores.

E. ROYLEANA. Bois.

Vernacular. J. *súlí.* C. *chúla.* R. *chún.* B. *chú, chiú, chúngha, súrs.* S. *súrú, tsúi.* S. R. *tordanda, danda, tor.* Bazár, dried juice, *afárbiún?*

Common wild in the Siwálik tract to 3,500 and occasionally found to 5,000 feet, up to the Jhelam only, as far as I have seen. Is frequently planted as a hedge to some little way from the hills, as at Jalandar, Seálkôt, &c., but does not grow very freely further out in the plains, although a few plants are at times seen at fakírs,' &c. In the tract where it is indigenous, when the accidental gaps are helped by thorns, &c., it forms a most formidable and impenetrable fence. In that tract it grows from cuttings with great ease, and I have seen these flourishing when stuck into ridges of shale splinters without a speck of soil. The stems are frequently 2 feet and sometimes reach 5 or 6 feet in girth, but do not often exceed 15 or 16 feet high. The structure of the wood is radiating and very loose, and it is of no use. Honigberger states that the milky juice, which abounds in the plant, is used in medicine, both externally and internally, but my enquiries have failed to elicit this, and I suspect he must have confused it with the next plant. This may, however, possibly furnish part of the officinal *afárbiún,* which is the inspissated juice of some EUPHORBIA. It was reported many years ago to the Agri-Horticultural Society, Punjab, that at Pind Dadun Khan the inspissated juice of this is used for adulterating opium, but otherwise I have not heard of this. An

European Engineer in the service of the Maharajah of Jummoo made some experiments on the milky juices of various plants in order to get a substitute for red lead in closing steam joints, and as a coating for cisterns, &c. He found that by boiling down the juice of this EUPHORBIA, adding dates and again boiling and skimming, he got a gutta-percha-like material better fitted for his purpose than from the FICUS INDICA or F. RELIGIOSA, &c. But practically the experiment does not appear to have had much result.

E. SP.

Vernacular. B. *gángíchú.*

A species which much resembles the last, but the stems are not hexagonal, as the rows of spines run spirally, not straight up and down. May be E. NERIIFOLIA, L. This I have nowhere seen wild, but an occasional specimen is seen with the other out in the plains, and it is not uncommon in' hedges in parts of the Siwálik tract. Its milk is applied to incipient abscesses, and is said to be effectual in preventing suppuration.

E. THYMIFOLIA. Bur.

Vernacular. *bara dodak* (Honigberger). Bazár, leaves and flowers, *hazárdána.*

A common weed in parts of the Punjab plains. Honigberger mentions that its juice is said to be a violent purgative. The fruit, &c., are officinal at Lahore.

FLUGGEA LEUCOPYRUS.

Vernacular. J. *karkún.* C. *ríthei, gulílí.* R. B. *girthan.*

A small tree occasionally seen wild in the Siwálik tract to 4,000 feet up to near the Indus. It appears only to be used for fuel.

F. VIROSA. Rox.

Vernacular. B. *girk.* T. I. *pereí pastáwane.* S. R. *báta, vanúthí.*

A small tree which occurs at low elevations in the Siwálik region, Salt Range, and Trans-Indus. The fruit is eaten by men and animals, and the wood is close-grained and strong, and is used for making part of a loom.

GLOCHIDION SP. (PHYLLANTHUS VELUTINUS. Mull. ?)

Vernacular. J. *gol kamíla, sama.* C. *bera.* R. *sama amblú.* B. *koamil, kalam.* S. *píndna.*

A small tree not uncommon in the Punjab Siwálik tract up to near the Indus. The wood is only used as fuel, the bark is employed for tanning.

JATROPHA CURCAS. Willd.

Vernacular. C. *rattanjot.* R. *japhrota.* B. *rattanjot, jablota, pín.* Bazár, seeds, *jumálgota.*

A soft-wooded shrub not uncommon planted by houses, &c., in or as a hedge in and near the Punjab Siwálik tract up to the Chenáb. It is said to be readily propagated by slips. The leaves are in some places applied to bruises, &c., and the milky juice is used to destroy maggots in sheep's sores. The seeds are commonly given as a purgative, probably furnishing part of the *jumálgota,* but are said to be less powerful than those of BALIOSPERMUM (q. v.) The fruit is stated to kill cattle that eat it.

LEPTOPUS CORDIFOLIUS. Dne. (ARACHNE CORDIFOLIA. Mull.)

Vernacular. J. *kurkni, gurgúlí.* R. *kurkúlí.* C. *bersu.* R. *barotri, madáre.* B. *mútkar, chírmútti, pín.* S. *tsatin.*

A slender shrub frequent in parts of the Punjab Himalaya at from 2,500 to 7,500 feet. The twigs and leaves are said to kill cattle when browsed in the early morning on an empty stomach.

PUTRANJIVA ROXBURGHII. Wall.

Vernacular. C. R. B. *putájan.* Bazár, seeds, *jiapota*; leaves, *pútrajívak.*

A tree which occurs in the eastern part of the Siwálik tract, and is occasionally planted in and near it. It is handsome, and has fine foliage, but does not generally reach a large size. I have seen one or two trees of 9 feet girth. The leaves, &c., are lopped off for fodder. The wood is white, strong, and durable, and in some parts of India is used by turners; in the Punjab it is only made into implements, &c. The leaves and the stones of the fruit are officinal in some parts of the Punjab, and the latter are used by Hindú fakírs, &c., as necklaces (*tasbih*), but most of the supply probably comes from the east.

RICINUS COMMUNIS. L.

Vernacular. C. *anerú.* S. R. *harnaulí.* Generally, *arand.*

This shrub is occasionally seen in waste ground in the Punjab plains throughout, and is not uncommon up to 3,500 and occasionally 4,000 feet in the hills. It is easily raised from seed, but seems to be liable to injury from frost. Animals are stated to be killed by eating its leaves, and in Harriána they are applied to guinea-worm to promote its expulsion. Elphinstone says that sweet oil is extracted from it at Peshawar, but it is not common there, and I do not find that the oil is extracted in the Punjab. As it grows well however, projects have been raised for cultivating it on the large scale for oil in the desert tract south of Lahore, &c., but have as yet failed. Bellew states that near Ghuzní (7,000 feet) in Affghánistán, the oil is used for domestic and culinary purposes, but I cannot find that in the Punjab it is ever used except medicinally. Aitchison mentions that in Jhelam the seeds are put into curries. They are commonly used for a purgative, half a dozen being sufficient for an adult. Bellew states that the flowers are given as a laxative, but this seems doubtful.

Rottlera tinctoria. Rox.

Vernacular. J. *kamíla*. C. *kembal*. R. *kámil*. B. *kámíl, kemal*. S. *reún*. U. *reini*. Bazár, powder off fruit, *kamela*; seed, *báobrang*.

An abundant shrub, growing sometimes to a considerable size (I have seen it of 3½ feet girth, though a size even approaching this is rare) throughout the Punjab Siwálik tract and outer hills occasionally up to 4,500 feet. The wood is poor, and is for the most part only used for fuel, though it is said that it is not subject to insects. The bark is in some places used by tanners. The red powder brushed off the capsules is employed as a red dye for silk, is a valuable vermifuge, especially for tape-worm, and is mixed with ointment for skin diseases. There is but a small quantity on each capsule, and there is some slight exaggeration in the recent statement in a newspaper that in Kángra enough could be collected to dye half the clothes and physic all the patients in the world. The seeds are officinal as *báobrang* (perhaps from some confusion with *bebrang*—see Myrsine), being given for uterine pains, &c.

N. O. BETULACEÆ.

Alnus sp. (Clethropsis nitida. Spach.) Alder.

Vernacular. J. *shrol, rikúnra*. K. *srol, sawálí, silein*. C. *chámp, tsápú, piák*. R. *koc*. S. *kúnsh, kúnich niú*. T. I. *gíra, ghuzhbe*. B. D. *rajáin*.

It seems to me that the Alders I have seen from 9,000 feet in the Punjab Himalaya to a few miles into the plains in the Bárí Doáb and in the Peshawar Valley, are all of one species or very nearly allied. The tree is handsome, attains a large size, specimens of 10 or 12 feet girth and 90 to 100 high, being frequent. The leaves appear to be sometimes used as fodder. The twigs are employed for binding loads and parts of bridges, &c. The wood is white, said to be weak, but is used for bedsteads, for the hooked stick of rope bridges, &c. Cleghorn states that it is also made into charcoal for iron-smelting, and into gunpowder charcoal. The bark is employed for tanning and dyeing, and Madden mentions that it enters into the preparation of red ink.

BETULA BHOJPUTRA. Wall. (B. JACQUEMONTII. Spach.) Birch.

Vernacular. J. *búrj, phúrz.* K. *búrjrí.* C. *búrzal, bhúj, shág, stagpa;* bark, *drowa.* R. *búrj.* S. *shag, shák, tagpa* (Longden). Lad. *takpa.*

The birch, found abundantly in the Punjab Himalaya at from 7,000 to 11,500 feet, appears to me to be all of the same or very closely allied species. It also occurs on the border of western Tibet. It grows to a higher elevation than most other trees, and may generally be seen occupying a tract above coniferous forests. The tree at times reaches 6 or 7 feet, and I have seen it 10 in girth and 35 feet high. The wood is almost valueless, and is only used for ploughs, small bridges, &c., at altitudes and in tracts where other trees are scarce. Mr. Watson, however, tells me that it is good for turning, and in Kanáwar poles of it are used for carrying and swinging a heavy kind of *ark* in religious processions, which implies some strength and elasticity. In Ladák the striking part of the stick for *polo,* "hockey on horseback," is made from it. In Kángra, "being sacred," the bark is used for funeral piles, and at the shrines of Umrnáth, in Kashmír, the pilgrims are said to strip and indue themselves with this. (?) In Kashmír and Kumaon it is found very durable put under the earthen roofs, and it is largely used for covering umbrellas and packing apples, pomegranates, tobacco, and drugs. It is also employed for writing paper, for which it is said to do excellently, and is exported to the plains for wrapping round hooka tubes. It sells for three rupees a *kharwár,* (ass-load) in Kashmír, according to Lowther. The price in Chumba was stated to me at ten to sixteen seers for a rupee. Longden mentions that the old bridge at Koksar (now replaced by a more civilized one) was made of birchen twigs—(see PARROTIA).

N. O. CUPULIFERÆ.

QUERCUS ANNULATA. Sm.

Vernacular. J. *bren, brán.* R. *banní, indrí.* B. *banní.* S. *bánní.*

A moderate sized tree occasionally seen on most of the rivers of the Punjab Himalaya in warm sunny situations at from 2,000 to 5,500 feet. The wood is white and similar to that of Q. INCANA, and is not valued.

Q. DILATATA. Lindl. (Q. FLORIBUNDA. Lind.)

Vernacular. J. *parúngí, barchar, káli ríng, chora.* K. *barάin.* C. *maurú, karsh.* R. *márú, banjí, banní.* B. *satrún.* S. *morú, marghang.*

This tree is abundant in many parts of the Punjab Himalaya (being more common within the outer ranges) from 4,500 to 9,000 feet. Bellew found it near the Sufêd Koh at 9,000 to 10,000 feet. It grows to a large size, trees of 8 and 10 feet girth and 80 to 100 high being not uncommon. I have noted one of more than 15 feet girth. Madden mentions a tree of 19 feet girth at 5 feet from the ground. It furnishes probably the best wood of any oak of the N. W. Himalaya, the timber being hard, heavy, durable, and much used for ploughs, axe-handles, house-building, &c. It is also said to be much used for *jámpán*-poles at some hill stations. The leaves are frequently given as fodder, for which purpose the trees are often very severely lopped and reduced almost to hop-poles.

Q. ILEX. L., (and Q. BALOOT. Griff. ?)

Vernacular. J. *chúr.* C. *írrí, yírú, khareo.* R. *bán, kathún bán.* S. *bre.* T. I. *spercherei, pargái, kharanja.* Aff., *sháh balút.*

This tree, which does not grow to such a large size as most of the others, is common in part of the arid tracts of most of the Punjab rivers at from 3,200 to 8,000 feet. It is also abundant on the eastern skirts of the Súlimán Range, Trans-Indus, and abounds in the northern part of Affghánistán. Bellew got it at 10,000 feet near the Sufêd Koh. These last and part of those Cis-Indus may be Q. BALOOT, Griff., if that species has stood. The tree is ordinarily about 5 or 6 feet in girth, but is not unfrequently seen of 9 or 10 feet girth and 60 to 70 high. Ploughs and handles are at times made of its wood, but it is not much valued, and is mostly used for fuel; a considerable part of that for the station of Peshawar is furnished by it. The leaves being very prickly, the branches are employed for fences, and the leaves are sometimes used for winter fodder. The fruit is said to be a favourite food of the *langúr* monkey (SEMNOPITHECUS).

Q. INCANA. Rox. (Q. LANATA. Sm.)

Vernacular. J. *ríng, rínj, banj.* C. *bánj, márú, kharshu, shindar.* R. *banj, bán, daghún-bán.* B. *ban, bán.* S. *bán.* T. I. *kharpata serei.* S. R. *vart.* Bazár, fruit, *bálút;* galls, *majú ?*

The commonest of all the oaks of the N. W. Himalaya, but more particularly affecting the outer ranges. It grows at from 3,000 to 8,000 feet, and reaches 7 or 8 and occasionally 9 feet in girth. It has at times been grown in the plains, and in Saháranpur Botanical Garden there is a tree of 2 feet girth and 25 high. The tree generaaay sheds its old leaves, and throws out new shoots in April, but in 1867 (an early year in India and Europe) it is stated to have retained the old leaves till June or even September, and to have thrown out no new shoots. The timber is reddish, heavy, and coarse, and is not much valued, but is sometimes used for ploughs, handles, beams, &c. Mr. Watson speaks well of it, but says—"I have never got it good;" and a large quantity of it, which was got down for locks on the Bárí Doáb Canal, was, I believe, never used. It may, however, have been cut at the wrong season, a mistake apt to occur in our Himalaya, where deodár, the chief tree, is felled in summer. A good deal of the fuel of some hill stations is furnished by this tree, and it is used for charcoal. The bark is employed in tanning, and the leaves are consumed for fodder. The *bálút* of the drug-sellers, which are considered diuretic and given in gonorrhæa, consists of its fruit. Part of the galls of the Bazárs, used as medicine, may be got from this or some of the other species noted, but I have never observed galls on the trees, and I believe the former are imported from the west. They are used as astringent in diarrhæa, &c., and in dyeing the hair.

Q. SEMECARPIFOLIA. Wall.

Vernacular. J. *banchar, jangal parúngí.* C. *khareu.* R. *kreu.* B. *karshú.* S. *khareo, kharshú, kharsúí.*

This grows to the largest size of any oak of the N. W. Himalaya, and may not unfrequently be seen in numbers up to 7 or 8 and occasionally 11 or 12 feet in girth, and 60 or 70 feet high. I have noted trees as much as 15 feet in girth. It is common in many places on all the rivers from 8,000 to 11,000 and occasionally 12,000 feet, and is abundant on the Sufêd Koh, &c., Trans-Indus, at 10,000 feet (Bellew). The large acorns ripen about August, and generally germinate within a very short time after falling. The timber is whitish, hard, and heavy, and one of the best furnished by these oaks, but is said to be apt to warp, and to be subjeet to the attacks of insects. It is used for plough-shafts, *jámpán*-poles, helves, door-frames, &c., and for charcoal. The leaves are stored for winter fodder for cattle and sheep.

N. O. CORYLACEÆ.

CARPINUS VIMINEA. Wall. Hornbeam.

Vernacular. R. *charkhre.* B. *shirásh.* S. *ímar.*

A moderate sized tree, which is seen occasionally in the Punjab Himalaya at from 5,500 to 6,000 feet up to the Rávi. Cleghorn states that its wood is esteemed by carpenters.

Corylus Colurna. L. var. b. lacera. (C. lacera. Wall.), and var. c. Jacquemontii. (C. Jacquemontii. Dne.)

Vernacular. J. *urrni.* K. *winri.* C. *wúria, wíri, thangoli.* R. *thángi.* B. *sharolí, sharoi.* S. *sharolí, shúrlí, ge.* Bazár, nut, *findak.*

A small tree common on some parts of the rivers in the Punjab Himalaya from 5,500 to 10,500 feet. It sometimes reaches 6 or 7 feet girth and 35 or 40 feet high, but most trees are much under these dimensions. Cleghorn states that the wood is light and compact, but I have not heard that it is particularly esteemed. The nuts are small, but fairly good, are largely eaten by the natives, and find their way in some numbers into several of the hill stations. Excessive rains are apt to lessen the crop of a season very much. The translator of Hoffmeister states that the kernels are not unfrequently pressed for oil, but I have not heard of this practice in the Punjab Himalaya. The nuts are not uncommon in drug-sellers' shops, being considered tonic. One authority mentions that the term *findak* is also applied to the apricot kernels and almonds—(see Amygdalus and Prunus Armeniaca)—imported from Affghánistán into Peshawar.

N. O. JUGLANDACEÆ.

Juglans regia. L. Walnut.

Vernacular. J. *akhrot.* K. *dún, chármaghz.* C. *than thán, khor, ká, darga.* R. *khor, akhori, krot.* S. *krot, ka-botang.* Lad., *starga.* T. I. *ughz, waghz.* Bazár, bark, *dindása.*

Not uncommon wild, and common cultivated in the Himalaya from 5,000 to 10,000 feet, and to nearly 11,000 feet in Tibet. Planted this may occasionally be seen in the outer hills down to about 3,500 feet, and young trees can be raised in the plains, though they generally die early; one, however, I have known to yield fruit in Peshawar. On the Chenáb and Sutlej the walnut does not ripen its fruit above 9,000 feet, but wild trees may be seen on the latter to 10,500. The tree also grows Trans-Indus, in Affgháuistán, &c., and there are said to be a few in Belúchistán. The largest trees I have noted were one of 28 feet girth in Kullú, and one of 22 feet in Chumba, and specimens up to 12 and 15 feet are not very rare. The produce of the wild tree is generally said to be very inferior, and hardly worth eating. The fruit ripens about August, and for some time forms a large proportion of the food of the people of those parts of especially Kashmír, and the Chenáb and Sutlej Valleys, where the tree is most abundant. It is mostly eaten raw, part being exported to the hill stations. A considerable quantity of the kernels are bruised by stones, and the oil expressed by hand. The oil is used for food, and at times for burning. In Kashmír the soft skin of the fruit is employed for dyeing drab (without a mordant), a little black being added to darken it if necessary. The wood of an old tree is dark, hardish, and strong, and takes a good polish, nor is it subject to warp or be attacked by insects. It is chiefly made into gun-stocks, cabinet-work, the shells of the Kashmír painted boxes, &c. Mr. Watson says that it is useful when got large. The bark is largely exported to the plains to be sold under the name of *dinddsa* for women's tooth-sticks, or for chewing to give a red colour to the lips; it is said to prevent the formation of tartar. It also seems occasionally to be used in medicine. The small branches and leaves are regularly and severely lopped to furnish winter fodder. On the Sutlej it is said that if the trees get a rest in this respect every fourth year, the quality of the fruit is not deteriorated. Honigberger states that a twig is recommended to be kept in a room to dispel flies.

N. O. MYRICACEÆ.

Myrica Sapida. Wall.

Vernacular. R. B. S. *kaphal.* Bazár, bark, *káiphal, káhí kahela ?*

Within Punjab limits the tree is by no means common except on the lower Sutlej, and a few trees may be seen at from 3,200 to 6,000 feet up to the Rávi. The fruit has not much flesh, but is a pleasant sour sweet. It is mostly used in *sharbats.* The bark is officinal in the plains, being considered hot, and given in rheumatism, and mixed in plaster.

N. O. PLATANACEÆ.

Platanus orientalis. L. Plane.

Vernacular. K. *búin, búna*; elsewhere, *chinár, chanár.*

I have never seen this tree wild, and statements to the effect that it is indigenous in or near Kashmír (as by Hugel), probably arise from some confusion with Acer, owing to the resemblance of the leaves. It appears to be tolerably common planted in Affghánistán, and is frequently seen at villages, &c., in the Punjab Himalaya, extending sparingly east to the Biás, and up to 8,300 feet in Tibet. In the Kashmír Valley it is abundant, the trees ranging up to 75 feet high, and I have noted seven or eight of about or more than 20 feet, the largest being 28 feet girth, in Srínaggar, Kashmír. The spread of two trees measured by me had a radius of 37 and 44 feet respectively in one direction. I have been told by an European Officer of one seen by another Officer near the Wúlar lake of 84 feet in girth, but this seems doubtful, and is possibly a corruption of Vigne's statement that he saw one of 66 feet girth under the Elburz near Teheran. The finest grove in Kashmír, or perhaps in the world, is the Nasím Bagh, on the banks of the lake, near the city of Srínaggar, which at one time consisted of 1,200 noble trees said to be planted nearly 200 years ago. The tree is propagated by cuttings (and occasionally by seed in Kashmír). In the Punjab plains trees may occasionally be seen, as at Peshawar and Lahore, there being one or two of fair size in old native gardens at the latter place. To the eastward it does not thrive; one small tree, dead at top, stands in Sahárànpúr Botanic Gardens. The wood has a peculiar and rather handsome grain, but appears not to be strong and is not valued. Yet, in Kábul, where timber is scarce, Irvine states that it is the only material for gun-carriages, and in Kashmír it furnishes part of the wood for making the small painted boxes. Honigberger states that the bruised fresh leaves are applied to the eyes in ophthalmia, and he mentions that the bark, boiled in vinegar, is given in diarrhœa. Attention has been drawn to a corky hypertrophy of the bark in Kashmír, and the substance might be useful, but seems to be far from common.

N. O. SALICACEÆ.

Populus Alba. L. White Poplar.

Vernacular. J. *safēda, chita bagnú.* K. *fras, janglí-frast, ríkkan.* C. *ríkkan, prastí, sannan, chanúní.* S. *mál.* T. I. *spelda, sperdor.* Plains, *safēda.*

A tree which grows wild to a considerable size in parts of the basins of the Jhelam and Chenáb, and is occasional on the Sutlej, ranging from 4,000 to 8,500 feet, reaching 9,000 in Tibet. Trees of 6 and even 8 feet in girth and 50 or occasionally 70 in height are seen, but they are mostly considerably smaller than these sizes. Of thousands of specimens I have never seen one in fruit. Wild trees are often seen uprooted by the wind. The tree is also common planted in parts at least of Affghánistán to 9,200 in Tibet (Thomson), is not uncommon planted at Peshawar, and grows at Lahore. It is propagated by cuttings. The timber is white and soft, but not strong or durable, and is not valued. In Affghánistán it (with perhaps that of P. fastigiata q. v.) is used for manufacturing the round boxes in which grapes are exported to India.

P. BALSAMIFERA. L. Balsam Poplar.

Vernacular. C. *yarpa*. Lad., *berfa, makal, maghal*. P. *máal, changma*.

This tree, which I have in part confused with P. FASTIGIATA (q. v.), is common planted in Lahoul (at 9—10,000 feet), and in Ladák (up to 14,000 feet), in Spiti (to 12,500 feet), and probably on the Sutlej. Aitchison mentions that in Lahoul it is never cut, as it is supposed to be the abode of the *dewa* (deity), and festivals are held under some of the finer specimens, which reach 50 feet in height. In Ladák they reach 60 or 70 feet, and I have there noted a plank of the wood 2½ feet broad, and seen one tree of 9 feet girth.

P. CILIATA. Wall. Himalayan Poplar.

Vernacular. J. *sufêdar, sháwa, bagnú, phalja*. K. *sufêdar, bagnú, suláli, dúdfras*. C. *supêda, ríkkan, ban frastú, flassú, chanún, pabe*. R. *chalon, tallon, falsh*. B. *chalonwa, falsh*. S. *chalonwa, kramalí*.

This tree grows to a large size, occasionally reaching 10 feet in girth, and from its leaves, resembling those of the *pípal*—(see FICUS RELIGIOSA)—is frequently called by that name by plainsmen. It is common wild in the Punjab Himalaya up to the Indus at from 4,000 to 10,000 feet. The wood is soft and not valued, but is used for water troughs, and in Hazára occasionally for gun-stocks. In some places the leaves are given as fodder. There is a plentiful floss round the seeds, which has at times been recommended for paper-making, &c.

P. EUPHRATICA. Oliv.

Vernacular. Lad., *hodung, hotung*. T. I. and S. P. *búhan, sufêda, sperawan ?*

This tree, which grows on the Jordan, Tigris, and Euphrates, is common wild in Sind and in the southern Punjab in the low land along near rivers. I have seen trees of it as high as Dera Ishmail Khan, and on the Indus it is said to be found occasionally in nooks up to Attock. Far above that on the Indus river or its tributaries, it is found in parts of Tibet (western) to 10,500 feet, and Aitchison mentions it in his Lahoul list, but this specimen may have been a Tibetan one, of which there appears to have been a few in the collection. In the southern Punjab (where planted specimens occur in Múltán, &c.,) the tree grows to no great size, specimens of 5 feet girth not being common, but this may partly depend on the excessive lopping to which it is subjected to provide fodder for goats. In Sind, where it is better cared for, trees of 7 or 8 feet girth are not uncommon. The leaves vary in shape to a considerable extent, especially in the plains, some being quite narrow, long, lanceolate, entire, and knife-like, and others excessively broad with a comb-like edge. The leaves of the Ladák trees vary much less. Thomson's statement, that the narrow leaves are found on young plants and pollarded shoots, and the broad ones on old trees, is to a considerable extent correct. These and intermediate varieties occur on both male and female trees, the latter being more common, so far as I have observed, in the Punjab plains. In places where the tree is subject to inundations, it is sometimes covered with short horn-like roots to 18 inches from the ground. (I have seen a similar growth on willows in like circumstances in Kashmír). From the wood of the tree on parts of the trunk, short spines project into the inner part of the bark (and see ULMUS EROSA). The wood is generally white, soft, and toughish, and, when unseasoned, is very subject to the attacks of white ants. But in old trees there is usually a large proportion of very dark strong heart-wood. In the southern Punjab the timber is for the most part only used for wells, &c., but in Sind it is largely employed for beams, &c., (not for planks), and in turnery. In Sind also the smaller trees are cut as coppice, and speedily spring again to furnish a fresh crop of rafters. The wood, being white (and so not *flesh*-coloured), is preferred for constructive purposes by Hindús, and for the same reason the twigs are used by them as tooth-sticks. The wood is rarely used for boats in Sind, but is said to be largely so employed on the Euphrates, &c. It is also employed for fuel in the south (in part even for steamers, although from its lightness it is not very suitable), and in parts of Tibet, where it grows, it furnishes much fire-wood. In Sind the bark is given as a vermifuge, and the liber is employed as a gun-match.

P. NIGRA. L. var. b. PYRAMIDALIS. Italian Poplar.

Vernacular. K. *frast.* C. *frast, prost, farsh, suféda, mak kal, pakhshú bút.* S. *kramalí, biúns.* Lad., *changma, yarpa, yúlatt, kabul, kaúll.* Plains, *sufêdar.*

This tree is common planted in Kashmír, on the Chenab, at from 3,000 to 11,500 feet, and on the Sutlej, and in Ladák, to 13,300 feet. Scattered specimens are not uncommon elsewhere in the hills, and it is occasionally seen at places in the plains, as Peshawar, Lahore, &c. I have never seen a wild tree or flower or fruit of this species. It appears to be common in Affghánistán, where the wood seems to be used as that of P. ALBA (q. v.) Elsewhere, I am not aware that it is employed for any special purpose. In Kashmír it grows in great luxuriance, being generally planted in rows, sometimes so very closely that two trees will grow together at the base (as seems to be the case in Affghánistán also). In Kashmír trees of 6 or 8 feet in girth are not uncommon, and some reach 10 and 12 feet. The celebrated "poplar avenue," close to Srínaggar, the capital, is probably one of the finest things of its kind in the world. It is perfectly straight, a row of trees on each side of a level road more than a mile long. They number about 1,700 in all. Most of them range from 90 to 105 feet high. A local guide-book says that these were planted by the Sikhs, but Lowther is much more likely to be correct in calling the avenue a "tasteful relic of the Moslems." In Ladák few of the trees exceed 50 or 60 feet high, with a proportionate girth. The bark is officinal in the plains, an *arak* being extracted from it, which is considered depurative. The tree is lopped in some places, probably for fodder.

SALIX.

The Himalayan species have not yet been thoroughly identified (Aitchison mentions nine undetermined species in Lahoul), and unfortunately I have not always sufficiently discriminated those I have seen or collected. I must here do the best with the data I have.

SALIX ALBA. L. (?)

Vernacular. J. *bis.* K. *vwir.* C. *yür, changma.* Lad., *chungmá, chámmá. málchang, kalchan.* P. *changma.* T. I. *kharwala.*

There is considerable doubt as to this species, but it or an allied one appears to be common in many parts of the Himalaya, as Kashmír, Pangí, Lahoul, and Ladák &c., from 5,000 up to 14,500 feet occasionally in the last, and it seems to occur Trans-Indus. It is generally planted, but is probably wild also in many places. It reaches 8 and 9 feet in girth when well protected. Moorcroft mentions one of 16 feet, but the largest trees are very often hollow. In Kashmír the willow is used largely for basket-making; and in Tibet Thomson mentions that many of the houses are made of willow wattle and dab. Twig bridges of willow are mentioned in Spiti, Zanskar, and Ladák, where PARROTIA (q. v.) is not found. In Kashmír the twigs are employed as tooth-sticks. There also, and still more on the Chenáb and in Ladák, the trees are severely and systematically lopped, the young shoots and bark of the larger, removed by hand, being used as fodder. It is worth consideration whether the great quantity of salicin the cattle must consume there ought not to have some effect on them. In Lahoul the branches are mostly cut for this purpose about every 3rd or 4th year only, just ere the grass springs up, but are acceptable to cattle at any time. (Moorcroft erroneously supposed that in Lahoul the willows are all pollarded for basket-work). Aitchison states that the timber is not much used in Lahoul, but Moorcroft says that in Tibet the whole plough (except the point, which is iron) is generally made of willow. Irvine notes that in Affghánistán willow wood is generally used for building, as insects do not attack it. On the Chenáb, pails, &c., are rudely cut from single blocks of the wood, and, according to Moorcroft, combs, to remove the fine goat's hair from the animal's back, are in Ladák made of it. In Spiti, &c., the poles and wattle-work of bridges are made of this. In Lahoul the tree is propagated in spring by cuttings up to 9 or 12 feet long, three of which are generally put in together along watercourses, &c. These are sometimes bound round with cord, cloth, &c., or surrounded by cut branches, to protect them from animals, but in many cases, where not so protected, the whole of the outer surfaces of the trees which are not nearly in contact, have the bark gnawed off by cattle, forage being very scarce in that tract. Mr. Jaeschke, of the Moravian Mission, Lahoul, informed me that all the cultivated willows there appear to be male.

S. Babylonica. L.

Vernacular. K. *bisa, giur*. C. *bidái, bitsú*. R. B. *badá*. T. I. *wala*. Plains generally, *bed majnún, laila* (?) *katira*. Bazár, leaves, *bed majú*.

This tree is very common planted in the plains throughout the Punjab, being fully more abundant to the west, and frequently being of the graceful "weeping" type. It also grows to 5,500 feet in the hills, including Kashmír. Near Chumba I have seen trees of 12 feet girth. It grows rapidly, and is easily raised in moist places by cuttings up to stakes of considerable size, which are often planted to consolidate the banks of water-cuts, &c. Its branches and twigs are largely used for baskets, wattles, weirs, &c. I do not know that the natives use its wood for any special purpose, but good cricket bats have been made from it. The leaves are officinal, being reckoned tonic, possibly from the salicin in them.

S. Caprea. L.

Vernacular. *bed mushk*. Bazár, distilled water, *bed mushk, khiláf Balkhí*.

The only two places where I have seen this tree cultivated are Lahore and Peshawar, but I am told it is grown at Umritsur and several other pleces in the plains. Elphinstone mentions it at Kohát, and I know of its having been cultivated at one place in Rohilkund. A native correspondent of the Agri-Horticultural Society states that the tree was introduced at Lahore from Kashmír by Harí Chund soon after he conquered that country for Runjeet Singh, but I think this is extremely doubtful. Close to Lahore there are a good many acres of it, and there it is raised by cuttings, which are plantedout in March. The tree, which is irrigated throughout the year, does not grow to a large size, and is said only to flourish for 11 or 12 years. The large yellowish catkins of flowers appear in February, and are collected and sold at about 6 or 8 rupees per maund to *attárs*, who at once distil a scented water from them. This is mixed with water and drunk as a *sharbat*, which has a rather pleasant though somewhat medicinal taste. It is a great favourite with well-to-do natives, and is much belauded by native writers on medicine, &c. It is considered cordial, stimulant, and aphrodisiac, and is applied externally for headache and ophthalmia. The ashes of the wood are said to be useful in hæmoptysis, and with vinegar are applied to hæmorrhoids, &c. The stem and leaves are considered astringent, and the juice and *gum (?)* also are said to be used medicinally.

S. TETRASPERMA. Rox.

Vernacular. J. *bis.* R. *bidá.* Plains, *bed leila, badha, safêda.*

This species is less common than S. BABYLONICA, planted in the plains, and is occasionally seen in the outer hills to 4,000 feet. Madden (?) mentions that it grows to 5,000 or 6,000 feet in Kumaon. It is readily raised by cuttings and grows rapidly to a considerable size. I have seen trees of 6 feet girth. I am aware of no special use to which the timber is put. The most frequent names of this and S. BABYLONICA, viz., *laila* and *majnún*, are supposed to allude to the story of the well-known eastern lovers of these names.

S. var. SP. Arboreous, including S. ELEGANS. Wall. S. FRAGILIS. L., and S. VIMINALIS. L.

Vernacular. C. *beis, bitsú, bed, bidá, belí, yír.* R. *badá.* S. *báshal.*

These grow at heights in the Punjab Himalaya from 6,000 and some of them in Ladák to 11,000 feet, and the twigs and leaves of many of them are used for fodder. The wood is not valued.

S. VAR. SP. Shrubby, including S. FLABELLARIS. Ands. S. HASTATA. L. S. OXYCARPA. Ands.

Vernacular. S. *bísa*. C. *bushan, jangal belí*. R. *ber, mathí*. B. *bak shel*. S. *shun, bháil*. P. *belí*.

These also are found at various elevations in the Punjab Himalaya and Ladák from 6,000 to 15,000 feet, and the leaves, &c., of several are used as fodder. In Spiti, baskets appear to be made from the twigs.

S. SP.

Vernacular. Bazár, manna, *bed khist*.

I have not met with this officinal substance, but it is mentioned by various writers, and may be noted here. It is used as a laxative. Irvine states that it is said to be produced on a dark-barked cultivated willow in Túrkistán, which may be one of those noted above.

N. O. ULMACEÆ.

CELTIS CAUCASICA. Willd.

Vernacular. J. *batkar*. K. *brímdú, brúmij, brimla*. C. *bigni, biúgú, kharg*. R. *khark*. B. *khirk, karík*. S. *kharak, khalk, kú*. T. I. *takhum, tágho*. S. R. *batkar, wattamman*. Bazár, fruit, *kanghol mirch, indarba*.

This fine tree is common wild from 2,500 to 8,500 feet in the Punjab Himalaya, and occurs Trans-Indus down to 1,500 feet, and appears from Griffith, &c., to be cultivated in Affghánistán. It is occasionally planted; there is a magnificent avenue near Chumba, composed chiefly of this tree, the largest specimen being 16½ feet in girth. Trees of 7 or 8 feet are not uncommon. Winter fodder is often stored in the forked boughs of this tree. Its timber is white, light, soft, weak, and subject to the attacks of insects. It is chiefly used for zemindárs' work, charcoal, and fuel. Bellew mentions that in the Peshawar Valley it is often made into charms to keep off the evil eye from man and beast. Cleghorn states that its bark is used for sandals, but I have not heard of this otherwise. The fruit, a small drupe, is eaten by the natives, who call it sweetish, but it has almost no flesh. Madden states that it has been supposed to be the Lotus of the ancients. The fruit is also officinal, being given as a remedy in amennorrhæa, and Bellew states that it is administered for colic.

2 D

C. Nepalensis. Planch.

Vernacular. J. *batkar*. T. I. *túgho*.

This is much more rare than the preceding. I have only found it in parts of the Jhelam basin and Trans-Indus at about 2,500 to 3,500 feet. The Patháns are said to use its tough wood for churn-sticks.

Sponia Wightii. Planch.

Vernacular. B. *mární*. U. *kanghí*.

A small tree found very sparingly in the Siwálik tract up to the Biás, and occurring also in the Salt Range. Locally I do not know that it is used for any special purpose, but in some parts of India its exceedingly harsh rough leaves are employed to polish wood and horn.

Ulmus campestris. L. (U. Wallichiana. Planch. ?) Elm.

Vernacular. J. *káin*. K. *brárí, brerí, brankúl*. C. *brorí, marazh, marárí*. R. *marál*. B. *marál, márún, hembar*. S. *imbir, marran, shko*.

This tree, which grows to a large size, is common wild in many parts of the Punjab Himalaya up to the Indus from 3,500 to 9,500 feet. It grows to a large size, trees of 10 and 11 feet girth and 60 high being occasionally seen. I have noted one more than 16 feet in girth. I may note that I have never observed flower or fruit of this or the following tree. The wood is not valued by natives, being reckoned less strong than that of the next species. But it is tough, and is used in Kanáwar for ark-poles—(see Betula)—and an European contractor in Hazára has found it light, strong, and useful for the panels of dog-carts, &c. The bark is very tough, and is used for bed-string, and sandals made from it will last for two days under hard work. The leaves are a favourite fodder, and the trees are often very severely lopped on this account.

U. erosa. ?
U. pumila. Pall. ?

Vernacular. J. *mánú, mannú*. K. *bren, bran, amrái*. C. *brannú, merú, chipál*. R. *marál, mandú*. B. *mányí, máúrn*. S. *mal dúng morún*. Lad., *yúmbok*.

This, which may include the two species named, is a much less common tree in the wild state than the last; is more frequently seen planted at villages, &c., and reaches a larger size. It attains 100 feet in height, and I have noted a good many of more than 20, one of 25, and one of 28 feet in girth. Madden mentions one of 29 feet girth at Chású, on the Sutlej, and Cleghorn one of 30 feet girth on the Biás. I have seen it as planted as low as 2,500 feet, and it occurs, introduced I believe, to 10,500 feet in Ladák. The wood is considered better than that of the last, but does not appear to have any special use. Short spines project from the wood of the trunk into the inner surface of the bark as in POPULUS EUPHRATICA (q. v.) In parts of the Jhelam basin, gun-fuse is made from the bark.

It is somewhat singular that I have never observed flower or fruit of either of the two above ELMS on any of hundreds of trees.

U. INTEGRIFOLIA. Rox.

Vernacular. B. *khulen, rajain.* U. *kachám.* D. *pápri.*

A handsome tree, rare in the Punjab Siwálik tract up to the Biás, and seen planted in the plains about Dehli, &c. The wood is light, white, and rather apt to splinter, but in parts of India is used for carts, door-frames, spoons, &c., and in the Punjab is employed for roof planks. At Mussooree, a wood called *pápri* is said to be employed for the same purposes as Box, but it can hardly be that of this tree. Near Dehli the bruised leaves of this are applied to boils.

N. O. URTICACEÆ.

ARTOCARPUS INTEGRIFOLIA. L. Jack-fruit tree.

Vernacular. R. *tiún.* B. *daheu.*

A large tree occasionally seen planted in the Punjab Siwálik tract up to the Rávi. The fruit is used for *áchár.*

FICUS CARICA. L. Fig tree.

Vernacular. C. *phagwára, fágú.* R. *jamír.* Plains generally, *anjír, phagwára.*

This fruit tree is not uncommon cultivated in (both English and) native gardens in the Punjab plains. I have also seen it as high as 5,000 feet on the Rávi. It reaches 7 feet in girth occasionally. Bellew says that it is common about Kandahár, mostly wild, (?) and that the white fruit is generally kept for home use, and the black exported. Davies gives 20 maunds of the fruit as annually imported from Affghánistán viâ Peshawar.

F. CARICORDES. Rox. (F. VIRGATA. Rox.)

Vernacular. J. *phág, phagwárí*. K. *kirmri*. C. *phagorú, fágú, phog, thapur*. R. *phagúra, jamír (?)* B. *fágú, dhúra, dhúdí, daholia*. S. *kak, kok, phedú*. U. *kimri*. T. I. *ínzar*. S. R. *phugwára, khabáre*. B. D., &c., *phugwárí, fagúrí*.

A small tree strongly resembling the former, which occurs wild occasionally in waste places in the plains Cis and Trans-Indus, and is not uncommon in the Himalaya to 6,000 feet. It not unfrequently reaches 5 or 6 feet, and I have noted one of more than 10 in girth. The fruit is eaten by the natives, and at 5,000 feet in the hills I have found it excellent, though it is generally poor.

F. CORDIFOLIA. Rox. (?)

Vernacular. R. *rúmbal, pulákh*. B. *pilkhan, badha*.

A tree which occurs occasionally in the Punjab Siwálik tract up to the Rávi. The fruit is eaten.

F. CUNIA. Buch.

Vernacular. C. *kath gúlar, trumbal*. R. *karndol*. S. *kúrí*.

A smallish tree occasional in the Punjab Siwálik tract up to the Chenáb. The fruit is not eatable, but in parts of India is used in medicine, and in the Peninsula the rough harsh leaves are employed for polishing wood-work.

F. ELASTICA Roxb. India rubber Fig.

Vernacular. ?

I do not know if this tree had been introduced by natives, nor have I heard of any specimens further west than Ambála, except quite small ones recently planted.

F. GLOMERATA. Willd.

Vernacular. R. *rúmbal*. S. R. *bat bar, palák*. B. D. *dadhúrí*.

(Common cultivated in the plains N. W. Provinces) rare in the Punjab plains, and occasional wild in the eastern part of the Punjab Siwálik tract, and in the Salt Range. In parts of India the coarse brittle wood is used for well-frames. The fruit is very inferior, but is occasionally eaten by the poor, raw and in curries, &c.

F. Indica. Rox. Banyan-tree.

Vernacular. C. *bera*. Plains, *bor, bargad*. Bazár, fibres of air-roots, *rísh bargad*.

This tree is common planted in most parts of the plains, and occasionally to 4,000 feet in the hills, wherever there are many Hindus. It is rare Trans-Indus, and in Hazára, &c., where there are few of the latter. It also occurs wild in the Siwálik tract and Salt Range, growing in the driest, rockiest places. I have noted trees of more than 30 feet girth, and have probably *seen* many larger. A correspondent of the Agri-Horticultural Society records a magnificent specimen, the *Pír ka bor*, which "covers many acres" in Jhang district, just under the junction of the Jhelam with the Chenáb. This tree is easily raised from cuttings. Dr. Henderson tells me that those trees which respectively have and want the characteristic root stems are called male and female by the natives. These root stems are in parts of India used for *dandy*-poles. The wood of the tree is said to be made into oil-presses in Kángra, although it, being coarse-grained and light, like that of the other figs, does not seem well adapted for this purpose. The fruit is said to be eaten by the starving poor in famines. The leaves are a favourite fodder for elephants, and the trees are sometimes severely lopped on this account. The milky juice of the tree is stated by Honigberger to be used in medicine by natives, externally and internally. It is in Lahore employed to aid in the oxidation of copper, &c. The root-fibres are officinal, being given in gonorrhæa, as they are considered by *bedaks* to resemble sarsaparilla. In the eastern and central Punjab, *lákh* appears to be occasionally collected on the tree, and in 1863 a single *bor* is mentioned in Proceedings, Agri-Horticultural Society, which brought a revenue of 12 rupees per annum on this account.

F. oppositifolia. Willd.

Vernacular. R. *dadúrí, rúmbal*. B. *degar*.

A small tree with very rough leaves not uncommon in the Punjab Siwálik tract up to the Rávi. The fruit is not eaten. In Kángra the milky juice is said to be used medicinally.

F. religiosa. L.

Vernacular. *pípal*.

This fine tree is common in most parts of the plains of the Punjab where there are many Hindús. It is also wild in the eastern part of the Siwalik tract, and I have seen a planted speci men of 25 feet girth at nearly 5,000 feet in Chumba. This tree is easily raised by cuttings, and is spread by birds on the tops of buildings, &c., where it grows from crevices with apparently not a particle of soil. It is seen in greatest numbers at old established cantonments, as at Loodiana and Ambála. At the latter place the tree (as well as some mangoes, &c.) have a tendency to decay, which kills them off at top, and often wholly, in some numbers each year. (I have also observed this in F. Indica in the southern Punjab). The timber is coarse-grained, and very subject to the attacks of white ants, and is not much used except for fuel and charcoal. The leaves furnish a favourite fodder for elephants, and complications are common from the resistance of the people to their trees being lopped for this purpose. *Lákh* is occasionally formed on this, as well as F. Indica. (Mr. Strettell, of the Forest Department, Sind, states that *lákh*, though common on Acacia Arabica (q. v.) in lower Sind, is never found on any Ficus there, which may possibly depend on the excessive drought of the climate).

F. reticulata. Miq. (F. scandens. Rox.)

Vernacular. J. *bat phagár, nágar jamián*. K. *thaur*. C. *phogrí*. R. *dúdagrú, mambre*. B. *dúgurú, shirúlí, matkágar*. S. *karambal, garelú*.

A climbing species found in the Punjab Siwálik tract and Himalaya at from 1,000 to 6,000 feet up to near the Indus. It is browsed by goats, &c.

F. Roxburghii. Miq. (F. macrophylla. Rox.)

Vernacular. J. *úrbúl, urmul, burh*. C. *túsi, trimbul*. R. *tremal, dadúrí*. B. *trimbal, tiamle*. S. *trímal, tirmí*.

A small tree not uncommon in the Siwálik tract and outer Punjab Himalaya, and seen occasionally to 6,000 feet. The wood is not valued. On the Sutlej I was told that the rk is used for ropes. The fruit is eaten, being sweetish with a pleasant flavour, and Cleghorn states that it is sold in the Simla Bazár.

F. venosa. Ait. (F. infectoria. Willd.)

Vernacular. J. *pákhar*. R. *palákh*. B. *trimbal*. U. *pilkhan*. S. R. *war, palkhí*.

Generally a small tree in the Punjab, though it reaches 6 or 7 feet girth at times. It is not uncommon in the low hills Cis and Trans-Indus, and in the Salt Range. The leaves are given as fodder to elephants, and in southern India the root is used as a red dye, and the root bark is made into bowstrings.

Nussiessya hypoleuca. Wedd. (Bœhmeria salicifolia).

Vernacular. J. *amrer, chenjúl, sandári.* C. *sansárú, súss.* R. *siárú, thána.* B. *siárú.* S. *siárú, píncho, prín.* T. I. *shakei.* Aff., *kharwala.*

A shrub which is common, generally near water, at many places in the low hills from 1,500 and occasionally to 6,000 feet, Cis and Trans-Indus, and which occurs in the Salt Range. In the eastern part of the Punjab, its bark appears, as in the N. W. Provinces, to be used for making ropes, but it is not generally employed in this way. It is browsed by sheep.

Procris sp.

Vernacular. ?

A species occurs in the Punjab Himalaya which may be the same as that which Madden states to be used as a pot-herb in Kumaon.

Urtica heterophylla. Willd. (Gerardinia. Wall.) Neilgherry nettle.

Vernacular. J. *kerí.* C. *kíngí.* R. *ein, sanoli.* B. *án, ján, kal.* S. *kárla, bhábar.*

A fine tall nettle with immense leaves and a vigorous sting, which is not uncommon in many places of the Punjab Himalaya, 2,500 to 7,000 feet. Its stems are often employed for making twine and ropes by the dry process, but these are not prized, and perish quickly from wet. At the Punjab Exhibition (December 1863), the offer of a prize of Rs. 250 did not elicit any specimen of the fibre worthy of reward.

U. hyperborea. Jacq.

Vernacular. Lad., *zatúd, dzátsutt, stokpo tsodma.*

A smallish species common in parts of Ladák from 11,500 to 17,000, and occasionally to nearly 18,500 feet. Its young leaves are eaten as a pot-herb.

N. O. CANNABINACEÆ.

Cannabis sativa. L. (C. Indica. Lam.) Indian Hemp.

Vernacular. K. *bangí.* C. *bhangí, bengí.* B. *bhang.* S. *bháng, kas*; seeds, *gúlú*; fibre, *chel.* Plains, *bhang.* Bazár, tops, *bhang, sabzí*; exudation, *charras*; seeds, *súka kí bíj.*

Common in waste places in many parts of the Punjab plains Cis and Trans-Indus, and much more abundant and large (reaching

9 or 10 and 12 or 14 feet in height at times) in many places in the Himalaya up to 10,000 feet. It appears to be more commonly cultivated in Garhwál, &c., than in any part of the Punjab Himalaya. But in the latter it is frequently grown in small patches on the Sutlej and Bías at 5,000 to 7,000 feet, and I have seen fields at 10,000 on the Chenáb, in Lahoul, and Aitchison's statement as to its fibre not being used there is incorrect. Within Punjab bounds the fibre of the stem, for which it is cultivated, appears only to be made into rope, bed-string, &c., and sandals (the latter are said to last for 8 or 9 days, *i. e.*, much longer than rice straw or elm bark, but to be less safe in difficult places than the latter), but further east it is made into sacking, as well as into cloth for wearing in the hot season. The wild plant also is used for making rope, &c., at places on the Jhelam, west of Kashmír, and on the Chenáb, &c. In Kashmír a proportion of the fibre is mixed with the material for paper-making. On the Sutlej the seeds of the cultivated plant are roasted and eaten in small quantity with wheat. The most important product of this plant is the resinous exudation, which does not appear to be produced below a certain elevation in the hills. It is used as a narcotic, as are the dried tops of the plant. The latter are gathered for home use in many parts of the hills, and also occasionally in the plains (they are largely used in Sind, where the plant appears to be grown in fields for this purpose), but the great source of the *charras* is Túrkistán. Dr. Cayley states that in October 1867, this drug to the value of Rs. 44,760 was imported from Yarkand into Lê, and Rs. 19,422 worth of *bhang* was exported from the latter to the Punjab in the same month. During 1867, 1830 maunds were imported from Yárkand to Lê, and 817 maunds were sent from the latter southward by various routes. The drug is mostly consumed with tobacco in a hookah, its use extending to Affghánistán, according to Bellew. Davies' Trade Report gives 75 maunds of *charras* as annually imported from Affghanistan viâ Peshawar, and two maunds by the Bolán. A cold infusion of the tops is generally used, and is in great favour with the Sikhs, who are debarred from tobacco, and so make up by the use of this, opium, and spirits. Bellew states that in the Peshawar Valley the tops, bruised into pulp, are applied to hæmorrhoids and other painful tumours. The tops, exudation, and seeds, are all officinal, on account of their narcotic qualities.

Humulus Lupulus. L. Hop.

Vernacular. ?

Lowther states that he had heard of the hop plant being seen in Kashmír (as others have done elsewhere in the Himalaya), but it is nowhere indigenous. In 1851 he proposed its introduction in Kashmír. It has been successfully cultivated in Dehra Doon for many years, so far as mere growth is concerned, but heavy rain at the flowering period prevents the flower from reaching perfection as to quantity and quality of the powder, on which its value depends, and the results have, on the whole, been unsatisfactory. Within the last few years, the plant has been tried at Kyelang and Kilár in the arid tract on the upper Chenáb, and it has flourished. But unfortunately it appears to have been found out, after several years care, that the sets, introduced at the latter place, were those of male plants! So that the experiment has still to get a fair trial there. At Kyelang, female flowers are sparingly produced. At the Murree Brewery, however, where the rain-fall is much lighter than further east, a considerable number of hop plants have been grown for some years with fair success as to quantity and strength of hops actually got. And it may be hoped that still better results will by-and-bye be attained.

N. O. STILAGINACEÆ.

Falconeria insignis. Royle.

Vernacular. B. *karálla, bilodar, ankhar*. S. *biloja*.

This tree only extends scantily along the Punjab Siwálik tract, as far as the Biás. The wood is occasionally employed for domestic purposes, but is of no special use.

N. O. MORACEÆ.

Morus alba. L.
M. Cashmeriana. Royle.
M. Indica. Rox.
M. lævigata. Wall.
M. Tatarica. Willd.
} Mulberry.

Vernacular. K. *túlklú, túti*; elsewhere, *tút, sháh tút*, &c.

There is considerable doubt as to the species of Morus, but all of the above appear to be cultivated in the Punjab plains, and some of them in the hills up to Kashmír, 5,000 feet, where they abound, and to 7,000 feet on the Chenáb. Vigne states that the mulberry grows in parts of Tibet, where Thomson mentions it at over 9,000 feet. From the accounts of Bellew and others, nine or ten kinds would appear to be abundant in parts of Affghánistán. In the plains of the Punjab, the mulberry varies much in frequency, and is more common than elsewhere in the northern Trans-Indus. Some of the trees attain a large size, specimens of 10 and 12 feet girth are not very uncommon, and I have noted one of 16 feet in the Salt Range. The wood of old trees is strong and useful, and is much employed for construction, implements, &c., in parts where the tree is common. About Peshawar it is the staple ordinary timber. The fresh twigs are in Kashmír used for tying loads. This tree is chiefly grown for its fruit, which is mawkish-sweet in flavour, and often very palatable. In Kashmír, Moorcroft states that the fruit, fresh or dried, furnishes much of the food of the inhabitants from June to September. In Affghánistán also it is consumed fresh, or dried in sacks, and eaten as a substitute for corn-flour, being, according to Bellew, found sweet, wholesome, and fattening. Davies' Trade Report gives 500 maunds of the dried fruit as annually imported from Affghánistán viâ Peshawar, but this is surely over the mark. Bellew states that in times of scarcity the leaves are often eaten raw by the poor. Lowther mentions that a strong spirit is in Kashmír distilled from the fruit, but I can find no other evidence of this. A considerable quantity of silk is got in Kashmír and near it from worms fed on the mulberry. And the raising of these is carried on upon a small scale, and has been at various times tried more extensively in Peshawar, Hazára, the Bárí Doáb, &c. These large experiments have as yet, however, not been successful; nor are the causes of failure always evident. But sometimes the obstacles are sufficiently patent, *e. g.*, in parts of Kángra the leaves are said to be attacked by an insect just at the time when they are most needed by the worms.

M. MULTICAULIS.
M. SINENSIS.

The cultivation of these two foreign species has been largely extended in the Punjab, chiefly from the Sahāranpúr Botanic Gardens, with a view to sericiculture, and now there are thousands of them in the Bárí Doáb, &c., ready for use, when the proper method of managing the worm has been found. At times the eagerness in certain quarters to cultivate these has been, on a small scale, like the maina for growing MORUS MULTICAULIS for silk, which prevailed in parts of the United States about 1835, and led to the ruin of many.

M. PARVIFOLIA. Royle.

Vernacular. C. *túl.* Plains, *tútrí.*

A small tree, which occurs wild in the plains of the eastern Punjab, and to 5,000 feet in Kashmír, &c. Its fruit does not appear to be valued. Cleghorn states that its leaves are prized as cattle fodder.

M. SERRATA. Rox. (M. CUSPIDATA. Wall.) Himalayan mulberry.

Vernacular. J. *krún, tút, sháh tút, túlukul.* C. *túlklú, kárt tút, túlklú.* R. *krún, krúm.* B. *krún, chímú, chún.* S. *chímú, kímú, soa, an.*

This tree is common in many parts of the Punjab Himalaya from 2,500 to 9,000 feet. It grows to a large size, trees of 10 and 12 feet girth being not uncommon; I have seen several over 20 feet, and at Barmaor, in Chumba, there is a magnificent specimen of 28 feet girth. The fruit of this species is not much valued. Its wood is yellow and strong, but is subject to the attacks of worms. It is used in construction and for ploughs, troughs, toys, &c. The twigs are in some parts largely lopped for fodder.

N. O. CONIFERÆ

ABIES SMITHIANA. Wall. Himalayan Spruce.

Vernacular. J. *kachal, kachan, ban lúdar.* K. *súngal, pústúl.* C. *sarei, salla, rág, re, kanlí.* R. *tos, re, bang, re.* B. *rái.* S. *re, ráiang kandre.* T. I. *wesha.* Bazár, young cone, *gaz pípal.*

A handsome but not a very useful tree common in many parts of the Punjab Himalaya at from 5,500 to 11,000 feet. From Griffith's notes it would appear that it also grows in Káfiristán, Trans-Indus. It does not as a rule attain quite such a large size as some of the other Himalayan conifers, but trees of 10 to 12 feet girth and 130 to 140 feet high are not unfrequent. Thomson notes one of 17; Madden mentions one of 20; and I have seen a specimen of 21 feet girth. The timber is soft and light, often with much sap-wood, and the fibres are frequently twisted. It is the least valued of all the conifers by the natives for construction. In some parts, however, especially on the Biás, it is largely used for shingles, which are said to last for two or three years, and under cover it will last twice that period. In houses built for Europeans it has been found to look and answer well for inside work. The resin of the tree is mentioned in Kángra, but I doubt if it is largely produced or used anywhere. Part at least of the officinal *gaz pípal* of Punjab Bazárs, generally attributed to POTHOS SCANDENS (and see PLANTAGO MAJOR), and said by the Lahore drug-sellers to be the fruit of the BORASSUS FLABELLIFORMIS, consists of the young cones of (apparently) this tree. It is in the Hindí system considered stimulant, warm, and tonic.

CEDRUS DEODARA. Loud. (PINUS. Rox.) Himalayan Cedar.

Vernacular. J. *diár, palúdar.* K. *diár, dewdár.* C. *diár, dadár, geyár, kilár, kelú.* R. *kelu, kilei, kelí.* B. *kelú, keolí.* S. *kenwal, keolí kelmang, giam.* T. I. *lmánza.* Aff., *nakhtar.* Bazár, wood, *dedwár Khatái*; oil, *diár ke tel.*

The existence of this noble tree in the Punjab Himalaya first became known to Europeans about the beginning of the century, when specimens were sent to Roxburgh, who named it a PINUS, but within a few years Gerard is said to have called it a Cedar. It is now believed by many to be specifically identical with the Cedar of Lebanon. It grows in many parts of the Himalaya at from 4,000 to 10,000 feet from the Ganges to the Indus, and beyond it on the Sufêd Koh (Bellew), and the mountains north of Jalálabád (Griffith), apparently at about the same elevations, but of smaller size than in habitats towards the centre of the Cedar region. The seeds of this tree were sent to England by Captain Gerard as early as 1819, and from the first it was a favourite in England owing to its very handsome and characteristic appearance. But for many years young plants sold high in England until shortly before 1852, when Dr. Jameson mentions that for years he had been sending home 400 or 500 lbs. of seed annually, so that the price of young plants had fallen to £1 a hundred. It does not seed in Europe, so that the demand for seed continues. In its native mountains it grows to a gigantic size, the finest specimens being generally seen near temples, &c., where they have been well-preserved. Several trees of 36 feet in girth have been noted, and a few of more than 200 feet in height have been felled. The *deodár* germinates very readily from seed, but the young shoots and plants are eagerly browsed by goats, &c., who with the forest fires keep down ruinously the reproduction of the tree.

Moorcroft appears to have been the first to note the exceeding durability of the wood, which has been so often commented upon since. The *deodár* pillars of the great mosque in the capital of Kashmír are said to be more than four hundred years old (the date 804 Hijrí is entered in an inscription over the door), and some of the bridges, where part of the timber is at times exposed to the influence of the water, are *said* to be still older. Madden mentions, but dubiously, temples in Kanáwar asserted to have been erected 600 or 800 years ago, and says there is no doubt that *deodár* in Gerard's house near Rámpúr was sound after being up 200 years. Lowther states that no subaqueous insect will touch the wood, and Colonel A. Taylor tells me that, when used as telegraph posts, the white ants never attack any but the sap-wood. The latter also mentions that when fairly tried along with ACACIA ARABICA, &c., as for the knees of boats, it answers better than any. It is strong, sufficiently elastic, and not too heavy, and, on the whole, may be reckoned one of the best coniferous timbers in the world. For many years it has been very largely exported from the Himalaya into the Punjab plains, where it is *the* constructive wood in general use for any but the most ordinary or temporary purposes. And so extensive have been the fellings, that whatever efforts are made to preserve what remains and aid reproduction (as a tree takes from 80 to 120 years to reach 6 feet girth, felling size) a period of great scarcity must inevitably begin before long, to last for some years. Indeed within the last few years the price of this excellent timber has doubled, and it must rise much higher still. Far down the Indus, in Sind, where its price is of course even greater than in the Punjab, it is not in use for many purposes for which cheaper timber will answer. Even there, however, as in the Punjab, the boats in use are mostly built of it: it is said that one of them will last for more than 20 years with fair usage. In the hills it is used for almost every purpose for which timber can be employed, indeed so lavishly that even the shingles for small native houses are in some parts made of it. In this shape, as in others, it outlasts all the other coniferous timbers of the Himalaya.

Many of the *deodár* trees, especially, as would appear, those growing on arid exposed situations, have very oily timber, which is frequently employed for the flambeaux *(jagní)* that are largely employed by the natives of the hills. From the wood, often that of the roots, is extracted by a process of destructive distillation, (accurately described by Hoffmeister) an oil, which is dark-coloured and thickish, with an empyreumatic odour, and resembles crude turpentine in its nature. Dr. Burton Brown has analysed this, and states that its specific gravity is 987, and that, when distilled, it gives off water and a little acetic acid, followed by a clear yellow oil sp. gr. 965, which leaves a dark resinous mass solidifying into a black brittle solid. The yellow oil is volatile, burning with a very smoky flame, and, though possessing a different odour, resembles oil of turpentine, and is likely to be useful for similar purposes. The *deodár* oil is used, on the Rávi and Biás at least, for anointing the inflated skins used in crossing rivers, and catching logs, &c., three seers it is said being put into each of the larger ones every month, and frequently shaken about. It is also a favourite and frequently effective remedy for eruptions and ulcers in man, and mange in horses, and sore feet in cattle, and is likewise administered internally. Quite recently several gentlemen have found that it possesses some at least of the virtues of carbolic acid as a dressing for sores, &c. In Lahore, from the knots of the *deodár*, I have been *told* that this oil is largely prepared, and sold for ordinary machinery purposes, &c., at a cheap rate. It is asserted, I know not with what truth, that this oil, rubbed on other wood, imparts to it some of the durability of the *deodár*.

Royle states that the leaves and young twigs of the tree are much used in native medicine, but I have found no trace of this within the Punjab. However, it may be quite correct opposite Saháranpúr, Royle's head-quarters, where the tree is rare or only planted by temples, &c., and therefore more revered. In Kángra, the wood is pounded with water on a stone, and the paste is applied to the temples for headache. The *dedwár Khatái* of the Lahore Bazár, which is officinal as a tonic, consists of chips of this wood.

CUPRESSUS SEMPERVIRENS. Willd. Cypress.

Vernacular. *sarú.*

This tree is seen planted in gardens in the Punjab plains, and in the outer Himalaya to 5,000 feet, attaining a girth of 6 to 8 feet and a height of 40 to 45 in the latter. Masson states that it also grows at Kábul. It is only planted for its sombre beauty, and its wood is of no special value.

C. TORULOSA. Don. Twisted Cypress.

Vernacular. R. *deví diár.* B. *deodár.* S. *galla, deodár.*

Of this tree, which in appearances has a considerable resemblance to JUNIPERUS EXCELSA (q. v.), there are only one or two patches on the Rávi, and rather more in one part of the Biás at 5,500 to 8,000 feet. On the former it reaches 6 to 7 feet girth and 60 to 70 in height, and I saw one tree of 15 feet girth and 120 high. On the outer hills, near the Sutlej, it is more common (as well as further east, including the forest at Nynee Tál at about 8,000 feet). In the Saháranpúr Botanic Garden, there is a tree about 20 feet high. In some of the eastern localities, Madden tells us the inhabitants believe that death would follow the felling of a tree for a secular purpose, so that its wood is only used as incense there. In Kúllú the people say it is chiefly used for making images, &c.; but elsewhere no such sanctity attaches to the tree. On the Rávi and Sutlej it is used for beams, &c., and Madden mentions that at Nynee Tál it is employed for roofs and indoor purposes, but is too flexible and weak to support much weight. He also states that it seems too soft to be durable, though the people assert that it lasts for centuries.

JUNIPERUS COMMUNIS. L.
J. SQUAMATA. Don. } Juniper.

Vernacular. J. *petthrí.* C. *petthar, betthal, wetyar, páma, giá shúk.* R. *betthal, lassar.* B. *mích, chích, betar, dhúp.* S. *lewar, langshúr, thelú, dhúp, gúgil.* P. *chúi shúpa.* Bazár, fruit, *haulber, abhúl.*

I have confused these two shrubby species, as the natives often do, so must give them together. They are common in many parts of the Punjab Himalaya from sometimes as low as 7,000 to at times as high as 13,000 feet (and occur near the Sufêd Koh, Trans-Indus), often forming a belt or more frequently patches above the upper limit of trees (although, as noted, seen at times very much below that). On the Sutlej I have seen the shrub planted at a temple. There and on the Bíás it is used as incense, whence some of the native names. The wood burns fairly well. and on the passes it is frequently the only decent fuel to be got within miles. Madden states that from the berries, with barley meal, a spirit is distilled, the former being probably only added to impart a gin flavour. The berries are officinal in the plains, and are used in decoction, being considered stimulant.

J. EXCELSA Bieb. Pencil cedar.

Vernacular. J. *chalái, chalei.* C. *shúkpá, shúr, lewar, (deodár).* S. *shúrgú.* Lad., *shúkpa.* P. *shúkpa.* Bel., *apúrs.*

This tree is said to be abundant in Nepál, and to occur below the Nítí Pass in Kumaon. In the Punjab Himalaya it is common in the upper and more arid parts of the basins of the Sutlej and Chenáb. It likewise occurs in Ladák. It is also found in some numbers on the Kúnhár, a tributary of the Jhelam, and occurs near the Sufêd Koh (Bellew), and on Cheheltán, in Belúchistán (Masson, &c.) Cleghorn gives the crest of the Dhauladhár, above Kángra, as a habitat, which is perhaps doubtful, as the climate there is moist. The elevational range may be put at 8,000 to nearly 15,000 feet. At the higher altitudes it is only seen as a shrub, but at 9—10,000 feet acquires a considerable girth. It tapers rapidly, however, and quickly divides into several trunks (in the manner of the yew), and with its frequently distorted boughs and short stature often presents a most grotesque appearance. The general size of the trees is from 4 to 8 feet in girth and 25 to 30 in height. On the Kúnhár I noted one of 14½ feet girth and 45 feet high, and a second 19½ feet girth and 25 high. The most remarkable and largest tree I have seen is one near the Moravian Mission station of Kyelang, in Lahoul, which is 33½ feet in girth and only 30 in height. The timber, which has the same fragrance as that (also produced by a Juniper) from which pencils are made, is light, and not strong, but is used for many purposes in the almost treeless parts where this generally grows. It is employed as supports for water channels, and I am told that the heart-wood, when in moist earth, is nearly imperishable. In Lahoul it is also used, alternating with stones, for the walls of houses, as well as for beams. And on the Sutlej some of the temples are built of it, and it is said to be in some request for boxes (at Simla). In Kanáwar also vessels made of it are much esteemed, and some charcoal is made from it. It gives a good fuel at elevations where little else is available, and is much used for this purpose in Lê, the capital of Laḍák, bits being collected from the Zanskar river, a few miles south. I have seen it planted at a temple in Kanáwar, and Thomson mentions a tree at the Lipa temple in the same tract, where, as well as in Lahoul, it is reckoned sacred. In the former the wood is used as incense, and offered by the Lamas to their deities, and in the latter the twigs are used by the priests in several religious ceremonies, and the fruit is regularly burnt as incense by the Buddhists. In Ladák, small branches of it are placed upon the cairns, &c. Masson states that on Cheheltán the fruit is employed medicinally, and is exported to Hindústán, so that it *may* constitute part of the *abhúl*—(see J. COMMUNIS). In Khágán, on the Kúnhár, the small branches under the name of *chalei ke dhúp* are burned near the patient as a remedy for the delirium of fever.

PICEA WEBBIANA. Lamb. (var. PINDROW and KHUTROW).

Vernacular. J. *palúdar, rewari.* K. *badar, búdar, túng.* C. *dhúnnú, rág, ráil, pe, salle, sgrá.* R. *dhúnnú, re.* B. *tos.* S. *spun, krok, pandrái kúlre.* T. I. *bajúr.*

This tree, of which the two varieties that have by some been called species probably depend on climate, and seem not to be very constant or well-marked, is abundant in many parts of the Punjab Himalaya from sometimes as low as 5,500 to 11,500 feet, frequently forming dense forests at or near the highest belt of arboreous vegetation up to the Indus. Griffith found it in Káfiristán, and Bellew collected it near the Sufêd Koh, Trans-Indus. It attains a great height (though I have nowhere seen it up to the 200 feet mentioned by Hoffmeister) and large girth. Trees of 10 to 12 feet girth and 130 to 140 high are not uncommon, and I have noted a specimen more than 17 feet in circumference. (Hooker mentions a tree in Bhotán of 30, and Madden one of 32 feet girth). The fibres of the trunk are often twisted, and the wood is white, soft, coarse-grained, and rots readily when there is much moisture, so that this is one of the least valued of Himalayan conifers. Even on the Biás, however, it is said to last as shingles for two or three, and under cover for five or six years. In Kashmír, Vigne states that it is used for door-frames. And in the drier climates of Kanáwar and Lahoul it is a good deal used. In the latter the Moravian Missionaries informed me that under shelter it would last as long as *deodár.* And in Murree, where the rain-fall is smaller than to the east, and where there is a dearth of the better timbers, this is frequently used for shingles and indoor-work even in European buildings, and is found to last fairly well. In parts of the Jhelam basin the twigs and leaves are much used as fodder.

Pinus excelsa. Wall.

Vernacular. J. *biár*. K. *yero, yárí, káiar, tser, chíl*. C. *chír, kachír, dárchír, keilrí, lhim, som shing*. R. *chíl*. B. *kail*. S. *káil, chíl, lim, somshing*. P. *sam, pálsam*.

This tree has recently been identified with P. peuce, which grows only in a confined locality in Macedonia at from 2,400 to 5,800 feet. It is common in many parts of the Punjab Himalaya, generally growing in mixed forests, from 5,000 to perhaps 11,000 feet; the 13,000 feet, given as a maximum by Aitchison, is probably a mistake. It also grows sparingly in western Tibet at 8,000 to 10,000 feet, Trans-Indus. Griffith found it in Káfiristán, and Bellew near the Sufêd Koh, at 9,000 to 10,000 feet. Trees of 8 and 9 feet girth are not unfrequent, but it rarely reaches 100 feet in height, although trees of 150 feet occur at times. It furnishes the best wood for most purposes of all our conifers next to *deodár*, and, where the latter is scarce or dear, this is used for all the ordinary purposes of construction. In Kúllú as shingles it is said to last 7 or 8, and inside 15 years. In the more moist eastern climate, however, it is stated to decay if not kept under cover, but even on the Sutlej it is often used for building. And at Murree, where it is the best wood procurable for shingles and ordinary purposes, the supply is rapidly getting exhausted. Mr. Watson tells me that it is the best of all for pattern-making, because it works well, and is non-resinous. But he must have had picked specimens, or perhaps got pieces of some of the other inferior conifers, for this is very inflammable, and is in most parts where it grows preferred to all (except the next) for torches. Its resin is mentioned in a Kángra Report, but I cannot find that it is largely produced or collected anywhere.

P. Gerardiana. Wall. Edible Pine.

Vernacular. C. *chírí, prita, mírri, galboja*. R. *kashti*. Aff., *chilghoza*.

This tree is said to be found below the Nítí Pass high in Kumaon, but the dried specimens at Saharanpúr hardly agree. It is common in a part of the upper Sutlej basin, at one spot on the Rávi, and on a short portion of the upper Chenáb and its tributary, the Marrú. It is also reported by Falconer and Winterbottom, as growing near Astor and Gilghit, not far from the Indus, is found near the Sufêd Koh (Bellew), and in Káfiristán, &c., north of Kábul (Griffith). Its range in the Punjab Himalaya may be put at from 5,800 to 8,800 feet (I believe there is some mistake in Cleghorn's 10,500 feet on the Sutlej). It does not, as a rule, exceed 6 or 7 feet in girth, although I have seen it up to

12 feet, and its height does not generally range over 50 or 60 feet. It is a short-trunked tree, and the boughs and often the stem are much curved. The timber is but little used for construction, but must be considered tough, for I have seen it used for the sticks on which the passenger by the swing-bridge sits, and on which his life depends. It is very resinous, and is generally reckoned the best of all for torches and fuel, but on account of the value of its fruit is not often taken for these purposes. Major Longden says that the Kanáwarís do not use its resin, as it "gets too hard," but he extracted excellent tar from the wood by destructive distillation. On the Sutlej, a rude basket is formed from a piece of the bark, having its corners fastened together by wooden pins. The chief product of the tree consists of the seeds, of which there are more than a hundred in a full sized cone. In the Himalaya they ripen about October, and are extracted from the unopened cones by heating. They are largely consumed by the inhabitants, which, as above noted, has probably caused the wood of the tree to be less used than it would otherwise have been. On the Sutlej they are said to be partly stored for winter use, and partly exported towards the plains. From Affghánistán they are extensively imported to the Punjab, Davies' Trade Report giving 250 maunds as annually brought down viâ Peshawar, and 50 maunds viâ the Bolán. They are oily and difficult of digestion, but have a rather pleasant flavour, and are by the natives "idly supposed to have many good qualities" (Irvine). They are officinal, being considered anodyne and stimulant, and an oil extracted from them is said to be applied externally in diseases of the head.

P. LONGIFOLIA. Rox.

Vernacular. J. *chír, chíl.* C. *chír, drab chír.* R. B. S. *chíl.* T. I. *nakhtar, ranzúrú (?)* Bazár, resin, *ganda biroza ;* purified ditto, *biroza, sat-biroza.*

This tree is common in parts of the Siwálik tract and outer hills from 1,800 to 5,000 and occasionally 6,000 feet, up to and beyond the Indus. In the part of the Súlimán range seen on the Mahsúd Expedition its lower level seems to be over 9,000 feet, probably depending on the peculiar aridity of the climate. It can easily be raised from seed in the Punjab plains, and there are occasional planted trees in the N. W. Provinces (down as far as Allahabád, I believe) some of them up to 6 feet girth. In the hills it does not reach the same size as most of our other conifers, and only occasionally now are there many trees up to 8 feet girth and 100 high (I have, however, seen trees of 11 and 12 feet girth). This partly depends on its growing for the most part in tolerably accessible places, which has caused very many of the larger trees to be felled. In some parts many of the trees have twisted trunks and fibres (so much so in parts of Kumaon, &c., that Jameson calls this a separate variety). The timber is resinous and strong, but is not very durable. It is used by the natives for construction, for roofs, &c., and (with the other inferior coniferous timbers) is largely employed in making the bottoms of boats on those (eastern) rivers where *deodár* is very dear. The heart wood is used for torches in some places. In some places baskets are made of thin slips of the wood. It is a favourite tree from which to make charcoal for export to the plains in places where the seignorage has been kept low enough to permit of this abuse of good timber. The bark is in many places employed by tanners, and Madden states that in Kumaon it is much employed for smelting iron, but these uses also are perhaps hardly in accordance with good conservancy. In parts of the Jhelam basin, the turpentiny seed is at times eaten when food is scarce, but it cannot be a pleasant, and is probably not a nutritious food. The resin of this tree is more largely collected and used than that of any other of the Himalayan conifers It is procured by incision, which is detrimental and ultimately destructive to the tree. Purified and unpurified it is used internally, and as a plaster, and is sometimes employed in coating timber which is to be exposed to water. The oil of turpentine is extracted from it, but probably the practice was introduced by Europeans, as has been that of extracting tar from the wood by destructive distillation, for applying to timber to be exposed to the weather, &c.

Taxus baccata. L.

Vernacular. J. *birmí, túng, thúnú.* K. *túng, sungal, postil.* C. *barmá, kautú.* R. *barmí, dhúnú, chogú.* B. *rakhal.* S. *rikhái, nyamdal, thona, kadenrú.* T. I. *saráp, badar.* Bazár, leaves, *birmí.*

This tree occurs in many parts of the Punjab Himalaya up to the Indus at from 5,000 to 10,000 feet, but sparingly in almost all except in parts of Hazára, where it is pretty common. It was also found by Bellew Trans-Indus, at 9,000 to 10,000 feet near the Sufēd Koh, &c. Its foliage is very like that of Picea, with which it is frequently confused by Europeans and natives. But otherwise it differs much even in appearance, as it generally divides into several trunks at a few feet up, and is never tall. The tallest yew in Britain is said to be 58 feet high, but I do not remember any in the Himalaya nearly so tall as this. I have in Hazára especially seen trees of 8 and 9 feet girth. Madden mentions one of 15 feet near the Sutlej, and quotes from Hooker another in Sikkim of 18 feet. Madden correctly remarks that the hard, heavy, strong wood of this tree has apparently been quite neglected in the Himalaya. It is tolerably elastic, and is used for making native bedsteads, and in some parts for *jámpán*-poles (Cleghorn mentions bows on the Sutlej). The wood of an old tree is of a fine red colour and polishes well, and seems adapted for upholstery purposes. Mr. Watson tells me that it is well fitted for turning, and Vigne states that in Kashmír it is used for making clogs. The branches seem in some places to be used for putting under the earth of the roofs of native houses. The berries appear to be eaten in most places (and once I was told they are collected for *pansárís*). Lindley states that in Europe they are not dangerous unless the seeds are crushed so as to break their hard shell. He also mentions that if the leaves are partially dried, they are a dangerous poison, but in the Punjab they are officinal, being reckoned stomachic. In Hazára I was told that they sell for their weight in coppers. Madden (?) states that the bark of the yew is imported from Kanáwar into Ladák to be used as tea, and for a red dye. And Hooker notes that the red juice of the bark is employed in Nepál as an inferior dye, and by the Brahmins for staining their foreheads.

N. O. GNETACEÆ.

Ephedra alata.

Vernacular. T. I. *bandúkái.* S. R. *kúchan, bráta, tandala, lastúk.* B. D. *nangarwal.*

Not uncommon in the southern part of the Bárí Doáb, in the Salt Range, and Trans-Indus. In the Salt Range it is used for scrubbing metallic dishes, and this may be the "Ephedra used for snuff," of Griffith near the Khyber, although I have not otherwise heard of its employment thus.

E. Gerardiana. Wall.

Vernacular. J. *ásmánia.* C. *bútshúr, búdshúr, chewa.* S. *khanna.* Lad., *tsapatl tsems.* P. *tse.*

This plant is found at places on the Sutlej and Chenáb, and in the Jhelam basin, at from 7,800 to 11,200 feet, and in Ladák to 15,000 feet. It is eaten by goats. On the Sutlej the pretty red berries are eaten. On the Jhelam they are not eaten, but I tried them, and found that there, as elsewhere, they have a not unpleasant mawkish-sweet taste, and are not unwholesome. In parts of Ladák the stems furnish fuel. Aitchison states that in Lahoul some part of the plant is used medicinally.

N. O. DIOSCOREACEÆ.

Dioscorea deltoidea. Wall. (D. bulbifera. L. ?)

Vernacular. J. *kniss*. K. *kniss, kriss*. C. *tar, kithí, kriss, khelí* R. *kithí, dharúr*. B. *tardí, tharrí*. S. *káns, gúngrú*. T. I. *kaspat, parwattí*. Bazár, leaves, *tarar pattr*.

There is some doubt as to whether all these are the same plant; but, if so, it grows abundantly in many parts of the Punjab Himalaya from as low as 2,000 up to 9,200 feet, and is found Trans-Indus. The root is used in Kashmír for washing the *pashm* for shawls, and there and on the Chenáb and Sutlej for washing woollen cloth. Vigne states that in Kashmír the shawls are washed with it, and that there is a smaller kind of the same name with which cottons are washed. I have also had it mentioned to me that silks are washed with it in Kashmír, but this is probably incorrect, as well as Honigberger's statement that there it is employed in dyeing *nafarmání* (blue). The root of this or a variety (?), a yam, which grows to several pounds weight, is largely eaten cooked, after steeping in ashes and water to remove acridity, by various classes in parts of the Siwáliks and outer hills, but in other places is not used, and once I was told that the tongue would rot from eating it! Honigberger says that it is used medicinally. The leaves, apparently of this species, are officinal in the plains under the above name.

D. sativa. Willd.

Vernacular. *ratálú*.

A cultivated yam much grown in parts of the eastern and central Punjab plains

N. O. MUSACEÆ.

Musa Paradisiaca. L.

Vernacular. *kela*.

This is largely grown in places towards the east of the Punjab plains, and in the Siwálik tract and outer hills (on the Sutlej it may be seen up to 4,000 feet). It becomes very rare towards the north-west. There are fewer varieties, and the quality of the fruit is less good in the Punjab than to the east and south. Unripe it is cooked as a vegetable, and ripe is eaten by natives, raw or made into pickle.

N. O. MELANTHACEÆ.

Colchicum sp.

Vernacular. J. *baphola.* S. R. *baphor, isafghol.*

It is somewhat doubtful if these are the same; that on the Jhelam growing at 8,400 and in the Salt Range at 2,000 feet (the latter not seen in flower). In the Salt Range the seeds were said to be medicinal under the name *isafghol*—(see Plantago).

Colchicum sp.

Vernacular. *harúntútiya.*

This is given on the authority of Masson, who states that its dried juice is used as an application in ophthalmia. (Honigberger supposes *harúntútiya* to be from Agathotes chiretta—(see A. sp.)

N. O. LILIACEÆ.

Allium ascalonicum. L. Shallot.

Vernacular. *gandhan.* Aff., *gandana.*

This is given by Firminger as cultivated. And it (or A. Porrum, L. leek) may be the plant mentioned by Masson, (?) as cultivated at and near Kábul for the leaves, and by Bellew as growing wild near Ghuzní (7,000 feet), where it is not eaten. The former states that the leaves may be cut two or three times a year for 25 or 30 years, and mentions one field at Kábul, dating from the time of Nádir Sháh, more than a hundred years before his visit.

A. cepa. L. Onion.

Vernacular. S. R. *gatta, janglí piáz, pad wassal.* Lad., *tsúng.* Plains generally, *piáz, ganthia.*

Commonly cultivated in the Punjab plains and in some parts of the hills. It is grown to 10,500 feet in Ladák. Cunningham states that there is a kind of onion grown on the Sutlej. A wild onion, found in the Salt Range, may be this species. The root of it is not eaten however, as it is said not to have the flavour of the cultivated plant.

A. rubellum. Bieb.

Vernacular. S. *lázhú.* T. I. *khakhoel, khokhán.* S. R. *janglí piáz, barání piáz, gad vassal.* Plains generally, *chirí piází.*

This slender-leaved species is common in the N. W. Punjab, including the Salt Range, and in the Siwálik tract, east to near the Sutlej, and the Kanáwar plant growing at 9,000 feet, as well as one found in Lahoul still higher, seem to be the same. In most places the root is eaten raw or cooked

A. SATIVUM. L. Garlic.

Vernacular. *lahsan.*

Commonly cultivated in the Punjab plains, to be eaten as a condiment. The root is also officinal, being given in confection for rheumatism.

A. SPHÆROCEPHALUM. L.

Vernacular.

This with another species is mentioned by Aitchison (and probably is that referred to in early records of the Agri-Horticultural Society for Spiti) as growing wild in Lahoul (10,000 feet), where the root and dried leaves are eaten, the former being exported to Kúllú in some quantity.

A. SP. (A. ODORUM. L.?)

Vernacular. J. *bhúk.* Lad., *skodze.*

A long-leaved species growing in Khágán at 12,000 to 12,500 feet, the root of which is eaten raw, and the leaves used as a pot-herb. The Ladák plant, growing about 10,500 feet, and all the parts of which are eaten, seems to be the same.

A. SP.

Vernacular. J. *khau.* P. *phúndú.*

With very broad leaves, growing in Khágán at 10,500 feet; the leaves are dried and eaten in winter with meat; the root is not eaten. What appears to be the same species occurs in Spiti at 12,000, but no part of it is eaten.

A. SP.

Vernacular. R. *kiúr.* Lad., *kosse gokpa.*

A much smaller species than either of the two last, growing in Chumba at 10,500 feet. The root is eaten. Of the Ladák plant, common at 10,000 to 13,000 feet, and apparently the same, a few leaves are added to flavour other vegetables.

A. sp.

Vernacular.

Mr. Jaeschke informs me that the bruised leaves of several species are exported from Lahoul to Kúllú to be used by the Hindús as a condiment. Also that towards the Kárakoram, the headache, caused by great elevations is attributed to an Allium— (see Pleurospermum and Artemisia sp.)

Aloe perfoliata. L. (A. Indica. Royle.)

Vernacular. *ghíkwár, kwár gandal, mastí*. Bazár, dried juice, *elwa ?*

Occasionally cultivated by *fakírs*, &c., throughout the Punjab plains, and in the outer hills, where I believe I have seen it to 4,500 feet. And it may possibly be the species Griffith mentions as cultivated in Káfiristán, having been brought thither from Bajaur to the north of Peshawar. The pulp of the leaves (after removing their skin) is eaten by poor people, and in famines. It is also applied to boils, and is used in veterinary medicine. One observer mentions that the root of this (or Gloriosa superba q. v.) is given in colic. I have been told that the seeds of the plant are eaten in times of scarcity. This is given by books as one of the sources of officinal aloes, which is, I think, very doubtful.

Agave Americana. L.

Vernacular. *wiláyatí kantála.*

Grows well as a hedge, &c., in many parts of the Punjab plains. The fibre of it yields a first-rate textile material, which has not yet been utilised on the large scale.

A. cuntala. Rox. (A. vivipara. Royle.)

Vernacular. *kantála, kítkí.*

Probably indigenous in India; common in parts of the Punjab plains. Yields a fibre as last.

Amaryllis grandiflora. Herb. (Brunsvigia. Lindl.)

Vernacular. *sukhdarsan.*

Cultivated for its flower. A correspondent of the Agri-Horticultural Society states that the strained juice of two drams, reduced to a pulp with water, is a good emetic, and that one drop into the ear will generally cure earache.

ASPARAGUS FILICINUS. Ham. (A. CURILLUS. Rox. ?)

Vernacular. *K. allí pallí.* R. *sanspaur.* S. *sensar pál, satzarra.* Bazár, root, ? *sitáwar, músli sufêd.*

Occurs frequently, though nowhere common in the Punjab Himalaya, from 3,000 to 8,500 feet. Its root is exported from Kanáwar to the plains, for which reason I have put the officinal root under this species. It is considered tonic and astringent, and thought to resemble salep—(see EULOPHIA)—in its effects. In Kanáwar a sprig of this (as of the next species) is put in the hand of small-pox patients as a curative measure!

A. (PUNJABENSIS).

Vernacular. S. *sensar pál, chutí.* T. I. *warchechúndi, chanjan wale, lashte.* S. R. *kúchan, banatha, chúrí saroch.* Plains generally, *dúz, soa gandal, sanmálí.* Bazár, leaves, *sitáwar patti.*

This plant, which has slender acicular leaves, and resembles A. OFFICINALIS (garden asparagus), is common in parts of the plains of the Punjab, east to the Sutlej (and apparently occasional to Thanêsar), as well as in the Salt Range, and on the Sutlej to 5,500 feet. It is frequent Trans-Indus, and may be the species mentioned by Bellew as growing high near the Sufêd Koh. He states it to be there eaten as a vegetable, and in the plains the young shoots are in some parts employed thus, but in others they are not eaten. In the Salt Range the twigs are used for scrubbing metallic vessels, and on the Sutlej a sprig of it (as of the preceding species q. v.) is put in the hand of small-pox patients. The leaves are officinal at Lahore. (For *chúrí saroj,* see ARTEMISIA ELEGANS).

A. RACEMOSUS. Willd.

Vernacular. J. *sabúni.* K. *sejpán.* C. *sanspaur.* R. *sansa phaur.* B. *sensafái.* S. *lashorí, chhota kelú.* S. R. *vinjanhora, phút kanda, jári kandiálí* U. *sitráwal.* Bazár, root, *bozídán*; fruit, *haliún.*

This species, which is furnished with small spines, is common in parts of the Salt Range, Siwálik tract, and outer hills, up to 5,000 feet. Its root is used medicinally for man and beast, and it probably supplies part of the officinal *sitáwar*—(see A. FILICINUS)—as well as the *bozídán.* The latter, which is given as an aphrodisiac, is by some authorities considered as identical with the former. The stems of probably this species have been used as garden Asparagus, and liked by Europeans, although Dr. Adams states that none of those growing in Kashmír have the esculent qualities of the latter.

ASPHODELUS FISTULOSUS. L. (A. CLAVATUS. ROX.)

Vernacular. *piázi, bokát.* Bazár, seed, *bínghár bíj.*

Abundant as a field-weed in most parts of the plains of the Punjab, so much so near Jhelam as to be troublesome to the cultivator (Aitchison). It is eaten as a vegetable in times of famine, and appears to be the plant which near the Bolán Pass Griffith describes the camp-followers as eating when the provisions of the Kandahár force ran scarce. The seed is officinal at Lahore.

CONVALLARIA MULTIFLORA. L. (POLYGONATUM. All.) Solomon's Seal.

Vernacular ?

Is common in many parts of the Punjab Himalaya from 6,000 to 11,000 feet, and occurs Trans-Indus near the Sufêd Koh (Bellew). Aitchison states that in Lahoul the powdered root is used as soap.

C. VERTICILLATA. L. (POLYGONATUM. All.) Solomon's Seal.

Vernacular. S. *shalgham misrí, dangshalts.*

This is still more common than the last over the same region from 6,000 to 11,000 feet. In Kanáwar the roots are collected and eaten. They have a not unpleasant flavour, and *shalgham misrí* may have some connection with *salib Misrí*—(see EULOPHIA)—which they slightly resemble.

EREMURUS SPECTABILIS. Bieb.

Vernacular. J. *shílí.* C. *bre, prau, ben.*

This magnificent plant, which grows to 5 or 6 feet high with close spikes of white flowers to half that length, is common at places on the upper Chenáb and in the Jhelam basin at from 6,000 to 9,000 feet. It is probably the "ORNITHOGALUM?" of 7 feet high, mentioned by Royle as having been found by Falconer, and called *prusterien* by the Kashmíris. The leaves when young are much eaten, both fresh and dry cooked as a vegetable, and the members of the Moravian Mission in Lahoul found them excellent treated "as spinach."

FRITILLARIA MELEAGRIS. L Fritillary.

Vernacular.

Is commonly grown in graveyards in Kashmír, along with IRIS, and is frequent on the hills near the valley to 11,000 feet.

GLORIOSA SUPERBA. L. (METHONICA. Lam.)

Vernacular. Bazár, root, *mulím, kariárí*.

This fine-flowered plant occurs sparingly in the Siwálik tract up to near the Jhelam, where Lowther states that he found it near Púnch. It also appears to grow out in the plains in Ambála, near the Jumna (Edgeworth). In some parts of India, the root is commonly used as a poison, but I do not know of its being thus employed in the Punjab.

NARCISSUS TAZETTA. Willd.

Vernacular. K. *nargis*. Bazár, root, *írisa ?*

Honigberger states that the roots of this are officinal, being brought from Kashmír. (I believe I have seen the plant alluded to, common along field-edges, &c., in and near the valley about 5,000—5,500 feet). The root has been found to be possessed of emetic properties by a French *savant*. The *írisa*, however, is generally referred to IRIS FLORENTINA (q. v.) I know not the grounds of either identification.

POLIANTHES TUBEROSA. L.

Vernacular. *gul shab bo*.

Very commonly cultivated for its flower, though not "indigenous" Trans-Indus, as stated by Masson.

TULIPA STELLATA Hook.

Vernacular. T. I. *shandái gúl, ghentol*. S. R. *bhúmphor, chamúní, padúna, jal kúkar*. Plains, *chamotí*.

With a pretty little flower is common in the Salt Range, Trans-Indus, and along the Siwálik tract and outer hills (to Kumaon). In many places the bulbs are eaten ; in some they are not (except by animals). They are regularly sold in the Bazárs of Peshawar, in the plains near which the plant is abundant, and Madden states that they are exported from Kumaon to the plains.

URGINIA INDICA. Kth. (SCILLA. Rox.) Squill.

Vernacular. S. R. *phaphor, kachwassal*.

What I take to be this plant (but good specimens have not been got) has been found in the Punjab only in the Salt Range at about 2,000 feet, although it probably grows in the Siwálik tract also in the Punjab as in the N. W. Provinces. In the latter the bulbs are used medicinally with the same effect as the Squill of Europe, and their juice is employed to give body to thread, but I have not found that they are applied to any special use in the Punjab.

N. O. ORONTIACEÆ.

ACORUS CALAMUS. L.

Vernacular. K. *barí*. S. *boj*. Bazár, root, *bach*, *ghorbach*.

Occasional in the Punjab Himalaya from 3,000 to 6,000 feet. The root is officinal in the plains, being given for rheumatism and flatulence, and is also used in veterinary medicine. Vigne mentions *buj*, a sweet reed from which sweetmeats are made, but as he says it is everywhere common in the ditches in Kashmír, he probably confused this with TYPHA (q. v.), or IRIS PSEUDACORUS (q. v.)

N. O. COMMELYNACEÆ.

ANILEMA TUBEROSUM. Ham. (COMMELYNA SCAPIFLORA. Rox MURDANNIA S. Royle.)

Vernacular. Bazár, root, *múslí siyáh*.

I have found this but rarely to the west of the Jumna, although it is common further east. Its roots are said to furnish the officinal *múslí siyáh*, which is considered astringent and tonic (and has been assigned to species of CURCULIGO by authors).

COMMELYNA BENGALENSIS. L.
C. COMMUNIS. L. ?

Vernacular. C. *chura*. Plains, *kanna*.

One or both of these species occurs in the Punjab plains, in the Salt Range, and in the outer hills, to 6,000 feet. The leaves are eaten as a pot-herb by poor people, and in times of scarcity.

N. O. ORCHIDACEÆ.

EULOPHIA CAMPESTRIS. Lindl.
E. HERBACEA. Lindl.
E. VERA. Royle.

Vernacular. Bazár, tuber, *sálib Misrí*.

The Botanical names given are Royle's, as I have no knowledge that any better identifications have been made since his time of the ORCHIDS, producing the officinal salep, *sálib Misrí*. The first is found in Oudh and Rohilkhund, and in the Siwáliks of the Gangetic Doáb, and I believe I have found it in low land by the Rávi, close to Lahore; the second in (southern India and) the outer Himalaya, near the Jumna; and the third (so named provisionally by Royle) "near the Jhelam river," in the Punjab Himalaya. The tubers of all three appear at times to be used or exported as salep, and those of the Lahore plant are collected for this purpose. Doubtless it is obtained from other species, as well in various places, as there are generally three or four different kinds of tubers found among the salep of the Bazár. The most valued kind, not the largest or nicest looking, has holes for stringing the tubers together, and is said by the dealers to really come from *Misr* (Egypt), the others being brought from nearer India. Cleghorn also mentions that the old residents of Simla and Ootacamund (in the Nílghiris) are in the habit of collecting the tubers of several ORCHIDS for family consumption as salep. The best kinds, however, are said by some authorities to come from Affghánistán and Kashmír. In the latter I heard nothing of the collectior of ORCHID roots, and the family is rare, but Dr. Adams mentions a "salep ORCHIS with large yellow flower" as common on the northern side of the Baltal Pass. Nor do ORCHIDS appear to be very common in Affghánistán, and Irvine (?) states that the salep of the Kábul Bazár is said to come mostly from Bokhára, and "a little from Russia." Davies' Trade Report gives one maund as annually imported from Affghánistán into Peshawar, and one maund by the Bolán Pass, and part of it would from Burnes' statements, &c., appear to come from beyond the former, which agrees with the dealers' information given above. By the natives the salep is chiefly esteemed as a tonic and aphrodisiac (on the "doctrine of signatures"), by Europeans it is frequently used for children as an easily digestible form of farinaceous food, consisting mostly of bassorin. In Europe, salep, consisting of the roots of ORCHIS MASCULA and other species, is used as an agreeable article of food.

ORCHIS SP.?

Vernacular?

Bellew mentions seeing on the hills around Ghuzní (8,000 feet), and about Hazrah near the Sufêd Koh (11,000 feet), an ORCHIS with thick fleshy leaves, which the natives cooked with *ghí*, and which the European Officers of the Kandahár Mission tasted as an experiment. This may, however, have been a member of some other family of plants, as I do not find noted any (other) instance of the leaves of one of these being eaten.

Zeuxine sulcata. Lindl.

Vernacular.

This small Orchid is common at places throughout the Punjab plains, as elsewhere in India. It generally grows in turfy ground in low parts. I have once been told that its tubers also are locally used as salep by natives.

N. O. ZINGIBERACEÆ.

Costus speciosus. Sm.

Vernacular. Bazár, *kút shírín?*

This plant, which is common in the Siwálik tract and elsewhere outside the Punjab, I have not found within the limits of the latter, but Edgeworth states that it grows out in the plains at Thanêsar, south-east of Ambála. The flowers are remarkably handsome, and the root is made into a preserve in some parts of India. To the root likewise some writers have assigned the officinal *kút shírín.* which has also been ascribed to various other species of C.—(see Aucklandia). It is given as a depurative and aphrodisiac.

Curcuma longa. Rox.? Turmeric.

Vernacular. R. *haldar.* S. *halia.* Bazár, root, *haldí.*

This is commonly grown frequently along the edge of fields of ginger—(see Zingiber)—in the Punjab Siwálik tract and outer hills from 2,000 to 4,000 and sometimes to 5,500 feet, up to the Rávi at least, and occasionally beyond that. Irvine is probably mistaken in stating that it is cultivated in Peshawar and Bunnú. The root is extensively used by natives as a condiment, and is employed as a dye. It is also applied to wounds and bruises. Some export takes place towards the west and north, as Davies' Trade Report gives 500 maunds as exported viâ Peshawar to Affghánistán. Cayley mentions that in 1867, 11 maunds were brought to Lê from Kúllú, to be sent on to the east and to Yárkand.

Elettaria Cardamomum. Maton.? Cardamum.

Vernacular. *illáchí.*

Specimens of what is said to be this plant are occasionally seen in gardens in the Punjab Siwálik tract, &c., but they never fruit.

HEDYCHIUM SPICATUM. Bot. Mag.

Vernacular. R. *ban kela, sáki*. B. *banhaldí, shlúi*. S. *khor, shalwi*. Bazár, root, *kapúr kachrí, kachúr*.

This plant is not uncommon in parts of the Punjab Himalaya up to near the Jhelam at least, at from 3,500 to 7,500 feet. Its large broad leaves are twisted and made into coarse mats for sleeping on, &c. The tuberous roots have, as "wild ginger," been tried by Europeans as a preserve, but without success. In Garhwál, I was told they are used in washing the newly married, and Madden states that they are pounded with tobacco for the hookah. They are officinal under the above names, being considered tonic and stimulant. Honigberger is apparently in error in stating that they are only used in veterinary medicine. Cayley mentions that there is some import from the south to Lê, and export from the latter to Yárkand of *kachúr*, which is probably this, but may be *tikia kachúr* or *nar kachur*, said to be the produce of CURCUMA ZERUMBET, Rox. Davies' Trade Report gives 25 maunds of *kachúr* as annually exported viâ Peshawar to Affghánistán.

ROSCOEA PURPUREA. Royle

Vernacular. B. *banhaldí*.

Occasional at 5,000 to 6,000 feet up to the Rávi. In Kángra its root is used in veterinary medicine.

ZINGIBER OFFICINALIS. Roscoe. Ginger.

Vernacular. *adrak, ada*.

Frequently cultivated in the outer hills apparently up to near the Indus at about 2,000 or 2,500 feet. The root is used as a condiment, and in medicine as a stimulant. Davies' Trade Report gives 100 maunds as annually exported to Affghánistán viâ Peshawar.

N. O. IRIDEÆ.

CROCUS SATIVUS. All. Saffron.

Vernacular. K. *kongs*. Bazár, stigmata, *kesar, zafarán*.

This plant, which is cultivated in the south of Europe, for the saffron which is used in colouring and flavouring, is grown in Kashmír, but only so far as I know in one small tract at Pámpúr, not far from the capital. On the spot I was informed that the bulbs are planted in June, that they are not irrigated, and that the crop is hurt by much moisture. When the bulbs have got old, after 10 or 12 years, they are all dug up, and a proportion of the younger ones are planted out in fresh ground. The pretty flowers are in bloom about October, when the crop of yellow stigmata is collected. I brought down some bulbs to Lahore in 1866, which flowered at Lahore in the following spring. The saffron is exported both to south and north from Kashmír. Vigne says it goes mostly to Yarkand, and Cayley mentions that in 1867 5¼ maunds reached Lê, which would be worth at Yárkand Rs. 8,640. Davies' Trade Report mentions that about 10 seers are brought annually to Peshawar viâ Affghánistán "from Persia" (Lumsden also states that it comes "from the west" to Kandahár), the buying price in the latter being Rs. 35, and the selling price at Peshawar Rs. 40 per seer. Davies gives 20 maunds as annually imported from Affghánistán by the Bolán. In India it is used as a condiment by the wealthy, and is officinal as a cordial and tonic. In large doses it is said to affect the head, and Vigne (I think) tells a story of one of the Mogul Emperors, who, having heard that an over-dose is poisonous, experimented with a large quantity on a condemned criminal, but the man escaped with his life.

Iris florentina. L.?

Vernacular. Bazár, root, *írisa*.

This officinal root, which is used externally in rheumatism, is attributed by some to the above plant—(see Narcissus).

I. Kamaonensis. Wall.

Vernacular. C. *piáz*. R. *karkar*. Lad., *tezma*.

This species, with narrowish leaves and purplish blue flowers, having a pleasant odour, is common in parts of the Punjab Himalaya from 5,000 to 12,000 feet, and apparently in Lahoul and Ladák, to at least 14,000 feet. In Chumba the root and leaves are given in fever. In parts of Ladák the leaves appear to be used as fodder.

I. Nepalensis. Wall.

Vernacular. J. *chalúndar*. K. *sosan*. B. *shotí*. S. *chilúchí*.

A broadish-leaved species occurring at various places throughout the Punjab Himalaya from 2,500 to 9,500 feet. In Kashmír and other parts of the Jhelam basin, and I think Trans-Indus, it is commonly planted in graveyards.

I. PSEUDACORUS. L.? Cornflag.

Vernacular. K. *krishun, imarjal, marjal.*

There is some doubt as to the identity of this plant, which I have only seen in and near the Kashmír Valley 5 000 feet—(see ACORUS).

I. SP.

Vernacular. B. *shrúl, skecho.*

A tall species with fine purplish lilac flowers found at 5,000—7,000 feet on the Biás. Its leaves are used as bedding for cattle, and for thatch.

N. O. HYDROCHARIDACEÆ.

HYDRILLA VERTICILLATA. Rich.

Vernacular. *jhanjh, jála ?*

This, which is common in water in parts of the Punjab plains up to Peshawar, is stated by Edgeworth to be used (with other aquatic plants) east of the Sutlej, for refining sugar, but at Múltán, west of that river, these are not obtainable.

VALLISNERIA SPIRALIS.

Vernacular.

This plant occurs occasionally within the Punjab, in the Salt Range, and elsewhere, up to Peshawar. But I have nowhere seen it common, and Honigberger may have been confusing it with other aquatic plants, where he states that it is used for sugar refining, "animal charcoal being forbidden by the Hindú religion."

N. O. FLUVIALES.

POTAMOGETON CRISPUS. L.

Vernacular. *sawál ?* Lad., *chúsbal.*

Not uncommon in the Punjab plains, and (apparently) abundant at 9,000 to 11,000 feet in Ladák. It is probably one of those used in refining sugar here as elsewhere. In Ladák it is used as fodder.

P. GRAMINEUS. L. (P. PECTINATUS. L. ?)

Vernacular. *sawáli ? jála.* Lad., *zímbil chupein, phús.*

As the last, and probably employed for the same purpose in the parts of the plains where it grows. I have seen it being carted into Jalandar, perhaps to be used thus. The name *jála* appears to be given to whatever aquatic plants are employed for this purpose. In Ladák this also (or a very similar species) is used for fodder.

P. LUCENS. L.
P. NATANS. L.

Vernacular ?

The former appears to be a species common in Kashmír, where also the latter, common in parts of the Punjab plains, seems to grow. In Kashmír, large quantities of these are used as fodder.

N. O. PALMÆ.

CHAMÆROPS RITCHIANA. Griff. Dwarf Palm.

Vernacular. J. *patha.* T. I. *mzarái, patha.* S. R. *patha, kilú, kaliún.* Bel., *pís ;* stones, *kaur.*

This plant, which Bellew calls "tiger grass," and Masson writes of as "aloe," has its chief habitats along the Súlimán Range, principally on and near the eastern skirts from the plains to about 3,000 feet. It is also common in a portion of the Salt Range near its centre, and occurs in the Siwálik tract in one place east of the Jhelam, near Súmání, above Bhimbur. The two young plants, mentioned by Aitchison as having been found by him near the river Jhelam, may have come down as seed from the last locality. I have seen the plant raised in Sind from Belúchistán seed, and in the Sahāranpúr Botanical Garden there is a fine specimen, with a trunk 10 or 12 feet high, said to have been grown from Trans-Indus seed, sown within the last 20 years. In the height of the trunk, and some points as to the leaves, the Sahāranpúr specimen appears to differ from the wild plant as ordinarily seen, but this may result from climate, and being grown in cultivated ground. The finer leaves are made into mats, and the more coarse ones into ropes, sandals, &c. A considerable quantity of them are exported from the places of growth as far at least as Jhelam to the east to be made into cordage for beds, well-ropes, &c. One season the supply of *múnj*—(see SACCHARUM SARA)—ran scarce, and the ropes for the bridge of boats were made of the *patha*, but are said to have snapped at once under a strain which *múnj* ropes could have resisted. The Patháns twist up spirally a segment of a leaf, to be used as a tobacco-pipe, for which purpose it answers better than the two holes in the ground—(see NICOTIANA TABACUM)—used at times by Patháns and some of the Himalayan tribes. On the frontier, a rude drinking vessel also is often formed by tying together the points of the segments of a leaf; these may frequently be seen lying by pools, &c., Trans-Indus. The red mossy-looking rete from the axils of the leaves is used for tinder, occasionally, as Bellew states, after being steeped in the juice of mulberry *leaves?* Bellew also mentions that the delicate young leaves, which have a sweet astringent taste, are in great repute for the treatment of diarrhæa and dysentery; and that at a later stage (?) when they become very sour, they are used as a purgative, chiefly in veterinary medicine. An official report states that large quantities of the stones of the fruit (which Trans-Indus ripens about July) are exported from Gwádur to Muscát *en route* to Mecca, to be manufactured into rosaries for the pilgrims.

PHŒNIX ACAULIS. Ham. Stemless Date-palm.

Vernacular. *pind khajúr*.

In this, which I take to be a distinct species, there is no stem whatever, and the clusters of fruit are half-buried in the ground. It is small but eatable. In parts of India a rope is made from the bruised leaves. I have not seen this species in the Punjab, except in the Siwálik tract, close to the Jumna.

P. DACTYLIFERA. L. Date-palm.

Vernacular. *khajúr khají*; fruit, *pind, chiriwi, bagrí*; cabbage of leaves, *gadda, gallí*; gum, *hokmchil*.

Much information as to this tree is given by Edgeworth in various papers and communications to the Agri-Horticultural Society of India, &c. He describes it as having been introduced into the southern Punjab in the 7th (or 9th) century, and states that the true Date is nowhere known in any quantity to the north or east of Tulamba and Jhang (both close to the Chenáb), although the tree has been tried in the districts of Lahore and Umritsur, and there are a few in the northern part of Jalandar, where, however, the chief use of the tree is for the sweet juice—(see P. SYLVESTRIS). He also mentions that there are some at Sahásranpúr, which give good fruit especially when the rains are late. The finest trees range up to 100 and 120 feet high, and the leaves are longer in this than in the following species. Edgeworth mentions that the natives assert that it will not grow except where the soil is or has been subject to inundation. There are now hundreds of the trees about various towns in Múltán and Mozaffargarh, but I think it is most abundant near Dehra Ghází Khan, Trans-Indus, where the country for ten or twelve miles from north to south has such numbers of trees that eight or ten thousand rupees are said to be annually got by Government from the small tax which is levied on each female tree (the sexes are on separate individuals). At Múltán and several other places, there are some trees which appear to branch, the most remarkable, according to Edgeworth, being one close to the *kachherí* at Jhang, which is 12 feet high, with a branch of 3½ feet. These have by some been assigned to the HYPHÆNE or Doûm Palm of Egypt, but I quite agree with Edgeworth that they merely result from seeds falling into and germinating in the axils of the petioles. Smaller specimens of such branches are not uncommon about Múltán, &c., generally growing near the top of the tree, whether the latter be short or tall. The male trees, in which the flower stalks are much shorter and less spreading than in the female, are frequently cut down, and as the roots don't readily rot and won't burn, they give some trouble. The stem lasts as a beam for five or six years in the arid climate of Múltán, and the wood is also used for rafters. It is likewise employed for water channels, and for supporting the earth of small bridges.

This, the true Date, has large bunches of orange, amber, or purple fruit, than which, as Edgeworth remarks "nothing can be more excellent when they are fresh," either eaten raw or cooked as a pudding. And for some part of the year they form a considerable proportion of the food of the natives of the parts where the tree is common. The outer leaves of the tree are often cut off to let the fruit get more sun and air. As taken from the tree, the fruit is called *pind*, and Coldstream mentions that when split up, *chirwí*, it is still more palatable, while *bagrí*, the produce of the poorer trees, boiled in oil and water, are much inferior to both. I do not know that the trees at Lahore and Peshawar (there are a good many about both places) are, as a rule, of this species, but near both the fruit is evidently valued, as each bunch has often a piece of mat tied round it (leaving only a small air hole) for protection from the birds. Cayley mentions dates as imported into Lê from the Punjab. Into the latter dates are brought from the west. And in the southern Punjab those from Kech (Mekrán) are reckoned so much superior to the ordinary fruit that they sell at five times the price of the latter. At Múltán there is a *bedána* (*i. e.*, seedless) fruit in which the stone and its kernel are represented only by a little shrivelled membrane, the rest of the fruit consisting of the pleasant sweet pulp. Edgeworth states that there is only one tree producing these, which was formerly reckoned *badsháhí*, "royal," *i. e.*, the produce was reserved for the ruler of the country. But Colonel Voyle (when Deputy Commissioner of Múltán) informed me, and I was told on the spot, that several trees produce these, which are the upper fruit ripening after the lower ordinary dates of the same tree.

Edgeworth, when Commissioner of Múltán, got men from Jessore in Bengal, who were acquainted with the method of extracting sugar from the juice of P. SYLVESTRIS there. They remained at Múltán for some time experimenting; and although they seem to have been hostile to the success of the scheme, and said there was less saccharine matter in the juice of this than of the other species, it seems to have been shown that the fruit of a female tree is much more valuable than its sugar was likely to be, and the male tree has but little juice. The rete forms a regular net round the base of each petiole, but it is difficult to remove, and is said to be taken from felled trees only. It is made into pack-bags for oxen, and ropes, and although I was told on the spot that it stands alternations of wet and dry, Coldstream mentions that it is rarely used for well-ropes. For these he states that the stalk and pinnæ of the leaf generally are used. The leaves set on end in the earth, and bound together, make a neat and good fence. The terminal bunch of young leaves, taken only when a tree is cut down, according to Coldstream, who notes that it is mentioned by Baber, is much eaten by the natives both raw and cooked. Edgeworth states that it is excellent, and Coldstream vouches for its making a good curry. Honigberger mentions that the "inspissated juice" of this tree is officinal at Lahore under the above name.

P. HUMILIS. Royle. Dwarf Date-palm.

Vernacular. *khajúrí*.

This I conceive to be merely a variety of the last. It grows in the Siwálik tract to some distance within Punjab limits, as further east.

P. SYLVESTRIS. Rox. Wild Date-palm.

Vernacular. *khajúr, khají*; juice, *sendhí, tárí*.

This tree, which strongly resembles the last, occurs wild in many places in and near the Siwálik tract up to and probably beyond the Indus, in the Salt Range, and out into the plains in the east of the Province. It is not seen much above 3,000 feet in the outer hills, and Vigne correctly points out that the "palms of Baramoule" in Kashmír were creations of Moore's imagination. Adams seems to note that Bernier also mentions palm in Kashmír, but I can find no such reference in that author. The fruit of this tree is small, and, though *eatable*, is not valued even by natives, but generally left to be consumed by birds. One man in the Salt Range told me that it is actually noxious, that he himself had eaten it, and been ill with head symptoms for days. (?) The most valuable product of the species is the saccharine juice got by incising below the tuft of leaves. It is largely extracted in many places, generally to be drunk fresh, when it is sweet and pleasant as a beverage, sometimes to be kept till it ferments into an intoxicating liquor. The wood and leaves are used for similar purposes to those of the last species.

N. O. TYPHACEÆ.

TYPHA ANGUSTIFOLIA. L.
T. LATIFOLIA. L. } Bulrush.

Vernacular. K. *pitz, yira*. B. *boj*. T. I. *lúkh*. Plains generally, *dib, kúndar, patíra, gond*.

The former species is common in marshes, &c., in most parts of the Punjab plains, at about 4,000 feet in Kúllú, and up to the Kashmír Valley (5,000 feet); the latter is much more rare. The roots are eaten in Kashmír—(see ACORUS)—and on the Sutlej I have seen the lower succulent part of the stem used for clearing the water of the swollen river, which it does speedily and effectually. The stems are used for making sieves in Kashmír. The leaves are in many parts used for roofs of houses; in Kashmír the thatch of the boats is constructed of them, and in the central and eastern Punjab and Kúllú (where CHAMÆROPS q. v. is not to be got) floor and other mats are generally made of them. In some places also they are made into boat-ropes, which it is said will last a month. In Peshawar, and probably elsewhere, the down of the ripe fruit (not the flower as mentioned by Vigne) is used to bind mortar for wall-plaster.

N. O. ARACEÆ.

ARUM CAMPANULATUM. Rox. (AMORPHOPHALLUS. Blume.) Yam.

Vernacular. *zamínkand*.

Commonly cultivated for its root, a kind of yam, in parts at least of the eastern and central parts of the Punjab plains.

A. COLOCASIA. L. (COLOCASIA ANTIQUORUM. Schott.) Yam.

Vernacular. B. *ráb, álú.* S. *kasaurí, gágli.* Plains, &c., *gwían, kachálú.*

This is very commonly cultivated in the plains by natives for its root, which they are fond of. Its leaves likewise are at times eaten. It is also grown at places in the hills to a considerable elevation; I have seen it at nearly 7,600 feet in Chumba and Kúllú.

A. CURVATUM. Rox. (ARISÆMA. Kth.)

Vernacular. J. *súrín.* C. *dor.* R. *kír kí chálú.* B. *kíra kál.* S. *jángúsh.*

There is some doubt as to the identity of these, but the species appears to grow at many places in the Punjab Himalaya from 4,000 to 6,500 feet. On the Jhelam and Sutlej it is stated to have poisonous qualities. In Kúllú the seeds are said to be given with salt for colic in sheep.

A. SPECIOSUM. Wall. (ARISÆMA. Mart.)

Vernacular. J. *samp kí khúmb.* R. *kírí kí kukrí.* B. *kírálú.*

This very handsome species, the coloured hood and protruding dark point of the spadix of which are, as Madden remarks, "alarmingly like a cobra," is not uncommon in parts of the Punjab Himalaya from 6,000 to 8,500 feet. In Hazára the root is stated to be poisonous, and in Chumba it is applied pounded to snake-bites, probably on the doctrine of signatures. In Kúllú, where the root is given to sheep for colic, the fruit is said to have deleterious effects on the mouth when eaten by children.

A. TORTUOSUM. Wall. (ARISÆMA. Schott.)

Vernacular. R. *kírí kí kúkrí.*

This, which was found in Chumba at about 7,000 feet, is much smaller than any of the preceding, and may be the above species, which also was found by Bellew near the Sufêd Koh. Its root is in Chumba applied to kill the worms which infest cattle in the rains.

A. SP.?

Vernacular. *núrialam.*

Mentioned by Bellew as growing in Swát, &c., north of the Peshawar Valley, where he states that the fleshy root is used as a cure for impotence and sterility. As he only gives "Arum ?" thus, and the properties ascribed are like those attributed to the orchids, I am inclined to think this must be a *sálib Misrí*—(see EULOPHIA).

N. O. GRAMINEÆ.

ŒLUROPUS REPENS. Trin.

Vernacular ?

Common in some saline tracts in the Punjab plains. Aitchison states that in certain of those near Jhelam it quite replaces CYNODON DACTYLON (q. v.)

ALOPECURUS PRATENSIS. L. (or A. AGRESTIS. L. ?)

Vernacular ?

This is common wild in many parts of the Punjab plains, and I believe I have seen it cultivated for fodder just to the east of the Jumna near the head of the Gangetic Doáb.

ANATHERUM MURICATUM. Beauv. (ANDROPOGON. Rets. VETIVERIA. Virey.)

Vernacular. *panní ;* roots, *khas ;* stem, *sink.* Bazár, tops, *sink, búra de járob.*

Not uncommon in the Punjab plains, but only locally, *e. g.,* Edgeworth mentions that it is not found within 80 miles north of Múltán, though abundant above that. And when the odorous roots have to be got in considerable quantity to make *tatties* for troops, it has sometimes to be brought from many miles off. This root is the best substance for making these *tatties,* or matted doors on which water is sprinkled to cool down the air within the room, and when it cannot be got, the twigs of ALHAGI (q. v.) are substituted. The stem of this grass is used for thatching, &c. The officinal *búra de jarob,* given as an alterative, is generally ascribed to SACCHARUM SARA (q. v.), but what I have seen seems to be the upper part of this grass.

ANDROPOGON ANNULATUS. Forsk.

Vernacular. *palwán, minyár.*

Abundant in many parts of the Punjab plains. It is considered excellent fodder for bullocks, &c., and for horses when green.

A. INVOLUTUS. Stend.

Vernacular. J. *baggar*. B. S. *múnjí, baggar*.

This grass is common in many parts of the Siwálik tract and outer Himalaya, at from 2,300 to 4,000 feet, up to the Indus, and occurs beyond that river also, though more rarely. It is commonly used for cordage, swing-bridges, &c., and probably supplies in the Punjab, as in the N. W. Provinces, most of the *bábar* or *baggar* fibre which is in part exported for making rope, &c.—(see ERIOPHORUM.

A. SP.

Vernacular. U. *bavú*.

This is mentioned by Edgeworth as occurring in Ambála, where it is considered poisonous. And it may be the same which Bellew alludes to as hurtful to cattle in the Peshawar Valley.

ANTHISTIRIA ANATHERA. Nees.

Vernacular ?

Abundant in parts of the Salt Range, Trans-Indus, and in the outer hills from 2,300 to 8,500 feet. Madden mentions that in Kumaon its roots are frequently luminous, whence it is there called *jyotishmatí*.

ARISTIDA DEPRESSA. Retz.
A. SETACEA. Retz.

Vernacular. T. I. *spín khalak, spín wege, jándar*. Plains generally, *lamba*.

This (or these) species is very common in many dry parts of the central and western Punjab and Trans-Indus, and in parts of the outer hills towards the west up to 2,500 feet. It is said to be a favourite food of cattle. In Madrás, A. SETACEA is stated to be used for *tatties*—(see ANATHERUM).

ARUNDINARIA FALCATA. Nees. (with A. UTILIS. Cleghorn).

Vernacular. R. *nirgál, nágre*. B. *nigál, nirgál, káthí, narrí, garrí, gero*. S. *spiúg, gorwa, spikso, pítso*.

It is difficult to disentangle the accounts of these, so I give them together, especially as Colonel Munro makes them one species in an elaborate paper on the BAMBUSACEÆ, in the last part of the transactions of the Linnean Society. I have, however, found two kinds always distinguished by the hillmen. The former is described as the smaller, and said to be the tougher of the two, and to have no hollow, and as growing at 9,000 to 12,000 feet, apparently up to the Biás only. The latter is stated to be larger and hollow, and to grow at 5,000 to 8,000 feet, and is found up to the Rávi. They are largely used for making baskets and other wicker-work and mats, and for putting under roofs, and the larger is employed for shepherds' pipes, &c., and is exported in some quantity to the plains for the *náicha* (hookah-tube).

Arundo donax. L. (A. Karka. Rox.) Reed.

Vernacular. J. *bag narri*. K. *nái*. C. *nar*. R. *nalú*. T. I. *dwárena, drúmbi, ghwarga*. Plains generally, *nar, naria, nal*.

I have made some confusion as to this plant, but it is common wild and frequently cultivated in the Punjab plains, and appears to occur in the hills, up to Kashmír (5,000 feet). The leaves are used for fodder, and the stems for hookah-tubes, *chiks* (screens), baskets, and hurdles, &c. About Calcutta, mats are constructed of the split stems of this or a similar species, and in Sind they are made into chairs, and a fibre is said to be extracted from the upper part of them (?)

A. Phragmitis. L.?

Vernacular. J. *díla*. Lad., *dámbú*.

A short species, growing on the Kishenganga at about 6,000 feet, appears to be this. Sandals are in winter made of its stems. It is abundant in Lahoul and Ladák, up to 14,000 feet, and reaches 6 or 7 feet in height. In Lahoul it is much used for roofing, but appears to be considered useless in Ladák, except that it is eaten by cattle.

A. sp.?

Vernacular. B. *phrol*. S. *rajal, táma*.

A smallish species of Arundo (?) common at places on the Biás and Sutlej from 3,000 to 9,000 feet. Baskets are made of its stems.

Avena fatua. L. Wild oats.

Vernacular. C. *gozang, kásumm*. Lad., *yúpo, úpwa*. Plains, *ganer, gandal, jei* (Hi.)

This is common as a field-weed in cereal crops throughout the Punjab plains, and in many places in the Himalaya, up to 9,500 feet,

Lahoul, and to 11,500 feet at least, Ladák. In almost all the places where it grows, it is pulled and gathered for fodder (Moorcroft mentioning that in Ladák it is given to the cattle "at night.") In Kumaon, Madden mentions that "the straw" is used as fodder, but is suspected of occasionally producing bad effects.

A. SATIVA. L. Oats.

Vernacular. *jei.*

Is occasionally cultivated in the plains of the Punjab by or for Europeans, to serve as horses' food. In the records of the Agri-Horticultural Society it is stated that in a trial at Jhang, nine maunds of seed gave 260 maunds of crop in the straw.

BAMBUSA ARUNDINACEA. Retz. Bamboo.

Vernacular. *magar báns, nál bans;* young shoots, *kalla báns.*

This species, which grows to 14 or 16 inches in girth and 50 or 60 feet high, is commonly cultivated in the Punjab Siwálik tract, and may be seen in the outer hills to 4,000 and occasionally 6,000 feet. It is rare out in the plains, and I doubt if it is this (but more probably the next) species which Edgeworth mentions as planted at Baghdád, 40 miles north of Múltán. The natives state that this (like the next, q. v.) grows to its full thickness and height in one year. It is used for *dooly*-poles and such-like purposes. The young shoots are made into pickle, &c.

B. STRICTA. Rox. (DENDROCALAMUS STRICTUS. Nees.) Male Bamboo.

Vernacular. *báns.* Bazár, silicious secretion, *banslochan, tabashír.*

This, a much smaller species, many of the stems of which are solid, and therefore called "male bamboo," is common wild in some parts of the Punjab Siwálik tract. Its chief habitats are near the Sutlej, above Hoshyárpúr and east from Núrpúr in a good many places, in one or two places on the Chenáb in fewer numbers, and north from Rawul Pindí, where it appears to be still more limited in extent. There are also a very few scanty clumps at two or three places in the eastern portion of the Salt Range. Its range in the Punjab may be from 1,500 to 2,500 feet. It generally occurs on arid shingly slopes, and where the clumps are pretty close together there is but little arboreous or shrubby vegetation among them. The natives assert stoutly that this bamboo accomplishes the *whole* of its growth in two or three weeks during the rains, and some experiments we have made seem to indicate that in its natural habitats a very considerable proportion of the whole growth as to size, though not as to consistency, takes place within the first season. The new stems of the year are of a much brighter green, and the sheaths remain on them. The seeding in quantity of some of the species of bamboo is believed by the natives to presage famine. Single stems, and not the whole of a clump of this, as of some other, species, generally seed, and in most cases such stems die after the seed ripens about June. The husks remain on the stems, so that those which have died in several successive years, being seen togther, are apt to deceive. The natives deny that there is any reproduction except from roots, and no doubt as conservancy has been, this is very much the case in most of our bamboo jungles, but this state of things results chiefly from the tender young seedlings being generally browsed or burned down. The stems are much valued for roofs, wattling, basket-work, &c., and the leaves are used as fodder (with wheat-straw, &c.) The silicious matter, found in the joints of some kinds of bamboo, though certainly inert, is officinal, being considered cooling, tonic, and astringent, but I do not know that any of it is produced in the Punjab from this or the preceding species.

CENCHRUS ECHINATUS. L.

Vernacular. *basla, leá, lapta, bhort* (Irvine).

This grass is not uncommon in the more arid parts of the Punjab plains. In some places it is called middling, in others it is said to be excellent fodder. The seed is frequently used as food in times of scarcity, and this seems to be the C. mentioned by Edgeworth as one of those which are swept up in the deserts of the southern Punjab for this purpose. The hooks on the fruit cause it to stick to the traveller's clothes in a troublesome way, but even in Bikanir the difficulty from it is probably not so great as to warrant Irvine in calling it "the chief annoyance to the traveller." The "considerable price" also which he mentions as at times paid for its seed (as food) would probably diminish on strict enquiry.

CHRYSOPOGON GLAUCOPTIS. Stend.

Vernacular. K. *shili ghá.*

This is found in parts of the Punjab Himalaya at from 2,500 to 9,500 (?) feet, and its stems, or those of a species very near it, are used for the sieves employed in paper-making in Kashmír, for which purpose they are very neatly tied together with horse hair. This also, or a nearly allied species, is noted in the Sahâranpúr Herbarium, as having luminous roots in the rains.

CYMBOPOGON IWARANCUSA. Schult. (ANDROPOGON. Rox. A. CALAMUS AROMATICUS. Royle.) C. LANIGER. Desf.

Vernacular. T. I. *sargara.* S. R. *san.* Plains generally, *khawí, panní, solára.* H. *búr.* Hí., *injaní.* Bazár, root-sheaths, *azkhar, mirchiagand, lámjak, katran.*

I have not been sufficiently careful to distinguish between these two species, which are not uncommon in many parts of the plains, and which are frequently confused by the natives. One or other is very abundant in some of the desert tracts of the Punjab, and the coarse lemon grass, mentioned by Bellew as growing among the ruins of old Kandahár, may be one of them. The smell of especially the former is that of lemons, but more turpentiny, and is sometimes very perceptible when a tract, covered by the grass, is being marched over by a body of men and animals. It is said to be much more powerful at certain seasons than others. The statements as to whether it is liked or not by cattle are most diverse in different places. Edgeworth, who suggests that this may possibly be the NARDUS of Arrian, mentions that in the Ambála tract it is much liked by them, and it is said to give a flavour to the milk and butter, and Royle asserts even to the flesh of animals feeding on it. Vigne states that near Hassan Abdál a stimulating oil is extracted from it, and in various parts this is extracted and used in medicine. The "grass oil" of Nimár, which is similar if not the same, is reckoned of great use in rheumatism. A spirit *(arak)* is also distilled from the grass with spices, &c., and is said to be useful in indigestion and fever. Madden mentions that the roots are sometimes luminous. They appear to be officinal under all the above names in the Punjab, where also the heads are officinal, both being considered desiccant.

C. SP.

Vernacular.

Madden mentions a species as common from 4,000 to 8,000 feet in Kumaon, which is so strongly aromatic that it is refused by cattle.

CYNODON DACTYLON. L.

Vernacular. T. I. *baráwa.* Plains generally, *khabbal, khabbar.* Hí., *dúb.*

This well-known grass, which is said to be held sacred by the Hindús on account of its tenacity of life, is abundant except in the lightest soils, and the most arid localities throughout the

Punjab plains, and at places to 6,000 feet in the Himalaya. On account of its rooting stolons and close growth when watered, it is well adapted for turfing, and is generally used for that purpose. From universal testimony it is the best of all our grasses for fattening and milk-producing powers. It seems to be peculiarly subject to smut in the Punjab.

DACTYLOCTENIUM ÆGYPTIACUM. Willd.

Vernacular. T. I. *chubrei*. Plains generally, *maddna, chimbarí*.

Common in many places throughout the plains of the Punjab. Its seeds are occasionally eaten in times of scarcity, and it is reckoned good as a fattening and milk-producing pasture.

DIGITARIA SANGUINALIS. Pers.

Vernacular. T. I. *khurdsh*. Plains generally, *motí khabbal, takkrí, farw*.

Occurs in many parts of the Punjab plains, and in the Himalaya to 9,000 feet. Is considered one of the best pasture-grasses.

ELEUSINE COROCANA. Gært.

Vernacular. C. *kodra, mandwa*. R. *mandal*. B. *kodra*. S. *kutra, kodon, mandwa*.

This, which is said by Cleghorn to be perhaps the most productive of all the Indian cereals, but is stated by natives to yield a somewhat bitter and indigestible grain, is not much cultivated in the Punjab plains. It is pretty frequent in the Himalaya as far west as the Chenáb, up to 6,000 and 7,000 feet. Monkeys are said to prefer it to other crops.

E. FLAGELLIFERA. Nees.

Vernacular. T. I. *chubrei*. Plains generally, *chímbarí, chemrí*.

Abundant in many of the more arid parts of the Punjab plains, especially towards the west. In some places it is stated to be a favourite with cattle.

ERAGROSTIS CYNOSUROIDES. R. and S.

Vernacular. *dab, dib*. Hi., *kúsa, davolia*.

This grass is frequent throughout the Punjab plains. It is coarse, but is said to be liked by buffaloes, and, having long roots, to remain pretty fresh throughout the year. The upper part of its stem is in some places used for making the sieves employed in paper-manufacture.

E. SPP.

Vernacular. *lamb, mirukar, kúri, chinka.*

There are several species common in the Punjab plains, which are considered good pasture-grass. One at least is used as a pot-herb, and the pounded seeds of several are eaten mixed with other flour in cakes, pottage, &c., the *lamb* particularly in certain Hindú fasts and festivals. A correspondent of the Agri-Horticultural Society mentions that the years 1809 and 1831, when wheat (flour?) rose to seven seers and ten seers per rupee, are respectively known near Lahore by the names of the *lambwála sál* and the *mirukarwála sál,* from the fact of the seeds of these two grasses being so largely employed for food by the starving poor. In the latter year, *mirukar* was fortunately abundant owing to the early (winter?) rains having been abundant.

HETEROPOGON CONTORTUS. R. and S.

Vernacular. T. I. *barweza, sarmal.* Plains generally, *suriála, surári.*

Is common in some parts of the Punjab plains, and abundant at places in the hills in some cases up to 7,000 feet. When young it is good fodder. The flowers are furnished with long twisted awns, which are troublesome to the traveller through their fixing themselves in his clothes, or still worse in his skin, from which they sometimes have to be cut out if they are not noticed in time. The humidity of the air affects the twist of the awn, and in the Bengal Asiatic Society Transactions of many years ago, there is a suggestion to employ one as a simple kind of hygrometer.

HORDEUM ÆGICERAS.

Vernacular. *oú?*

A peculiar species of barley grown in some parts of the inner Himalaya, mentioned by Thomson at 11,500 feet in Tibet.

H. CÆLESTE. (Viborg.?)

Vernacular. C. *grim? elo?* S. *úá, újan.* Lad., *grim, nas?*

This grain is cultivated on the Sutlej to 13,600 feet (Gerard), and to 15,000 (? Cleghorn). Moorcroft appears to mention it in Lahoul, and I believe I have seen it in Pangí further down on the Chenáb to 8,000 feet. In the latter place it is said to be hardy but not very digestible. I am not sure that the *grim*, grown in the Wurdwan Valley in the Chenáb basin at 7,000 feet, and that of Ladák common to over 14,500 feet, are this species. In the latter, dough made from it and used as food (like the *sattú* of the outer hills) is called *ampe*.

H. HEXASTICHUM. L. Barley.

Vernacular. C. *thanzatt, nái, jawa*. S. *chák*. Plains, *jau*; cut as fodder, *kawíd, kasíl, patha*. Lad., *soá, jhotak, shiroka*; (bearded, *shrúk*; beardless, *yangma*, Cayley). P. *tro, ne*. C. *chung*. Beer, *lúgar*. S. *búza*. Lad., *chang*. Spirits C. and Lad., *arrak*. Bazár, ashes, *jáwa-khár*.

This species of barley is frequently cultivated as a cold-weather crop in the plains of the Punjab, as it requires less labour, and gives more produce than wheat, even in inferior soil, and where the water is deep below the surface. Varieties of it are also cultivated to great elevations in the Himalaya. In some parts above 8,000 feet, it is much more common than wheat, while at lower levels it is less grown. In Lahoul and Ladák it is abundantly cultivated with FAGOPYRUM (q. v.) up to 13,000 feet; in the latter some kinds of barley may be seen to over 14,000 feet, about Hanle, near the Tsomorírí lake. On the Chenáb, in some places when ripe, it is pulled up, not cut. In the plains it is frequently cut two or even three times, when young, as fodder, with little or no injury to the ear, which is formed afterwards. In Lahoul and on the Sutlej, a kind of beer is made from its grain, the ferment in the former being brought from Tibet as little farinaceous looking cakes, the size of a fig, called *pab* or *phap*. In Ladák also a similar beverage is made by the aid of the same substance which is said to be made in Drás to the west, from barley flour, mixed with cloves, cardamoms, ginger, and an herb which is probably an Umbellifer (and then fermented ?) On the Sutlej, Moorcroft states that in the preparation of the beer rice is mixed with it, and the root of a "bitter aromatic from high"—(see *budkes*, UMBELLIFERA)—is added to prevent indigestion. In Lahoul, Aitchison mentions that spirits made from barley are used by some of the richer inhabitants, and spirits are also made in Ladák. In some parts of the hills, sandals are made of barley-straw. The ashes of barley stalks, which consist chiefly of an impure carbonate of potash, are officinal in the plains, being given for indigestion.

IMPERATA KŒNIGII. Beauv. (I. CYLINDRICA. Beauv. SACCHARUM CYLINDRICUM. Lam.)

Vernacular. *sir, sil.* Hí., *bnarwí.*

A silky-headed small grass abundant at low spots in many parts of the Punjab plains. Its leaves are coarse, and Edgeworth states that it is not eaten by cattle when any other forage can be got.

MELICA SP.?

Vernacular. Lad., *chípkian.*

A tall grass (mentioned by Thomson) reaching 5 and 6 feet in height. Abundant in Ladák from 10,000 to 12,000 feet. It is used for basket-work.

NARDUS STRICTA. L.

Vernacular. T. I. *samá.*

A small grass, which is found Trans-Indus, and to considerable elevations in the Jhelam basin, &c. It may be the N., mentioned by Adams as a favourite food of the Ibex in Kashmír.

OPLISMENUS FRUMENTACEUS. Kth. (PANICUM. Rox.)

Vernacular. S. *sámúka.* Plains *samá, sánwak.*

A cultivated cereal, uncommon out in the plains except Cis-Sutlej, and common in places in the eastern part only of the Punjab Himalaya. Its grain is considered heating, and is one of the poorer of the millets.

ORYZA SATIVA. L.

Vernacular. J. *tái.* K. *dein, tání.* C. *dhán.* S. *dhán,* and plains generally; varieties, *básmati, chita,* &c.

Commonly cultivated in the plains where the soil is low and good, and water abundant, throughout the Punjab, especially in the upper part of the Jalandar Doáb. It is also abundantly grown throughout the Siwálik tract, and up the valleys to an elevation in places of 6,000 or even nearly 7,000 feet. The varieties of it are very numerous, the best of all in each locality being generally called *básmati* (literally, "the odorous.") Very large quantities of the grain are exported to the plains from Kángra, &c. In Kúllú and Lahoul, a kind of beer is stated to be prepared from rice, and on the Sutlej some rice appears to be mixed with barley for making beer—(see HORDEUM HEXASTICHUM). In Kashmír and elsewhere, sandals are made of the straw; they only last about one day's hard-work, on a heavy European foot at least. In the Punjab I have not seen or heard of a wild rice, such as in the N. W. Provinces and elsewhere is stated to grow in wet places, the seed being collected and eaten in times of scarcity.

PANICUM ANTIDOTALE. Retz.
(P. MAXIMUM. Jacq.?)

Vernacular. T. I. *male, shamúkha.* Plains generally, *garm, girúí, mangrúr.*

A tall grass common in many parts of the Punjab plains and Siwálik tract. In some places it is said to be good forage for cattle; in others it is called bitter, and is not relished, and this seems more likely. Near Lahore the smoke of it is used to fumigate wounds.

P. COLONUM. L.

Vernacular. *sánwak, janglí sámak.*

Common wild in most places throughout the Punjab plains. It is one of the best grasses for forage. I have never seen it cultivated in the Punjab, as Aitchison states it to be near Jhelam. The seeds are often eaten by the poorer classes, being swept off the ground in the rains by a brush to which it is said the moisture makes them adhere. Bellew mentions that in the Peshawar Valley this seed is especially eaten during Hindú fasts, and that it, with milk, has for 30 years constituted the chief food of the Akhoond of Swát, for whom it is cultivated.

P. HYDASPICUM. Edge.

Vernacular ?

This grows wild in the southern Punjab, where Edgeworth mentions that its seeds are swept up from the ground to be eaten by poor people.

P. MILIACEUM. Willd.

Vernacular. J. *chína.* K. *chinwa.* C. *chíní, anne, sálan.* R. *chena.* S. *rad, chíní.* Lad., *tsedze.* Per., *arzan.*

This is cultivated in some parts of the Punjab plains, as about Múltán, for its grain and for fodder, and is common in many parts of the Himalaya up to the Indus, being most common from

3,000 up to 8,000 feet (at places on the Chenáb). It is also grown at 10,000—11,000 feet in Ladák. Its grain is considered digestible and nutritious, and in some parts is mostly consumed unground.

P. MILIARE. Lum.

Vernacular. *kútkí.*

Does not appear to be common in the Punjab, but Edgeworth mentions it at Múltán.

PASPALUM SCROBICULATUM. L.

Vernacular. C. *kodra.*

I have not observed this in the Punjab plains, but Edgeworth notes it at Múltán. Unless it has been confused with ELEUSINE (q. v.), it is grown on the Chenáb at about 6,000 feet. Edgeworth, however, states that it is not cultivated in the hills, further east, and I may have been misled. The grain is one of the poorest of the millets.

PENICILLARIA SPICATA. Willd.

Vernacular. *bájra.*

Largely cultivated in some parts of the Punjab plains, and in the high and dry tract, south from Rawul Pindí, constitutes the chief cereal crop. Its grain is considered heating. In many parts it is much grown as fodder. Its stems sometimes reach to a great height; I have seen fields of it to 12 or 14 feet high.

PENNISETUM CENCHROIDES. Rich.

Vernacular. T. I. *taura.* Plains generally, *dhaman, táman, kúrkán.*

Common in many parts of the Punjab plains, and reckoned one of the best of all the wild grasses for forage, both for cows and horses. It would appear from Edgeworth that near Múltán its seeds are swept up from the ground to be used as human food.

P. ITALICUM. R. Br. (PANICUM. L. SETARIA. Beauv.)

Vernacular. J. *kangní, chiúrr, kher.* K. *shálí, pingí.* C. *kauní, shálú, sálan. (?)* R. *kauní.* S. *shak, kusht.* T. I. *gal.* Plains generally, *kangní.*

This is rarely seen grown in the Punjab plains, but is commonly cultivated in the Himalaya, occasionally up to 6,500 feet. The grain is reckoned rather heating. At places on the Chenáb the leaves are used as a pot-herb. This plant is common wild or acclimatised in many parts of the Punjab Himalaya, and is collected to be given as fodder to goats, &c.

SACCHARUM OFFICINARUM. L. Sugar-cane.

Vernacular. *ganna, kamánd,* with *paunda* and other varieties. Products, *chíní, misrí, gúr,* &c.; refuse cane, *pachí.* Roller-mill, *belna, kulharí (?)* pestle-mill, *kolhú.*

Is grown extensively in parts of the Punjab plains, especially towards the east, or where the soil is low and good, manure plentiful, and irrigation abundant. The chief sugar tracts are in the northern part of the Jalandar Doáb, and there is a considerable quantity grown at places along the Western Jumna Canal, and in the southern parts of Múltán and Mozaffargarh. There is even a good deal cultivated in limited localities in the Peshawar Valley, but much sugar is carried from the east up to Peshawar, and beyond it into Affghánistán. Kupar Rám, when governor of Kashmír, is stated by Vigne to have tried the cane in the valley, but the elevation is much too great, and he found that although the plant *grew*, that was all. Indeed, when cultivated in other than low rich lands, the stalks are often markedly thinner. Curious enough, a good deal of the cane is grown in Ambála (and perhaps elsewhere) where there is no irrigation whatever, but I am told that most of it is used as *charí*, fodder for the Commissariat elephants. In the N. W. Provinces, the *kolhú*, pestle-mill, which is employed for extracting oil all over northern India, is used for sugar-pressing also; but about half way between the Jumna and Sutlej, the *belna* or roller-press (is the name *kulharí*, given for this by Edgeworth in Ambála, Journal Agri-Horticultural Society of India, 1838, a mistake) takes its place for sugar, and is in general use throughout the central Punjab. Trans-Indus, however, the *kolhú* again appears. One authority states that the latter is more effective and less expensive, and it is mentioned that for certain soft canes (as the *paunda*, which is juicy and generally eaten, and not pressed) it alone will do, while another says the *belna* is the better of the two.

No doubt, the cultivation of sugar-cane has been much increased by the extension of canals under British rule; but about Rohtuk, near the Western Jumna Canal, I was told that the natives blame the canal for making the *gúr* (unrefined product) sink in in weight within some months, which good *gúr* will not do for years. But Colonel Voyle, an officer of experience, assured me that the fault lay with the cultivators, who in that tract overcrop and under-manure their land. In places like Múltán, where the aquatic weeds—(see HYDRILLA and POTAMOGETON)—employed elsewhere to refine and remove the moisture from the raw produce, are not procurable, the latter has to be used unrefined, or to be sent to other places for purification. In Shahpúr it is reported that much *gúr* is brought to certain marts in order to be refined. A correspondent of the Agri-Horticultural Society states that the long *leaves* of the cane make the best well-ropes, but he probably refers to the refuse crushed stalks, which are sometimes used for cordage, and on the Chenáb, ropes of this *pachí* are preferred for tying the logs into rafts, to those made of *babbar*—(see ANDROPOGON INVOLUTUS).

S. SARA. Rox. (S. MUNJA. Rox.)

Vernacular. T. I. *daryá, karre.* S. R. *sarút.* S. P. *kánda, kúra, sacha.* Dc. *jhúnd.* Plains generally, *sar, sara, sarár, surpat, sarkara, sarkanda, múnja, baunkar.* Parts of plant, *kána, sentha, sirkí, sarka, múnj.* Bazár, root, *garba ganda.*

I have probably confused here, at least two species, to one or other of which these remarks may be understood to imply, and which are common in low sandy places and along canals, &c., in many parts throughout the Punjab plains, and are occasionally planted as fences, &c., and for their products. They are very tall, often raising their white silky heads to 16 or 17 feet. The sheaths of the upper leaves are by beating made into fibre for the *múnj* cordage, which is a favourite for track-ropes, &c., as it stands moisture and strain well. The leaves themselves are in some parts of India made into mats. Bundles of the stems are used for floating heavy timber on the rivers. The stems are made into blinds, chairs, *tatties*, and basket-work, and are used for thatch, and they are laid down on sandy roads in default of macadamizing. Coldstream states that the tops, just before flowering, are reckoned good fodder for milk, and that in the southern Punjab the delicate pith, contained in the upper part of the stem, is eaten by the poor. The root of this or of the next appears to be officinal under the name of *garba ganda.* It is burned near women after child-birth, and near burns and scalds, as its smoke is considered beneficial.

S. SPONTANEUM. L.

Vernacular. *kán, káhí.*

A smaller species which is common on islands, &c., throughout the Punjab plains. It is used for *chiks*, thatch, &c., and pens are made from its stem. It is also given as fodder to buffaloes.

S. SPP.

Vernacular. C. *nau.* R. *ká.* B. *jab.*

Various other species are found in the Punjab Himalaya up to 8,500 feet, some of which are used for similar purposes with the former, such as thatch, &c.

SECALE CEREALE. L. Rye.

Vernacular ?

Various early writers on Affghánistán mention rye as being cultivated in that country, but I can find no recent or definite intelligence as to its being grown there or in the Punjab.

SORGHUM HALEPENSE. Pers.

Vernacular. J. *barú.* K. *brahám.* T. I. *barúa.* S. R. *barwa.*

I have not observed this large grass in the plains of the Punjab, but it is common in parts of the Siwálik tract, and in the outer hills to over 5,000 feet. It is at times browsed by cattle, but I was told in Hazára that after eating it they sometimes have fatal head affections.

S. VULGARE. Pers.

Vernacular. *joár;* close sown for fodder, *charí;* stalks, *karbi.*

Is cultivated in many parts of the Punjab plains, closely sown for fodder, or grown for food, chiefly in the same tracts as PENICILLARIA (q. v.) The grain is reckoned heating.

STIPAGROSTIS PLUMOSA. Munro. ? (ARISTIDA. L.)

Vernacular. *ronák, lonak.*

A very handsome little grass which occurs in the central and southern Punjab, and is common in places up to the base of the Súlimán Range. It is said to be an indifferent fodder. A similar species occurs in Ladák to 18,000 feet.

TRITICUM DURUM. Desf.

Vernacular. *pambhan kanak, barkanak.*

T. ÆSTIVUM. L.
T. HYBERNUM. L.

Vernacular. C. *rozatt dro, do.* S. *zud.* Lad., *tro, shruk ?* (*tokár* (white), *tomár* (red) Cayley). P. *nís, to.* Plains, &c., *kanak.* Per., *gandum;* red rust, *kúngi;* smut, *siyáhí, kalyattí.* Bazár, starch, *nishasti gandum.*

Wheat is cultivated abundantly as a winter crop throughout the Punjab plains, T. ÆSTIVUM being the common species, and

T. DURUM frequent about Loodiana, Múltán, &c. (Edgeworth). It is of many varieties, white or red, generally bearded, but beardless wheat is common in some parts. Some kinds are also grown to great heights in the Himalaya, it being one of the chief crops up to 9,500 feet on the Chenáb, and occurring to 15,000 feet on the Sutlej ? (Cleghorn), good to 11,500 feet, and grown to 13,000 feet in Ladák. The quality of the crop is excellent in many places, and I think the finest fields of wheat I have ever seen were in Sind, where the standing grain was about 5½ feet high, close and with fine ears. Edgeworth mentions that in Ambála, wheat (as well as barley) is sometimes sown as early as August or September, so as to be in flower by December, but that thus treated it is frequently killed by frost. He also states that white ants and rats are very destructive to it in irrigated lands. It is subject to red rust, and more frequently to smut, which is said to prevail most when much rain has been followed by cloudy weather. It is often cut as *kasíl*—(see HORDIUM HEXASTICHUM)—or green fodder, generally once only if the grain also is wanted, but otherwise several times. Irvine, however, states that taking *kasíl* even once is said by many to injure the grain. The starch of wheat is officinal, being considered astringent and tonic, and used in plasters.

VILFA SCABRIFOLIA. Hochst.

Vernacular ?

The seeds of this are said by Edgeworth to be swept up by the poor in the southern Punjab, in order to be used as food.

ZEA MAYS. L.

Vernacular. *makkí, makkei, mak, kúkrí, bará joár.*

A common hot weather crop in the Punjab plains as elsewhere in India, and abundant towards Rawul Pindí. In some parts of the Province it forms a staple food of the people, ground and made into bread, a much smaller proportion of it being eaten roasted in the ear than elsewhere in northern India. It is of many kinds, red and white, &c. It is frequent also in parts of the Himalaya, being grown to 7,500 and even 8,000 feet on the Chenáb and Rávi. It is a favourite food of the black bear. In parts at least of the Kashmír Valley, I observed that this crop was not over 3 feet in height, and Moorcroft notes that near Kábul it is not generally more than that height (instead of 5 or 6 feet, which it reaches or exceeds in the plains).

N. O. CYPERACEÆ.

Carex Indica. L.?

Vernacular. C. *múter, charí.*

A fibre under the above botanical name (I know not on what authority), and with the former vernacular appellation, was sent to the Punjab Exhibition as "used for snow shoes in Pangí and Lahoul." In the Wurdwan Valley at 8,000 feet, a Cyperus called *charí*, which may be the same, is used for making sandals.

Cyperus juncifolius.?

Vernacular. Bazár, root, *nágar motha, mutran sialián.*

This root is officinal, being considered cordial, stomachic, and desiccant, and is used for washing the hair. The books give the above as the botanical name of the plant.

C. tuberosus. Rottb.

Vernacular. *kaserú, díla.*

In the N. W. Provinces the root is used as food, and is officinal as *kaserú.* The *díla* root, mentioned by Bellew as eaten in the Peshawar Valley, may be the same. *Díla,* however, appears to be a generic name for the Cyperaseæ, the roots of several of which are eaten by pigs, and their stems, &c., browsed by cattle, as is one called *múrg,* which may be Scirpus (q. v.)

Eriophorum comosum. Wall. (E. cannabinum.?)

Vernacular. J. *bújí babbar, baggí babbar.* C. *babbí.* R. *ban baggar.* B. *kásh, múnja, baggar, gorbagra.* S. *klúnji, múnzí, úchí.* S. R. *babúr*

This grows throughout the Punjab Siwálik tract and outer hills to 5,000 feet, and in the Salt Range. Although most of the *baggar* or *babbar* rope appears to be made of Andropogon involutus (q. v.), yet in some places part of the cordage for bedsteads, Persian wheels, &c., is unquestionably made of this, which, however, is, I believe, not so much valued as the other.

Malacochæte pectinata. Nees.?

Vernacular. K. *búd.*

This is a common aquatic sedge in the plains, and is, I think, that one which in Kashmír is used for mats, &c.

SCIRPUS MARITIMUS. L.

Vernacular. *múrak, díla.*

Is common in marshes, &c., in the Punjab plains, and when fresh is fair forage, but soon gets too dry. It also appears to grow in Ladák at 10,500 feet.

N. O. FILICES.

ADIANTUM CAPILLUS VENERIS. L. Maiden hair.

Vernacular. K. *dúm túlí.* T. I. *kúwatzei, bisfáij* (?) S. R. *parshawarsha.*

Not uncommon along ditches, &c., in the extreme north-west, and occasional in wells further east in the Punjab plains, and common in the Siwálik tract and lower hills occasionally up to 8,000 feet. In the Salt Range it is given with pepper as a febrifuge, and it may occasionally be the officinal *pareseoshán*—(see A. VENUSTUM). Bellew mentions *bisfáij,* a fern growing in wells in the Peshawar Valley, of which the leaves and stems are purgative, which may be this (the only other ferns I got in the valley were NEPHRODIUM MOLLE and PTERIS LONGIFOLIA, neither of which grow in wells). But for the ordinary *bisfáij,* see POLYPODIUM.

A. CAUDATUM. L.

Vernacular. J. *adhsarita ka jarí, kanghái, gunkíri.*

Common in the Punjab Siwálik tract and outer hills to 4,000 feet, and occasional in the Salt Range, growing often on arid rocks in hot sunny places. Near the Rattan Pír it is called by the first of the above names, significant of its use there, viz., as a medicine in hemicrania.

A. VENUSTUM. Don.

Vernacular. R. *ghás.* Bazár, plant, *hansráj, pareseoshán.*

This graceful little fern is very common in many parts of the Punjab Himalava from 5,000 to 11,000 feet. In Chumba it is pounded and applied to bruises, &c., and the plant appears to supply in the Punjab most of the officinal *hansráj,* which is administered as an anodyne in bronchitis, &c., and is considered diuretic and emmenagogue.

NEPHRODIUM ERIOCARPUM.

Vernacular ?

Madden states that this is commonly eaten and occasionally brought to market in spring in Kumaon—(see PTERIS). It also appe s to grow in the Punjab Himalaya.

"POLYPODIUM VULGARE." L.

Vernacular. Bazár, root, *bisfáij.*

This officinal root is common in the drug-venders' stores, and is by the books ascribed to the above species. I have no clue as to which of our Himalayan ferns it is generally derived from, or whence it is brought, but Kábul is given by one authority, and Honigberger says "the hills." It is used as an alterative.

PTERIS AQUILINA. L. ("ASPLENIUM POLYMORPHUM." Madden.) Brake.

Vernacular. C. *kakhash.* R. *kákei, liúngra.* B. *lúngar.* S. *dío, liúngra.*

This fern is abundant in many parts of the Punjab Himalaya from 4,000 to 12,000 feet. It is certainly eaten at times as a pot-herb in various parts. But I am by no means certain that others also are not thus employed. The fronds are generally used in quite a young state, so that it is not easy or possible to identify them. Cleghorn states that when cooked it is juicy, but rather insipid; another officer informs me that it is exactly like Asparagus, but that one kind, sometimes taken by mistake, is apt to cause colic. The fronds are sometimes used to put under the earth of roofs.

N. O. MARSILEACEÆ.

MARSILEA QUADRIFOLIA. L.

Vernacular. K. *paflú.* Plains, *tripattra ?*

Abundant growing in water throughout the Punjab plains and in the hills to 5,000 feet. This is the *nardoo* so often mentioned as furnishing a sort of food from its tubers to famished travellers in Australian wilds. The plant is eaten as a pot-herb in some parts of India, but I have nowhere heard of its being so used in the Punjab. Nor have I ever noted it in flower or fruit.

N. O. EQUISETACEÆ.

Equisetum debile. Rox. Horse tail.

Vernacular. K. *matti*. S. *skinung*. T. I. *bandukei*. Plains generally, *nari, trotak, búki*.

This is abundant in wet places throughout the Punjab plains, and (the same species I think) to at least 10,500 feet in the Himalaya. The plant is administered as a cooling medicine, and near Jhelam is given for gonorrhæa. I believe it is also at times given to cattle as fodder.

N. O. FUNGI.

Agaricus campestris. L. Common Mushroom.

Vernacular. K. *máns khel*. C. *moksha*. Plains, *khúmbah, khámbúr, chattri*. Aff., *samarogh*. Bazár, *kúmbh, samarogh*.

It is by no means *certain* that these are all the same species; at the same time it is not unlikely that most or all of them are identical. The common mushroom is abundant in cattle fields in many parts of the central Punjab after the rains, and also abounds in the desert tracts of the central and southern Punjab. Coldstream describes it near Mozaffargarh as pure white, with a powdery surface, and, so far as he had seen, no gills. It is largely eaten by the natives in most places where it grows, and is described as excellent, and equal to the English mushroom by those Europeans who have eaten it. It is also extensively dried for future consumption, and is said to preserve its flavour tolerably well. The same species also appears to grow commonly in Kashmír and Kúllú, sparingly in Lahoul, and abundantly in Affghánistán, where Bellew states that the poor use it largely as food. In Kashmír I was told by the people that the edible mushroom is always white, and the non-edible or poisonous kinds, called *herar*, are always dark-coloured, and that they have no other test of the quality. Dried mushrooms (generally small) are officinal in the Punjab.

Boletus igniarius.? (Agaricus albus.?)

Vernacular. K. *bulgar jangli*. C. *búti ka mochka*. Plains, *kiáin*. Bazár, *ghárikún*.

I have put together here two Fungi mentioned separately by Honigberger under the above botanical names, as they are probably the same. The *ghárikún* appears to come from the west,

Davies' Trade Report giving 15 seers as imported viâ Peshawar annually. It is officinal, being given for internal disorders, and Honigberger states that the Boletus is got in Kashmír, where its tinder (?) is used to stop hæmorrhage. The Chenáb Fungus, which appeared to be a Boletus, I saw in Lahoul growing on willow trunks at about 9,500 feet. It is cooked with salt and eaten by the natives.

Lycoperdon gemmatum. Batsch. Puffball.

Vernacular. Bazár, spores? *kúnba.*

What appeared to be this I have seen repeatedly in the Punjab Himalaya up to 11,500 feet, and in Ladák at 13,000 feet. I do not know that it is used in any way. But the black spores of this or some other Fungus are officinal at Lahore, being considered warm.

Morchella semilibera. (M. esculenta. L.) Morel.

Vernacular. *kána kach, kan gach, kánha bíchu, girchhatra.* Plains, *khúmb.*

This appears to be abundant in and near Kashmír, from which considerable quantities are after drying exported to the plains. I have only once noticed it growing, fresh, at 6,000 feet, near Chumba. It is much eaten by natives, both fresh and dry, and is said to be preferred by them to the mushroom. Dried it is a not unsatisfactory addition to a stew even for an European taste. I have no proof that a morel, which is found abundantly in the desert about Jhang, &c., and is said to be got near Hoshiárpúr, &c., is the same species. It is considered a great dainty by natives, and relished by those Europeans who have tasted it.

Tuber cibarium. Sib. Truffle.

Vernacular.

There has been a good deal of debate at times as to whether truffles really are found in the Punjab Himalaya. But it is certain that they do grow there, for I have once at least seen genuine specimens got down to settle the point from towards Kashmír. They are said to be found also above Kángra.

Fungus sp.?

Vernacular. J. *shirían.* R. *bat bakrí.*

A thin, flat, ragged-looking Fungus, yellow above, and with white gills below, which is got on dead trees in various parts of the Punjab Himalaya at 8,000 to 8,500 feet. The natives slice and cook them either fresh or dry, and eat them as a relish with bread. I have tried them in stews, &c., but found them leathery and flavourless.

F. SP.?

Vernacular. *boenphal.*

An underground mushroom, mentioned by Edgeworth as found in cultivated ground near Múltán, and eaten by natives, and which he states he did not find at all palatable.

N. O. ALGÆ.

LAMINARIA SP.

Vernacular. *gillar pattr.*

An algal marine plant, consisting of long ribbon-like pieces, which is found in most Bazárs, being brought from the northward to be administered for goitre (*gillar* or *gal*), a common disease in many parts of the Himalaya. Cayley states that 16 seers of this were imported from Yárkand to Lê in 1867. Honigberger mentions that the natives say it is produced in a salt lake in Tibet, but it is probably brought from the sea through China.

N. O. LICHENES.

PARMELIA KAMTSCHADALIS. Esch.

Vernacular. *chalchalíra, charcharíla, aúsneh.*

A lichen found in the Punjab Bazárs, and probably gathered in the Himalaya. It is used as a dye, and is also officinal, being given as a stimulant to digestion, and on the Yúnání system in mania. Honigberger states that it is also administered in disorders of the stomach and womb, and in cases of calculus.

P. SP.?

Vernacular. R. *hiúnsew.*

This lichen I saw common on rocks at various places in Chumba from 11,500 to 15,000 feet. It is applied to burns.

FINIS.

INDEX,

BOTANICAL AND ENGLISH.

A.

B.

C.

D.

E.

N.

O.

P.

Q

R

S

W.

X.

Y.

Z.

INDEX,

VERNACULAR.

A.

C.

changmá, Salix alba, 206.
chanjan wale, Asparagus Punjabensis, 233.
channa, Cicer arietinum, 63.
channí, Daphne oleoides, 189.
chanún, Populus ciliata, 204.
chanúní, Populus alba, 203.
(*ban*) *char*, Quercus semecarpifolia, 200.
char, Valeriana Hardwickii, 118.
chár maghz, Juglans regia, 201.
charúnglí, Boucerosia Aucheri, 143.
charcharíla, Parmelia Kamtschadalis, 269.
charí, stalks of millet, &c., for fodder, 260.
charí, Sorghum vulgare, 262 ; Carex Indica ? 264.
(*rang*) *charí*; Elsholtzia polystachya, 168.
charka, Letsæa sp., 188.
charkhre, Carpinus viminea, 200.
charras, Cannabis sativa, 215.
chástang, Faba vulgaris, 69.
chaterní, Rhamnus Purpureus, 42.
chatní, a compound spiced, acid, condiment, 42, 50, 184.
chatra, Leucas Cephalotis, 168.
chatríwal, Euphorbia Helioscopia, 193.
chattr, Rhamnus virgatus, 42.
chattrí, Agaricus campestris, 267.
chau, Artemisia sp., 121 ; Machilus odoratissimus, 188.
chauláí, Amaranthus mangostanus, and A. polygonoides, 181.
(*lál*) *chauláí*, *chaulei*, Amaranthus anardana, 181.
cháunsh, Berchemia sp., 41.
cháyang, Brassica sp., 13.
chechar, Rhus Buckiamela, 48.
chel, Cannabis sativa, 215.
chemrí, Eleusine flagellifera, 254.
chena, Panicum miliaceum, 258.
chenjúl, Nussiessya hypoleuca, 215.
(*sper*) *cherei*, Quercus Ilex, 199.
cherkúsh, Prunus Armenica, 81.
chetí búta, Abelia triflora, 113.
chewa, Ephedra Gerardiana, 228.
(*gir*) *chhatra*, Morchella semilibera, 268.
chhota, small.
chhota kelu, Asparagus racemosus, 233.
chhota lewar, Andromeda fastigiata, 133.
chhotí láne, Suæda fruticosa, 180.
chhotí maúharí, Solanum xanthocarpum, 161.
chhotí ván, Salvadora Indica, 174.
(*maí*) *chhotí*, Tamarix orientalis, 92.
chichinda, Trichosanthes anguina, 99.
chichra, Butea frondosa, 59.
chichrí, Plectranthus rugosus, 171.
chijákrí, Podophyllum Emodi, 8.
chijla, Fraxinus Xanthoxylloides, 139.
chik, a kind of screen for doors, &c., 250, 261.
chíkan, Euonymus fimbriata, 41.
chíkí, Gouffeia holosteoides, 20.
chíkní, *chíkrí*, Buxus sempervirens, 192.
chil, Pinus excelsa, 225 ; P. longifolia, 226.
chíla, Casearia tomentosa, 44.
Chilássí tamákú, Nicotiana rustica 157.
chilghoza, Pinus Gerardiana, 225.
chilkí, a rupee of Kashmír, value ten annas, 122.
chílla, Casearia tomentosa, 44.
chilotá, Litsæa sp , 188.
chilúchí, Iris Nepalensis, 240.
chimbarí, Doctyloctenium Ægyptiacum, 254.
chímbarí, Eleusine flagellifera, 254.
chimkaní, Cathartocarpus fistula, 62.
chímú, Syringa Emodi, 140 ; Morus serrata, 219.
chimyáka, Podophyllum Emodi, 8.
chín, Fagopyrum esculentum, 184.

H.

I.

J.

L.

M.

N.

pashm, fine wool, or hair, 229.
pashmaran, Thalictrum foliolosum, 5.
pastúwanna, Grewia oppositifolia, 27.
pastú wanne, Grewia villosa, 27.
(*perei*) *pastúwanne*, Fluggea virosa, 195.
pat, *patta*, *pattr*, &c., a leaf.
pat, Corchorus capsularis, 26.
(*ban*) *pat*, Corchorus olitorius, 26
(*tez*) *put*, Cinnamomum albiflorum, 187.
pataka, Abutilon Indicum, 21.
patákí, Cissampelos Pareira, 6; Gymnosporia spinosa, 41
patákhen, Cratægus oxyacantha, 79.
patang, Cæsalpinia sappan, 60.
páth, Cissampelos Pareira, 6.
patha, Chamærops Ritchiana, 242; Hordeum hexastichum, 256.
pathor, Marsdenia Roylii, 145.
patíra, Typha angustifolia, 246.
patís, Aconitum heterophyllum, 1.
patpatúla, Oreoseris lanuginosa, 128.
(*ban*) *patrak*, Saxifraga ligulata, 103.
patrawála damá, Solanum gracilipes, 159.
patsan, Hibiscus cannabinus, 22.
patrís, Aconitum heterophyllum, 1.
(*haiza ka*) *patta*, Kalanchoe varians, 100.
(*mít*) *pattar*, Machilus odoratissimus, 188.
(*til*) *pattar*, Acer Creticum, and A. cultratum, 80.
pattharman, Callicarpa incana, 165.
patthra, Malcolmia strigosa, 14.
pattí Kashmírí, Rhododendron campanulatum, 134.
(*sitáwar*) *pattí*, Asparagus Punjabensis, 233.
(*gillar*) *pattr*, Laminaria sp., 269.
(*tarar*) *pattr*, Dioscorea deltoidea, 229.
(*til*) *pattra*, Marlea begonifolia, 93.
(*tre*) *pattra*, Trifolium pratense, 76.
(*tri*) *pattra*, Marsilea quadrifolia ? 266.
patwa, Hibiscus sabdariffa, 22.
paunda, Saccharum officinarum, 260.
pawanne, Clematis Nepalensis, 3; Boucerosia Aucheri, 143.
pe, Picea Webbiana, 224.
peil mundí, Tanacetum vulgare, 181.
pek, Plectranthus rugosus, 171.
pekkar, Adhatoda Vasica, 164.
peni, Abelia triflora, 118.
penma Potentilla Inglisii, 81.
perei pastúwanne, Fluggea virosa, 195.
perkhatúna, Cocculus Leæba, 6.
pesho, Nima quassioides, 39.
petha, Benincasa cerifera, 95.
petthar, *pettharí*, Juniperus communis, 222.
pewand, a graft.
pewandí, Zizyphus Jujuba, 43.
phág, Ficus caricoides, 212.
(*bat*) *phagár*, Ficus reticulata, 214.
phagorú, Ficus caricoides, 212.
phágrí, Loranthus sp., 112.
phagúra, Ficus caricoides, 212.
phagwára, Ficus carica, 211; F. caricoides, 212.
phagwárí, Ficus caricoides, 212.
phal, a fruit.
(*boen*) *phal*, Fungus sp. ? 269.
(*dákú*) *phal*, Elæagnus conferta, 189.
(*kái*) *phal*, Myrica Sapida, 202.
(*mend*) *phal*, Randia dumetorum, 116.
phalá, Acacia modesta, 54.
phaláhar, lawful to be eaten in Hindú fasts, 89, 184.
phalí gudr, Cyamopsis psoraloides, 65.
(*maror*) *phalí*, Helicteres Isora, 25.
phalja, Populus ciliata, 204.
(*múng*) *phallí*, Arachis hypogæa, 57.

S.

T.

U.

V.

W.

Y.

Z.

INDEX OF USES, &c.

INDEX OF USES, &c.